Current Issues in Monetary Economics

Contributions to Economics

Christoph M. Schneider
Research and Development Management: From the Soviet Union to Russia
1994. ISBN 3-7908-0757-5

Bernhard Böhm/Lionello F. Punzo (Eds.)
Economic Performance
1994. ISBN 3-7908-0811-3

Lars Olof Persson/Ulf Wiberg
Microregional Fragmentation
1995. ISBN 3-7908-0855-5

Ernesto Felli/Furio C. Rosati/Giovanni Tria (Eds.)
The Service Sector: Productivity and Growth
1995. ISBN 3-7908-0875-X

Giuseppe Munda
Multicriteria Evaluation in Fuzzy Environment
1995. ISBN 3-7908-0892-X

Giovanni Galizzi/Luciano Venturini (Eds.)
Economics of Innovation: The Case of Food Industry
1996. ISBN 3-7908-0911-X

David T. Johnson
Poverty, Inequality and Social Welfare in Australia
1996. ISBN 3-7908-0942-X

Rongxing Guo
Border-Regional Economics
1996. ISBN 3-7908-0943-8

Oliver Fratzscher
The Political Economy of Trade Integration
1996. ISBN 3-7908-0945-4

Ulrich Landwehr
Industrial Mobility and Public Policy
1996. ISBN 3-7908-0949-7

Arnold Picot/Ekkehard Schlicht (Eds.)
Firms, Markets, and Contracts
1996. Corr. 2nd printing 1997.
ISBN 3-7908-0947-0

Thorsten Wichmann
Agricultural Technical Progress and the Development of a Dual Economy
1997. ISBN 3-7908-0960-8

Ulrich Woitek
Business Cycles
1997. ISBN 3-7908-0997-7

Michael Carlberg
International Economic Growth
1997. ISBN 3-7908-0995-0

Massimo Filippini
Elements of the Swiss Market for Electricity
1997. ISBN 3-7908-0996-9

Giuseppe Gaburro (Ed.)
Ethics and Economics
1997. ISBN 3-7908-0986-1

Frank Hoster/Heinz Welsch/Christoph Böhringer
CO_2 Abatement and Economic Structural Change in the European Internal Market
1997. ISBN 3-7908-1020-7

Christian M. Hafner
Nonlinear Time Series Analysis with Applications to Foreign Exchange Rate Volatility
1997. ISBN 3-7908-1041-X

Sardar M.N. Islam
Mathematical Economics of Multi-Level Optimisation
1998. ISBN 3-7908-1050-9

Sven-Morten Mentzel
Real Exchange Rate Movements
1998. ISBN 3-7908-1081-9

Lei Delsen/Eelke de Jong (Eds.)
The German and Dutch Economies
1998. ISBN 3-7908-1064-9

Mark Weder
Business Cycle Models with Indeterminacy
1998. ISBN 3-7908-1078-9

Tor Rødseth
Models for Multispecies Management
1998. ISBN 3-7908-1001-0

Michael Carlberg
Intertemporal Macroeconomics
1998. ISBN 3-7908-1096-7

Sabine Spangenberg
The Institutionalised Transformation of the East German Economy
1998. ISBN 3-7908-1103-3

Hagen Bobzin
Indivisibilities
1998. ISBN 3-7908-1123-8

Helmut Wagner (Ed.)

Current Issues in Monetary Economics

With 26 Figures
and 16 Tables

Springer-Verlag Berlin Heidelberg GmbH

Series Editors
Werner A. Müller
Martina Bihn

Editor
Prof. Dr. Helmut Wagner
Chair of Macroeconomics
University of Hagen
Feithstr. 140
D-58084 Hagen, Germany

Cataloging-in-Publication Data applied for
Die Deutsche Bibliothek – CIP-Einheitsaufnahme
Current issues in monetary economics: with 16 tables / Helmut Wagner (ed.). – Heidelberg; New York: Physica-Verl., 1998
(Contributions to economics)

ISBN 978-3-7908-1127-8 ISBN 978-3-642-99797-6 (eBook)
DOI 10.1007/978-3-642-99797-6

Originally published by Physica-Verlag Heidelberg in 1998

Softcover Design: Erich Kirchner, Heidelberg

SPIN 10683371 88/2202-5 4 3 2 1 0 – Printed on acid-free paper

Contents

Introduction

Helmut Wagner
University of Hagen, Feithstr. 140, D - 58084 Hagen

In the last few years decisive methodological and thematic focal points which are important for practical economic policy have been developed in the theory of monetary and exchange rate policy. This book is concerned with these developments, their assessment and the open questions which have still not been solved. It is divided into four parts. The first part deals with central bank design, the second with strategies of monetary policies and their implementation. Part III is concerned with theoretical aspects of exchange rate policy and monetary union, and part IV with selected issues of monetary and exchange rate policy in developing and transition countries. In the following pages I will provide an overview of the individual articles[1]. With the exception of the article by Nobel Laureate James Tobin, the contributions contained in this book were all introduced and discussed at an academic symposium I organized in Castrop-Rauxel on 8 and 9 September 1997. James Tobin agreed spontaneously to my suggestion that he should write a comprehensive article especially for this publication.

A short summary of the comments or supplementary papers and of the general discussions will be given in the last section of this book, titled „Conclusion and Supplements". There I will also provide some supplements respecting the issues which were the subject of the greatest amount of debate at the symposium.

Following the introduction, the book starts with a survey of the recent theory and practice of monetary policy by **James Tobin**. It deals with several key issues of monetary economics. Tobin commences with an assessment of the rise and fall of monetarism. Then he turns to the current orthodoxy in monetary and fiscal policy which he views as dedication solely to price stability (representing the dominant trend in the theory and practice of monetary policy over the last two decades) and official indifference to real macroeconomic outcomes that, as he emphasizes, refers to fiscal policy as well. Afterwards he considers the macroeconomic theories underlying these policies.

In a further chapter Tobin presents the United States as a striking exception to the "fashion" of designating price stability as *the* target of monetary policy and explains the US's obviously better macroeconomic results over the past years as against Europe and Japan by means of the non-orthodox policy there. Tobin then

---

[1] I would like to stress here the help provided by my assistants, namely Wolfram Berger, Claudia Goldschmidt, Friedrich Kißmer, Ralf Sonnenfroh and Florian Späte.

turns to the question of "rules versus discretion" in monetary policy. He argues that a mechanical rule blind to actual economic events and outcomes cannot work. And in fact even supporters of rules such as John Taylor would interpret "rules" in a way that requires large doses of discretion in their application. Tobin also emphasizes that, if the Fed had implemented the so-called Taylor-rule, as good as it is, from 1993 through 1997, the US economy would have suffered unnecessarily high unemployment and output losses, so that the Fed was right to use discretion.

In the last chapter, Tobin analyzes the "spectacular" success of the US economy over the last years and discusses the question, or as he states the "mystery, fully understood by neither central bankers nor economists", why and how monetary policy rules the economy. In his tentative answer, he refers to two lines of explanation: substitution chains and policy expectations, whereby expectations are claimed to be very powerful, but unable to work unless chains of asset substitution really do occur. Finally he states that nowadays, where fiscal policies are no longer eligible for counter-cyclical stabilization, and the globalization of financial markets threatens national financial sovereignty, innovative thinking about the tactics and the structure of monetary operations is urgently necessary, in particular in Europe.

The first part of the book deals with central bank design. A central methodological focal point of modern economic theory is the game theoretic approach. The essay by **Gerhard Illing** is concerned critically with solutions based on game theoretic models of central bank design. He refers in particular to two empirical trends: the increase in the independence of central banks in many countries, and the transition to inflation targeting in a series of countries. Illing shows that both trends can be supported by game theoretic models; but he also points out that the suspected credibility problems cannot be solved simply through the institutional implementation of these policies. It is claimed in particular that the previously much-discussed solution concepts of Rogoff and Walsh in part displace the credibility problem to another level. Illing first analyzes the time inconsistency problem of monetary policy in the Barro and Gordon (1983) model, and then goes on to discuss different options of institutional solution. Following a comparison of the results achieved by monetary targeting with those achieved by strict inflation targeting, Illing then turns his attention to two rival concepts of central bank independence. He first discusses the solution in the Rogoff (1985) model, which provides a rationalization for an independent central bank that sets its own policy goals and chooses its policy instruments independent from government interference. His criticism of this approach concerns the fact that the government still has an incentive to renege on delegation. Rogoff's approach assumes implicitly that the costs of doing so are infinitely great. The credibility of delegation is therefore only assumed and not substantiated. In addition, the costs of longer-term delegation are not specified.

Finally, Illing turns to Walsh's (1995) approach, in which the central bank is given instrumental independence but no goal independence. In addition, the contract design itself is assumed but not substantiated. The lack of government credibility is replaced by the assumption, that the government is able to commit to keep contracts. An adequate analysis must take the costs of reneging the contract into account. But this means that the analysis must take into account the verifiability of different policies. Illing then comments on the Persson and Tabellini (1993) findings on the theory of incomplete central bank contracts. Once again he criticizes the constitutional solution (i.e. an incomplete contract) for merely assuming the government's capability of commitment. Illing shows that the theory of incomplete central bank contracts stresses above all the trade-off between democratic accountability and robustness against political distortions.

Following Illing's extensive theoretical representation of the "Central Bank Design", **Dietmar Kath** and **Wolfgang Filc** provide an outline of their controversial assessment of the question of central bank autonomy.

Kath pleads in his paper for strict independence of central banks. First of all he takes up the theoretical discussion on the pros and cons of central bank autonomy and puts forward arguments for both positions. The most important argument of opponents of central bank autonomy consists in the danger of stabilization policy conflicts between the monetary and the fiscal authority. Supporters of central bank independence on the other hand deny that there is a (long term) conflict between macroeconomic targets. They also argue that even an existing trade-off does not support the above position, because it would be exploited by selfish politicians maximizing their individual utility. Kath states that the results of such a policy consist in exclusively temporary increases to output and employment which are purchased in the long term by accelerating inflation.

With these arguments in mind, the autonomy of central banks, combined with the statutory commission to keep the price level stable, appears to be the rational solution. However, Kath goes on to argue that central bankers also act to maximize their own self-interest and that therefore central bank autonomy cannot guarantee a monetary policy orientated towards social welfare. He draws the conclusion, therefore, that the independence of central banks should not be anchored merely in a statute, but that it should encompass additional elements. With this in mind he defines the term independence using three criteria. Firstly, the central bank must be statutorily obliged to aim for price level stability; secondly, decision-makers must be independent; and thirdly, there must be a prohibition on granting the government credit and complete freedom to make decisions on exchange rate policy. In the light of these criteria, Kath regards the foundation of the autonomy of the European Central Bank in the Maastricht Treaty as inadequate, and sees the risk that future European monetary policy will be predetermined by national governments.

Filc on the other hand argues in favor of only a "conditional independence" of central banks. He criticizes the fact that Kath's approach focuses exclusively on a microeconomic consideration of central banks from the point of view of the economic theory of bureaucracy and ignores macroeconomic problems. In particular with regard to the European Central Bank, Filc demands that banks should not be simply given the aim of monetary stability, but that it should also be charged with concerning itself with growth and employment. In his opinion, monetary policy autonomy must be restricted to prevent the target of price stability being pursued irrespective of the (social) costs. Central banks should not be subject to government directives, but at the same time the inclusion of additional macroeconomic variables in the catalogue of targets should be used to prevent central banks taking up an isolated position. Filc therefore favors cooperation between monetary, fiscal and income policy. In his opinion, this is the only way to achieve a combination of interest rates, exchange rate and wage levels which will enable inflation-free growth with high employment. As the foundation of a cooperative strategy of this nature Filc formulates a "code of economic behavior" which replaces the delegation of each of the macroeconomic targets in the sphere of responsibility of only one of the stabilization policy authorities.

Summing up, Filc pleads for a monetary policy that is not subject to any government directives but which is orientated towards socially desirable macroeconomic targets and follows a simple, operational and systematic rule here, whereby he proposes a modified Taylor rule.

The second part of the book is concerned with monetary policy strategies and their implementation. At first, the article by **Alexander Karmann** deals with the question of how the proposal for simple linear central bank contracts can be modified so that the contract becomes more credible as an institutional mechanism. With recourse to McCallum (1995) and with reference to recent experience with the Central Bank Act in New Zealand, Karmann recognizes a credibility problem for simple contracts in the lack of an ex-post incentive for the government actually to impose the prescribed sanctions in the event that the contractual targets are not reached. Karmann argues that the structure of the underlying distribution of information between the central bank and the government must be taken into account when the contract is drawn up, so that more flexible and therefore more credible solutions can be found.

The article begins with a general introduction to linear rational-expectations models, in the scope of which central bank policies are usually examined in a formal way. Following the tradition of Barro and Gordon (1983) the commitment solution is contrasted with the discretionary solution and simple rules are introduced, which can be found in the literature, in order to come closer to the commitment solution. In the third section the results are compared that are found when these rules are applied in the scope of an AS/AD model. Karmann points out that the relative assessment of the rules depends to a great extent on the respective model parameters and on the type of shock that is assumed. In addition, the question must be put with all these rules as to how a central bank can be obliged credibly to comply with the rules if it always finds itself exposed to a subsequent incentive to deviate from them.

The fourth section then presents contractual agreements which extend the loss function of the central bank by a transfer element as a possible approach to the solution of this credibility problem. This contractual transfer may be interpreted as a monetary parameter or as a threat of dismissal which is based on the target inflation rate and the actual inflation rate.

Karmann then introduces a specific information structure. This structure is based on the assumption that signals on supply shocks are equally available as public information to private individuals and to the central bank, while the central bank is in possession of private, if imperfect information with regard to the velocity of money circulation. Starting from this assumption Karmann comes to the conclusion that a simple, state-independent contract can only lead to the objectives under special assumptions regarding the process of the formation of expectations among private individuals. For this reason he examines another type of contract in which a scheme of targets is set as a function of public information on supply shocks and with which those responsible in the central bank are threatened with dismissal on any deviations from the state-contingent targets. While demand shocks do not affect this type of inflation target, so that the central bank should react in a discretionary manner to them, in the case of observable information on supply shocks the defined goals and objectives can be adjusted in a manner stipulated in the contract. Karmann comes to the conclusion that the government could use a suitable scheme of targets to induce the central bank to provide a socially optimal money supply by controlling the probability distribution on the dismissal of those responsible in the central bank in a contractually stipulated and observable manner.

The next two articles examine the problems of implementing monetary policy strategies. First, **Stephen Cecchetti** discusses questions that arise if the central bank is bound to policy rules. He first introduces a framework which interprets the rule followed by the central bank as the solution of a control problem. The rule indicates a time path for the instrument (in this case, the interest rate), subject namely to the occurring shocks and to the model parameters (such as discount rate, weighting parameters, etc.). Cecchetti then discusses various aspects of policy rules. He shows that inflation targeting, in contrast to nominal income targeting, can be derived as a possible policy rule from the previously developed framework. Intermediate targets, according to Cecchetti, are only meaningful if they contribute to the transparency of the policy. In so far, he regards money supply aggregates as being less suitable. He then refers to his own empirical surveys to show that the trade-off between output variability and inflation variability is very steep, i.e. a reduction of the inflation variability leads to a clear rise in output variability. He interprets the introduction of inflation targeting as an implicit change of relative importance in the loss function with the consequence that now real variables will fluctuate more. Cecchetti goes on to examine the possible impact of uncertainty on the effect of monetary policy measures, which he himself assesses as low. He then discusses the question of the optimum level of inflation. In particular he discusses whether it is more suitable to pursue a low positive inflation rate than zero inflation. The argument put forward recently by Lawrence Summers (1991) that zero inflation also demands a positive real interest rate, and therefore affects the possibilities of reacting to shocks negatively, is assessed as not being particularly relevant empirically. Cecchetti also shows that it can be optimal not to adjust the policy instrument immediately to the full amount as a reaction to a shock, but to smooth the adjustment.

In the concluding section Cecchetti discusses the question of the necessity of policy rules. He sees the reasons for rules on the one hand in the time inconsistency problem, and on the other hand in increased transparency and an accompanying increased accountability of policies. He also sees in this an important benefit of inflation targeting, which has been adopted by a number of countries recently.

In the following article, **Gabriel Fagan** describes and discusses problems of implementing monetary policy strategies, whereby he restricts his discussion to money supply strategies and direct inflation targeting. The fundamental premise of the article is that the primary target of monetary policy is to pursue price stability. First of all Fagan questions the specification of price stability. The final goal may be defined as a price level target or as an inflation rate target. If a defined price level is aimed for, deviations in a period have to be reversed in the following period by means of appropriate measures by the central bank. This reduces long-term uncertainty, as could be seen in Cecchetti's article, because the price level is stationary, but this takes place at the cost of increased short-term price volatility. If on the other hand the aim is an inflation rate target, the price level follows a random walk and uncertainty regarding the price level increases as the prognosis horizon is enlarged. Fagan, like Cecchetti before him, then discusses the question of whether it is suitable to aim for a low positive inflation rate, or whether zero inflation is optimal. Possible theoretical foundations for a low positive inflation rate, which is preferred by central banks in practice, are, firstly, nominal rigidities, which can turn into real rigidities with zero inflation, secondly, the rate of inflation as part of an optimal tax structure, thirdly, the necessity of negative real interest rates (Summers effect), and fourthly, a bias in the calculation of inflation.

The practical aspects of the implementation of a monetary policy strategy, which form the core of this article, are dealt with in the fourth section. Fagan discusses some aspects which are in part interdependent. First of all, he goes into the question of the choice of variables for the final goal (price index) and for the intermediate goal (money supply aggregate). He then examines the time horizon and the range of a possible target. The longer the time horizon and the wider the range, the greater is the flexibility of monetary policy, and the more likely it is to hit the target. At the same time, the possible disciplinary effect of a defined goal may be weakened and the transparency of the monetary policy reduced. He then shows the problem of target deviations. This problem is created not only in the case of a disinflation (pace at which the optimal rate is to be achieved) which may indeed be necessary at the start, but also in the case of subsequent deviations from the target as a result of the shocks that occur. The central bank sees itself confronted here with conflicting goals. On the one hand, a rapid and sharp adjustment of the instruments reduces the deviation of the inflation rate from the target rate, but on the other hand, this may increase output variability. Finally,

Fagan stresses the importance of communication with the general public with regard to the building of credibility and an increase in accountability as well as the importance of an extensive analysis of the macroeconomic environment, of the use of various indicators and of drawing up own inflation forecasts.
In conclusion, Fagan discusses necessary requirements for monetary policy strategy in a European Monetary Union, whereby it becomes clear that not only a money supply strategy but also direct inflation targeting can be a suitable candidate for a European Monetary Union.

The above articles have all been concerned with innovations in the theory of monetary policy. A second group of articles deals on the other hand with more recent aspects of the theory of exchange rate policy.

The first article of part III by **Michael Frenkel** deals with the advantages and disadvantages of alternative exchange rate systems, which have been the subject of discussion among economists for some time. This work summarized selected aspects of this discussion with the background of the latest findings.

In a first step Frenkel discusses above all three controversial aspects of flexible exchange rates: a) the volatility of exchange rates; b) the insulation properties of flexible exchange rates to seal itself off; and c) the effectiveness of central bank interventions in foreign exchange markets.

On a): the core findings of empirical studies is that the volatility of nominal and real exchange rates after the collapse of the Bretton Woods system was greater than during the system's lifetime. In addition, it is claimed that exchange rate fluctuations were greater than might have been expected on the basis of the fundamental data. Furthermore, structural economic exchange rate models are scarcely able to explain these fluctuations. Frenkel therefore stresses the relevance of more recent approaches in the theory of exchange rate policy, which take into account heterogeneous information and the use of technical analyses in the currency markets (the microstructure of the foreign exchange market). He regards the existence of noise trading, and the induced destabilizing bandwagon effects, as one of the most important objections to flexible exchange rates. Frenkel then checks whether the relatively high volatility exchange rate has harmful effects for international trade, for investments and growth and for the integration of capital markets. He basically comes to the conclusion that damaging effects of exchange rate volatility cannot be clearly proven either theoretically or empirically.

On b): In fact, according to prevailing opinion, flexible exchange rates should insulate a country from foreign inflation and output shocks. According to Frenkel, the empirical findings show that individual countries are able to insulate from foreign inflation trends over the long run, whereas flexible exchange rates do not eliminate the transmission of business cycles. This can probably be explained by the occurrence of a symmetrical shock. However, these findings can also be explained in the scope of Keynesian two country models, if the latter assume different dynamics for assets and goods prices.

On c): The efficiency of foreign exchange market interventions remains controversial according to Frenkel. Sterilized interventions appear to be successful in the short term. This corresponds to the findings of the asset-market approaches. In addition, the interventions can contain new information on future monetary policy and become successful via this signaling effect. In almost all theoretical approaches on the other hand, the success of non-sterilized interventions remains undisputed.

In the second main part of this work Frenkel is concerned with selected aspects of fixed exchange rate systems. At first the question is whether fixed exchange rates exercise a disciplinary effect on monetary and fiscal policy. Again Frenkel's results are inconclusive. It is true that a monetary restriction can be shown theoretically and empirically (for Europe), but the differences to flexible exchange rate systems are less than was originally thought. In both exchange rate systems the target of price stability can only be reached through credible policies, whereby credibility is also determined through long-term fiscal policies. Finally, Frenkel deals with approaches for explaining currency crises in fixed exchange rate systems. Here, two directions can be roughly differentiated: the theory of speculative attacks explains the collapses of fixed exchange rate systems with inconsistent policies, while a second theoretical approach stresses the credibility problems of fixed exchange rate systems. According to Frenkel, currency crises are difficult to foresee, because a great number of factors influence the occurrence and timing of a crisis.

Frenkel then turns to the question of whether choosing a fixed exchange rate for developing countries and emerging markets is a possibility to realize low inflation rates. In addition, Frenkel deals with the business cycle associated with exchange-rate-based stabilization. What is remarkable in this context, among other things is whether exchange-rate-based stabilization programs lead to a recession only after some delay and even trigger a boom immediately following their implementation. Frenkel also discusses the question of which factors form the basis of successful exchange-rate-based stabilization programs. He comes to the conclusion that fixed exchange rate systems do not necessarily eliminate inflationary pressure. Once again, the role of credible policies, and in particular of a fiscal policy, compatible with fixed exchange rates is stressed. Finally, Frenkel discusses target zones for exchange rates. The author provides an overview of the theoretical and empirical positions in the literature. In addition, Frenkel discusses the suitability of target zones for industrial countries. He provides reasons why the implementation of target zones would not be a practical reform of the international monetary system.

The following article by **Paul De Grauwe** deals with a particular problem in the field of exchange rate theory in the context of the realization of EMU. According to the schedule specified in the Maastricht Treaty for the realization of European Economic and Monetary Union, on 1 January 1999 the exchange rates of the participating states will be irrevocably fixed not only bilaterally but also against the common currency, the euro. The decision on the conversion rates is to be taken in 1998, after the group of participating states has been announced early in the year. The following restrictions must be taken into account for this decision.

Firstly, according to the Maastricht Treaty the external value of the ecu must not be affected by the conversion rates, and secondly, according to a resolution of the Madrid Summit Meeting in 1995 conversion from ecu to euro must be in the ratio 1:1. To sum up, this means that the conversion rates for the euro on 1 January 1999 must correspond to the ecu rates on the previous day. A premature fixing of the euro conversion rates for the participating states is not possible, because the value of the ecu expressed in a national currency continues to fluctuate because of the non-fixed ecu rates for non-participating countries. This would infringe against the demand in the treaty for consistency of the external value of the ecu on transition to the euro. The euro conversion rates cannot be determined either by premature fixing of bilateral parities. According to De Grauwe, this situation results in an indeterminacy problem with regard to euro conversion rates, because on 31.12.1998 there may be an unlimited number of ecu rates and therefore of conversion rates.

De Grauwe fears that these problems can lead to turbulence in the foreign exchange markets in the run-up to European Economic and Monetary Union. The indeterminacy of the DM/euro and of the dollar/euro exchange rate has a direct influence on the DM/dollar exchange rate. A defined DM/dollar exchange rate can be assigned to each possible combination of DM/euro and dollar/euro exchange rates because of arbitrage considerations. The indeterminacy of the latter two exchange rates therefore leads via spill-over effects to indeterminacy of the first exchange rate. Because each possible ecu exchange rate on 31.12.1998 determines the conversion rate to the euro, the creation of speculative bubbles cannot be ruled out. Each movement of the ecu rate can lead to the creation of self-validating exchange rate fluctuations with instability of general price levels as a consequence.

De Grauwe finally examines several possibilities for solving the problem of indeterminacy of euro conversion rates. One possible procedure is the premature announcement of the euro conversion rates. Because the ecu exchange rates can diverge from the fixed exchange rates until the start of EMU, it is necessary to compensate for these movements. De Grauwe suggests here that the composition of the ecu currency basket is changed constantly. A second solution would be to fix the exchange rate temporarily between countries taking part in EMU and a non-participating currency, e.g. the dollar. The question arises, however, how far such an agreement is politically desirable or enforceable. A third solution is based on a different interpretation of the relevant provisions of the Maastricht Treaty to that usually used. The required stability of the external value of the ecu/euro can also be regarded as being solely related to the non-participating currencies. In this way, euro conversion rates for EMU currencies could be chosen which do not have to be orientated towards the ecu rates derived from the market on 31.12.1998.

In part IV on monetary and exchange rate policy in developing and transition countries, **Friedrich Sell** first deals with the causes of currency crises and the role of monetary and exchange rate policies in preventing such crises. He examines first of all the currency crisis in Thailand. The trigger for this is thought to be the collapse of the Thai real estate sector. A considerable part of credit growth, principally funded by foreign capital, went into this sector. To a large extent, the boom of the real estate sector was financed by non-performing loans. To sum up, the following stylized facts emerge: foreign capital was absorbed almost exclusively in the non-tradable sector and the Thai central bank was extremely negligent in its task of supervising the banking sector.

Sell then analyzes the Mexican currency crisis of 1994/1995 and draws parallels to the present Bath crisis. The following common causes are shown: firstly, not fiscal deficits did trigger the crises but prior lending booms. Secondly, financial vulnerability was quite obvious before the crisis, and this resulted from the discrepancy between the amount of foreign exchange reserves on the one hand and the total of government debt or the quantity of money in circulation respectively on the other. A third problem lays in the adverse effect of a strong real overvaluation of the currencies on the prices of the non-tradables. As the fourth and last point Sell introduces the consequences of globalization, in particular the circumstance that a small amount of negative news can provoke a radical reaction by investors. This is magnified by stampede effects.

In a subsequent chapter Sell introduces a model of speculative attacks on the same lines as the model from Sachs, Tornell and Velasco (1996), whereby a lending boom with a proportion of non-performing loans is explicitly examined. The findings of this study can be summed up by stating that a country with poor fundamentals and low international liquidity is the probable victim of speculative attacks.

In a following chapter Sell points out the common features and differences between developing countries and transformation countries. He points out that transformation countries can learn from the new tigers that liberalization of the financial markets is only possible with strict bank supervision.

In the final part Sell summarizes the consequences for monetary and exchange-rate policies. From the aspect of monetary policy, extensive bank supervision is decisive. In addition, attention should be paid to the monetary aggregate M2 as an important early-warning indicator of speculative attacks. In front of the background of his examination of currency crises Sell then emphasizes two points. On the one hand he raises the principal question whether any fixed rate system is only optimal for a while; on the other hand he points out that the choice of an anchor currency must be reconsidered.

The final conference contribution to this volume, from **Wilfried Fuhrmann**, deals with the theoretical foundations of a currency board (CB). After stating that there is no general theory of a CB, Fuhrmann gives reasons for the recent interest in this institution. In particular, a consideration is made of the expected costs and benefits of CB, which already point to the conclusion that it can only be successful if accompanied by an adequate institutional framework.

First, it is pointed out that a CB is generally seen as a non-state-contingent rule, which can be analyzed in the tradition of Kydland and Prescott (1977) and Barro and Gordon (1983). In this interpretation of a CB as a specific form of delegation, a number of assumptions are explained which set the formal framework for confronting the CB case with the case of a central bank with discretionary power and a commitment solution respectively. Fuhrmann concludes that a CB can lead to a second-best solution. If the results of an optimal monetary policy can be realized with a CB, Fuhrmann identifies advantages of this institution as against other institutional mechanisms as being above all the easier realizable and the greater credibility that are assumed with a CB. Credibility is regarded as depending to a large extent on the choice of the anchor currency, on the consensus regarding the intended structural change, and the ability to defend the fixed exchange rate. However, Fuhrmann emphasizes that a CB is not an optimal solution in all cases.

Fuhrmann goes on to discuss the effects of (transitory and permanent) disturbances and the implications of inside-money creation as aspects which influence the stability of a CB.

In a system without money creation, the stability and credibility seem perfect at a first glance, still they are restricted by a number of factors such as the parliament's ability to change the parity, the governance of fiscal policy and the flexibility of prices and wages. Using a target zone approach, a CB is to be understood as a target function defining an admissible range for the exchange rate. In this context, the target zones for all fundamental variables of the economy are determined by this parity, whereas stabilization tasks have to be performed by non-monetary policies. Therefore, Fuhrmann argues, the establishment of a CB has to be understood as a social strategy which requires the integrative development of the domestic economy.

In a system with inside-money, it is noted that the money supply process by commercial banks can have a destabilizing effect. Therefore, an effective banking supervision and discretionary monetary measures become necessary, which could be put in effect by a modified CB or a central bank consisting of a pure CB and a banking board.

With regard to the dynamics of the system, Fuhrmann underlines that the CB represents a strategy which, in contrast to other possibilities of an exchange rate fixing, is not imposed on a given market system, but takes into account that implementing countries are in a process of endogenously developing or optimizing market structures. Therefore, he concludes, it is part of a future-orientated strategy that is effective and stable only within a comprehensive institutional framework which allows for the structural adaptation of the entire domestic economy.

References

Barro, R. J. and D. B. Gordon (1983), Rules, Discretion and Reputation in a Model of Monetary Policy, *Journal of Monetary Economics* 12, 101-20.

Kydland, F. E. and E. C. Prescott (1977), Rules Rather than Discretion: The Inconsistency of Optimal Plans, *Journal of Political Economy* 85, 473-91.

Mc Callum, B. T. (1995), Two Fallacies Concerning Central Bank Independence, *American Economic Review* 85, Papers and Proceedings, 207-11.

Persson, T. and G. Tabellini (1993), Designing Institutions for Monetary Stability, *Carnegie-Rochester Conference Series on Public Policy* 39, 53-84.

Rogoff, K. (1985), The Optimal Degree of Commitment to an Intermediate Monetary Target, *Quarterly Journal of Economics* 100, 1169-90.

Sachs, J., A. Tornell and A. Velasco (1996), Financial Crises in Emerging Markets: The Lesson from 1995, *Brookings Papers on Economic Activity,* 1, 147-215.

Summers, L. H. (1991), How Should Long-Term Monetary Policy Be Determined?, *Journal of Money, Credit, and Banking* 23, 625-31.

Svensson, L. E. O. (1997), Optimal Inflation Targets, Conservative Central Banks and Linear Inflation Contracts, *American Economic Review* 87, 98-114.

Walsh, C. E. (1995), Optimal Contracts for Central Bankers, *American Economic Review* 85, 150-67.

Monetary Policy: Recent Theory and Practice

James Tobin
Yale University, P.O. Box 208281, New Haven, CT 06520-8281, USA

1 The Demise of Monetarism

Milton Friedman's monetarism provoked hot debates on the conduct of monetary policy from the 1950s through the 1970s. The monetarists wanted the central bank to stop setting interest rates and instead to target growth in a monetary quantity, a stock of money by one or another definition, from the monetary base to intermediate aggregates as inclusive as M2 and M3. For hitting at least some of these monetary targets setting a money-market interest rate might be the operating mechanism. (The alternative could be quantitative control of the bank reserves portion of the monetary base, as practiced by the Federal Reserve 1979-82.)

Monetarist proposals differed in the horizon over which a money stock growth rate would be fixed. Friedman himself sometimes advocated setting it permanently, once for all at the estimated growth rate of the real economy. In practice, numerical money stock growth targets were reconsidered every year or even every quarter. The Full Employment and Balanced Growth Act of 1978, the „Humphrey-Hawkins" Act, required the Fed to report them to Congressional committees every six months. Thus they could themselves be intermediate instruments designed to achieve the broader economic goals of the legislation. The use of money stock targets spread throughout the central banks of the world. The main purpose was to overcome the inflationary bias alleged to result from operating by discretionary movements of interest rates.

In the last two decades the sway of mechanical monetarism of this kind faded away. A principal reason was institutional change, which made the velocities of the various M's even more variable and uncertain than they already were. Money substitutes multiplied, and definitions of M's couldn't keep up. Regulatory reforms and market developments allowed market-determined interest to be paid on deposits that had formerly been interest-free or subject to legal ceilings.

One proposal to avoid the problems created by volatility of money velocity V was to target nominal Gross Domestic Product, that is M times V, instead. The implicit terms of trade between rates of growth of price level P and real GDP Y, in responding to a shock to MV would then be one percent to one percent, and this might result in excessive short-run volatility of Y and P. This whole approach to monetary policy seems to have lost support, as it came to be understood that central banks did not need the discipline of intermediate M-growth targets to achieve more fundamental goals, including the control of inflation.

2 Current Orthodoxy in Monetary and Fiscal Policy

The dominant trend in the theory and practice of monetary policy over these last two decades has been its dedication to price stability. Central banks from New Zealand to the Finland have undertaken this commitment, either by mandates of their governments or by exercises of independent discretion granted them by their governments. Now the new European central bank will be bound by its charter to maintain the purchasing power of the *euro*, the coming single currency of the European Union (EU).

It is significant that these targets are stability of the price *level*, not of the rate of inflation. Inflation is not to be stabilized at a positive rate, by holding unemployment at the „natural rate“ or the NAIRU (the „Non-Accelerating-Inflation Rate of Unemployment“) - or at a negative rate either. No, it is to be stabilized at zero. This implies that any inflation that occurs as a result of supply or demand shocks, domestic or foreign, must be sooner or later expunged. A less draconian monetary strategy would accept price level increases resulting from big shocks as permanent and seek to avoid subsequent inflations. Even if inflation stability were accepted as a target, it is likely to be asymmetrical. That is, monetary policy would oppose a shock increasing the rate of inflation but would welcome a disinflationary shock.

The corollary to dedicating monetary policy to price stability is official indifference to real macro-economic outcomes - employment and unemployment, real domestic product and its growth rate. These are likely to be ignored or drastically subordinated in the priorities of most central banks today. At best, they will suffer from lexicographic ordering. That is, real outcomes become a policy concern only after the central bank, and the government too, are confident that the price stability target is met.

Fiscal policy, reflecting the same values and priorities, and the same macro theory, is also unavailable to stabilize real national output against cyclical fluctuations. The same orthodoxy that minimizes the role of real economic performance in monetary policy insists on fiscal discipline regardless of the state of the economy. Indeed, not only is active fiscal stimulus to reverse cyclical recession and promote recovery outlawed, but also active fiscal contraction is required to overcome deficits that arise endogenously from recessions and feeble growth. Formal rules to enforce fiscal as well as monetary austerity in the coming *euro* regime of the EU are provided in the Treaty of Maastricht.

Under the Treaty the member states will have no autonomous macro policy instruments, not monetary policy, not exchange rate depreciation or appreciation, not budgetary policy. Their governments' debt interest rates will be those of the EU central bank plus allowances for maturities and risks reflecting judgments of rating agencies and financial markets. Absent the governmental, political, and fiscal institutions possessed by the authorities of federations like the United States, Canada, and Germany, the EU's macro policy will be limited to its central bank's tough stance. They are bound to be both Europe-wide and inter-regional shocks, both demand and supply. The architects of the new regime are placing extraordinary faith in the flexibility, mobility, and resourcefulness of the peoples of the continent.

The Bank of Japan has long followed monetarist policies, pursuing price stability via intermediate targets for non-inflationary growth of monetary aggregates. At the same time, the Japanese Ministry of Finance is extremely allergic to budget deficits, even those produced by economy-wide slowdowns. The Ministry especially disdains Keynesian counter-cyclical fiscal policies. Thus Japan, like Europe, eschews macro policy, in faith that the economy will achieve optimal results on its own.

3 Orthodox Macroeconomic Doctrine

The macroeconomic theories underlying these policy rules are those of the anti-Keynesian counter-revolutions, Monetarism and the New Classical Macroeconomics. The fundamental proposition of these new orthodoxies is that real outcomes are invariant to price levels and inflation rates. Actually this was a pre-Keynesian old classical proposition, though more modestly interpreted to refer to long-run tendencies rather than to be literally true every day of the year. The old „classical dichotomy" is now read to mean not only that real outcomes cannot be improved by monetary policies that increase prices and inflation - you can't ride up Phillips's famous curve - but also to imply that counter-inflationary austerity will be costless in real income, consumption, and social welfare.

Acceptance of New Classical doctrine in official financial policy-making circles was mightily promoted by the unhappy macro-economic history of the 1970s. Prices accelerated first as a consequence of demand shocks from the Vietnam war, then as a result of supply shocks, the two oil price boosts of 1973-4 and 1978-79. Counter-inflationary monetary policies led to four recessions, in 1969-70, 1973-75, 1979-80, and 1981-82, and to postwar record highs in United States unemployment rates in 1975 and 1982. „Stagflation," the simultaneous occurrence of high unemployment and high inflation seemed to be a 180-degree refutation of Keynesian Phillips-curve predictions. In the New Classical version of these events, easy monetary policy - notably Federal Reserve expansionary measures in the election year of 1972 - received the blame. The supply shocks, unprecedented in peacetime, are completely omitted from the ideological histories of the period. Yet the deep and lengthy recessions that accompanied the central banks' concerted attacks on inflation, beginning in 1979, were scarcely confirmations of the New Classical claim that disinflation is costless.

4 The United States, an Exception in Monetary Policy and in Results

The United States is a striking exception to the fashion of designating price stability as *the* target of monetary policy.

Faced with inflation rates above 10 percent in 1979, it is true, the Federal Reserve shifted its tactical operating instrument from money-market interest rates (the Treasury bill rate, and the market rate on overnight interbank loans of „federal funds“ - bank reserve accounts in Federal Reserve Banks), to bank reserve aggregates. For three years 1979-82 the ultimate policy target of the „Fed“ was to bring down inflation. By mid-1982 inflation had fallen to 5 percent and unemployment had risen from 6 percent to 10.5 percent. At this point the Fed under Chairman Paul Volcker reversed course, returned to its previous interest-rate operating procedure, and initiated and managed a six-year recovery, which reduced unemployment below 6 percent while inflation continued to decline.

Under Volcker's successor Alan Greenspan, United States monetary policy has continued to be balanced and pragmatic. It has been directed to reduction of unemployment rates and of the „gap“ between potential and actual GDP, as well as to stabilization of inflation. Indeed Congress has mandated such an approach. The Employment Act of 1946 commits the Federal government, including the Federal Reserve System, to pursuit of „maximum employment, production, and purchasing power.“ The „Humphrey-Hawkins Act“ specifically directs the Fed to aim at both unemployment and inflation goals. This Act's numerical targets, 4 percent for each, were long ignored as impractical, but now they don't seem so outlandish. Radical Right Republicans have in recent years introduced legislation to repeal these Acts and to replace them with a pure price stability mandate. The proposal has supporters within the Federal Reserve System and in private financial circles. However, it seems unlikely to be adopted, anyway so long as the economy's macro performance in the present regime continues to be so spectacularly successful.

In contrast to the United States, European and Japanese central banks and governments did not try to return to the high growth rates, with low unemployment and inflation, which characterized their spectacular quarter century of postwar reconstruction and prosperity 1947-1972. They did not even try to recover the real economic ground they lost in the 1970s and early 1980s. Instead they concentrated on eliminating the slightest chance of any resurgence of inflation. European unemployment has risen to 12 percent in 1997, compared to 4.7 percent in the United States. Inflation in Europe is no lower than in America.

Japanese unemployment numbers are chronically low, because redundant workers are kept on payrolls; but the increase in under-utilization of workers is comparable to Europe. Indeed Japan has managed to have a full-blown depression for the past four years, with periods of negative growth and negative inflation. As a result of lack of demand, not because of deliberate expansionary monetary policy, short interest rates have fallen virtually to zero. Thus monetary policy has become impotent, even if the central bank should want to use it to rescue the economy. Thus has Keynes's *liquidity trap*, thought even by Keynes himself to be an anomalous and rare curiosity confined to severe depressions, come to life once more. The Finance Ministry, unwilling to fill the breach in aggregate demand and distressed by the fiscal cosmetics of a stagnant economy, acts perversely to raise taxes and cut spending. Japanese savers move the funds no one wants to borrow at home into dollars, causing the yen to depreciate (losing 40 percent of its dollar value since 1995), generating an ever larger trade surplus, welcome within Japan as needed demand but unwelcome to the U.S. and other trading partners. It would be hard to find a case of worse macro-economic policy. As terribly costly as it has been to Japan itself, it has been much more disastrous to other economies of East Asia, as events in late 1997 have shown.

5 Applying Rules with Discretion

"Rules versus discretion" in monetary policy has long been a topic of debate and research. In Tobin (1983), I argued that a mechanical rule blind to actual economic events and outcomes could not work, and for that reason alone would not be tolerated by central bankers, governments, and electorates. Any rule would have to be responsive to observed economic information. However, it would be impossible to anticipate all events that might require policy adjustments and to specify in advance the correct direction and size of the response to each. Actual responses would have to depend on the best estimates and judgments of the policy makers at the time - in that sense discretion. For this reason, I stressed, as I have here, the prime importance of choices of targets and operating procedures for monetary policy, rather than „rules," counting on the central bank to find, in varying circumstances, the ways of pursuing the goals.

According to Taylor (1993), "If there is anything about which modern macroeconomics is clear...- and on which there is substantial consensus - it is that policy rules have major advantages over discretion in improving economic performance." At the same time Taylor interprets "rules" in a way that allows, indeed requires, large doses of discretion in their application. Starting from the side of the debate opposite to mine, he seems to arrive at the same place. Follow the spirit, the intent, of a rule, he says, and do not be bound by a particular quantitative formula. Use such a formula perhaps, but as just one element in the set of indicators considered in periodic decisions on settings of the operating variables of monetary policy, whether quantitative aggregates or interest rates.

A major reason for the modern consensus for rules over discretion, as Taylor remarks, is to sustain the "credibility" of the policy-makers, specifically avoiding "dynamic inconsistency". I have never believed that monetary policy makers are organically vulnerable to such irrationality or addicted to playing a deceitful game to override public preferences. I am sure that they do not consciously seek to mislead the public into expecting future price stability in order to fool workers into working more than they really wish to. On the contrary, central bankers are obsessively concerned with the future consequences of their actions and the possibility that something they do now will set a bad precedent. Anyway, Taylor agrees that formal rules are not essential to credibility.

Taylor suggests a simple monetary policy formula for the United States:

$$r = p + .5y + .5(p - 2) + 2$$

where

r is the federal funds rate in percent per year.

p is the rate of inflation (of the GDP deflator) over the past four quarters.

y is the percent deviation of real GDP from target.

Target GDP would be its value at full employment, i.e. NAIRU. Potential GDP in this sense has been growing at 2.2 to 2.5 percent per year. This "rule" embodies the balanced pragmatic two-goal policy I above attributed to the Fed since 1982. Taylor shows that his "rule" fits actual data quite well. As he recognizes and illustrates, nevertheless, its message has to be modified in case of observed or expected exogenous shocks, and the formula itself has to be corrected as new data accumulate. In fact, if the Fed had implemented his equation from 1993 through 1997, the economy would have suffered unnecessarily high unemployment and lost about two percent of GDP per year. The reason is that in 1993 and indeed until 1996 the NAIRU defining Potential Output was thought to be at least 6 percent, whereas in the event it turned out to be at most 5 percent and probably lower. Greenspan was right to use discretion, as new observations suggested that more output could be produced without inflationary danger.

6 The Mystery: Why and How Does Monetary Policy Rule the Economy?

The interest rate on overnight loans of federal funds is, as explained above, the Fed's instrument of policy. It is a market rate, which the Fed controls by buying or selling Treasury bills (in usual practice with agreements to repurchase them) at its intervention rate, nowadays publicly announced. At scheduled meetings eight times a year - and occasionally at other times - the Federal Reserve System's „Federal Open Market Committee" (FOMC) reconsiders and sometimes changes the intervention rate, generally by 25 or 50 basis points, rarely by more.

The tail wages the dog. By gently touching a tiny tail, Alan Greenspan wags the mammoth dog, the great American economy. Isn't that remarkable? The federal funds rate is the shortest of all interest rates, remote from the rates on assets and debts by which businesses and households finance real investment and consumption expenditures counted in GDP. Why does monetary policy work? How? It's a mystery, fully understood by neither central bankers nor economists.

There are two lines of explanation: substitution chains and policy expectations. Expectations are very powerful, but they cannot work unless chains of asset substitution really do occur. That is, FOMC actions today, in conjunction with other economic observations, convey information about future monetary policies and future federal funds rates and thus affect the entire current spectrum of interest rates and asset prices. The process involves reshufflings of portfolios in response to changes in market interest rates and asset prices, actual and expected: banks' reserves and loans; bank deposits, bonds, and equities; debt instruments, equities, and real properties.

It would do portfolio managers, entrepreneurs, and consumers no good to understand Alan Greenspan if his actions really do not matter - unless they matter **just** because everyone thinks they do. We think we know that monetary policy is not just a bubble. We think we know from experience, as in 1931-33, 1973-74, 1979-83, that the Fed can if it wants take really big actions with immense consequences, and these demonstrations support the belief that even its modest everyday measures are important. That belief makes the central bank's job much easier. But it does not permit us, or the central bank, to expect precision from formula rules like Taylor's, as good as his is.

Why do the Federal Reserve and other central banks intervene only in financial markets for the shortest and most liquid nominal assets, those closest to the monetary base, far from the frontiers between financial markets and economic agents' expenditures on GDP goods and services? It was not always thus. In the past, central banks have discounted illiquid commercial loans, and even brokers' customer loans, and have conducted open market operations in long-term government bonds. In the present free-market mood of capitalist democracies, central banks want to be as unobtrusive and neutral as possible.

However, there are times when interventions closer to the real economy would be desirable. The present impasse in Japan is an example. Central bank operations in short safe liquid assets are mired in the „liquidity trap." Because of the unfavorable and risky business outlook and the unsound balance sheets of the banks, loans to businesses and households are expensive or unavailable. The Bank of Japan has operated in the stock market in the past, and maybe the time has come again for bold moves.

More generally, operations in long-term bonds could help get cyclical recoveries going when lenders are slow to reflect easing of short-term rates. Inflation-indexed government bonds are desirable instruments for open market operations, because they are closer to real goods and services than are nominal bonds. With fiscal policies no longer eligible for counter-cyclical stabilization, and with the globalization of financial markets threatening national financial sovereignty, innovative thinking about the tactics and structure of monetary operations is urgently needed. This is especially imperative in Europe, given the novel challenges facing the new EU central bank.

References

Taylor, J. B. (1993), Discretion versus Policy Rules in Practice, *Carnegie-Rochester Series on Public Policy* 23, 194-214.

Tobin, J. (1983), Monetary Policy: Rules, Targets, and Shocks, *Journal of Money, Credit, and Banking* 15, 506-18.

Part I:

Central Bank Design

1. Game Theoretic Analysis of Monetary Policy Institutions

Mechanism Design for Central Banks - Results and Unsolved Issues

Gerhard Illing
University of Frankfurt, Mertonstr. 17, D - 60054 Frankfurt/Main

1 Introduction

The question how monetary institutions should be designed attracted considerable attention during the past years. In the context of the Maastricht Treaty, there has been a surge of papers on the adequate design of the European Central Bank; the breakdown of the Rouble-zone created a strong demand for policy advice about what kind of monetary institutions should be adapted in Eastern European countries; finally, after the breakdown of stability of money demand in many countries, there was a need to redesign monetary policy instruments.

For those searching for theoretical foundations of policy advice, game theory has been a popular candidate for obvious reasons: A specific branch in game theory is concerned with the issue of mechanism design (that is, the search for adequate rules). The mechanism design approach turned out to be extremely successful in the theory of industrial organization, yielding important insights in issues such as the optimal regulation of firms under asymmetric information. One of the most spectacular applications was the design of auctions for selling radio waves by the federal government in the US.

It seems natural to try to adopt these methods also to monetary policy, and so it is not surprising that game theoretic models play a major role in the present debate on the design of monetary policy. Indeed, these models provide helpful insights about what rules of the game monetary policy should follow. During the past years, there have been two significant trends in monetary policy: central banks became increasingly independent across many countries, and inflation targeting has been adapted as a new framework for monetary policy in a growing number of countries.

Game theoretic analysis gives a theoretical foundation for both trends. In particular, it supports moves to delegate policy to an independent central bank. In the literature, however, different paradigms can be found which give quite contradictory policy advice for essential details. On the one hand, Rogoff (1985) suggests that monetary policy should be delegated to a conservative central banker. On the other hand, Walsh (1995) - in a much cited paper - argues that monetary policy should be specified in a transparent contract between government and central banker.

In a rough, over-simplified, but provocative way one could argue that these two concepts give theoretical support to two quite different forms of central bank independence both of which are hotly debated recently: Rogoff's idea is frequently cited as a justification for the model of the Bundesbank (which is the prototype for the design of the European Central Bank). Crudely speaking, it suggests that the central bank should be independent from government interference both when formulating its goals and when choosing its instruments. On the other hand, the Walsh contract can be interpreted as justifying movements towards inflation targeting as experienced in New Zealand and Great Britain (see Fischer 1995). According to Walsh, a democratic parliament should specify the final targets the central bank is supposed to implement in a contract, and then let the bank choose the instruments to implement these goals on her own (she gets operational independence). The central bankers should be paid according to the performance achieved, and the contract has to be designed to give the appropriate incentives.

It turns out that - at least in theory - the Walsh contract performs much better than the Rogoff delegation mechanism. Remarkably, it can eliminate completely all inefficiencies caused by a lack of credibility. Thus, the Walsh contract presents a challenge for those who consider incentives for surprise inflation to be one of the major issues for monetary policy. The contract approach is also of interest because it suggests a quite different route than the one chosen for the European Central Bank (obviously, there will be no single democratic parliament which could specify the targets).

The present paper gives a critical survey about the main results of game theoretic models of central bank design. In section 2, the problem of dynamic consistency is discussed. Then, the main section compares the Rogoff and the Walsh mechanism and discusses some issues which have not been solved. The main drawback of the standard mechanism design approach is that it leaves a crucial question unanswered: Why should the specific rules defined be credible? In the literature on mechanism design, it is, in general, taken for granted that the rules of the game, once defined, will be binding - the only question is which rules should be chosen. This approach makes sense for certain issues - such as the design of optimal auctions. In that case, it is very easy both to define and to enforce specific rules. Credibility of the mechanism itself is no issue.

In the case of monetary institutions, however, things are much more complicated. Here, the most challenging task is to find ways to make credible that the rules designed will be adhered to. Some rules are more credible than others, and adaptation to a different mechanism, in general, involves learning costs. Thus, a mechanism which seems to be inferior from the view of mechanism design may be superior once these learning costs are taken into account. The final section speculates on how this problem may be approached.

2 The Problem of Dynamic Consistency - The Basic Model

The framework of dynamic inconsistency formulated by Kydland and Prescott (1977) and Barro and Gordon (1983) has become the workhorse for game theoretic analysis of monetary policy. The famous Barro-Gordon model analyzes a world with sticky private wage and debt contracts. Private agents arrange their contracts for a fixed term, based on inflationary expectations. During that period, contracts cannot adjust to shocks. In contrast, monetary policy can respond flexibly to shocks. Thus it can play an active role in stabilizing output fluctuations.[1]

If, however, because of structural inefficiencies in the economy, the natural output rate is below the socially optimal rate, there is a strong incentive to abuse this flexibility by carrying out a surprise inflation.[2] The essence of the argument can be captured in a simple three stage game: In stage 1, monetary policy is announced; in stage 2, private agents form their expectations about inflation and arrange their contracts; finally, in stage 3, monetary policy is carried out.

In the last stage, with given contracts, policy can exploit the short-run Phillips curve trade-off, in order to stimulate output above the natural level. Private agents anticipate this incentive already in the second stage; as a result, they form high inflation expectations from the beginning. Consequently, in an economy with rational, forward looking agents, monetary policy cannot be used successfully to stimulate output to cope with structural inefficiencies; but since the incentive prevails, equilibrium is characterized by an inefficiently high average rate of inflation. All agents in the economy would be better off if policy could commit to low inflation.

The standard example assumes that deviations from the desired targets for inflation π^* and output y^* cause quadratic welfare losses:

(2.1) $$L = (\pi - \pi^*)^2 + b(y - y^*)^2,$$

---

[1] Usually, monetary policy is assumed to have immediate control about inflation and output. As emphasised by Goodhardt and Huang (1995), considering the time lags in the monetary transmission mechanism, there must be enough persistence in the stickiness of the contracts. Obviously, if policy did not become effective before the contracts expire, the consistency problem would disappear.

[2] It is no coincidence that this model became popular during the period of high inflation in the beginning of the eighties. Now, when some see „the end of the inflation era" coming, empirical support gets much weaker. So Alan Blinder (1997) states: „During my brief career as a central banker, I never once witnessed nor experienced this temptation (*that is, to carry out a surprise inflation*). Nor do I believe my colleagues did." Nevertheless, in the academic discussion there is a strong feeling that the Barro-Gordon model captures an important aspect of monetary policy. The world-wide reduction of inflation rates during the nineties may simply be a result of having established efficient mechanisms to restrain this incentive as discussed below.

with π^* as inflation target and y^* as output target.

Output deviates from its natural level $\bar{y}$ according to a short run supply curve:

(2.2) $$y-\bar{y}=\pi-\pi^e+\varepsilon\,;\ \text{with}\ E(\varepsilon)=0\,;\ Var(\varepsilon)=\sigma_\varepsilon^2,$$

(2.3) $$\Delta=y^*-\bar{y}.$$

Actual output rises above (falls below) the natural level $\bar{y}$ when inflation is higher (lower) than expected. In addition, shocks ε disturb the supply curve. The degree of structural inefficiency in the economy is captured by Δ - the difference between target and natural output.

In stage 1, when inflationary expectations can be influenced, it would be optimal to announce a contingent policy $\pi(\varepsilon)$ - the rate of inflation π as a function of the shock ε. On average, the policy should correspond to the target rate of inflation π^*. If policy can commit to carry out in stage 3 the policy announced in stage 1, the optimal commitment solution is obtained by differentiating the loss function :

(2.4) $$L=(\pi-\pi^*)^2+b(\pi-\pi^e-\Delta+\varepsilon)^2,$$

with respect to $\pi(\varepsilon)$ and to π^e subject to the constraint $\pi^e=E(\pi)$. The first order conditions give:

(2.5) $$\pi_C^e=\pi^*,\ \pi_C=\pi^*-\frac{b}{1+b}\ \varepsilon\,;\ y_C-\bar{y}=\frac{1}{1+b}\ \varepsilon,$$

(2.6) $$L_C=\frac{b}{1+b}\sigma_\varepsilon^2+b\Delta^2.$$

The commitment solution is derived under the assumption that the policy announced in stage 1 will indeed be carried out in stage 3. Once inflationary expectations have been set in stage 2, however, the optimization problem for a social planner trying to maximize welfare has changed. Given low inflationary expectations, there is an incentive to raise inflation above the announced level. This incentive problem is essentially a dynamic moral hazard problem. In a rational expectation equilibrium, private agents will form expectations in stage 2 such that cheating is no longer worthwhile. The optimization problem has to be modified to take into account this incentive constraint. The discretionary solution is characterized by:

(2.7) $$\pi_D^e=\pi^*+b\cdot\Delta,\quad \pi_D=\pi^*+b\cdot\Delta-\frac{b}{1+b}\varepsilon\ ,\ y_D-\bar{y}=\frac{1}{1+b}\varepsilon,$$

(2.8) $$L_D = \frac{b}{1+b}\sigma_\varepsilon^2 + (1+b)b\Delta^2 = L_C + b^2\Delta^2.$$

Figure 1 gives a graphical representation of the discretionary solution (see Fecht and Illing, 1997). Temporary supply shocks cause fluctuations of the short run supply curve around the natural level $\bar{y}$. Those short run supply curves shift upwards with increasing inflationary expectations: with $\pi^e = \pi^*$, they fluctuate around point C, whereas with $\pi^e = \pi_D^e$, they fluctuate around D. But regardless of the level of the curves, the optimal policy response for given expectations is always characterized by a point of tangency between the short run supply curve and a social indifference curve. Thus, the stabilization curve $f(\varepsilon, \pi^e)$ represents all policy solutions for given π^e and ε. Since $E(\varepsilon) = 0$, average inflation is characterized by the intersection of the stabilization curve $f(\varepsilon, \pi^e)$ and the natural output rate $\bar{y}$ (point D). In a Nash equilibrium, $\pi^e = E(\pi)$, so π_D^e is the only rational expectation of inflation under discretionary policy.

Figure 1: Discretionary Policy

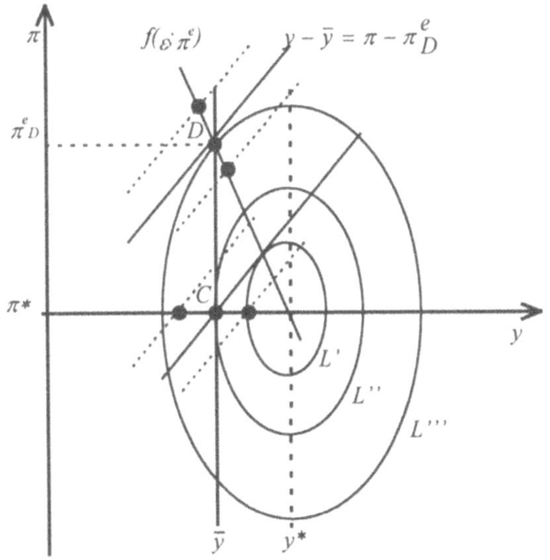

Discretionary policy is subject to the inflationary bias $b \cdot \Delta$. If structural inefficiencies get worse ($\bar{y}$ shifts further to the left from y^*), this bias increases (on the other hand, the bias disappears when $\bar{y}$ coincides with y^*). Similarly, if the weight b of output losses in the welfare function increases, the stabilization curve becomes steeper and so point D shifts upwards. Since the bias is anticipated, there is no output-gain.

Under commitment, the stabilization curve would shift downwards crossing point C as the average outcome. Figure 1 immediately illustrates the incentive problem caused by dynamic inconsistency: Given low inflationary expectations, the short run supply curves would fluctuate around C. Since ex post, with given expectations, the optimal policy is always characterized by the stabilization curve $f(\varepsilon,\pi^e)$, there is a strong incentive to deviate from the announced policy in order to get closer to the output target y^*. Obviously, welfare would be higher if some commitment mechanism could guarantee in a credible way that policy will not give in to this incentive for surprise inflation.

What kind of mechanism could enforce such a commitment? It is well known that in a repeated game, such commitment may be feasible via reputation. The folk theorem shows that the commitment outcome can be sustained as equilibrium, given that there is perfect information, and agents have an infinite time horizon and are sufficiently patient. The theory of repeated games, however, does not provide a convincing argument for the view that the commitment solution will actually be achieved. According to the folk theorem, in a repeated game an infinite number of equilibria exist - both the commitment and the discretionary solution may be sustained as equilibrium, but also any outcome in between.

The repeated game framework is helpful in showing what solutions can possibly be achieved, but it does not help to answer the question which one of all these possible equilibria will actually be chosen. For that issue, it is necessary to analyze specific institutional structures in detail which may guarantee that a superior equilibrium will be picked out of all feasible ones. This *institutional approach* is complementary to the *reputation approach*: By designing specific rules, particular solutions can be sustained. The following section compares different institutional arrangements which may improve upon the discretionary solution. Of course, these rules (resp. mechanisms) cannot be credible unless the institutions enforcing them have sufficient reputation to stick to the rules. Problems involved in designing credible rules will be discussed.

3 Designs for Commitment

The crucial issue is to what extent different institutions can get close to the commitment outcome. Obviously, they should be able to provide some binding commitment power. Work in industrial organization shows that delegation of tasks to an outside agent can serve as an effective commitment mechanism. Not surprisingly, many monetary arrangements found in the real world fit well within this framework.

As an example, pegging the exchange rate can be interpreted as effectively delegating monetary policy to some outside authority - at least within limits (that is, usually escape clauses allow for cancellation of the commitment). Another mechanism, becoming increasingly popular, is the delegation of monetary policy to an independent agency (the transfer of decisions to an independent central bank). Rogoff's (1985) famous model of delegation to a conservative central banker gave theoretical support to movements to make central banks more independent.

The delegation mechanisms discussed so far do reduce the *inflation bias*, but there is always a cost involved: Since output fluctuations are no longer stabilized efficiently, a *stabilization bias* is introduced. Beginning with Rogoff (1985), the literature seemed to suggest that the trade off between inflation and stabilization bias is unavoidable. That is, even though delegation mechanisms can improve upon the discretionary solution, they will be unable to sustain the commitment solution.

In a much cited paper, Walsh (1995) showed that - contrary to conventional wisdom - the commitment solution may indeed be obtained by a properly designed contract. His approach is a straightforward application of principal agent theory to the monetary policy game. The government (the principal) signs a contract with the central bank (the agent) specifying the goals and monetary incentives. The central bank has the task to implement the policy. By giving proper monetary incentives, the desired outcome can be obtained. The Walsh set up attracted considerable attention, esp. since recent moves to inflation targeting have some resemblance to his idea: Under inflation targeting, governments formulate a specific target and delegate implementation to the central bank, which is given independence concerning the instruments it may use. The most explicitly formulated contract is New Zealand's central bank governor's contract. Narrowly interpreted, inflation targeting appears to be a definite example of an extremely inflexible rule. But by allowing for escape clauses, inflation targeting can mimic the optimal contract. Svensson (1997) even argues that inflation targeting can be equivalent to the optimal contract.

Before comparing the Rogoff and the Walsh solution, implications of strict targets are analyzed first.

3.1 Strict Targets

The most extreme type of rules would be to tie the hands of monetary authorities so that monetary policy has no flexibility at all to respond to shocks. There are, however, quite different ways for tying the hands. A famous example of such a strict, passive rule is Friedman's proposal to reduce monetary policy to a simple exercise: money supply should grow at a steady, fixed rate. An alternative would be a passive rule of inflation targeting without adjustments to output shocks. Fixing exchange rates (or, as a more extreme version, currency boards) are comparable mechanisms. Obviously, alternative strict rules will yield quite different outcomes, depending on the nature of the shocks. With a stable money demand, money supply targeting provides - in contrast to inflation targeting - some automatic stabilization for supply shocks. On the other hand, inflation targeting can offset demand shocks, whereas a strict target of money supply implies high volatility under unstable money demand. As a reference, we briefly compare the outcome of these rules in the present framework.

3.1.1 Targeting Money Supply

To analyze implications of a policy of money supply targeting, we need to characterize equilibrium on the money market. Let μ be the growth of money supply, y the rate of output growth. η represents shocks to money demand with $E(\eta) = 0$; $Var(\eta) = \sigma_\eta^2$. Then, we get according to the quantity theory:

(3.1) $$y = \mu - \pi + \eta$$

A policy of strict money growth $\bar{\mu}_M$ aims at accommodating demand arising both from target inflation π^* and potential output growth $\bar{y}$:

(3.2) $$\bar{\mu}_M = \pi^* + \bar{y}$$

By inserting (3.1) and (3.2) into (2.2), this policy yields the fluctuations:

(3.3) $$\pi_M - \pi^* = \tfrac{1}{2}(\eta - \varepsilon),\ y_M - \bar{y} = \tfrac{1}{2}(\varepsilon + \eta).$$

(3.4) $$L_M = \frac{1+b}{4}\left(\sigma_\varepsilon^2 + \sigma_\eta^2\right) + b\Delta^2.$$

Targeting money supply eliminates the inflation bias; in addition, it provides some automatic stabilization of supply shocks. Stabilization of supply shocks is excessive (relative to price stability) under money supply targeting for $b < 1$, whereas it is insufficient for $b > 1$. Evidently, a strict policy not adjusting for „special factors" (money demand shocks) introduces additional noise. $L_D > L_M$ if:

(3.5) $$\frac{4}{1+b} b^2 \Delta^2 > \sigma_\eta^2 + \left(\frac{1}{4} - \frac{b}{(1+b)^2}\right)\sigma_\varepsilon^2$$

The strict rule (3.1) improves upon the discretionary solution (2.7) if the loss arising from inflation bias exceeds the loss due to volatility of money demand and inadequate stabilization of supply shocks ($b \neq 1$). When volatility of money demand is high, (3.1) gives a worse performance relative to discretion. Obviously, the commitment solution (2.5) can be obtained provided demand shocks are small ($\sigma_\eta^2 \to 0$) and deviations from both targets are weighted equally ($b \to 1$).

3.1.2 Strict Inflation Targeting

A policy of strict inflation targeting keeps inflation at the target π^*. Supply shocks are completely absorbed by output fluctuations (compare figure 1). We get:

$$(3.6) \qquad \pi_F = \pi^* \ , \ y_F = \bar{y} + \varepsilon.$$

$$(3.7) \qquad L_F = bE(\varepsilon - \Delta)^2 = b\left[E(\varepsilon)^2 + \Delta^2\right] = b\sigma_\varepsilon^2 + b\Delta^2.$$

The inflexible rule (3.6) is superior to the discretionary policy (2.7) if the loss due to lack of stabilization is more than compensated by the elimination of the inflation bias. For that to hold, obviously, the variance of the shocks has to be low enough. More precisely, $L_D > L_F$ if

$$(3.8) \qquad \Delta^2(1+b) > \sigma_\varepsilon^2.$$

Pegging the exchange rate to another country can also be interpreted as a strict rule (cf. Giavazzi and Pagano (1988)). The fixed exchange rate regime may serve as mechanism to achieve the commitment solution, if the monetary authority in the leading country has commitment power and if shocks are perfectly correlated across countries. Obviously, this leaves open the question why the leading country should be able to commit to the optimal policy whereas the pegging country can only commit to a policy of fixed exchange rates (see also section 4).

In case of asymmetric shocks, in general, a better solution can be achieved by an exchange rate regime with escape clauses. Such clauses allow for a flexible response in case of large asymmetric shocks. Of course, again this poses the question how such clauses may be implemented in a credible way. Furthermore, fixing the exchange rate cannot be used as commitment device for all countries, so it does not give a final answer to the commitment problem.

3.2 Delegation to a Conservative Central Banker (Rogoff)

In the context of monetary policy, Rogoff (1985) was the first to adopt the idea that delegation of policy to an independent agent may serve as mechanism to gain commitment power. In his setting, agents differ by the weight b_i they attach to the target of output stabilization. There is a density distribution $g(b_i)$ across all agents i. Let b_m be the weight of the representative agent in the economy (b_m may either be the mean of the distribution, if a utilitarian social planner delegates policy, or it may represent the weight of the median voter in a democracy).

Rogoff's famous and intuitively appealing result is that a social planner (the representative agent) has a strong incentive to delegate monetary policy to a banker who is more conservative than he is himself in the following sense: The banker should give less weight to the output target. The social planner tries to minimize the loss $L_m = (\pi - \pi^*)^2 + b_m (y - \bar{y} - \Delta)^2$. An agent with weight b_k carries out the policy:

$$(3.9) \qquad \pi_k = \pi^* + b_k \Delta - \frac{b_k}{1+b_k}\varepsilon \; ; \; y_k = \bar{y} + \frac{1}{1+b_k}\varepsilon.$$

with $E(\pi_k) = \pi^* + b_k \Delta$. The more conservative the banker (the lower b_k), the lower inflation will be on average, but at the same time the higher the volatility of output shocks (in the extreme, with b_k =0, policy is equivalent to (3.6)).

Figure 2 illustrates the effect of a conservative central banker graphically. The dotted indifference curves give the representative agent's preferences, whereas the continuously drawn indifference curves L_k represent preferences of the conservative banker who gives less weight to output stabilization. Since a conservative banker's stability line is less steep, average inflation rate is lower and at the same time the response to output shocks is weaker. Thus, inflation bias will be reduced at the expense of a stabilization bias.

Figure 2: Delegation to a Conservative Banker

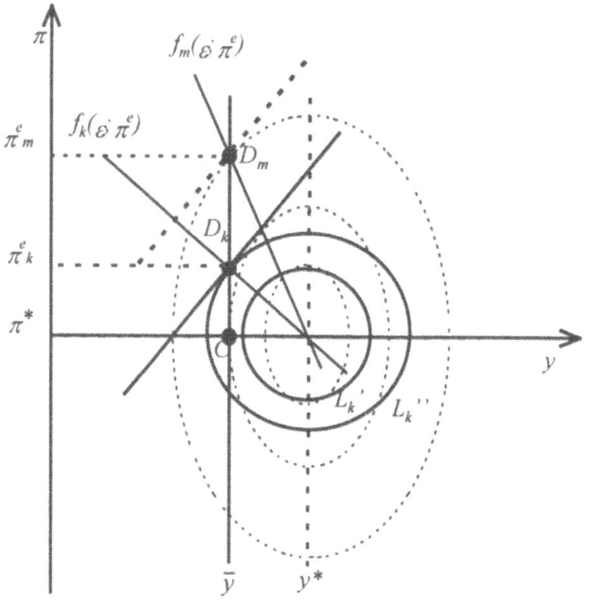

The expected loss of such a policy, calculated from the point of view of the representative agent, is:

$$(3.10)\quad L(b_k)=b_k^2\,\Delta^2+\left(\frac{b_k}{1+b_k}\right)^2\sigma_\varepsilon^2+\frac{b_m}{(1+b_k)^2}\sigma_\varepsilon^2+b_m\,\Delta^2 .$$

The representative agent b_m will choose the type b_k as central banker which minimizes (3.10). This gives the first order condition:

$$(3.11)\quad F(b_k)=2\,b_k\,\Delta^2+2\,\frac{b_k-b_m}{(1+b_k)^3}\sigma_\varepsilon^2=0\ .$$

$F(b_k=b_m)>0$, whereas $F(b_k=0)<0$. With F being continuous, there is an interior solution. The solution is given by the condition:

$$(3.12)\quad \frac{b_m-b_k}{b_k(1+b_k)^3}=\frac{\Delta^2}{\sigma_\varepsilon^2}>0.$$

Policy should be delegated to a more conservative central banker, the lower the variance of supply shocks and the stronger the structural (and thus the inflationary) bias. But it should never be delegated to an extreme conservative unless $\sigma_\varepsilon\to 0$ resp. $\Delta\to\infty$. On the other hand, if $\sigma_\varepsilon\to\infty$ resp. $\Delta\to 0$, there is no gain in delegation.

Rogoff's paper became popular because his idea goes very much conform with intuition about central bank policy: Central bankers usually behave in a conservative way, and Rogoff gives a mathematical proof that this is exactly what they should do. So, at first sight, his approach seems to provide a convincing answer to the problem of mechanism design. To make this solution work, the central bank, once appointed, should be given both target and operational independence for the following reason: obviously, in stage 3, there is a strong incentive for the government to renege on the delegation - as soon as private agents formed their expectations, it would be in the interest of the representative agent to cancel the arrangement. Thus, delegation to a conservative banker makes sense only if, once appointed, the banker is free to do what she wants. The government should not be allowed to interfere with her policy.

At the same time, however, the argument illustrates that - in contrast to all sophisticated calculations involved - the commitment problem is solved rather by hand waving than by specifying a proper game form. Certainly, the conditions derived show what could be obtained in case the government sticks to the delegation mechanism. But it tells nothing about the reasons why it will not renege on its commitment in stage 3. More bluntly: why should it not be feasible for the government to stick to the own announcement made in stage 1, whereas it is feasible to stick to the process of delegation?

Of course, to motivate the story, one can argue that there are costs to renege on delegation.[3] If, for instance, the term length of the central bank appointment is written in a legal constitution, it may be very costly to cancel this arrangement. As Persson and Tabellini (1993) put it: „Clearly, it is possible to change the central bank law, but only according to a preset procedure which requires time." But now, implicitly, the structure of the game has been changed dramatically compared to the initial 3 stage game. Presumably, there are also costs involved in not sticking to an initial announcement. The whole story, even though intuitively appealing, is not fully convincing as long as the nature of commitment costs of different mechanisms is not specified. For delegation to be a credible mechanism, some repeated game story must be hidden behind. Rather than telling the story explicitly, the model resorts to some unspecified belief in the functioning of rules.

The fact that the nature of commitment costs is not modeled in a precise way turns out to be a serious drawback once we accept that there are also good arguments for at least some degree of accountability of monetary policy. To see that, the model has to be made only a little bit more realistic. As shown in condition (3.12), the optimal degree of conservatism does depend on the weight b_m the representative agent attaches to output stabilization. With decreasing weight b_m policy should be delegated to an increasingly conservative banker. Assume now that, initially, there is some uncertainty about b_m which will be resolved after stage 2, but before stage 3. If the actual b_m deviates too much from expected value $E(b_m)$ (if there is a significant change in preferences), there will be considerable gains from reneging on the delegation mechanism, the more so if the game is repeated for several periods. Now, the advantage of reduced inflation bias has to be traded off against inflexibility of the mechanism to respond to a change of the environment.

A similar point: what should happen if the appointed banker turns out to be inadequate or simply incompetent? The easiest way to capture this within the model is to introduce uncertainty about the weight the central banker attaches to output stabilization. It seems to be an impossible task to pick out exactly the person with the desired preferences. Realistically, preferences are private information. Assume there is a probability distribution around b_k. At what point should the government fire the central banker, if it turns out that $b_k \neq E(b_k)$? To

---

[3] In Rogoff (1985), these costs are assumed to be infinite. With finite costs, delegation would be cancelled in case of large shocks. Lohmann (1992) shows, that welfare increases by appointing a conservative banker, but threatening her to be fired in case deviations from target inflation become too large. Given the threat, the central banker adjusts her policy in case of large shocks more to the preferences b_m. Thus, if policy could choose the cost for reneging on delegation, it would always incur some finite costs. Essentially, by mixing two commitment mechanisms (delegation and escape clause), a superior outcome is achieved.

make matters even more complicated: how should we cope with committee decisions in this context?

To summarize: Rogoff's story is quite helpful as a first step in demonstrating the advantage of central bank independence; yet it is not much more than that. It certainly gives no justification for demands to make monetary policy completely resistant against democratic control, and it does not give much guidance for how far independence should go. There have been quite some fruitful extensions of the approach - such as Lohmann (1992) and - for the trade off between independence and accountability - Fratianni, von Hagen and Waller (1997) and Waller and Walsh (1996). The latter paper also considers the impact of political distortions on monetary policy. As in Alesina and Gatti (1995), it is shown that both inflation and output variability may be reduced via delegation to an independent central banker if policy run by parliament decisions followed partisan interests. Waller and Walsh (1996) also show that term length should be limited if shifts in the long run median preferences are likely. But these papers again simply assert that the rules they analyze can be implemented credibly; the important issue how the functioning of such rules can be made credible is not tackled in a satisfactory way.

3.3 The Optimal Central Bank Contract (Walsh)

Rogoff's basic and intuitively appealing message is that delegation to an independent central bank can improve upon the inflation bias, but only at the cost of introducing a stabilization bias. When policy is guided by partisan interests, independence may also reduce output volatility. For quite some time, this message has been accepted as „common knowledge“ among researchers in monetary policy. This established wisdom has been challenged by Walsh (1995). Applying the theory of optimal regulation of firms, he models monetary policy as a principal agent problem between government (the principal) and central bank (the agent). The problem is to design an efficient contract between the two parties. At first sight quite surprisingly, the optimal contract between principal and agent turns out to have an extremely simple form, provided the agent is risk neutral. It can completely overcome the trade off between inflation and stabilization bias. A crucial condition for this result is, however, that preferences of the central banker are known.

The idea is fairly straightforward. When deciding about policy, central bankers are directed by their preferences, but in addition, they also care about their own monetary payoffs. For a start, assume that the central banker has the same preferences as the government (b_i=b_m=b). Then, even in the absence of any incentive payments, she would take care optimally for stabilization of output. The only difference to the commitment solution is that - benevolent as she is - she cannot resist the temptation to inflate, thus causing an inflationary bias. Intuitively, if the banker gets punished for the social cost imposed by high inflationary expectations, she internalizes these costs and refrains from cheating. So, if a contract gives adequate monetary incentives, it may correct for this bias. As it turns out, payments depending simply on the inflation outcome are sufficient to sustain the commitment outcome. To see why, we analyze the banker's optimization problem

(3.13) $L_i = (\pi - \pi^*)^2 + b_i (y - \bar{y} - \Delta)^2 - T(\pi, \varepsilon)$.

After observing the shock ε, the first order condition for discretionary policy is:

$(\pi - \pi^*) + b(\pi - \pi^e + \varepsilon - \Delta) - \frac{1}{2}\frac{\partial T}{\partial \pi} = 0$ for all ε. This gives:

(3.14) $\pi = \frac{1}{1+b}\pi^* + \frac{b}{1+b}\left[\pi^e - \varepsilon + \Delta\right] + \frac{1}{2}\frac{1}{1+b}\frac{\partial T}{\partial \pi}$.

Taking the average and imposing $\pi^e = E(\pi)$, (3.14) reduces to:

(3.15) $E(\pi) = \pi^* + b\,\Delta + \frac{1}{2}\frac{\partial ET}{\partial \pi}$.

The inflation bias can be completely eliminated if $\frac{\partial ET}{\partial \pi} = -2\,b\,\Delta$. If we impose the condition that on average transfer payments should cancel out (e.g. *E(T)=0*), we get as condition for the optimal transfers by integrating (3.15):

(3.16) $T(\pi, \varepsilon) = c - 2\,b\,\Delta\,\pi = 2\,b\,\Delta\,(\pi^* - \pi)$.

In contrast to Rogoff, according to Walsh, the representative agent should appoint a central banker with the same preferences. In addition, he should pay her a transfer if actual inflation deviates from the target. If inflation exceeds the target, she gets punished, whereas she gets a reward if inflation is below the target. These transfer payments are not meant as punishment for misbehavior, rather they are supposed to correct for the extra welfare cost imposed by higher inflationary expectations. The Walsh contract works like shifting preferences downwards (see figure 3).

The transfer payments should be linear because expected inflation increases linearly with actual inflation. The extent to which deviations should be punished resp. rewarded (the power of the transfer) depends on the inflation bias $b\,\Delta$: the greater the bias, the stronger the payments should react to deviations. The neat thing about the contract is that payments do not depend on the realization ε of the shock. Transfer payments depend only on the inflation outcome π: $T(\pi, \varepsilon) = T(\pi)$. So if the central bank has private information about ε, the contract is not affected at all. Similarly, the nature of the contract is unchanged if inflation control is stochastic, as long as the central bank is risk neutral.

Figure 3: The Optimal Walsh Contract

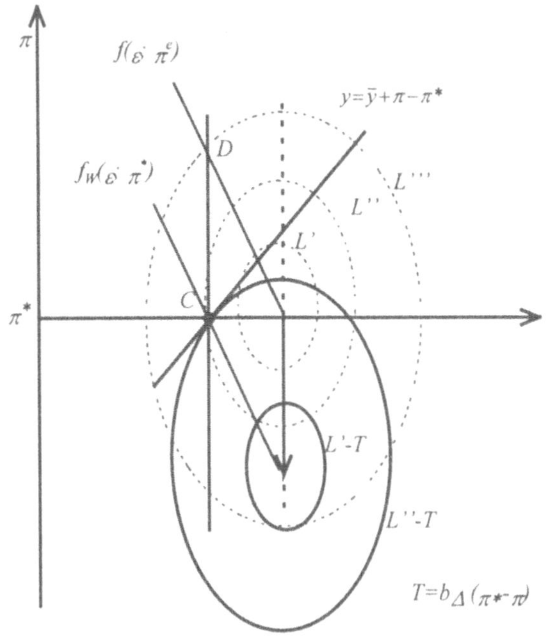

The fact that the Walsh contract can eliminate the inflation bias without the cost of introducing a stabilization bias makes it extremely attractive. The idea is particularly appealing because the contract has some resemblance to inflation targeting. Proponents of such a policy frequently cite it as theoretical foundation. Taken literally, however, inflation targeting is an instruction to the central bank to care only about price stability - an extremely inflexible rule exactly as modeled in section 3.1. The government (the median voter) sets a specific target. The central bank is given operational independence to use the best instruments available to achieve the target. It is held accountable for failing to reach the target (as extreme case, the central bank governor might get fired).

In practice, however, there are lots of escape clauses allowing for adjustments in case of supply shocks (see Leiderman and Svensson (1995) and Bernanke and Mishkin (1997)). As shown by Walsh (1995b), the threat of firing the banker, combined with such escape clauses, can mimic the optimal contract. So implicitly, inflation targeting may be interpreted as approximation of the optimal contract. Svensson (1997) even argues that inflation targeting, appropriately designed, is equivalent to the Walsh contract - at least for the quadratic loss function.

His argument is that even when central bankers have the clear mission to aim at price stability, they certainly care also about other variables besides inflation such as output and employment. Suppose the central banker weights output stabilization in the same way as the government ($b_i = b_m = b$). Now, consider an inflation target $\hat{\pi}$ which undercuts the desired target π^* by some amount k (that is: $\hat{\pi} = \pi^* - k$). When k is chosen appropriately, the mission to enforce such an over ambitious target will effectively implement the optimal contract. Since the banker implicitly cares also about output stabilization, her preferences are:

(3.17)
$$L_i = (\pi - [\pi^* - k])^2 + b_i (y - \bar{y} - \Delta)^2 = (\pi - \pi^*)^2 + 2\,k\,(\pi - \pi^*) + k^2 + b_i (y - \bar{y} - \Delta)^2$$

For $k = b\,\Delta$ the loss function is - up to the constant k^2 - identical to the loss function of the optimal contract in (3.13) (taking into account (3.16). Thus, with an inflation target $\hat{\pi} = \pi^* - b\,\Delta$, the commitment solution can be sustained. As evident from figure 3, the appropriate choice of inflation target $\hat{\pi}$ shifts preferences downwards in the desired way.

It seems doubtful that such a procedure can serve as a strong justification for inflation targeting. The most obvious problem: the actual policy carried out will systematically overshoot the target $\hat{\pi}$. That is exactly what it is supposed to do, but it is hard to see how such a strange arrangement can give credibility to the mechanism. When Svensson (1997) cites the fact that up to now inflation targets have been imperfectly credible as empirical support for the model, that is stressing the whole approach a bit too far.

More general, it is certainly true that inflation targeting, softened via escape clauses, may approximate the Walsh contract. But obviously, the link between optimal contract and inflation targeting is rather loose. Again, it is supported more by hand waving than by sound game theoretic analysis. The reference to escape clauses begs the question of their credibility. But there are even more fundamental problems involved: (1) the credibility of contract design itself; (2) the question of implementing the contract when preferences are private information.

Since the Walsh contract yields a better outcome, it seems superior to Rogoff's delegation mechanism:[4] so a fairly simple and rather robust contract appears to solve for the inflation bias at no cost. At a closer look, this is not so surprising any

[4] Because a conservative banker (decreasing the weight b_i) is formally equivalent to incurring a quadratic penalty $\alpha_i\,(\pi - \pi^*)^2$ with $\alpha_i = (b / b_k - 1)$, one might argue that Rogoff's delegation mechanism is nothing else than proposing quadratic penalties. In that view, the main lesson of Walsh (1995) is that linear penalties (as derived in (3.16)) are superior to quadratic ones. This interpretation (as in Persson and Tabellini (1993) and Svensson (1997)), however, is contrary to the spirit of delegation of policy to a conservative person. Particular contractually arranged transfer payments do not conform to this idea. The fact that formally they are equivalent in the set up presented, once more confirms the point that this set up is not able to capture essential differences of mechanisms in an appropriate way.

more. The driving force behind the result is that the government is assumed to be able to commit to keeping the contract. Without specifying the commitment mechanism, this assumption is rather ad hoc (just as the assumption that delegation can serve as credible mechanism).

Why can the government commit to keep contracts, whereas it cannot commit to public announcements? Once inflationary expectations are fixed, there is a strong incentive to forget about the punishments initially written into the contract. Private parties writing contracts can go to court to enforce the contract, but here, dynamic inconsistency is an inherent problem of benevolent rulers, and so a court interested in maximizing social welfare would have no reason to punish the government in case it does not charge fines in stage 3. From the perspective of mechanism design, the story is nothing more than moving the commitment problem a step further (see also McCallum (1996)).

Again, costs of reneging the contract can serve as motivation. Obviously, there are costs involved (such as loss of reputation, and the danger of not getting reelected), if the public has clear evidence that the government does not stick to the contract and forgets about fines initially arranged - but presumably similar costs have to be borne if public announcements are not kept. Again, the need for specifying the game form which gives credibility to the mechanism itself is obvious. Evidently, an important way to make specific mechanisms enforceable is *public accountability* - if deviations from initial arrangements can easily be observed by the public, the danger of fooling is reduced. Certainly there may be good arguments that explicitly written contracts can be checked more easily than oral announcements, but not necessarily so. In any case, the reasons should be made explicit.

The theory of incomplete contracts provides a partial answer to this problem. The idea is that the higher the complexity of contracts, the more difficult they are to enforce. This suggests that only simple contracts can be implemented; it is not feasible to write complex state contingent contracts, because they cannot be verified by court. Several papers adapted this approach to the Walsh contract (see Canzoneri, Nolan and Yates (1996) and Persson and Tabellini (1993)).

In contrast to the simple setting presented above, complex contingencies have to be faced in reality, and contracts soon get much more complex. A simple modification may illustrate the basic point. Assume that at the stage of framing a constitution for the central bank, the exact nature of structural inefficiency is not yet known. At that stage, Δ is a random variable with $E(\Delta)=\overline{\Delta}$; $Var(\Delta)=\sigma_{\Delta}^2$. The uncertainty is resolved when private agents write their contracts (before stage 2 of the game), so structural inefficiency Δ gets incorporated in inflationary expectations. If complete contracts could be written, the obvious solution to the additional uncertainty introduced would be to write contingent contracts depending on Δ (as derived in (3.16), the slope of the transfer payments should depend on Δ). If however, such detailed contracts are not feasible, transfer payments as laid down in the constitution can only depend on the average expected distortion $\bar{\Delta}$. When transfers are restricted to $T(\pi) = 2\,b\,\bar{\Delta}\,(\pi^* - \pi)$, an efficiency loss is unavoidable: Since the contract cannot adjust to the contingency, realized inflation rate will deviate from the commitment solution: $\pi - \pi_C = b\,(\Delta - \bar{\Delta})$. The deviation does not introduce a systematic bias, but it imposes an additional expected loss:

$$L_{\bar{\Delta}} = b^2\,\sigma_{\Delta}^2\ .$$

Persson and Tabellini (1993) suggest the following alternative: Society may either frame an incomplete constitution for the central bank (the legislative solution); alternatively, it may delegate the task of contract design to the government. Since the government has flexibility in reformulating the contract, it may be able to impose specific targets once, before stage 2, the uncertainty about Δ has been resolved. Thus, a benevolent government would be superior to the inflexible (incomplete) constitution. If, however, partisan interests distort the government incentives, the outcome of a policy run directly by the government may be inferior. For example, there may be a political bias to overstimulate the economy. Partisan interests may introduce a distortion χ for stabilization effort. If, due to political pressures, reaction to stabilizing output is too strong ($\hat{b} = b + \chi$),we get:

$$\text{(3.18)}\qquad \pi_P = \pi^* - \frac{b+\chi}{1+b+\chi}\,\varepsilon\ ;\ y_P - \bar{y} = \frac{1}{1+b+\chi}\,\varepsilon\,,$$

$$L_P - L_C = \frac{\chi^2}{(1+b+\chi)^2\,(1+b)}\,\sigma_{\varepsilon}^2\,.$$

Constitutional inflexibility may lead to a superior outcome relative to government flexibility if there is the risk of a strong bias due to political distortions. In this view, dynamic consistency problems are rather irrelevant; the real choice is between either *inflexible institutions* which cannot respond to all contingencies, but are not subject to political pressure or on the other hand flexible arrangements which run the risk of allowing too much scope to political distortions. The argument of Persson and Tabellini (1993) gives a nice illustration how the incomplete contract approach can yield interesting insights. It seems, however, rather ad hoc to assume that a government subject to partisan pressure will still be able to commit to a Walsh contract before stage 2. If commitment at that stage is not feasible, we get back to the Rogoff mechanism, and then both political and dynamic incentive constraints have to be taken into account.

So, again, the question of implementability of the Walsh contract is at issue. One problem with the approach is that, evidently, the optimal transfer in (3.13) depends on the exact preferences of the central banker. As long as they are known, the contract can easily be adjusted. If the central banker attaches a different weight b_i to output stabilization than society (b), transfers will correct for that; they will be adjusted to $T(\pi,\varepsilon) = 2\,b\,\Delta\,(\pi^* - \pi) + C + (b_i - b)(y - \bar{y} - \Delta)^2$. If she does not care at all about social welfare, but is only interested in cash, she will simply be paid $T(\pi,\varepsilon) = 2\,b\,\Delta\,(\pi^* - \pi) + C - (\pi - \pi^*)^2 - b\,(y - \bar{y} - \Delta)^2$.

Preferences, however, are private information, not verifiable by the public. Then things get rather complicated. Beetsma and Jensen (1997) analyze the impact of private information. They do not derive the optimal contract under asymmetric information, but they show that linear payments can no longer achieve the commitment solution. As a consequence of private information, the contract introduces again a stabilization bias. But now, there is no longer a systematic bias; rather, there may be over- or under-stabilization, depending on the exact preferences.

The incomplete contract approach suggested by Persson and Tabellini (1993) points to a trade-off between democratic accountability and robustness against political distortions. In a democratic society, policy should respond to changes in the median voter's preferences. If the median voter herself were to decide about policy, she would adjust for changes in preferences. In contrast, when policy is delegated to an independent agency, being not accountable to democratic institutions, such changes will not be taken into account properly. On the other hand, it is well known from public choice theory that the political process itself introduces distortions due to partisan interests.

The trade off involved can be modeled in a straightforward way. To simplify, in the following stylized model we abstract from the problem of dynamic consistency and from other shocks. For illustration, assume that - at the stage of constitution - there is uncertainty about the median voter's optimal inflation target $\pi_M{}^*$. It may differ from her initial judgment by a random component ϕ:

(3.19) $\quad \pi_M{}^* = \pi^* + \phi$ with $E(\phi) = 0;\quad Var(\phi) = \sigma_\phi^2$

At the stage of designing the institutional set up for monetary policy, the alternative is to delegate policy either to an independent central bank or to a bank dependent on government's instructions. An independent central bank, appointed before the realization of shocks, will - in the absence of democratic accountability - react neither to preference changes nor to political pressures. Thus, it pursues the inflexible target

(3.20a) $\quad \pi_{CB}{}^* = \pi^* + \zeta$ with $E(\zeta) = 0;\quad Var(\phi) = \sigma_\zeta^2$

ζ represents uncertainty about the precise preferences of the central bank - there may be a risk that she deviates from the mandate. In contrast, if monetary policy is run on government instructions, it will respond to changes in the median preferences. In addition, however, there is the risk that the government yields to political pressure. According to public choice models, the government is likely to follow partisan policy. The danger of political distortions is captured by the random component χ:

(3.20b) $\pi_P{}^* = \pi_M{}^* + \chi$ with $E(\chi) = 0;\quad Var(\chi) = \sigma_\chi^2$

So, if the government runs monetary policy itself, it can - on the one hand - adjust its policy to specific preference shocks ϕ, but on the other hand, this flexibility comes at the cost of political distortions χ. Its target is:

(3.20c) $\pi_P{}^* = \pi^* + \chi + \phi$.

In general, even an independent central bank is subject to some political pressure. If θ represents the impact of political pressure, the actual target will be a compromise between the two targets (3.20a) and (3.20c):

(3.20d) $\pi_\theta{}^* = (1-\theta)(\pi^* + \zeta) + \theta(\pi^* + \chi + \phi) = \pi^* + (1-\theta)\zeta + \theta(\chi + \phi)$

Among the alternative institutional arrangements, the median voter will choose the mechanism maximizing her expected welfare. The realization of the shocks ϕ, χ and ζ is unknown at the stage of mechanism design and also when inflationary expectations are formed. The shocks are assumed to be independent: E(ϕ, χ)=E(ϕ,ζ)=E(χ, ζ)=0. Expected losses are:

(3.21) $L_M = (\pi - \pi_M{}^*)^2 + b(y - \bar{y})^2$ with $y - \bar{y} = \pi - \pi^e$

Given the target $\pi_\theta{}^*$, the optimal policy after realization of the shocks is characterized by:

(3.22) $$\pi = \frac{1}{1+b}\pi_\theta{}^* + \frac{1}{1+b}\pi^e$$

Imposing the equilibrium condition $\pi^e = E(\pi)$ gives:

(3.23) $$\pi = \pi^* + \frac{1-\theta}{1+b}\zeta + \frac{\theta}{1+b}(\chi + \phi)\,;\; y - \bar{y} = \frac{1-\theta}{1+b}\zeta + \frac{\theta}{1+b}(\chi + \phi)$$

with expected losses for the median voter:

(3.24) $$EL_\theta = \frac{(1-\theta)^2}{1+b}\sigma_\zeta^2 + \frac{\theta^2}{1+b}\sigma_\chi^2 + \left[\left(\frac{\theta}{1+b} - 1\right)^2 + b\frac{\theta^2}{(1+b)^2}\right]\sigma_\phi^2$$
$$= \frac{(1-\theta)^2}{1+b}\sigma_\zeta^2 + \frac{\theta^2}{1+b}\left(\sigma_\chi^2 + \sigma_\phi^2\right) - \frac{2\,\theta}{1+b}\sigma_\phi^2 + \sigma_\phi^2$$

Giving monetary policy in the hand of an independent central bank $(\theta = 0)$ yields a superior outcome compared to leaving it to political parties $(\theta = 1)$, provided $\sigma_\chi^2 > \sigma_\phi^2 + \sigma_\zeta^2$ - volatility of the median voter's preferences plus central bank uncertainty have to be less than the volatility arising out of political distortions. In general, allowing for some political pressure $(0 < \theta < 1)$ can improve upon this arrangement. The optimal degree of pressure is (by minimizing EL_θ):

$$(3.25) \quad \theta = \frac{\sigma_\phi^2 + \sigma_\zeta^2}{\sigma_\chi^2 + \sigma_\phi^2 + \sigma_\zeta^2}$$

The lower the volatility of the median voter's preferences and the uncertainty of central bank actions relative to partisan bias, the less room should be given to political pressure. Obviously, if there is no partisan bias ($\sigma_\chi^2 \rightarrow 0$), the flexibility of the political process gives the better outcome ($(\theta \rightarrow 1)$).

4 Unsolved Issues

Game theoretic models helped to make considerable progress in understanding the impact of specific mechanisms on monetary policy. The problem of dynamic consistency stresses the importance of credibility. Historically, starting with Kydland and Prescott (1977), the debate has been phrased in terms of rules vs. discretion - implying a trade-off between flexibility and credibility. In the literature, two competing mechanisms have been suggested to enhance credibility: (1) Delegation to an independent conservative central banker and (2) the arrangement of explicit, accountable contracts between government and central bank. Whereas the former mechanism can reduce the inflationary bias only at the expense of incurring a stabilization bias (thus confirming the notion of a trade-off), the latter promises to achieve the commitment solution at no cost, provided it can be implemented in a credible way. Political incentive constraints, however, may reverse the ranking between both mechanisms.

The analysis of different rules is helpful in organizing thoughts about what are the relevant issues involved, but it cannot provide final answers to the questions posed by mechanism design. It would be rather naive to try to implement the mechanisms discussed directly when designing real monetary institutions. The main reason is that the comparison of different rules does not address an issue which is crucial for those seeking monetary policy advise: how can adherence to the rules itself be made credible? Whereas the approach discussed in the paper provides a clear understanding about specific implications of different rules, it does not say much about which mechanisms are enforceable and by what means (see also Jensen (1997)). But exactly that issue may be the most important one to policy makers.[5]

An analogy may be helpful to emphasize the basic point: Comparing different, well functioning institutions is like comparing different steady state equilibria. But if one is interested in the process how a specific equilibrium is reached, understanding of the out of equilibrium process is called for. Building up credible institutions is a slow learning process, and trying to start with the optimal mechanism may give the wrong answer in case the mechanism lacks credibility. If multiple equilibria (different steady state solutions) exist, it may well be the case that aiming at an overly ambitious transition path ends up in a suboptimal trap compared to a gradual build up of reputation.

As an example: simply to prescribe independence is nonsense unless there exists a reliable legal and political infrastructure which makes moves to independence credible. It is no coincidence that the most popular mechanism used in reality to contain the inflation bias is exchange rate pegging. It seems fairly evident that the exchange rate mechanism is the superior institutional arrangement for developing countries (or transition economies) lacking a tradition of no interference with independent central bank. In a similar vein: one could argue that simply signing a contract which explicitly states the target of price stability is of not much help, as long as there is no institutional and economic background, giving support to „*stability culture.*" This concept, admittedly, is rather vague and hard to formalize - but not more so than the idea that an optimal contract can be enforced via inflation targeting. As emphasized by Posen *(1995)*, pressure for price stability from financial markets may be a more efficient enforcement mechanism than any abstract legal rules (see also Eijffinger and De Haan (1996)).

A clear advantage of the mechanism of pegging exchange rates certainly is the straightforward public observability of adherence to the rules. This aspect plays no role at all in the analysis of the mechanisms discussed above (except, in a rather crude way, in the incomplete contract approach). To give an example: When they claim superiority of direct inflation targeting as compared to intermediate targets, Persson and Tabellini (1993) completely neglect the issue of observability. In their set up, stochastic inflation control poses no problem. In a real world context, when learning via signals plays an essential role, public observability of adherence to announced rules can be a decisive element of the whole process. Robust, transparent mechanisms should minimize the opportunities for cheating, and it may well be that credibility rises by use of intermediate targets which can be hit more precisely without long time lags.

Another question not properly understood up to now: under what conditions can a central bank afford to deviate from announced targets without loosing her reputation? Just as with exchange rate bands, there is a trade-off between an

---

[5] This fact helps to explain some scepticism about the insights gained out of the models surveyed here for the issue of designing the European central bank - see also Winkler (1996).

ambitious narrow target range (with a high probability of missing the target) and a rather wide band which does constrain behavior not much and thus hardly improves upon credibility. The issue how reliable, accountable targets should be designed, is a challenging area for future research. As Walsh (1996) shows in a recent paper, if the central bank is required to announce an inflation target herself rather than accepting a target imposed on her by government, that can induce her to reveal part of her private information and at the same time impose discipline for price stability.

The critical comments are not meant as argument against the use of game theoretic methods for monetary policy. Quite the contrary. Up to now, the mechanism design literature has done only the first step in understanding the problem of credibility. Game theory (esp. the branch of information economics) provides sufficient tools for the next step, the question of how specific rules can be made credible. Signaling models seem a natural starting point for analyzing the process of building up credible institutions. There is already much promising work in progress (such as the analysis of central bank's private information in Beetsma and Jensen (1997) and Walsh (1996)). No doubt there will be more exciting research in this area in the future.

References

Alesina, A. and R. Gatti (1995), Independent Central Banks: Low Inflation at No Cost?, *American Economic Review* 85, 196-200.

Barro, R. J. and D. B. Gordon (1983), Rules, Discretion, and Reputation in a Model of Monetary Policy, *Journal of Monetary Economics* 12, 101-20.

Beetsma, R. and H. Jensen (1997), Inflation Targets and Contracts with Uncertain Central Banker Preferences, CEPR Discussion Paper No. 1562, London.

Bernanke, B. and F. Mishkin (1997), Inflation Targeting: A New Framework for Monetary Policy?, *Journal of Economic Perspectives* 11, 97-116.

Blinder, A. (1997), What Central Bankers Could Learn from Academics - and Vice Versa, *Journal of Economic Perspectives* 11, 3-19.

Canzoneri, M. B., C. Nolan and A. Yates (1996), Mechanisms for Achieving Monetary Stability: Inflation Targeting versus the ERM, CEPR Discussion Paper No. 1418, London.

Eijffinger, S. C. W. and J. De Haan (1996), The Political Economy of Central-Bank Independence, Special Papers in International Economics No. 19, Princeton, New Jersey.

Fischer, S. (1995), The Unending Search for Monetary Salvation, in: Bernanke, B. S. and J. J. Rotemberg (eds.), NBER Macroeconomics Annual 1995, Cambridge, MA, 274-86.

Fecht, F. and G. Illing (1997), Konservativer Zentralbanker vs. optimaler Zentralbankkontrakt - Eine spieltheoretische Analyse der Unabhängigkeit der Zentralbank, mimeo, Frankfurt.

Fratianni, M., J. von Hagen and C. Waller (1997), Central Banking as a Political Principal Agent Problem, *Economic Inquiry* 35, 378-93.

Giavazzi, F. and M. Pagano (1988), The Advantage of Tying One's Hands: EMS Discipline and Central Bank Credibility, *European Economic Review* 32, 1055-82.

Goodhardt, C. and H. Huang (1995), What is the Central Bank's Game?, LSE Financial Market Group, Discussion Paper 222.

Jensen, H. (1997), Credibility of Optimal Monetary Delegation, *American Economic Review* 87, S. 911-20.

Kydland, F. E. and E. C. Prescott (1977), Rules Rather than Discretion: The Inconsistency of Optimal Plans, *Journal of Political Economy* 85, 473-91.

Leiderman, L. and L. E. O. Svensson (eds.) (1995), Inflation Targets, London.

Lohmann, S. (1992), Optimal Commitment in Monetary Policy: Credibility versus Flexibility, *American Economic Review* 82, 273-86.

McCallum, B. T. (1995), Two Fallacies Concerning Central Bank Independence, *American Economic Review* 85, Papers and Proceedings, 207-11.

Persson, T. and G. Tabellini (1993), Designing Institutions for Monetary Stability, *Carnegie-Rochester Conference Series on Public Policy* 39, 53-84.

Rogoff, K. (1985), The Optimal Degree of Commitment to an Intermediate Monetary Target, *Quarterly Journal of Economics* 100, 1169-90.

Svensson, L. E. O. (1997), Optimal Inflation Targets, Conservative Central Banks and Linear Inflation Contracts, *American Economic Review* 87, 98-114.

Waller, C. and C. E. Walsh (1996), Central Bank Independence, Economic Behavior and Optimal Contract Length, *American Economic Review* 86, 1139-53.

Walsh, C. E. (1995), Optimal Contracts for Central Bankers, *American Economic Review* 85, 150-67.

Walsh, C. E. (1995b), Is New Zealand's Reserve Bank Act of 1989 an Optimal Central Bank Contract?, *Journal of Money, Credit, and Banking* 27, 1179-91.

Walsh, C. E. (1996), Announcements, Inflation Targeting and Central Bank Incentives, Working Paper No. 353, Santa Cruz.

Winkler, B. (1996), Towards A Strategic View on EMU: A Critical Survey, *Journal of Public Policy* 16, 1-28.

Comment

Hans-Peter Grüner
University of Bonn, Adenauerallee 24-42, D - 53113 Bonn

1 The Walsh Contract: A Perfect Solution for a Fictitious Problem?

The time inconsistency of optimal policy plans is today's most popular theoretical explanation for the existence of positive inflation rates. Among academics, incentive mechanisms for central bankers are becoming a very popular solution concept for this particular problem. The appealing feature of incentive mechanisms is that they solve the credibility problem of the central bank without reducing monetary policy flexibility. Gerhard Illing has provided an insightful survey of this recent literature. And he raises a couple of interesting questions for further research. In my comment I want to make some additional skeptical remarks.

The theoretical analysis of monetary policy rests on a set of assumptions with relatively weak justifications. There are several open questions which need to be answered before we can think about the practical implementation of incentive mechanisms for central bankers. The first obvious problem is that we do not have the data needed to implement a Walsh contract. There is a considerable lack of knowledge about magnitudes which - in theory - we treat as known parameters. Secondly, we do not know enough about whether „flexible“ central banks perform better in stabilizing output. If they don't then the flexibility versus credibility trade-off is a fictitious problem rather than a real one. Thirdly, monetary theory in its current state provides us with little reliable knowledge about desirable objectives for monetary policy. Hence there is considerable uncertainty about what central bankers should achieve and about what one should write into the contract.

Before I discuss those points in more detail, I would like to make a remark on Illing's major concern about contracts: that the government may wish to forget about them once inflation expectations are formed. Accordingly the credibility problem would just be transposed to a higher level (credibility of contracts) but it would not be solved.

2 Are Contracts Credible?

I agree that the renegotiation proofness of central bank contracts is an interesting theoretical problem. However, I also believe that there are a number of reasons why contracts for the central bank should in deed give low inflation more credibility than a simple announcement by the monetary authority.

In Walsh's game, there is a first stage where the government chooses the contract for the central bank. In stage 2 inflation expectations are formed by the public. In stage 3, the central bank observes a shock and chooses the rate of inflation. Payments from the contract are realized in the final stage, stage 4.

Forgetting about the punishment would have to be made credible *before* the central bank chooses monetary policy, i.e. between stages 2 and 3. Otherwise, this would have no impact on inflation. The only way to achieve credibility would be to remove the incentive mechanism from the central bank law. Otherwise the central bank can not rely on the fact that the government will forget about the punishment in the final stage. Changing the central bank law, however, is a process that takes time. It may take more time than is left between the stages 2 and 3. And it is a very clear (and bad) signal to the markets.

Moreover, recent experiences in Germany tell us that the political costs of an attempt to change the central bank law might be prohibitively high. It should be even more difficult to abandon a potential incentive mechanism for the European Central Bank since this would require the consensus of all participating countries.

Central banks that deviate from their own announcements often justify this on grounds of „money control errors". Hence there remains some uncertainty whether a deviation was indeed intended by the monetary authority. A government that breaks or removes a contract instead very clearly admits that it no longer pursues a policy of monetary stability. For these reasons I believe that contractual arrangements for monetary policy should make low inflation policies more credible than oral announcements by the monetary authority.

In the rest of my comment I would like to concentrate on some other - mostly practical - problems with the implementation of incentive mechanisms for monetary policy. These problems can be summarized in three questions:

1. Do we have the data needed to implement a Walsh contract?
2. Do flexible central banks really reduce employment volatility?
3. What is the optimal rate of inflation?

3 Do We Have the Data Needed to Implement a Walsh Contract?

My major concern about the practical usefulness of our theoretical achievements is our lack of knowledge about magnitudes which - in theory - we treat as known parameters. The implementation of an optimal contract would require the following information:

1. A description of central bankers' preferences over macroeconomic objectives and private income.

2. A specification of the probability distribution of macroeconomic shocks.
3. A specification of the probability distribution of measurement errors of the consumer price index (c.f. Walsh (1995)).
4. An exact measure of how central bank policies affect economic activity and inflation rates.
5. A specification of "society's preferred inflation rate".

It is needless to say that our knowledge of all these parameters and magnitudes is far from satisfactory. The uncertainty about central bankers' preferences is most obvious if we compare the various assumptions about central bank objectives in the theoretical literature. Some authors assume welfare maximization while others (e.g. Fratianni, von Hagen and Waller (1997), Grüner (1997), Herrendorf and Neumann (1997)) postulate private macroeconomic objectives, the desire to be reappointed or simply income maximization. Blinder (1997) argues that welfare maximizing central bankers automatically turn conservative when they are in office.[1]

Our uncertainty about central bank preferences implies that any numerical specification of a contract will be a rough guess that has little to do with the exactness of the underlying theoretical literature. Today we have no idea what an optimal contract for the central bank would look like in monetary terms. We need more information about the objectives of central bankers and about their willingness to pay for different macroeconomic outcomes. Only a detailed empirical analysis of central bank decisions - including unconventional methods such as interviews with the decision makers - can help to improve our knowledge in this field.

4 Do Flexible Central Banks Really Reduce Employment Volatility?

But I do not want to be too pessimistic. The famous credibility vs. flexibility trade-off only arises if the central bank must actively accommodate economic shocks. This role makes it so difficult to calculate the optimal incentive scheme or (in the Rogoff paper) to find the best intermediate type of central banker. If accommodation was not an objective of the central bank then the best policy would just consist of appointing the most conservative central banker, or,

[1] His view is supported by some interesting theoretical work by Caillaud, Cohen and Jullien (1994). They argue that credibility problems are simply solved by internalizing that whatever is done today in a given state of the world, will also be done tomorrow if the state of the world is the same. A central banker would then *understand* that discretionary behavior is in vain and chooses state contingent low-inflation policies.

alternatively to implement the most rigid contract. Both procedures would lead to the same result: low inflation.

Two questions must be answered before we can assume that a central bank should react to shocks:

(i) Does accommodation really work?
(ii) Aren't there other ways to achieve output stability?

Let me begin with the first point. Given the long and variable time lag between monetary policy implementation and its real effects[2], one may doubt whether central bankers are able to stabilize the economy in the way assumed in the Rogoff and Walsh papers. Recent empirical research points out that there is no link between the degree of central bank independence and the volatility of output although there is some impact on inflation (Grilli, Masciandaro and Tabellini (1991), Cukierman (1992) and Alesina and Summers (1993)). The most simple explanation for this is that government dependent central bankers do not succeed in stabilizing output. There are many reasons why the government's ability to fine-tune the economy is limited (see Siebke and Thieme (1981), for a list). If this holds for monetary policy as well then the Rogoff-Walsh credibility vs. flexibility trade-off simply disappears.

Secondly, there may be better ways to stabilize output. One of them is to remove nominal rigidities, especially on labor markets. The interaction between nominal rigidities and inflation is a topic which is too often neglected. It might be a better institutional mix to assign the role of output stabilization to (flexible) labor markets and to fight inflation with a conservative monetary policy (see Grüner and Hefeker (1995)).

Once we stop seeing the central bank as an agency with a mission to fine tune the economy, the credibility vs. flexibility trade-off disappears. Both, a conservative central banker or a contract that punishes deviations from low inflation rates would then achieve an optimal outcome. The contract may still be helpful to avoid the emergence of a political business cycle. Recent empirical investigations suggest that such a cycle may arise even when the central bank is formally independent. The variability of society's inflation target may require a contract which does not foresee an irrevocably fixed inflation target. This can be achieved by a contract which relies on monetary or inflation target announcements by the central bank (Grüner (1997)).

[2] Figure 1 in Stephen Cecchetti's contribution to this volume gives a measure of the impact of monetary policy innovations on output in the U.S. The lag between the time of the innovation and the peak of the output response is 17 months and the variance of the estimated output response is also considerable.

5 What Is the Optimal Rate of Inflation?

My last point is that there is still considerable disagreement in the profession about what an optimal inflation rate might be. Akerlof, Dickens and Perry (1997) recently argued that - with downward wage rigidity - zero (or negative) inflation rates create considerable welfare losses. Lucas (1997) who calibrated several monetary macro models in order to estimate the welfare maximizing inflation rate for the U.S. arrives at very different results. His estimates are below zero percent but depend upon the underlying theoretical framework. Needless to say that Lucas' values differ from what we are used to think of as price stability. If we accept these values then we see that a lot remains to be done about disinflation.

The main problem, however, is that we still do not possess a satisfactory theory of the relationship between money and prices. In his 1992 EEA presidential address Martin Hellwig has argued most convincingly that the fundaments of monetary theory are very weak. The use of money is usually justified on the basis of ad hoc assumptions such as the famous cash-in-advance constraint. An exemption are attempts to microfound the use of money as a medium of exchange by Kiyotaki and Wright (1989) and also by Hellwig (1976). Without a satisfactory monetary theory, our knowledge about the welfare costs of inflation is very limited and objectives for monetary policy can not be easily specified.

Over the last 15 years, the game theoretical analysis of monetary policy has become a fashionable business. The basic assumptions of this vast literature certainly need a better empirical and theoretical foundation before we can think about turning the solution concepts into institutions for monetary policymaking.

References

Akerlof, G., W. T. Dickens and G. L. Perry (1996), The Macroeconomics of Low Inflation, *Brookings Papers on Economic Activity*, 1, 1-59.

Alesina, A. and L. Summers (1993), Central Bank Independence and Macroconomic Performance: Some Comparative Evidence, *Journal of Money, Credit, and Banking* 25, 157-62.

Blinder, A. S (1997), What Central Bankers Could Learn from Academics - and Vice Versa, *Journal of Economic Perspectives* 11, 3-19.

Cukierman, A. (1992), Central Bank Strategy, Credibility and Independence: Theory and Evidence, Cambridge, MA.

Caillaud B., D. Cohen and R. Jullien (1994), Towards a Theory of Self Restraint, CEPREMAP Discussion Paper No. 9421, Paris.

Fratianni, M., J. von Hagen and C. Waller (1997), Central-Banking as a Political Principal-Agent Problem, *Economic Inquiry* 35, 378-93.

Grilli, V., D. Masciandaro and G. Tabellini (1991), Political and Monetary Institutions and Public Financial Policies in Industrialized Countries, *Economic Policy* 13, 341-92.

Grüner, H. P. (1997), A Comparison of Three Institutions for Monetary Policy when Central Bankers have Private Objectives, *Public Choice* 62, 172-93.

Grüner, H. P. and C. Hefeker (1995), Domestic Pressures and the Exchange Rate Regime: why Economically Bad Decisions are Politically Popular, *Banca Nazionale del Lavoro Quarterly Review* 194, 331-50.

Hellwig, M. (1976), A Model of Monetary Exchange, Econometric Research Programme Research Memorandum No. 202, Princeton University, Princeton NJ.

Hellwig, M. (1993), The Challenge of Monetary Theory, *European Economic Review* 37, 215-43.

Herrendorf, B. and M. J. M. Neumann (1997), A Positive Theory of Central Bank Independence, University of Bonn.

Kiyotaki, N. and R. Wright (1989), On Money as a Medium of Exchange, *Journal of Political Economy* 97, 927-54.

Lucas R. E. (1997), The Welfare Costs of Inflation, Presidential Address, Econometric Society North American Meeting, Pasadena, CA.

Siebke, J. and J. Thieme (1981), Einkommen, Beschäftigung, Preisniveau, Vahlens Kompendium der Wirtschaftstheorie und Wirtschaftspolitik, Verlag Vahlen, München.

Walsh, C. E. (1995), Is New Zealand's Reserve Bank Act of 1989 an Optimal Central Bank Contract?, *Journal of Money, Credit, and Banking* 27, 1178-91.

2. Outline of Two Controversial Positions on Central Bank Autonomy

Central Bank Autonomy and Political Decision Process

Dietmar Kath
University of Duisburg, Lotharstr. 65, D - 47048 Duisburg

1 Introduction

Since a couple of years central bank independence is a very popular topic in economic literature as well as in the political discussion. There are several reasons for this actual interest:

- the different proposals concerning the institutional status of the European Central Bank (ECB) as a part of the European Monetary Union (EMU) during the time the Maastricht Treaty was prepared;
- the critical analysis and the political discussion of the specific regulations of the treaty itself concerning the status of the ECB;
- the necessity of reforming the banking system and to establish a new central bank law in post-socialist countries in accordance with the transformation of the economic system.

Indeed a considerable number of empirical articles during the last years have shown a negative correlation between the degree of central bank autonomy and the level of inflation across countries.[1] As a consequence of these investigations central bank autonomy sometimes is considered not only as a prerequisite but also as a sufficient condition for achieving price stability. But this opinion is doubtful. On the contrary, by applying the economic theory of political behavior of bureaucracies it can be demonstrated that central bank autonomy is not a guarantee for an efficient anti-inflationary policy, unless the central bank is obliged by law to achieve price stability. Yet according to standard economics even the legally fixed combination between the autonomy of the central bank and its responsibility for price stability is at most a necessary condition for achieving stable money.

With respect to the economic theory of democracy it is argued that monetary stability will be realized especially in those countries where price stability is the primary economic goal in the opinion of the public. This opinion is also defended by Pollard (1993), who interprets low rates of inflation as the outcome of the

---

[1] The problems of measurement of central bank autonomy were first discussed and empirically investigated by Bade and Parkin (1982) and Grilli, Masciandaro and Tabellini (1991). Further empirical studies were presented by Alesina. and Summers (1993) and by Cukierman (1992).

preferences of the majority of the people. An independent central bank therefore represents the institutionalization of the public fear of inflation. In this view, central bank autonomy is no prerequisite for a low level of inflation.

In what follows this hypothesis is discussed with respect to its consequences for the coming EMU currency, euro. For this purpose in the first step the pros and cons according to the actual theoretical discussion are described. The second section elaborates on the legal, the institutional, and the economic criteria by which central bank autonomy in its comprehensive sense may be defined. In the two following sections, firstly the Bundesbank's autonomy is critically analyzed and afterwards the status of the ECB is evaluated on the basis of those criteria for central bank autonomy.

2 The Controversial Discussion about Central Bank Autonomy

The question whether central bank autonomy is an efficient institutional arrangement for an optimal solution with respect to the system of macroeconomic objectives is analyzed in numerous models. The basic idea of this approach consists in the hypothesis that macroeconomic goals as low unemployment, steady growth, and price stability are arguments of a common social welfare function and the government is interpreted as the agent of the social wealth of the citizens as the principal. According to this principal-agent approach governments ideally have an essential interest to hit the target on the highest possible level. This is because in democracies governments can only survive if they are re-elected. In representative democracies the parliament has the function to control the government. In extreme cases parliaments even have the competence to eliminate the government from office.

On the other hand governments have an interest to transfer the responsibility for monetary stability to a specialized institution called central bank.[2] At this level there too exists a principal-agent relation: the central bank acts as the agent of the government as the principal. In this model the central bank plays the role of the executive of the government and as a consequence it is obliged to fulfill the government's directions.

In political and economic reality most of the assumptions of this ideal model are not realized. On the political level it is assumed that the parliament is efficient in controlling the government, i.e. the government can be released whenever it has failed to achieve its objectives. But in reality parliaments are constituted by different parties and the government is elected by the majority in the parliament. Consequently the function of controlling the government is weakened. The true principal, i.e. the public, is able to penalize the government for its failures only by electing another party at the end of the election period.

---

[2] For a detailed discussion of the principal-agent-problem see, e.g. Fratianni, von Hagen and Waller (1997).

On the economic level it is assumed by the standard model that the arrangements of the objective function, i.e. the levels of prices, production and employment are at least independent variables or can even be considered as supporting each other. This of course is true - at least in the short run - for the aggregates of production and employment, but it is not with respect to price stability. Consequently in the standard model production is often used as a synonym for employment. On the other hand between this variable and the price level as a measure for stable money a negative relationship cannot be denied. What consequence has this negative relationship concerning the connection between the government and the central bank? Answers with respect to this questions are controversial.

The advocates of a dependent central bank argue that stabilization policy necessarily will be driven into conflicts if monetary policy and fiscal policy are delegated to independent institutions which follow different targets, i.e. the central bank pursues the goal of price stability and the fiscal authority the goal of high output and full employment. In order to avoid conflicting strategies resulting from non-cooperation between the two authorities, it is argued that monetary and fiscal policy have to be coordinated.[3] As cooperation between autonomous institutions is at least very difficult, the competence for all macroeconomic goals has to be concentrated in the hands of only one authority. Two pre-conditions for achieving this concentration have to be fulfilled:

- the definition of a common and unambiguous goal function and
- a central bank, which has to execute the instructions of the government.

At a first sight this reasoning seems plausible, but a deeper investigation reveals the weakness of the underlying hypothesis, i.e. the existence of a trade-off between the rate of inflation and the percentage of unemployment, known as the Phillips-Curve theorem.

The opposite opinion which supports the idea of central bank independence denies at least for the long run any possibility of choice between a higher rate of inflation and a lower degree of unemployment and vice versa. Furthermore it is argued that a possibly existing temporary trade-off between the two goals of stabilization policy is misused by the political majority in parliament. The government party like all politicians always acts in its own selfish interest to improve its chances of being re-elected.

This conclusion is based on the hypothesis that the system of parliamentary democracy is characterized by a conflict concerning political rationality and economic efficiency. To achieve economic efficiency with respect to economic policy only those decisions are required which guarantee the best possible performance of the economic target variables. The decision-making politicians on

[3] The coordination problem is discussed in Alesina and Tabellini (1987) and in Sargent and Wallace (1981).

the contrary try to satisfy their individual goal function that is keeping their office and stabilizing or even expanding their political influence. From the economic theory of political behavior we learn that the procedures of a parliamentary democracy are extremely sensible for misusing monetary expansion.[4]

Of course the representative democracy in principle is the most effective procedure for the transformation of people's preferences into political decisions. As individuals are eager to maximize their utility they will elect only those politicians who promise to achieve the goals of the public. On the other hand the policymakers′ chance to be re-elected depends on his successful work during the past.

As far as this "mechanism" is concerned parliamentary democracy is a very effective procedure. But this effectiveness is questionable if the full consequences of a political decision occur only after a considerable time lag or - more seriously - the bad long run consequences of a political action are totally in contrast with the good short run performance of the same measure and vice versa. In these cases the public will have difficulties to find out that the events of today are the delayed but unambiguous results of a specific activity of some years ago.

It is this pattern in the reaction of various macroeconomic aggregates which is characteristic for monetary acceleration and deceleration processes. As we know from modern macroeconomic theory as well as from many empirical investigations monetary growth which exceeds the growth of real potential output has a positive impact on goods production and employment in the short run. But in the long run the result is an inflationary process which in its final stage is characterized by a rate of inflation equal to the difference between the growth rates of money and real output. Or putting it in another way: the positive short run effects on actual production and employment are only temporary episodes and hence are vanishing as time goes on, and the real economic target variables will finally be located at their initial levels.

These divergencies of the different time paths may be a temptation for policymakers to demonstrate their ability to fight unemployment successfully. They consequently foster monetary expansion in such a manner that the positive real effects occur right in time before the election while the higher rate of inflation will emerge with a considerable time lag after the event. Of course there is the hope that the voters are short-minded and do not detect or will forget the maneuver until the next election.[5] If the policymakers are successful in this respect they will repeat the same procedure with the result of accelerating inflation.

---

[4] This idea was elaborated by Nordhaus (1975). A special type of political business cycles based on different ideological positions of the various political parties concerning the goal of income distribution was introduced by Hibbs (1977).

[5] If the voters are not short-minded, there will arise the problem of time inconsistency. As a result there may exist an incentive for the government inflating wages to reach a higher level of employment. As soon as the economic actors recognize this strategy they will anticipate a higher rate of inflation. Consequently this lack of credibility of the government produces an inflationary bias.

Against this backround an independent central bank which by legislation is obliged to maintain price stability seems to be a rational solution.[6] But considering the possible conflict between the central bank pursuing a stable-money policy and the government expanding their expenditures by debt financing there may arise an unfavorable macroeconomic situation. The conflicting strategies lead to an increasing public debt and to a higher level of interest rates. This conflict creates problems for private capital formation, because there arises uncertainty for the public of either inflation or higher tax burden. Either the central bank is set under pressure to finance the budget deficits with the result of inflation or the government gives in and increases taxes.

As a consequence it is possible that an autonomous central bank can also be set under pressure to follow an accommodating monetary policy. Therefore the question arises whether an autonomous central bank is overcharged when it is expected to withstand the pressure executed by the highest political authorities. Is it indeed a realistic assumption that central bankers always make their decisions in accordance with the common sense while politicians maximize their individual utility? These questions were already asked and answered by the same author (Downs (1957)), who had formulated the basic theoretical approach for the analysis of the behavior of politicians. According to the economic theory of bureaucracies (see Downs (1965), Niskanen (1971) and Tullock (1965)) - and of course central banks are bureaucracies, too - bureaucratic institutions try to maximize the self-interest of their head officers. The corresponding utility function contains as goals the maintenance of status, the expansion of competence, and the increase in reputation. There is no a priori accord with the commandment of maximizing the societies utility.

A successful strategy for central banks to satisfy their utility function according to this theoretical approach is to avoid any conflict with the fiscal authority. If central bankers are convinced that supporting government policy is the best strategy to maximize their own selfish interest, than central bank autonomy is no efficient weapon against the political misuse of the competence for monetary control by political agents. To exclude such indirect political pressure on monetary authorities the installation of additional elements for central bank independence is required.[7]

This so called problem of time inconsistency was analyzed by Kydland and Prescott (1977) and by Barro and Gordon (1983). For a detailed discussion of possible solutions of this problem see Rogoff. (1985), Walsh (1995) and Persson and Tabellini (1993).

[6] An independent central bank is also seen as a solution for the time inconsistency or credibility problem, see Rogoff (1985)

[7] One additional element could be an „optimal contract" which reduces the principal-agent-problem between the society and the central bank, see Svensson (1997) and Walsh (1995).

3 Criteria for Central Bank Authority

To strengthen the ability of a central bank for pursuing independently and strictly the goal of price stability it is necessary to eliminate any potential influence of the government on the decision making authority. Independence in this comprehensive understanding means that the autonomy status has not to be defined by legislation only but also has to incorporate institutional and economic criteria. Central bank autonomy therefore consists of three different elements:

- At first it must be guaranteed by central bank law - or even better: in the constitution - that price stability is the main goal of the monetary authority and that it is independent from government instructions in fulfilling this objective. This legal criterion often is misunderstood as a synonym for central bank autonomy in general.
- Secondly the members of the body, which is responsible for the decisions in monetary policy have to be appointed for a period of time, which exceeds the election period of the parliament and of the government. Furthermore, suspension from their duty must be excluded. If central bankers are appointed for a limited time period only there should be a legally fixed minimum age, so that the end of their term of office coincides with the age of retirement. The purpose of this arrangement is to relieve the officers from the fear of not being re-elected if their decisions are against the interests of the government. So their economic independence would be strengthened. A further element of institutional independence is the level of their personal income. Consequently central bankers must be paid top salaries. On the other hand they should suffer reductions of their individual income whenever they failed the goal of price stability - defined as two percent annual increase in the consumer price index - equivalent to the rate of inflation. In general the following conclusion may be drawn: Every step towards more independence of central bankers will favor the possibility for achieving price stability.
- Thirdly the central bank must be unrestricted in defining those assets which it accepts to buy with its own central bank money. And it must be autonomous in limiting the quantity of each of those assets. Ideally this means that the central bank is free of any obligation to grant credit to central, state and local governments and other public authorities as well as of supporting fixed exchange rates by interventions in foreign currency markets. This third element can be characterized as the economic criterion of autonomy.

Central bank autonomy in its purest form contains all of the aforementioned components.[8] In existing central bank laws however we do not find all of them

[8] The three elements discussed above are the main components of central bank independence. Additional aspects are discussed in Cukierman (1992) and Grilli, Masciandaro and Tabellini (1991).

included. Even in the German central bank legislation (Gesetz über die Deutsche Bundesbank (1957)) - which often is considered as a good example for a statute of autonomy - the third criterion is hurt. This fact and its consequences in the past are subject to the next section. In the next but one chapter it will be analyzed to what extent these criteria for autonomy are realized for the coming ECB according to the Maastricht Treaty. As a result of this analysis an answer will be given to the question whether the Euro can be expected to become a stable currency.

4 Deficits in the Autonomy Status of the Deutsche Bundesbank

In the German central bank law the legal criterion and the institutional conditions for a monetary authority which is independent from government are regulated in a sufficient manner, but the third criterion is hurt. While the Bundesbank on the one hand is legally forbidden to finance government deficits it is not allowed on the other hand to choose the exchange rate system. The competence to make exchange rate arrangements is given to the government. The Bundesbank only has the right to a hearing.

This deficit of competence with respect to exchange rate arrangements is illustrated by three historical events:

- The foundation of the EMS in 1979 by the German Chancellor and the French President against the resistance of the Bundesbank;
- the creation of the German monetary union in 1990 on the basis of the one-to-one exchange rate, while the Bundesbank had recommended a relationship of one-to-two, and
- the ratification of the Maastricht Treaty by which the Bundesbank will lose its competence to create a national currency.

Despite the fact that institutional regulations of the German central bank law are designed to prevent central bankers from being economically dependent on central government pressure concerning their monetary decisions several empirical studies[9] have investigated the performance of German monetary policy in the past with respect to good conduct of central bank decisions. The results were not convincing. In a recent study Vaubel (1993) found some evidence for the hypothesis that decisions of the central bank council can be explained as the outcome of the preference of its members with respect to political parties.[10] But there are some doubts why central bankers should make decisions according to their general political preferences which as a result are detrimental for the reputation of the decision body as well as of that of their members. This consequence would diminish the utility of the officers - which according to the

[9] See Basler (1978), Basler (1979), Frey and Schneider (1981) and Baum (1983).

[10] Vaubel's hypothesis originally is based on Hibbs (1977).

economic theory of bureaucracy is the relevant variable for their decisions - instead of increasing it. Central bank activities in favor of government policy would be qualified as rational behavior only if the members of the decision body had to consider government benevolence as the pre condition of not losing their jobs.

In fact the hypothesis that the Bundesbank could have tried to satisfy its specific utility function by cooperation with the government is not very plausible. There is no need for the members of the central bank council to catch the government's favor in order to keep their office. The German central bank law stipulates for the Council members an eight-year-period of office, while the election period, which is relevant for the government, is only four years. Because of this difference and because of the rules with regard to the election of these members the hypothesis that the central bank council is dependent on government influence for economic reasons must be rejected as not realistic.

Besides these regulations given by law there is of course the phenomenon of overlapping periods of office among members of the body of directors themselves. As a consequence of all those legal and institutional facts it may take the government remaining in office up to three periods of election to reach the most desirable constellation, viz. that all members of the board of directors of the Bundesbank will have a preference for the parties in government.

Indeed this situation existed in the FRG from 1958 until 1972 and again in 1980 and 1981. During the first period of 14 years all members of the board - with the exception of the vice president and later on the president - were members of or had a preference for one of the government parties under the leadership of the CDU. The same situation was due during the years 1980 and 1981 at the end of the government period of the social-liberal coalition, when the SPD was the leading party. Since 1990 the party preference of the board members - again with one exception - anew is in line with government parties. As these experiences show it is possible for the German Federal Government to determine the personal composition of the board of directors of the Deutsche Bundesbank provided that it is being re-elected at least twice.

But the board of directors constitutes only one part of the central bank council[11], the other part is the group of the Presidents of the State Central Banks. Each of them is appointed by the proper State Government, but political equalization is attainable only if the government is being re-elected at least once. This condition again is due to differing periods of office. It was fulfilled in all Federal States until the middle of the eighties. Consequently during the period 1977 to 1988 a constant relationship could be realized of six LZB-Presidents with

---

[11] According to the Bundesbankgesetz §§ 5, 6, 7, 8 the Central Bank Council consisted from 1957 to 1992 of twenty members from which nine members - including the President and the Vice-President - had special functions in the board of directors of the central administration. Some of the positions of the board of directors were vacant. Especially during the period from 1980 to 1988 only six of them were occupied.

a preference for the CDU-party and five LZB-Presidents in favor of the SPD-party.[12]

As a result of the German re-unification and of the establishment of five new Federal States there was a need for restructuring the Central Bank Council. In order to reduce the number of members to a reasonable dimension, in 1992 the German central bank law was changed with respect to the number of State Central Banks and their locations. Since that time only four Federal States - Baden Würtemberg, Bayern, Nordrhein Westfalen and Hessen - are equipped with a State Central Bank which is responsible exclusively for its own territory. The other twelve Federal States must share in one of the remaining five Federal Central Banks. It would have been interesting to learn the consequences of this new constellation for the appointment and the election of the candidate for the common Federal Central Bank President. If the majority in the parliament of those Federal States which participate in the same Central Bank are in the hands of different political parties with all probability there would have been chosen a political neutral person. As a result of the foundation of the EMU and the establishment of the ECB this problem will be of minor interest, because regarding the European Central Bank System these Presidents are not equipped with decisional competence anymore.

The empirical experience of the party-political selection of the Bundesbank council members offers no proof that the monetary decisions in Germany are decided by party-political preferences. Independence, competence and authority of the Bundesbank could grow, if it resists demonstratively against the governments' interests and on that it gets the confirmation and acknowledgment from other social or economic groups. The central bank would gain more acceptance from the credit institutions, which are the direct addressees of their policy. The non-bank public, with their prior interest in price stability, and the foreign central banks also are authorities, where the governors of the Bundesbank may earn reputation. The degree of estimation of a central bank by these authorities will grow proportionally with its ability to avoid inflation and - if it is necessary - even resist the pressure of the government. But this motivation is no guarantee for price stability; the members of the council will gain international reputation, if the rate of inflation is less than the long-term average of the rate of inflation in the other countries. In the international ranking the Deutsche Bundesbank is situated at one of the top positions with respect to monetary stability. Since 1955 Germany has one of the lowest inflation rates in the world but the purchasing power of the Deutsche Mark actually had reduced to 25 p.c. of its value in 1949, the year of its birth.

---

[12] The legal procedure for the appointment of a State Central Bank President requires a majority of the votes of the Federal Council (Bundesrat), the second chamber of legislation in the FRG. But in reality this majority always accepts the candidate of the respective federal state government.

5 The Autonomy of the European Central Bank - A Critical View

Finally it has to be investigated to what extent the future European Central Bank will fulfill the criteria for an autonomous central bank discussed in section 3 above. Concerning the first criterion it has to be ascertained according to Article 107 EC-Treaty that the European Central Bank is not allowed to follow nor to receive instructions of another community organization, an institution or a national government. Additionally, Article 105 EC-Treaty stipulates that price stability is the primary goal of the future ECB. The first criterion for an autonomous central bank therefore is fulfilled without any restriction.

With respect to the third criterion, the economic dimension of central bank autonomy, the ECB is equally restricted as the Deutsche Bundesbank. According to Article 109 of the EC-Treaty the competence for the choice of the exchange rate system vis-à-vis foreign countries is due to the Council of the European Union. On the other hand the ECB is not allowed to grant credits to public authorities. And this definition is stronger than the respective restrictions of the law about the Bundesbank.

The judgment of how the second criterion of autonomy is regularized in the Maastricht Treaty is even more unfavorable. It refers to the question, whether the legal and institutional arrangements for an independent status of the members of the European Central Bank Council are sufficient to guarantee that monetary decisions are always in favor of the stability of the purchasing power of the euro. With regard to this problem the arrangements of the treaty are not satisfactory. The objections refer to the composition of the decision body as well as to the regulations concerning the independence of the board members from their national governments. The central bank council consists on the one side of four to six members who constitute the board of directors and on the other side of the presidents of the national central banks. The period of office of the former is eight years without being restricted by a minimum age and without the possibility of re-election. The period of office of the latter is five years; further regulations are left to the national governments.

A realistic hypothesis is: Most of the EU-countries will restrict the period of office of their national central bank governors to the legal minimum, and their re-nomination will not occur automatically. The decision about the prolongation of the period of office may be used as an instrument to enforce a good conduct with respect to the national governments interests. Consequently officers who have to consider their occupational career must respect the interests of their national governments. In recent theoretical models analyzing the relationship between a central bank and the national government the monetary decisions are treated as a strategic game (Debelle (1996)). But referring to the ECB, monetary policy cannot be interpreted as a game between one national government and its central bank as the agent of the society's fear of inflation. Whenever the number of parties of the

EMU will be completed this strategic game will be played by 21 players from 15 countries. These 15 „parties“ are representing different preferences of the governments by which they are nominated as well as of the citizens with regard to their respective interests concerning the goal of price stability.

Considering the long-term experiences in Europe it can be expected that aversion against inflation differs from country to country. This means that there does not exist a homogenous objective function of a homogenous society and of all members of the monetary decision body. The famous Becket-effect cannot be used as an argument in favor of the resistance of the members of the council because they are not economically independent and because there are 15 Beckets and 15 Henry IIs. For this reason political business cycles can be excluded for the EMU.[13]

But concerning this scenario it has to be feared that the decisions of the ECB will be influenced and controlled through informal channels by the national governments. This statement may be illustrated as follows: Monetary policy decisions will be decisions with respect to the interest rate level. This is true for the Bundesbank and can be expected for the ECB too, irrespective to the question whether the ECB follows an inflation goal or chooses a monetary aggregate as a target variable. As far as the differences in the levels of public debt in the various countries are concerned the national governments have diverging goals with respect to the level of interest rates. Consequently monetary policy will always be under strong political pressure. Therefore it is to be feared that ECB decisions will be protracted, and that they finally will be compromises as a result of a time consuming bargaining process.

What measures are suitable to avoid or to curb these dangers? Possibly the following:

- strengthening the personal independence of the members of the ECB Council;
- a higher degree of political unification in Europe and
- a harmonization of fiscal policies.

[13] The same conclusion is drawn by Holzmann (1997). But there is disagreement concerning his further statement that „ ... political pressures on the ECB similar to that on the Bundesbank through the German federal setting ... is excluded.“

References

Alesina, A. and L. H. Summers (1993), Central Bank Independence and Macroeconomic Performance: Some Comparative Evidence, *Journal of Money, Credit, and Banking* 25, 151-62.

Alesina, A. and G. Tabellini (1987), Rules and Discretion with Noncoordinated Monetary and Fiscal Policies, *Economic Inquiry* 25, 619-30.

Bade, R. and M. Parkin (1982), Central Bank Laws and Monetary Policy, unpublished Paper.

Barro, R. J. and D. B. Gordon (1983), Rules, Discretion and Reputation in a Model of Monetary Policy, *Journal of Monetary Economics* 12, 101-21.

Basler, H. P. (1978), Die wirtschaftspolitischen Zielpräferenzen der Deutschen Bundesbank. Eine empirische Analyse des Zentralbankverhaltens für die Zeit von 1958-1974, *Kredit und Kapital* 11, 84-108.

Basler, H. P. (1979), Wirtschaftspolitische Zielpräferenzen und theoretische Orientierungen in der Geldpolitik der Bundesrepublik Deutschland, Tübingen.

Baum, T. M. (1983), Empirische Analysen der Bundesbankautonomie, *Konjunkturpolitik* 29, 163-86.

Cukierman, A. (1992), Central Bank Strategy, Credibility, and Independence: Theory and Evidence, Cambridge, MA.

Debelle, G. (1996), Central Bank Independence: A Free Lunch?, IMF Working Paper No. 96-1, Washington, D.C.

Downs, A. (1957), An Economic Theory of Democracy, New York.

Downs, A. (1965), Inside Bureaucracy, Washington, D.C.

Fratianni, M., J. von Hagen and C. Waller (1997), Central Banking as a Political Principal-Agent Problem, *Economic Inquiry* 35, 378-93.

Frey, B. S. and F. Schneider (1981), Central Bank Behavior: A Positive Empirical Analysis, *Journal of Monetary Economics* 7, 291-315.

Grilli, V., D. Masciandaro and G. Tabellini (1991), Political and Monetary Institutions and Public Financial Policies in the Industrial Countries, *Economic Policy* 13, 341-92.

Hibbs, D. (1977), Political Parties and Macroeconomic Policy, *American Political Science Review* 71, 1467-87.

Holzmann, R. (1997), Political Pressures on the Future European Central Bank, Comment to Susanne Lohmann, *Aussenwirtschaft* 52, 179-82.

Kydland, F. E. and E. C. Prescott (1977), Rules rather than Discretion: The Inconsistency of Optimal Plans, *Journal of Political Economy* 85, 473-91.

Lohmann, S. (1997), Political Accountability in an Economic and Monetary Union, *Aussenwirtschaft* 52, 159-77.

Niskanen, A. W. (1971), Bureaucracy and Representative Government, Chicago.

Nordhaus, W. (1975), The Political Business Cycle, *Review of Economic Studies* 42, 169-90.

Persson, T. and G. Tabellini (1993), Designing Institutions for Monetary Stability, *Carnegie-Rochester Conference Series on Public Policy* 39, 53-84.

Pollard, P. S. (1993), Central Bank Independence and Economic Performance, *The Federal Reserve Bank of St. Louis Review* 75, 21-36.

Rogoff, K. (1985), The Optimal Degree of Commitment to an Intermediate Monetary Target, *Quarterly Journal of Economics* 100, 1169-90.

Sargent, T. J. and N. Wallace (1981), Some Unpleasant Monetarist Arithmetic, *Federal Reserve Bank of Minneapolis Quarterly Review* 11, 1-17.

Svensson, L. E. O. (1997), Optimal Inflation Targets, „Conservative“ Central Bankers and Linear Inflation Contracts, *American Economic Review* 87, 98-114.

Tullock, G. (1965), The Politics of Bureaucracy, Washington, D.C.

Vaubel, R. (1993), Eine Public-Choice-Analyse der Deutschen Bundesbank und ihre Implikationen für die Europäische Währungsunion, in: Duwendag, D. and J. Siebke (eds.), Europa vor dem Eintritt in die Wirtschafts- und Währungsunion, Berlin, 23-79.

Walsh, C. (1995), Optimal Contracts for Central Bankers, *American Economic Review* 85, 150-67.

For a Monetary Policy that is Independent, yet Subject to Rules

Wolfgang Filc
University of Trier, Universitätsring 15, D - 54286 Trier

1 Introduction

Dietmar Kath gives an excellent digest of the arguments in favor of an independent central bank exercising its responsibilities without being subject to direction by government. Taking the Deutsche Bundesbank as an example he then points out deficiencies in the extent of its autonomy, for instance with respect to international currency agreements and in connection with monetary union between the two German states before reunification. However, intolerably high inflation in Germany - which is the concern of all those who, like Dietmar Kath, favor a central bank with unrestricted autonomy - did not result from this event. In the run-up to European Monetary Union, which is due to come into force in 1999, Kath pleads for a future European Central Bank which will have a greater degree of independence than the Deutsche Bundesbank currently has. He argues his case above all on the basis of the theories of Public Choice and of Institutional Economics. Both of these concepts are able to offer interpretations of the actions of bureaucracies; but to the analysis of developments in the economy as a whole they scarcely make any useful direct contribution. This requires macroeconomic paradigms. And so this article, on the basis of Keynesian elements of macroeconomics such as sluggish price adjustment and incomplete information, pleads for a future European Central Bank with conditional independence, which will be required to pay due regard not only to monetary stability but also to economic growth and employment. And this is only possible within a concept of cooperation, and not if monetary policy is to have unrestricted autonomy with the aim of maintaining only price stability at any cost.

2 Macroeconomic Prerequisites for Reducing Unemployment

Monetary policy, fiscal policy and incomes policy ought together to ensure a constellation of interest rate, exchange rate and wage levels that are able to bring about inflation-free growth with a high level of employment. This requires that the central bank, all tiers of government and the two sides of industry should agree to pursue jointly all three macroeconomic aims, namely stable prices, an appropriate level of growth and full employment. A central bank can only attempt to keep interest rates low if it is backed up in its fight against inflation by incomes policy and by fiscal policy. Substantial rises in unit labor costs must endanger price stability, and therefore demand a restrictive use of interest rates; rising interest rates depress production, increase unemployment and create budget deficits. An increasing public-sector borrowing requirement makes the financial markets expand at rates of growth far higher than those of the formation of real capital. But if portfolios are overloaded with monetary assets, then even the slightest rumors will provoke substantial processes of redeployment, with sharp fluctuations of interest rates and exchange rates as the consequences. These in turn affect the markets for goods, rendering the problem of undesirable effects on the macroeconomy even more acute.

What is therefore required is a "code of economic behavior" to replace the straightforward allocation of responsibility for each of the individual macroeconomic goals to one of the instances involved in stability policy. This code of behavior should include the following elements:

- those responsible for incomes policy should bear in mind that the amount to be distributed depends upon the level of real income,
- those directing fiscal policy should ensure that public debt is kept at a level which is sustainable in the long term,
- and those conducting monetary policy should be aware of its substantial effect on the real economy.

Those responsible for monetary policy must be induced to play their part in such a stability pact. They must remember that the upheavals that have taken place in international finance also affect any monetary concept that is orientated towards a stable value of money. With the progressive globalization of financial markets, the rates of change in monetary aggregates - which are the target figures for monetary policy - have deviated further and further from the patterns that were familiar in the past and from the rate of growth of the economic product. In addition, the velocity of money circulation is now fluctuating more strongly. But if central bank policy is to be strictly tied to a monetary target, it requires the velocity with which money circulates to be constant and predictable. This means that the rate of growth of the money supply can no longer be the major factor governing activity in the field of monetary policy: the money supply has lost much of its importance as an indicator of the course monetary policy should take and of future price developments, whilst the performance of interest rates, which is largely determined by central banks, has gained in weight. For this reason, a close look must be taken at interest, as the primary control factor in monetary policy and as a monetary target. Interest here means the interest rate that can largely be determined by central banks, namely the rate for call money. The aim must be to achieve interest rates that are only slightly higher than the inflation rate. The experience of the last few years in Switzerland, the USA and Japan proves that an interest-rate policy that is so orientated can stimulate the forces of growth without jeopardizing price stability. But this assumes a largely inflation-free environment, i.e. also wage and fiscal policies that are directed towards stability.

How can a central bank be induced to enter into a national stability pact? How can a situation be achieved in which the Bundesbank follows a policy of low interest rates for liquidity provided by the central bank when the value of money is stable, when there is no indication of future inflation, when unit labor costs are falling, when the public sector is engaged in consolidating its budgets and import prices are constant? The Bundesbank refuses to be drawn into a national stability pact. In doing so, it puts forward two lines of defense. The first is its credo: it professes to be the sole repository of wisdom with regard to the rates of growth of the money supply that can be reconciled with price stability, yet refuses to accept any responsibility for incomes or employment because it appears that the long-term real rate of interest which in its view is relevant to economic growth and employment cannot be influenced by monetary policy. The second line of defense is for the Bundesbank to stand upon its autonomy. But is the autonomy of an institution at any price to be attributed greater weight than the opportunity to make a contribution towards reducing mass unemployment by involving the Bundesbank in a national stability pact?

3 Central Bank Independence and Economic Growth

Institutional arrangements are supposed to be a way of achieving efficient solutions; in the present case this would mean a way of contributing to the better management of macroeconomic performance. It is no doubt impossible in the long term to maintain economic, social and political stability without adequate price stability. And in order to maintain price stability, money must be kept scarce. That is the task of central banks. They have to decide upon the amount of liquidity that the central bank will make available, and on the rates of interest they will charge for it, in accordance with the requirements of the macroeconomy. This requires a central bank which is not subject to government directives in the exercise of its responsibilities. Otherwise, if the central bank *is* subject to directives from state bodies, a monetary potential for inflation can scarcely be avoided. Central bank autonomy that is derived from this principle is functionally-related and therefore limited. Thus the Bundesbank is independent of direction by the federal government, and is not subject to any legal or prudential supervision in the exercise of its responsibilities, is not under the control either of the government or of parliament. At the same time, however, the Bundesbank is required to support the federal government's general economic policy, to fulfill international tasks on behalf of the government, and to advise the government; and the statutes of Bundesbank have to be approved by the government. The autonomy of the Bundesbank is therefore relative, and rests upon social consensus.

The results of empirical studies on the relationship between the degree of independence enjoyed by different central banks and the overall economic performances of the countries concerned do not allow any unambiguous conclusions to be reached as to the degree to which autonomy is a necessary prerequisite for economic growth and stable prices. It does appear that countries in which the central bank is highly independent generally also achieve a high degree of price stability, without it however being possible to establish any clear causality.

But it also appears that there is no empirically established basis for the claim put forward by the Bundesbank to justify its obvious fixation with the objective of price stability, namely that this is essential to satisfactory economic growth. It does appear that high and sharply fluctuating rates of inflation detract from economic growth. However, more recent studies have come to the conclusion that inflation rates of less than around 8 - 10% do not exert any significant positive or negative effects on economic growth (Bruno and Easterly (1995), Barro (1995), Sarel (1996)).

Similarly, there is no significant correlation between the degree of independence of central banks on the one hand and the level or the variability of economic growth on the other (Alesina and Summers (1993), Schiemann and Alshuth (1994)). A high level of central bank autonomy is linked to a high degree of price stability, but not to high economic growth.

However, this does not mean that measures of monetary policy are of no significance to economic growth and employment. In every cycle of the American economy since 1953 only monetary policy has been in the position to put an end to recession and to create the conditions for renewed growth (Romer/Romer, (1994)). It is also indisputable that inflation can be stopped by a monetary squeeze: but that route leads directly to recession. Incentives are therefore necessary if an independent central bank that is orientated towards price stability is not to overreact and force a stabilization crisis without any manifest need to do so.

4 The Bundesbank's Conditional Independence

The Bundesbank is a legal entity created by statute and incorporated under public law: it is a quango.[1] The Bundesbank is the only administrative body in Germany that is not subject to any restrictions imposed from without; it is the example *par excellence* of a quango that is outside democratic control. The consequence: "Anyone who is so independent that he is allowed to do anything will do what he wants to and not necessarily what he should" (Vaubel (1992)). Implicit in this is a danger that during periods of inflation monetary policy will overreact, upping interest rates excessively and so depressing income and employment, but without

[1] Abbreviation for: Quasi-autonomous non-governmental organization.

thereby managing to put the lid on prices any more quickly. Olaf Sievert's commentary on the raising of the discount rate by three-quarters of a percentage point to a record level of 8.75 % in July 1992, in the midst of a recession and with every indication that inflation would soon start to decline anyway, was as follows: "But we are in danger, out of sheer impatience, of thrashing the economy back into stability, although ... a recession, for God's sake, is the last thing it needs ..." (Sievert (1992)). Sievert here identifies an overreaction in interest rate policy that was out of step with the challenges of the social situation and thus with what were viewed by the majority of the population as desirable goals.

A central bank as an institution in society that is not involved in the struggle for the distribution of wealth is particularly well-suited to serve the cause of monetary stability. This is why it should never allow itself to get into a state of dependency upon social groups that are fighting each other for shares in the economic product. Only if it observes this rule can the central bank exercise its function as a body that can impose sanctions if other players in the macropolitical arena act in such a way as to put stability at risk. This is the position in Germany, and the Bundesbank exercises this function uncompromisingly. Whenever it observes that price stability is in danger it drives up interest rates, depresses economic activity, imposes wage restraint, and deprives the government of room to manoeuvre in its fiscal policy. Its restrictive course is not relaxed until the inflationary pressure has subsided.

There can be no objection to such a concept of a stability-orientated monetary policy. The Bundesbank represents an external control upon fiscal policy and incomes policy. But there is no such external control on monetary policy. Nothing and nobody can impose sanctions upon the Bundesbank if it fails to act correctly. And since not even the governing council of the Bundesbank are exempt from human frailty, this cannot be the optimum institutional arrangement for stability policy. There are various kinds of duty that may be imposed upon a central bank from outside, while still leaving it free to determine monetary policy without being restricted by directives from the state. The attitude in France is this: "But independence does not mean being isolated from democracy, from the French people. Accountability is a necessary complement to independence. The Independence Act requires the Banque de France to report to the President of the Republic and to Parliament. It maintains very close relations with the finance committees of the Senate and the National Assembly, and the members of the monetary council regularly explain their policy to the people in lectures and publications" (Trichet (1997)).

In Germany, things are different. "This political independence of the Bundesbank does not however in any way mean freedom from responsibility. It is true that, in contrast to the situation in many other countries, the Bundesbank, for well-considered reasons, does not have any duty of accountability towards the government or parliament imposed upon it. But it has nevertheless, from the very beginning, always regarded itself as having a duty to lay open to the public and to justify both its policy and its assessment of events that affect stability" (Tietmeyer

(1997)). But why is there no duty of accountability towards the government and parliament, towards the people? What are the "well-considered reasons" for this? Why is the Bundesbank completely free to decide which "events that affect stability" it will comment on and which not? Why does the Bundesbank only very rarely allow the public an insight into its monetary laboratory? Why is there in Germany no forum in which all those responsible for the macropolitical situation, i.e. including the Bundesbank, can exchange information, consult with each other and explain their measures of policy? Without cooperation, that is to say without consultation upon measures of incomes policy, fiscal policy and monetary policy, a constellation of interest rate, exchange rate and wage levels that will lead to a high level of employment while maintaining price stability can be achieved only by pure chance.

5 A Concept for Interest Rate Policy

Monetary policy cannot be used to intervene in wage bargaining, and it has no systematic influence on the evolution of exchange rates. But it does govern interest rates on the money market. It thereby exerts substantial influence on economic growth and employment, and only as a consequence of this, if at all, on general price levels. It is clear that what is central to the further repercussions of measures of monetary policy is the interest rate band, and not the effect on exchange rates or the granting of credit (Taylor (1995)).

The interest rate referred to here is that interest rate that can be determined by central banks, namely the rate for call money. The outstanding quality of the call-money rate as a source of information on production and real incomes has now been extensively documented (Bernanke and Blinder (1992), Döpke, Krämer and Langfeldt (1994), Filc (1992), Filc (1994), Juchems, Langmantel and Nerb (1994), Sims (1992)). As far as the causality is concerned, there are some well-founded assumptions (Filc (1992), Sandte (1994)).

An example of excessive control through a restrictive interest rate policy with the aim of holding down inflation, but resulting in a deep recession, is to be found in the phase following German unification. As an indicator of monetary policy the difference can be used between the money-market rate, adjusted for inflation (cost of living), and the monthly year on year of change in the net output of manufacturing industry. The net interest burden calculated in this way increased from the middle of 1991 onwards, initially as a consequence of rising money-market rates, and from the middle of 1992 onwards principally as a result of the slump in production. Around the turn of the year 1992/1993 interest rate policy assumed a degree of restrictiveness that had never been seen before in the history of the Federal Republic (see Fig. 1). There was an associated decline in real income, but only minor success in re-establishing price stability.

Figure 1: Monetary Restraint Following German Unification

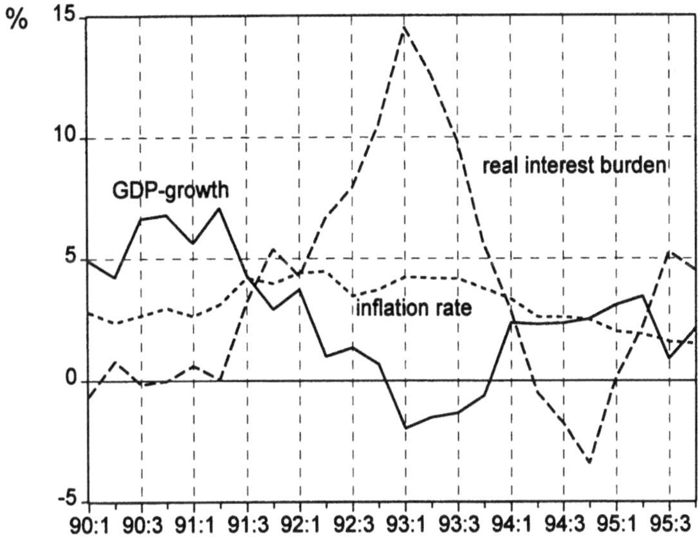

Source: Deutsche Bundesbank - Monthly Reports; own

Indicators in the real economy - production, incomes and employment - reacted markedly to this flexing of interest-rate muscles on the part of the Bundesbank; the inflation rate reacted less. This is proof of the distinct effects on the real economy of measures of monetary policy that at least from the spring of 1992 onwards were excessively restrictive. If this is to be avoided in future, there must be a harmonization of measures of incomes policy, fiscal policy and monetary policy on the basis of an overall stability concept, in order to achieve a constellation of interest levels, wage rates and exchange rate levels that can be reconciled with a high level of employment while maintaining price stability.

6 The Taylor Rule for the Establishment of a Monetary Policy Directed Towards Price Stability and High Employment

Price stability and an appropriate level of economic growth with high employment rank highly on the scale of socially desirable goals for the overall economy. From this is derived the demand that monetary policy should minimize a social loss function by keeping any deviations of the inflation rate and of real incomes from their respective target values as small as possible (Green (1996), Illing (1998)).

The action parameter for monetary policy is the interest rate for liquidity provided by the central bank, which the central bank itself determines. In addition, there is need for an operational, simple and systematic rule for monetary policy which will be accepted as credible by private players and will therefore eliminate possible problems of time inconsistency in the implementation of measures of monetary policy. Taylor suggests that "... good policy rules typically call for changes in the federal funds rate in response to changes of the price level or changes in real income" (Taylor (1993)). And he has identified such an implicit rule underlying the US central bank's interest rate policy in the period between 1987 and 1993. According to his calculations, the federal funds rate (r_T) was adjusted every time that discrepancies arose between a target value of 2% for the inflation rate (p') and the actual inflation rate (p) and/or between actual economic growth (y) and the long-term trend of economic growth (y') of 2.2%. In both cases, the adjustments amounted to half of the discrepancy between actual values and target values. In addition, a basic interest rate of 2% was put into the equation as constant:

$$(6.1) \qquad r_T = p + 2\% + 0.5\,(y - y') + 0.5\,(p - p')$$

And using this simple formula it does indeed turn out to be possible to reconstruct the trend of the federal funds rate with astonishing accuracy. And the result in terms of the economy is also remarkable: high and stable economic growth with almost stable prices in the USA.

It is therefore only logical to apply the Taylor Rule of a systematic interest rate policy on the part of the central bank to Germany too, with the aim of identifying possible discrepancies between actual money-market rates and the figures that are derived from the application of such a rule. The reference figures to be used for monetary policy would be firstly a measure of the amount by which economic growth deviates from the target value, and secondly a figure which gives information on inflationary pressure. Which figures it would be expedient to use is an open question. The modified Taylor Rule for Germany that will be presented below is therefore to be regarded merely as a research experiment, and not as a rule for a systematic interest rate policy that ought to be followed.

The Taylor interest rate for Germany (i_T) is the interest rate for call money that would be desirable if monetary policy were to react to the current rate of inflation, inflationary pressure and high economic growth which looks liable to endanger price stability. An interest rate premium of $\Delta y'$ is used here, representing the discrepancy between an economic growth target of 3%, above which level a substantial effect on employment can be identified, and any higher rates of actual economic growth. In addition, it is assumed that the makers of monetary policy will relate changes in interest rates to the average of the rise in the cost of living (p_L) and the rise in industrial producers' prices (p_P) as an indicator of future price rises at consumer level. Finally, a constant real core call-money rate of 2% is included in the equation:

(6.2) $i_T = 0.5\,(p_L + p_P) + 2\% + \Delta y'$

If the required interest rates determined in this way are compared with actual call-money rates, then it can clearly be seen that the modified Taylor interest rate and the actual money-market rate run contrary to each other from the first quarter of 1991 until the middle of 1992 (see Fig. 2). It can thus be seen once again that the Bundesbank's interest rate reaction was excessive, being directed solely at the current inflation rate and neglecting its repercussions on the real economy. The consequence for the real economy of an interest rate policy whose restrictiveness can be measured in terms of the difference between the call-money rate and the required rate as per Taylor was the recession of 1992/1993, which did not end until interest rate policy was relaxed (see Fig. 3).

These provisional results relating to a central bank interest rate policy that follows systematic and clear rules cannot of course be interpreted as a manual of method that will apply at all times. In a constantly changing environment, there is no prospect of finding mechanical rules that can be applied automatically in any economic situation. This applies to money supply rules just as much as to the indicators that might guide an interest rate policy which is required to take account of its powerful influence on economic growth and employment.

But there is every reason to plead that the monetary policy of a central bank that is not subject to political direction should follow logical rules and to be directed towards the attainment of objectives for the macroeconomy which correspond to what is socially desirable. For monetary policy to be thus independent and yet subject to rules might be a way of obviating overreactions of interest rate policy in one direction or the other, and so of avoiding the undesirable economic effects that occur when the central bank pays regard only to one single objective.

Figure 2: Overnight Money Rate and Required Rate According to a Modified Taylor-Rule (Germany, 1988:1 - 1997:1)

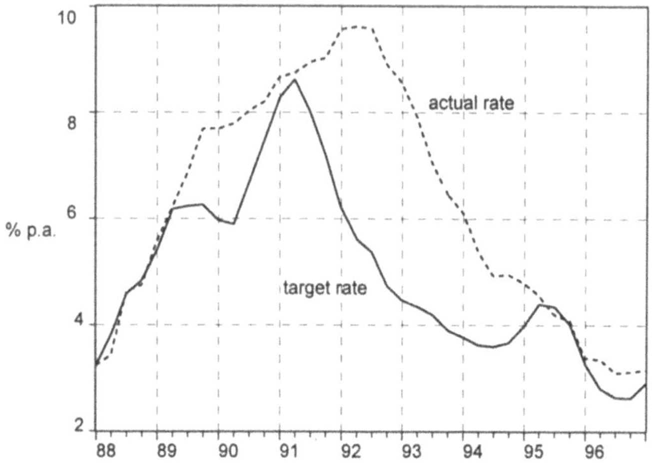

Source: OECD - Main Economic Indicators; own calculations

Figure 3: Deviation of Actual from Target Interest Rate and Economic Growth (Germany, 1988:1 - 1997:1)

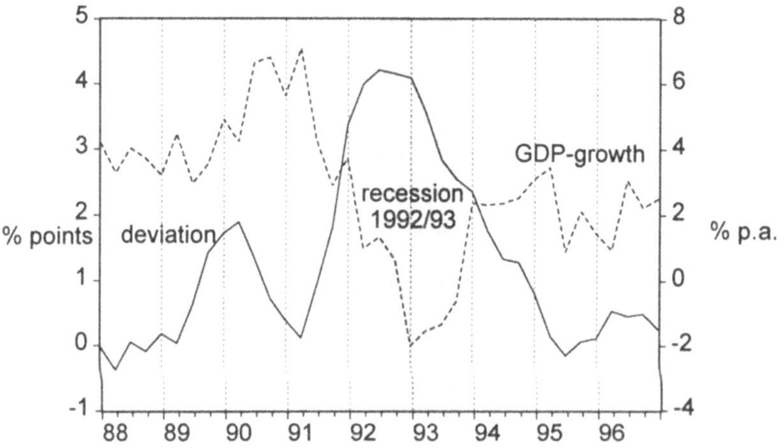

Source: OECD - Main Economic Indicators; own calculations

References

Alesina, A. and L. H. Summers (1993), Central Bank Independence and Macroeconomic Performance: Some Comparative Evidence, *Journal of Money, Credit, and Banking* 25, 151-62.

Barro, R. J. (1995), Inflation and Economic Growth, *Bank of England Quarterly Bulletin* 35, 166-76.

Bernanke, B. S. and A. S. Blinder (1992), The Federal Funds Rate and the Channels of Monetary Transmission, *American Economic Review* 82, 901-21.

Bruno, M. and W. Easterly (1995), Inflation Crises and Long-Run Growth, NBER Working Paper No. 5209, Cambridge, MA.

Filc, W. (1992), Monetäre Fundierung einer angebotsorientierten Stabilisierungspolitik, *Konjunkturpolitik* 38, 316-39.

Filc, W. (1994), Geldpolitik, Bankpolitik und Konjunktur, in: M. Bodin and L. Hübl (eds.), Banken in gesamtwirtschaftlicher Verantwortung, Stuttgart, 5-23.

Döpke, J., J. W. Krämer and E. Langfeld (1994), Konjunkturelle Frühindikatoren in Deutschland, *Konjunkturpolitik* 40, 135-53.

Green, J. H. (1996), Inflation Targeting: Theory and Policy Implications, *IMF Staff Papers* No. 43, 779-95.

Illing, G. (1998), Mechanism Design for Central Banks - Results and Unsolved Issues, this volume.

Juchems, A., E. Langmantel and G. Nerb (1994), Geld- und Fiskalpolitik - Vernichten sie Arbeitsplätze?, *Ifo-Schnelldienst* 47, 20-27.

Romer, C. D. and D. H. Romer (1994), What Ends Recessions? NBER Working Paper No. 4765, Cambridge, MA.

Sandte, H. (1994), Kurzfristige Zinssätze, Kreditkosten und Konjunktur, *Sparkasse* 111, 307-11.

Sarel, M. (1996), Nonlinear Effects of Inflation on Economic Growth, *IMF Staff Papers* No. 43, 199-215.

Schiemann, J. and S. Alshuth (1994), Der Grad der Zentralbankautonomie und sein Einfluss im gesamtwirtschaftlichen Prozess. Eine international vergleichende Rangkorrelationsanalyse, *Aussenwirtschaft* 49, 579-600.

Sievert, O. (1992), Einspruch gegen Übertreibungen, *Wirtschaftsdienst* 72, 455-56.

Sims, C. A. (1992), Interpreting the Macroeconomic Time Series Facts. The Effects of Monetary Policy, *European Economic Review* 36, 975-1000.

Taylor, J. B. (1993), Discretion versus Policy Rules in Practice, *Carnegie-Rochester Conference Series on Public Policy* 23, 194-214.

Taylor, J. B. (1995), The Monetary Transmission Mechanism: An Empirical Framework, *Journal of Economic Perspectives* 9, 27-48.

Tietmeyer, H. (1997), Die Europäische Währung ist kein Selbstzweck, *Sparkasse* 114, 13-16.

Trichet, J.-C. (1997), Die Europäische Währungsunion aus französischer Perspektive, *Sparkasse* 114, 9-12.

Vaubel, R. (1992), Das Ende der Preisstabilität, *Frankfurter Allgemeine Zeitung* from 3-28-1992, 13.

Part II:

Monetary Policies: Strategies and Implementation

3. Theoretical Considerations on Strategies in Monetary Policy

Monetary Policy Strategies: From Rules to Central Bank Contracts under Contingent Target Agreements

Alexander Karmann
University of Dresden, Mommsenstr. 13, D - 01062 Dresden

1 Introduction

The rules-versus-discretion debate in monetary policy is at least 150 years old, as Stanley Fischer (1990) points out. For a long time, until 1977, the advocates of discretionary policy strategies could refer to the fact that, methodologically, any rule could be adopted by some discretionary policy. Due to the problem of time inconsistency, as in the Barro-Gordon model of 1983, a simple rule seems to be superior to discretionary policy, at least in deterministic models. But simple rules do not solve the trade-off between optimal, i.e. flexible, and credible policies in models with stochastic supply disturbances. The rules debate still touches on the recent discussion of credible institutional arrangements for monetary policy like central bank contracting in the presence of informational asymmetries (Walsh (1995a)). The question to be answered in designing optimal institutional mechanisms is to what extent discretionary power should be given to the central bank to engage in stabilization, based on its private information. McCallum (1995) already pointed out that even central bank contracting may not solve the credibility problem since there is no ex-post incentive for the government to realize the sanctions included into the contract when not achieving the contracted targets. This view seems to be supported by recent historical experience with the New Zealand 1989 Act. When New Zealand inflation rate exceeded the current PTA (Policy Target Agreement) of 0-2 percent CPI inflation in January 1997, the Central Bank's governor, who is held accountable by the Charter, was not fired by the government. This, at first sight time-inconsistent decision, harks back to theoretical reasoning that the preannounced inflation targets should be state contingent on supply shocks. Hence, the PTA to be published ex-ante should specify a functional relationship between supply disturbances and target levels (Walsh (1995b)). A contractual arrangement, using contingent PTAs and assigning discretionary power to the central bank to use private information on demand shocks, will allow to achieve the socially optimal commitment solution.

The paper is organized as follows. We start by describing the general modeling framework (sect. 1), introducing the different solution concepts and defining the terminology related to the topic (sect. 2). Within a standard aggregate supply/aggregate demand model we compare the relative performance of simple rules w.r.t. the socially optimal solution (sect. 3). In section 4, we show that informational asymmetries between the public and the central bank will lead to optimal contractual designs by using PTA inflation target schemes instead of constant target levels. We conclude by drawing on this result when commenting New Zealand's PTA revision in January 1997 (see Brash (1997)).

2 The General Approach

Modeling central bank policy typically consists of three elements. First, we formulate the functional relations describing the structure of the economy. Typically, a *linear rational-expectation* (LRE) model is considered. The assumption of homogeneous expectations is a standard one when we disregard effects resulting from informational asymmetries. Let X be the vector of (present and/or past) relevant data, X^e the corresponding vector of expected variables and $\overline{X}$ denote a vector of target levels. Then, taking $Y^T := (X, X^e, \overline{X})$, the LRE model may be written as

(2.1) $$Y = AY + \eta_Y$$

for some matrix A where η_Y denotes the disturbance vector. Typically, as variables are considered output, employment, price level or inflation rate, monetary aggregates or money growth, interest and exchange rates. Thereby, at least one of the variables included is assumed to be a control variable of the policy maker, e.g. the inflation rate or short run interest rates. The equations describing supply and demand relations constitute the constraints in the optimization approach considered below.

The specification of the *social loss function L*, respectively its expectation

(2.2) $$E\,L(Y),$$

constitutes the second element of the model. Until the 80's, the literature focused especially on losses based on deviations of the output from its equilibrium level $\overline{y}$. Later on the analysis was expanded by considering, in addition, an inflation (or price) target level π^*

(2.2') $$L = g_y(y - \overline{y})^2 + g_\pi(\pi - \pi^*)^2$$

where g_i are nonnegative weights. The combination of output and inflation considerations within the loss function, as in (2.2'), is called *flexible inflation targeting* (Svensson (1997)). The third element of the model is a reaction function (target rule) which links the target (or *instrument*) variable(s) Z, as element(s) of the X-vector, to the target levels $\overline{X}$. More generally,

(2.3) $$Z = \Lambda Y + \eta_Z$$

where η_Z is the disturbance vector in the reaction function. Thereby, the reaction function is either deduced from optimizing expectations of (2.2), given the constraints (2.1). (Optimal rules are defined uniquely as long as target levels in (2.2) and (2.1) are consistent, claiming for $\bar{y} = y^*$. The '*time inconsistency*' case of $k := y^* - \bar{y} > 0$ is discussed in section 3). Or it is assigned a priori to the policymaker as a *fixed target* (i.e. non-state contingent) rule or a *flexible target* (i.e. state contingent) rule. This enables us to mimic the optimal (time consistent) solution by an appropriate target rule in setting the Λ-coefficients accordingly. The relative performance of alternative rules is measured in terms of (2.2). A list of well known simple rules and their performance will be considered in the following section.

3 Solution Concepts and Simple Rules

The time inconsistency debate starts from arguing that governments tend to increase employment figures and thereby produce output values which exceed equilibrium values in order to improve social welfare. Barro and Gordon (1983) show that if private expectations are set on the base of levels announced by the policymaker, the social welfare can be improved, in terms of (2.2), by fooling private expectations. In a rough critique, Blinder (1997) classifies this reasoning as a nonproblem in practical central banking: responsible behavior would simply prevent central bankers from lowering unemployment below the natural rate. Blinder's position, though well suited for a large majority of central bank behavior, does not convince with regard to casual temptations to use inflationary tools in situations of political distress. The problem of time inconsistent behavior is an important issue, even for central bankers. Central bank contracting under contingent PTA, as discussed in section 4, seems to constitute a credible mechanism to overcome time inconsistent behavior under discretion.

In the following we deal with the standard concepts discussed as alternative solutions to the problem of time-inconsistency in LRE models. Beside concepts derived from optimization calculus, we also consider simple rules, like the Friedman money-supply rule, nominal income targeting or interest rate smoothing, whose relative performance is discussed even in recent contributions (Svensson (1997); see also Cecchetti, this volume). The explicit discussion of the relative performance of these concepts in a straightforward aggregate supply/aggregate demand setting will be referred to the next section.

The problem of credible monetary strategies, as formalized in Barro and Gordon (1983), starts by considering different preferences for the government ('*flexible inflation targeting*'), i.e. $L^G = L$ as in (2.2'), and for the privates ('expectation stabilization'), i.e.

$$L^P = (\pi - \pi^e)^2. \tag{3.1}$$

Given a standard AS/AD model, the *commitment solution* (π^C, π^{eC}) is the 'socially optimal' or 'ideal' (Canzoneri (1985)) solution, i.e.

$$\text{(C)} \qquad (\pi, \pi^e) \in \arg\min \; L^G(\Pi, \Pi^e; \pi^*)$$

$$(\pi, \pi^e) \in \arg\min \; L^P(\Pi, \Pi^e),$$

and any information (w.r.t. shocks) is public. The discretionary solution (π^D, π^{eD}) is described by the Nash equilibrium

$$\text{(D)} \qquad \pi \in \arg\min \; L^G(\Pi, \pi^e; \pi^*) \quad \text{for given } \pi^e$$

$$\pi^e \in \arg\min \; L^P(\pi, \Pi^e; \pi^*) \quad \text{for given } \pi,$$

and, typically, information is asymmetric. In the *cheating solution* (π^F, π^{eF}) the privates are fooled. While building their expectations π^e in accordance with the governmental announcement, the government chooses the inflation rate π^* that optimizes its objective function

$$\text{(F)} \qquad \pi^e = \pi^*$$

$$\pi \in \arg\min \; L^G(\Pi, \pi^*; \pi^*).$$

From the above definition, it is easy to see that the commitment solution, in general, is superior to the discretionary solution, in terms of L^G: this is an immediate consequence of the simultaneous choice of realized and expected values. Moreover, under discretion (i.e. in the noncommitment case) there is an incentive for the government not to stick to announced targets as the commitment solution would claim for, but to improve its welfare by cheating. As the cheating solution is not stable (the privates would react in adjusting their expectations) the process ends in the Nash equilibrium (D). The question related to these solution concepts is to which extent simple, transparent rules allow to approach, if not to achieve, the commitment solution in a credible way.

In the literature, a number of different flexible and fixed rules are proposed. The most prominent fixed rule is the constant growth rate rule, introduced into the discussion by Friedman (1959). He proposed to increase the monetary base each period at a certain, constant rate (explicitly at the expected rate of average real growth). The Friedman rule, further called *money-supply rule* (MS) can be stated as

$$\text{(MS)} \qquad m - \overline{m} = 0\,.$$

The *interest rate rule* (IR), as an alternative rule introduced by Poole (1970), pegs interest rates to a certain level i*

$$\text{(IR)} \qquad i - i^* = 0.$$

(IR) is of special importance if stabilization of financial markets is regarded to be a goal of monetary policy. The *nominal income rule* (NI) proposed by Bean (1983) and others, gained most emphasis from analytical reasoning

$$\text{(NI)} \qquad (\pi + y) - (\pi^* + \bar{y}) = 0.$$

Price- or *inflation target rules* (IT) disregard from any instrumental consideration in reaching the target:

$$\text{(IT)} \qquad \pi - \pi^* = 0.$$

Its counterpart, an *output target rule* (OT) is described by

$$\text{(OT)} \qquad y - \bar{y} = 0\,.$$

The above simple rules, and any mix of them, can be stated in terms of a reaction function with appropriate nonnegative weights λ by using money growth *m* as an instrument variable:

$$m = \sum_i \lambda_i \,(x_i - \bar{x}_i)\,.$$

Any fixed rule, pegging a variable x_{i0} to its target $\bar{x}_{i0}$, can be represented by choosing $\lambda_i = 0$ for $i \neq i_0$ and λ_{i0} 'big enough'. As will be demonstrated below, there is no simple, fixed rule to provide an overall 'good' solution. The relative performance quite considerably hinges on the structure of the model and the nature of the shocks prevailing within the economy.

4 On the Relative Performance of Simple Rules

To demonstrate the properties of the above cited alternative rules and their performance relative to the commitment and discretionary solution, we use the following standard AS/AD model (see, e.g. Karmann (1993)):

$$\text{(4.1)} \qquad y - \bar{y} = a(\pi - \pi^e) + \eta_1$$

$$\text{(4.2)} \qquad y = -\,b(i - \pi^e) + \eta_2$$

$$\text{(4.3)} \qquad m - \pi = cy - d\,i + \eta_3,$$

where y denotes the (log of) output, π the (log of) price level (i.e. inflation rate) and i the short term nominal interest rate. Cancelling out the interest rate i, eq. (4.2 - 4.3) can be rewritten as

$$\text{(4.2')} \qquad y = B(m - \pi) + C\pi^e + \eta,$$

where $B := b/(d+bc)$, $C := db/(d+bc)$, and $\eta := (d\eta_2 - b\eta_3)/(d+bc)$.

The derivation of the price- and output processes corresponding to the different concepts considered in section 2 is a standard technique. Given the model (4.1) - (4.3), the commitment solution (C) is given by

$$\text{(4.4)} \qquad \pi^C = \pi^* - \eta_1 (g_y a)/(g_\pi + g_y a^2)$$

$$y^C = \bar{y} + \eta_1 g_\pi/(g_\pi + g_y a^2).$$

Inserting this into (2.2'), the corresponding expected loss under commitment can be calculated as

$$\text{(4.5)} \qquad EL^C = [\sigma^2_{\eta 1} g_\pi/(g_\pi + g_y a^2) + k^2] g_y$$

which tends to zero if the relative weight g_y/g_π on output is high. The denominator $(g_\pi + g_y a^2)$ shows the stabilization effect by allowing supply shocks η_1 to be partly offset by price fluctuations.

The discretionary solution (D) is given by

$$\text{(4.6)} \qquad \pi^D = \pi^* + (g_y/g_\pi) a k - \eta_1 g_y a/(g_\pi + g_y a^2)$$

$$y^D = \bar{y} + \eta_1 g_\pi/(g_\pi + g_y a^2),$$

where $(g_y/g_\pi)a k$ is called the *inflation bias*: the output variations are the same as in the commitment case but the inflation rate is higher and causes higher social costs. The resulting expected loss is

$$\text{(4.7)} \qquad EL^D = EL^C + g_\pi[(g_y/g_\pi) a k]^2.$$

The money-supply rule (MS) results in the processes

$$\text{(4.8)} \qquad \pi^{MS} = \pi^* + (\eta - \eta_1)/(a + B)$$

$$y = \bar{y} + (a\eta + B\eta_1)/(a + B),$$

where π^* is determined by the money supply $\bar{m}$, $\pi^* := (B\bar{m} - \bar{y})/(B - C)$. Together with the definition of the aggregate demand shock η in (4.2'), the money-supply rule implies a complex pattern of reactions to IS-, LM- and AS-disturbances. Besides, the values of the structural parameters play an important role. Finally, expected losses are given by

$$\text{(4.9)} \qquad EL^{MS} = \sigma^2_{\eta 1}(g_\pi + g_y B^2)/(a+B)^2 + \sigma^2_\eta (g_\pi + g_y a^2)/(a+B)^2 + g_y k^2$$

showing that, in general, MS cannot mimic commitment policy.

To solve for (IR), we first have to explain how private expectations are formed in our model. Given the interest target level $\bar{i}$ to be known publicly and equating (4.1) and (4.2), expectations π^e consistent with the equilibrium (i.e. $y = \bar{y}$, $\eta_1 = \eta_2 = 0$) are given by $\pi^e = \bar{i} + \bar{y}/b =: \pi^*$. Then we get

$$\text{(4.10)} \qquad \pi^{IR} = \pi^* + (\eta_2 - \eta_1)/a$$

$$y^{IR} = \bar{y} + \eta_2.$$

Thus,

$$\text{(4.11)} \qquad EL^{IR} = \sigma^2_{\eta 1}\, g_\pi / a^2 + \sigma^2_{\eta 2}\,(g_\pi + g_y a^2)/a^2 + g_y k^2.$$

A flexible rule, closely related to the outcome under commitment, is the nominal income rule (NI). Assuming $\bar{y}$ and $\pi^e = \pi^*$ to be consistent with an AD equilibrium, we get $\bar{y} = (C\text{-}B)\,\pi^*$. Inserting the reaction function $m = -\lambda\,[(\pi + y) - (\pi^* + \bar{y})]$ into (4.2') and taking λ 'high enough', finally results in

$$\text{(4.12)} \qquad \pi^{NI} = \pi^* - \eta_1/(a+1)$$

$$y^{NI} = \bar{y} + \eta_1/(a+1),$$

hence

$$\text{(4.13)} \qquad EL^{NI} = \sigma^2_{\eta 1}\,(g_\pi + g_y)/(a+1)^2 + g_y k^2.$$

Under inflation targeting (IT) we get

$$\text{(4.14)} \qquad \pi^{IT} = \pi^*$$

$$y^{IT} = \bar{y} + \eta_1,$$

where $\bar{y} := (C\text{-}B)\,\pi^*$, and

$$\text{(4.15)} \qquad EL^{IT} = \sigma^2_{\eta 1}\, g_y + g_y\, k^2.$$

Output targeting (OT), on the other hand leads to

$$\text{(4.16)} \qquad \pi^{OT} = \pi^* + \eta_1/a$$

$$y^{OT} = \bar{y}$$

where again $\pi^* := \bar{y}\,/\,(C\text{-}B)$. Accordingly,

$$\text{(4.17)} \qquad EL^{OT} = \sigma^2_{\eta 1}\, g_\pi / a^2 + g_y k^2.$$

The performance of rules is based on comparing the resulting expected losses with the ones resulting from the commitment solution (C). According to (4.7), the discretionary solution (D) is always inferior to (C) as long as there is an inflation bias due to $k = y^* - y > 0$. It is easy to see that under certain circumstances, simple rules, like the inflation target rule or the nominal income rule, may perform better than (D). More precisely

$$(IT) \succ (D)$$

if and only if $\sigma^2_{\eta 1} < (1+(g_y/g_\pi)a^2)k^2$. Or

$$(NI) \succ (D)$$

if $a = 1$ and output- and inflation deviations are equally weighted, i.e. $g_y = g_\pi$. In this particular case, (NI) is equivalent to the commitment solution. On the other hand, under strict inflation targeting, i.e. g_π / g_y is 'high enough', (IT) becomes equivalent to the commitment case. The objection against an inflation target rule comes from the fact that under (IT), there is an undamped reaction to any supply shock in the production sphere (see eq. (4.14)). The counterpart to (IT) is the output rule (OT) where fluctuations affect inflation rates but not real output.

Within the class of simple rules, from a theoretical point of view, the NI-rule created much attraction. Especially, we find

$$(NI) \succ (MS)$$

if and only if $B < 1$. The latter holds for $c < 1$, i.e. if money demand is inelastic w.r.t. income. Similarly,

$$(NI) \succ (IT)$$

holds if and only if $(g_\pi + g_y) / g_y < (a + 1)^2$. Under equal weights, this reduces to $\sqrt{2} - 1 < a$ for which empirical evidence can be found (Funke (1995)).

The objection against interest rate pegging comes from the price-indeterminacy problem due to infinitely elastic money supply. But, at least from a modeling perspective, the problem can be solved by allowing privates to form their expectations when the reaction function of the authority is known (McCallum (1986)). In the literature, the issue of financial innovations and their impact on the (stability of the) money demand led to the question whether 'interest rate stabilization' may be a good policy advice. The presence of large LM shocks (η_3), steep LM curves ('$d \rightarrow 0$') or flat IS curves ('$b \rightarrow \infty$'), as seen to be accompanied with the process of financial innovations, worsens the performance of traditional money-supply rules. (IR) or a policy mix of (IR) and (MS) can be shown to produce 'smaller' social losses in terms of (2.2'). (For a detailed discussion, we refer to Karmann (1993).)

There are two major concerns a monetary authority has to face when adopting a certain simple rule as discussed above. First, the relative performance of the rule to be adopted crucially depends on the relevant parameters of the model and on the nature of shocks the economy is exposed to. Second, how can the authority credibly commit to the announced rule being aware of the fact that there is always an ex-post incentive for the authority to deviate from the announced rule. An institutional mechanism to solve this credibility problem is the design of a central bank contract between the government and the central bank.

5 Contracting, Shocks, and Target Agreements

Among others, inflation contracting is a prominent approach to the solution of the time-inconsistency problem. Thereby, the government (the 'principal') offers an incentive contract to the central bank governor (the 'agent') permitting discretionary responses of the central bank to new information but making remuneration to depend on achieved levels of inflation. In a standard modeling framework, this design is shown to eliminate the inflation bias of discretionary policy (Walsh (1995a, b)).

Contractual mechanisms originate from industrial economic concepts to deal with informational asymmetries between uninformed parties (principal) and informed parties (agent). By assumption, the principal is able to observe a certain outcome but cannot infer directly to which extent the existence of random shocks or the amount of the agent's effort have determined the observed result. The design of appropriate contracts is shown to offset the effects of informational asymmetries by linking the agent's reward to the achieved outcome. This approach can be generalized to multiple-task problems in the presence of multiple goals (see Karmann (1995)).

The applicability of this approach to the problem of time-inconsistent behavior is straightforward: The government or the public can observe, ex-post, macro indicators like CPI but does not have full information on the use of instruments by the central bank. There is one specific assumption typically met in modeling central bank contracting: both, the government and the central bank governor share the same preferences over inflation and output deviations. Hence, the central-bank utility function U^{CB}, loss function L^{CB} resp., can be written as

$$(5.1) \qquad U^{CB} = -L^{CB} = -L^{G} + T,$$

where $T = T(\pi, \pi^*)$ is the *monetary transfer contracted*, based on the observed inflation and its target level.

There are several points of criticism which we will neglect in our modeling approach below, too. First, we add up welfare losses and money transfers in (5.1), as it is done usually in utilitaristic models. Second, the society's preferences between stabilizing output and inflation are equally adopted both by the government and the central banker. Third, and for simplicity, we also disregard from any effects resulting from different effort levels as they are considered in the literature on industrial organization.

The specification of the financial contract deserves a closer look to the issue of incentives to central bankers. The use of linear contracts imposing unlimited financial fines in case of missing targets seems to be a somewhat adhoc modeling approach. The issue of dismissal rules where agents are fired whenever the target variable exceeds a critical level seems to be a more appealing alternative, here. Central bankers are seen to be less motivated by financial gains than business managers usually are, and to be concerned more about reappointment. Moreover, the presence of complex information structures typically leads to conditions for state-contingent contractual responses. Such responses can be handled more naturally within the class of dismissal contracts.

To describe informational asymmetries, we focus on three elements constituting the information structure of our model. First, the public as well as the government is less informed than the central bank with respect to shocks in money supply. In controlling this process, the central bank gathers information for 'guestimating' changes in velocity. These velocity innovations may be understood as resulting from financial deregulation, innovations, portfolio operations or from foreign political instabilities affecting currency circulation. Professional forecasts of changes in velocity provide the informational advantages of the central bank. Velocity forecasts will be used by the central bank before setting money growth rates. Second, and on the contrary, informational asymmetries between the central bank and the public with respect to supply shocks are more unlikely to exist. Supply shocks resulting from changes in the terms of trade, from technological innovations or from other sources may affect the demand side, but when identified, they are public knowledge (up to some measurement error). Hence, we will assume that there is informational symmetry with respect to supply disturbances. Third, any information concerning innovations is imperfect. Finally, we allow the public to react on information news to be incorporated in their expectations formation.

Our first assumption is in line with Canzoneri (1985) putting emphasis on aggregate demand shocks (but neglecting supply shocks). Supply shocks will enter the underlying economic relations as in Walsh (1995a) but are no longer private information to the central bank. The information structure used here is more in line with Walsh (1995b) but without assuming perfect information on signals. The latter results in a simple signal extraction problem in our model.
The aggregate supply relation is given by

$$(5.2) \qquad y - \bar{y} = a(\pi - \pi^e) + \eta,$$

where η is a (white noise) supply shock with known distributional parameters. The price process is determined according to some quantity reasoning by

$$(5.3) \qquad \pi = m + \nu - \lambda\eta,$$

where ν is a velocity (white noise) shock uncorrelated to η where again, the distributional characteristics are assumed to be known. The money supply m is the central bank's instrument (or control) variable. There is a direct negative effect of supply shocks on inflation. The central bank has private information ν^f

('*forecast of the velocity shock*') which together with an error term ε_v constitutes the innovation v by

(5.4) $$v = v^f + \varepsilon_v.$$

Furthermore, the signal $\theta_1 := \eta + \phi$ on supply shocks is publicly observed where ϕ is white noise, uncorrelated to η, with known variance. The *information structure* Θ on disturbances differs for the central bank, θ^{CB}, and for the public, θ^P:

(5.5) $$\theta^{CB} = (\theta_1, v^f)$$

$$\theta^P = \theta_1.$$

By E_Θ^{CP} we denote the central bank's expectations conditioned on Θ, by E_Θ^{CP} the expectations of the *public*, i.e. the privates and the government. In the case of public information we simply write E_Θ, instead. Especially, the expectation on the supply shock η, conditioned on information Θ, can be modeled as a *signal extraction* problem. This leads to identical expectations on supply shocks for the public and the central bank as given by

(5.6) $$E_\Theta \eta = \gamma\eta,$$

where $\gamma := \sigma^2_\eta / (\sigma^2_\eta + \sigma^2_\phi)$ is the share of the supply shock variance relative to the total variance of the observed signal θ_1.
From (5.2) - (5.6), the commitment solution which characterizes minimal expected social losses $E_\Theta L$ conditioned on information Θ, is derived by

(5.7) $$m^C(\Theta) = \pi^* - v^f + \lambda(\gamma\,\theta_1).$$

Hence, the central bank reacts on supply and demand shocks. As an expected increase in velocity tends to increase inflation, the money supply will be reduced. Similarly, as there is a negative impact of supply shocks on inflation, the corresponding term has a positive sign. Due to direct unobservability of the supply shock η, its conditional expected value $\gamma\,\theta_1$ enters into the money supply reaction function.

To derive the optimal contractual design we proceed as follows. For a given contractual payment scheme T, private expectations conditioned on Θ are derived by maximizing $E_\Theta^P L^{CB}$ subject to the constraints (5.2) - (5.6). Setting the weight g_y equal to one, the first-order condition results in the following condition for the money supply m^{CB} and the corresponding price process $\pi(m^{CB})$:

(5.8) $$E_\Theta^P \pi(m^{CB}) = \pi^* + (\partial / \partial m(E_\Theta^P T)) / (2\, g_\pi).$$

Under the assumption of rational expectations π^e equals the left hand side of (5.8). Inserting this into (5.2) and maximizing $E_\Theta^{CB} L^{CB}$ subject to the constraints, results in the first-order condition

$$m^{CB}(\Theta) = \pi^* +$$

(5.9) $$+ \left[ak - a\gamma\theta_1\right] / (a^2 + g_\pi) + \lambda\gamma\theta_1 - \nu^f + \left[(\partial/\partial m)(E_\Theta^{CB}T + (a^2/g_\pi)E_\Theta^P T)\right] / (2(a^2 + g_\pi)).$$

The optimal contract T^{CB} must allow to achieve the commitment solution (5.7). Hence, comparing (5.9) with (5.7), the second term in (5.9) must be offset by the last one, or

(5.10) $$2(ak - a\gamma\theta_1) = -(\partial/\partial m)[E_\Theta^{CB}T + (a^2/g_\pi)E_\Theta^P T]$$

As the left hand side of (5.10) depends on the signal θ_1, marginal contractual benefits have to be state-contingent. So, as a result of the underlying information structure, we cannot stick back to the use of linear noncontingent contracts. But changing the expectations building process by assuming private expectations to be set before information arrival, we get conditions for commitment behavior and money supply, corresponding to (5.7) and (5.9), both implying non-contingent marginal benefits of the optimal contract

(5.10') $$2\,ak = -\,\partial/\partial m\,(E_\Theta^{CB}T)$$

Eq. (5.10') can be solved by using simple *linear contracts* (Walsh (1995a)).
The class of contracts we consider in solving eq. (5.10) are PTA *dismissal rules*

(5.11) $$T(\pi, \pi^{PTA}) = I \quad \text{for } \pi \le \pi^{PTA}$$
$$= 0 \quad \text{elsewhere,}$$

where I is a positive constant denoting rewards from holding office, and π^{PTA} is the inflation target level the central bank has to commit to under the policy target agreement (PTA). We show that for a solution of (5.10) to exist the PTA inflation level has to be contingent on the public information but not on the private one. Hence, π^{PTA} is a target agreement scheme relating the inflation target level to the supply shock. The arguments follow equations (7) to (11) in Walsh (1995b).

First, for given public observation θ_1 and *probability* P *of reappointment* the following holds: if there is any PTA level solving (5.12), the government is able to control the money supply process $\mu = m + \nu^f$, unverifiable for the public, by setting π^{PTA} to depend on θ_1 such that the induced inflation $m + \nu^f - \lambda\gamma\theta_1 - \varepsilon$ does not exceed the PTA level with probability P, or

(5.12) $$P = \operatorname{Prob}\left\{\varepsilon:\ \pi^{PTA}(\theta_1) - (\mu - \lambda\gamma\theta_1) \ge \varepsilon\right\},$$

where $\varepsilon := \varepsilon_\nu + \lambda(\eta - \gamma\theta_1)$. As the expected revenues $E_{\theta 1}T$ of the central banker, conditioned on θ_1, are equal to $P \cdot I$, eq. (5.10) can be rewritten as

$$(5.13)\qquad 2\beta(ak - a\gamma\theta_1)/(I(a^2+\beta)) = f(\pi^{PTA}(\theta_1) - \mu - \lambda\gamma\theta_1),$$

where f denotes the publicly known density function of the money supply error term ε. By choosing the PTA scheme π^{PTA} appropriately, the government can enforce the socially optimal money supply $\mu^C = m^C(\Theta) + v^f$ leading to the inflation level $\pi^C = \pi^* - \lambda\gamma\theta_1$ under the commitment policy, and π^{PTA} and π^C solely depend on θ_1 but not on v^f. Thereby, the second-order condition of the central banker's maximization problem requiring $f' \leq 0$ (hence, $\pi^{PTA} \geq \pi^C$ by assuming f to be symmetric, single-headed), is assumed to hold.

Again, as in Walsh (1995b), PTA-schemes do not depend on demand shocks, more precisely, on the central bank's unverifiable forecast v^f of the velocity shock, and the private information of the central bank has not to be revealed by the government.

The effect of supply shocks on PTA levels, i.e. $d\pi^{PTA} / d\theta_1$, can be calculated using the implicit function theorem, as follows

$$(5.14)\qquad d\pi^{PTA}/d\theta_1 = -\ [\lambda\gamma f' + 2\beta a\gamma/(I\,(a^2+\beta))]\,/\,f',$$

which is typically negative (for λ-values not close to zero). Hence, negative supply shocks cause inflation targets to increase under optimal PTA schemes and the adjustment mechanism is known a-priori to the public.

The basic feature of the above approach is the mechanism that the government can control the distributional function of the central banker's reappointment and, thereby, can enforce the central bank to provide the socially optimal level of money supply even under discretion. Thus, dismissal rules seem to be an efficient instrument to handle informational asymmetries in the process of money supply.

6 Conclusion

We have taken up the rules-versus-discretion debate by considering the performance of simple rules. A simple rule, generally accepted as a policy reaction function superior to others for a broader set of macro models, is not at hand as the relative performance quite substantially depends on the structure of the relevant economic relations as well as on the specific nature of shocks prevailing within the economy. Even nominal-income targeting, though neutralizing demand- (but not supply-) shocks completely, has to be qualified in so far as the magnitudes of surprise- and income elasticities play a considerable role. Moreover, the use of specific monetary rules depends on the relative weights attached to potential target variables in the social loss function. If concern is given to stabilize, in addition, financial markets by smoothing or by stabilizing interest rates, policy response functions have to be reformulated to count for effects resulting from interest rate movements. Most likely, simple rules can be formulated as convex combinations of some standard fixed rules.

The discussion on commitment and credible policy announcements shifted the academic debate to the design of institutional mechanisms when information is asymmetric, thus allowing for discretionary monetary policy.

Our analysis shows that the more conventional linear-contracting approach reestablishes the commitment solution only under quite specific assumptions. More complex information structures ask for contracts to be state-contingent in the sense that policy target levels have to be adjusted to (verifiable) shocks from the supply side but not from the demand side. Thereby, the functional relationship between targets and shocks have to be formulated a-priori.

It is interesting to contrast the idea of contingent PTA schemes with the recent New Zealand experience on inflation targeting. Since the first PTA in February 1990, the CPI inflation rate twice exceeded the agreed 0 - 2% range. In June 1995, the index increased temporarily up to 2,2 % due to unfavorable agricultural conditions. In early 1996, the inflation rate again exceeded 2 % as a consequence of unexpected increases in demand following governmental announcements to cut down taxes. As the first event can be seen as resulting from a supply shock and the second as resulting from demand innovations, the New Zealand example illustrates the issue of state-contingent policy reactions. In the light of our analysis, the Central Bank should react discretionary to demand shocks while PTA levels remain unchanged. Supply shocks, on the other side, should be accounted for by adjusting PTA in an a-priori defined way. The New Zealand's second PTA in December 1996 increasing the 0-2 % range to 0 - 3 % seems to be a less convincing policy response opening the field to renegotiation and discretion.

References

Asako, K. and H. Wagner (1992), Nominal Income Targeting versus Money Supply Targeting, *Scottish Journal of Political Economy* 39, 167-87.

Barro, R. J. and D. B. Gordon (1983), Rules, Discretion, and Reputation in a Model of Monetary Policy, *Journal of Monetary Economics* 12, 101-20.

Bean, C. R. (1983), Targeting Nominal Income: An Appraisal, *Economic Journal* 93, 806-19.

Blinder, A. (1997), What Central Bankers Could Learn from Academics - and Vice Versa, *Journal of Economic Perspectives* 11, 3-19.

Brash, D. T. (1997), The New Inflation Target, and New Zealanders' Expectations about Inflation and Growth, Speech, January 23, Reserve Bank of New Zealand.

Canzoneri, M. B. (1985), Monetary Policy Games and the Role of Private Information, *American Economic Review* 75, 1056-70.

Cecchetti, S. G. (1998), Central Bank Policy Rules: Conceptual Issues and Practical Considerations, this volume.

Fischer, S. (1990), Rules Versus Discretion in Monetary Policy, in: B. M. Friedman and F. H. Hahn (eds.), Handbook of Monetary Economics, Vol. II, Amsterdam, 1155-84.

Friedman, B. M. (1990), Targets and Instruments of Monetary Policy, in: B. M. Friedman and F. H. Hahn (eds.), Handbook of Monetary Economics, Vol. II, Amsterdam, 1185-1230.

Friedman, M. (1959), A Program for Monetary Stability, New York.

Funke, N. (1995), Nominale Anker als geldpolitische Koordinationsziele, Tübingen.

Karmann, A. (1993), Financial Deregulation and Macroeconomic Stabilization Rules, in: W. E. Diewert e.a. (eds.), Mathematical Modelling in Economics, Berlin, 622-31.

Karmann, A. (1995), Multiple-Task and Multiple-Agent Models, Annals of Operations Research No. 54, 57-78.

McCallum, B. (1986), Some Issues Concerning Interest Rate Pegging, Price Level Determinacy, and the Real Bills Doctrine, *Journal of Monetary Economics* 17, 135-60.

McCallum, B. (1995), Two Fallacies Concerning Central Bank Independence, *American Economic Review* 85, Papers and Proceedings, 207-11.

Poole, W. (1970), Optimal Choice of Monetary Policy Instruments in a Simple Stochastic Macro Model, *Quarterly Journal of Economics* 84, 197-216.

Svensson, L. E. O. (1997), Inflation Targeting: Some Extensions, Working Paper, Stockholm University.

Walsh, C. E. (1995a), Optimal Contracts for Central Bankers, *American Economic Review* 85, 150-67.

Walsh, C. E. (1995b), Is New Zealand's Reserve Bank Act of 1989 an Optimal Central Bank Contract? *Journal of Money, Credit, and Banking* 27, 1179-91.

Comment

Norbert Funke
OECD, Financial Affairs Division, 2 rue André Pascal, F - 75775 Paris

1 Introduction[1]

There is no simple monetary policy rule that dominates all other strategies under all circumstances. This is one essential finding of traditional theoretical analyses, which have focused on the capacity of the various policy strategies to absorb micro- and macroeconomic shocks. The superiority of a specific rule depends on a number of factors, including the structure of the economy (the rigidity of labor markets), the objective function of the authorities and society, the size and correlation of shocks, as well as the openness of the economy. Under certain circumstances a discretionary policy may dominate simple rules, though discretion is typically associated with a higher average rate of inflation. More recently, a number of proposals have been made to reduce the inflationary bias with the help of institutional arrangements, such as the implementation of inflation contracts.

The objective of this note is to supplement Karmann's (1998) concise overview of traditional and recent developments, mainly by looking at the assumptions of standard models, extensions of the basic theoretical framework to an international setting as well practical problems associated with the various strategies. Following this introduction, the second section looks again at the assumptions underlying the existence of an inflationary bias. The third section reviews essential findings of the theoretical literature. The fourth section discusses escape clauses, inflation contracts and the proposal to adjust target levels of inflation to (verifiable) supply shocks. It is suggested that a preferable alternative might be to target a modified price index which is appropriately adjusted for the impact of supply shocks. Section five argues that, in practice, many policy strategies differ less markedly than theory might suggest. An important issue, which has only recently achieved more attention, relates to the transparency and the appropriate communication strategy of central bank policy.

[1] The views expressed in this paper are those of the author and do not necessarily reflect those of the OECD.

2 Inflation Bias

Much of the recent theoretical discussion has focused on the time-inconsistency problem. The crucial assumption in all standard models is that the natural rate of unemployment is inefficiently high, for example due to existing distortions in the economy. Because of these distortions and because the Phillips curve implies a trade-off between unemployment and unanticipated inflation, authorities would be tempted to inflate surprisingly in order to reach short-term output gains. As rational agents anticipate the authorities' temptation, discretionary policy leads to higher average inflation and no employment gains.

Widespread agreement exists that a removal of existing distortions would represent a first best solution to the time- inconsistency problem. In this case average output would be higher, the natural rate of unemployment lower and the inflationary bias would disappear. However, political and practical constraints are often cited as major reasons that work against achieving a first best solution (Svensson (1997)).

As Karmann (1998) points out, it has been questioned whether the assumption that authorities intend to stimulate activity by surprise inflation is plausible. A "simple" second-best solution appears to be to accept the existing distortions. Recognizing the impact of forward-looking expectations, central banks could choose not to start playing the game (Blinder (1997)). The emergence of a low inflation environment in many industrialized countries during the 1990s might also suggest that monetary authorities have been able to eliminate, or at least substantially reduce, the inflationary bias.

Though the relevance and extent of the time-inconsistency problem may be country-specific and may have declined in some countries, the underlying assumptions should not be discredited. It may not be sufficient that monetary authorities are willing to accept the distorted natural rate of unemployment. As long as private agents attach some probability to the occurrence of surprise inflation, these expectations will be built into the wage- and price setting process. Under these circumstances monetary authorities may, ex post, want to accommodate that policy and as a result inflation will be higher than intended. Although inflation has been reduced substantially during the last few years, average inflation rates are in many cases still close to the upper limit of explicit or implicit target ranges. In addition, at least a full business cycle may be necessary to evaluate the recent inflation performance. To conclude, the time inconsistency literature points to two important insights: First, central banks that are not fully credible may experience higher inflation. Second, there may be pressures on central banks to accommodate inflation expectations (McDonough (1997)).

Actual rates of inflation may also depend on the precise shape of the short-run Phillips curve, which has implications for the conduct of monetary policy. In particular the curve may be asymmetric in the sense that expansionary demand shocks would generate relatively little output gain in response to higher inflation, while contractionary demand shocks would deliver little inflation reduction in the short-term, but large output losses. There is not yet any conclusive empirical evidence on the slope of the short-run Phillips curve and the inflation-unemployment trade-off. Some evidence points in the direction that there may be asymmetries. Laxton et al. (1993) test this proposition by estimating Phillips curves for Canada with inflation depending on an expected inflation proxy, an output gap term, and an additional term which is a function of positive output gaps only. In most of the specifications tried, the coefficient on the positive output gap is reported to be statistically significant and positive, suggesting an asymmetric short-run Phillips curve effect. Turner (1995) also provides some support for asymmetries in five of the G-7 countries, although a linear Phillips curve is decisively rejected only for the United States, Japan, and Canada.

A further issue is the possibility that the Phillips curve becomes flatter on average when inflation is low. This might arise from a greater importance of nominal rigidities when inflation is low, due to price and wage adjustments becoming less frequent in such an environment. A flattening of the Phillips curve would imply that nominal demand shocks in either direction would have relatively less impact on prices, and more on output, as inflation slows. The short-run costs of disinflation would thus become progressively greater as zero inflation was approached.

3 Monetary Policy Rules: Major Theoretical Findings

The implementation of monetary policy rules is seen as one possibility of reducing the inflationary bias of discretionary policies. In traditional models a number of strategies are compared in light of their capacity to absorb various shocks (e.g. Karmann (1998, 1993)). Typically, the strategies include a money supply rule, a nominal income rule, a price level (inflation) rule and, in an open economy context, an exchange rate rule. Though output rules are, at times, also analyzed, not too many economists appear to believe that monetary authorities are able to influence output in any systematic manner over time. From a standard theoretical perspective, nominal GNP-targeting has a lot of attractive features. In contrast to a money supply rule, but similar to an inflation rule, demand shocks may be fully neutralized. Less clear-cut are the results in the case of supply shocks. However, a nominal GNP rule dominates an inflation target, a monetary target as well as a discretionary policy as long as authorities attach equal weight to inflation and output stabilization and the supply elasticity with respect to unexpected inflation is 1. The first condition may represent roughly the split that a discretionary policy would favor anyway. Despite some variability in estimates, the second condition is close to some empirical findings. For example, Frankel and Chinn (1993) calculated on the basis of two alternative methods a supply elasticity of 1.60 and

1.36 for the US, 0.33 and 0.59 for Germany, 0.69 and 1.07 for Japan, and 0.22 and 0.46 for the UK.

From a theoretical perspective nominal GNP targeting not only has attractive features in a closed economy context but also in an open economy. In a two-country model, simultaneous nominal GNP targeting is in most cases preferable to a simultaneous money supply rule, simultaneous inflation rules as well as discretionary policies in both countries (Funke (1995)). These analyses as well as simulations in large macro-econometric models show, however, that the potential gains from co-ordinating monetary policy strategies may in many cases be small. Further, these results do not yet take account of the potential costs of policy co-ordination, which may be associated with both the negotiations and implementation of such a regime as well as compliance with such an agreement. Co-ordination may even be counterproductive, for example if the political negotiations result in suboptimal policy agreements. Multicountry analyses thus tend to show that a single country may well be able to reap most of the benefits when implementing a policy strategy that reflects the preferences of this country.

In actual policies, nominal GNP targeting has so far attracted little explicit attention. However, it may be argued that in deriving their policy targets a number of central banks make use of variables which would also allow for the calculation of an implicit nominal GNP target. For example, monetary targets in Germany are set on the basis of estimates for the growth of the long-run production potential in the coming year, the so-called "unavoidable" rate of inflation as well as estimated changes in trend velocity. With estimated changes in velocity and a target path for the monetary aggregate M3, comparable nominal GNP targets can be easily derived. However, a number of factors are typically brought forward against an explicit nominal GNP target. Nominal GNP itself is not easily controllable by monetary authorities. Changes in policy instruments in pursuit of a nominal GNP target take effect only with a lag, thus it may be very difficult to achieve the target accurately. In addition, it remains debated how large the difficulties would be to explain such a target to the public and whether and in what way the wage bargaining process may be influenced by such a change.

Following the breakdown of stable relationships between monetary aggregates and the goal of price stability in some countries since the last decade, direct announcements of inflation targets have become an increasingly popular strategy. Countries, such as New Zealand, Canada, the UK, Sweden, Spain, and Australia have started to announce numerical inflation targets (see e.g. Wagner (1997)). From a standard theoretical perspective, the advantages of inflation targets are similar to those of a nominal GNP target in the case of demand shocks. The well-known disadvantage of a rigid inflation target may arise in the case of a supply shock, such as a drastic increase in oil prices. In this case, an inflation rule would require a restrictive monetary policy to prevent inflation from rising. Monetary policy would dampen output and the undesired effect on output would be larger than in the case of a nominal GNP target or money supply targeting. Recognizing the potential disadvantage of inflation targets in the case of supply shocks and acknowledging the difficulty of targeting inflation precisely, most existing inflation targeting regimes allow for some degree of flexibility. Examples of a built-in flexibility include the announcement of target ranges instead of point targets and/or the implementation of some type of escape clauses. For the determination of the appropriate target ranges, one open issue is to what extent there is an upward bias in the measured inflation rate and how the bias should be taken into account in the formulation of monetary policy. An upward bias may, for example, arise if indexes do not appropriately incorporate effects of quality improvements, product substitution by consumers, the emergence of new products, and outlet substitution, which may arise if consumers substitute in favor of lower-cost retail outlets (Edey (1994)). Empirical estimates for the size of the upward bias in the CPI vary across countries and are up to around 1.5 percentage points for the US.

4 Escape Clauses, Inflation Contracts and Contracts under Contingent Target Agreements

More recently the theoretical debate shifted to the design and implementation of a rule-based framework in which discretion may be exercised under certain extreme and undesired conditions. The general idea behind escape clauses is that monetary authorities are allowed to deviate from the rule, if an unfavorable large shock occurs. Escape clauses aim at allowing for the possibility of obtaining the benefits of a discretionary policy at difficult times. In practice, an escape clause may take several forms. The circumstances under which the authorities are allowed to deviate from the announced strategy may either be known ex ante, decided upon on an ad hoc basis, or authorities may ex post have to justify any deviation from planned policies.

The initial inflation targeting regime in New Zealand may be seen as having some similarities with the case, where escape circumstances are known ex ante. As formalized in the 1989 Reserve Bank Act the primary objective of monetary policy is to achieve "stability in the general level of prices". Operational targets that reflect this objective are to be agreed between the Minister of Finance and the Governor of the Reserve Bank at each election or re-election of a governor. The "Policy Targets Agreement" (PTA) has to be made public. It specifies objectives for CPI inflation which are subject to a number of escape clauses that include "significant" changes in the price level resulting from changes in the terms of trade, indirect taxes, a major natural disaster and changes to government or local authorities levies on the CPI (Mishkin and Posen (1997)). The first PTA stated that if the caveats took place and had an impact on the price level of at least one half of a percentage point, the agreement could be renegotiated. However, in the following the Reserve Bank used the caveats as a justification to focus its operations on "underlying" inflation, a measure which is calculated by the Bank itself and which excludes from the "headline" CPI effects which relate to the caveats.

Escape clauses can only be successful, if they are not implemented in such a way that they undermine the credibility of monetary policy. To ensure credibility, escape clauses have to be transparent and easily verifiable. In this respect, an ex ante definition of circumstances under which authorities may deviate from their target or re-negotiate the target appears desirable. However, it is almost impossible to foresee all possible circumstances that may justify a deviation from announced policies. On the other hand, ad hoc decisions as to whether it is appropriate to change the policy objective bear the risk that they may lack transparency. An ex post justification on why the central bank deviated from the announced target, emphasizes the crucial role of the communication strategy, which will be analyzed in section V.

In a simple standard theoretical framework, escape clauses may not be necessary, as a second-best solution can be achieved by Walsh-type contracts. A linear inflation contract, where the central bank governor's salary depends on the target achievement, represents an elegant option to eliminate the average inflation bias. As Karmann (1998) shows, a challenge is to construct the appropriate contract in practice and traditional contracts lead only under specific circumstances to the commitment solution. With asymmetries in the information structure, state contingent contracts are needed, where target levels are adjusted in the case of supply shocks. The regime advocated is called "a contingent PTA scheme". Again, crucial is that the adjustment mechanism is known ex ante to the public. An a priori definition would require that all types of possible supply shocks as well as their impact on prices would be known. If it were possible to gauge the correct functional form of the adjustment, an alternative solution might be to calculate and make public a modified inflation rate which is adjusted for these effects. Such an underlying rate of inflation would deviate in particular in the case of supply shocks from a traditional inflation measure, such as the CPI. The inflation target would then be related to the underlying inflation rate. The advantage would be that in the ideal case, the public would have to focus only on one price index for which an adjustment of the target range would no longer be needed. The economic effects of a policy shift towards an underlying inflation rate will, however, also depend on the wage adjustment process, i.e. whether wages are adjusted to traditional measures of inflation or the underlying rate of inflation. As noted above, the Reserve Bank of New Zealand already makes use of an underlying rate of inflation. One drawback is, however, that the calculation "includes a significant judgmental element" (OECD (1996)). The measure is calculated by the bank itself and lacks transparency. The credibility of monetary policy could clearly be enhanced by more transparency with respect to the calculation of this measure.

5 Transparency and Communication Strategy

Most central banks do not follow pure strategies. In practice, the outcome of monetary policy differs less markedly between countries which have adopted inflation targets and those which follow other strategies, e.g. those who use a monetary aggregate as intermediate target. In those cases in which central banks deviate on purpose from their announced objectives, they have to devote considerable resources to explain to the public the reasons for that deviation in order to maintain credibility. The communication strategy of the central bank, i.e. by which means does the central bank signal its policy intentions to the public, is presumably almost equally important to the choice of the policy strategy (Borio (1997)). Strategies can hardly be compared without talking at the same time about the communication strategy. Appropriate signals may be crucial in order to reduce financial market volatility. Signaling is becoming more important, as interest and exchange rates appear to be increasingly sensitive to shifts in private expectations as well as shifts in macroeconomic fundamentals (Funke (1996)).

The German experience, where monetary targets have been missed in roughly half of the cases indicates that the anti-inflation reputation of a central bank can remain fairly high, if considerable efforts are devoted to explaining the reasons for the deviations (Mishkin and Posen (1997)). In this respect, it may be argued that one advantage of inflation targeting is that it requires authorities to explain more intensively to the public how the objective will be achieved. Inflation targets are not very direct targets for monetary policy. Policy has to rely on predictions of inflation over the following year or two. Such estimates must be credible, yet they are inevitably complex and therefore not necessarily easy to explain. Thus, there is a greater need to invest in transparency and the communication strategy. A shift towards greater transparency and changes in the communication strategy are already visible. For example, some countries started to publish inflation reports or give a more explicit inflation assessment in their regular bulletins. Because authorities publish inflation reports including forecasts and explain how they will achieve the targets, their analysis is more open to scrutiny and public debate.

Transparency and an appropriate communication strategy will also be of crucial importance for the future European Central Bank (ECB). The ECB can not inherit credibility from any central bank but will have to establish policy credibility quickly. The current low inflation environment and the institutional framework as laid down in the Maastricht treaty should be helpful in this regard. However, financial market analysts will initially lack reliable euro area-wide indicators to assess the stance of monetary policy in the single currency area. Given the lack of such an indicator, major bilateral exchange rate developments may be seen by market participants as useful substitutes. Although the ECB does not follow an exchange rate policy, the ECB may thus be tempted or even forced to place a larger weight on exchange rate movements than its medium-term strategy would require. A transparent and clear communication strategy could reduce the time period until the authorities' anti-inflation reputation is established.

On theoretical grounds, a move towards greater transparency along with changes in the communication strategy may have effects which are similar to a shift from a discretionary policy towards a more rule-based strategy. Greater transparency and improvements in the communication strategy should help to support the credibility of monetary policy.

References

Blinder, A. S. (1997), What Central Bankers Can Learn from Academics - and Vice Versa, *Journal of Economic Perspectives* 11, 3-19.

Borio, C. E. V. (1997), Monetary Policy Operating Procedures in Industrial Countries, Bank for International Settlements, Working Papers No. 40, March.

Edey, M. (1994), Costs and Benefits of Moving from Low Inflation to Price Stability, *OECD Economic Studies* 23, 109-30.

Frankel, J. and M. Chinn (1993), The Stabilizing Properties of a Nominal GNP rule in an Open Economy, University of California, Working Paper No. 91-166, March.

Funke, N. (1995), Nominale Anker als geldpolitische Koordinationsziele, Tübingen.

Funke, N. (1996), Vulnerability of Fixed Exchange Rate Regimes: The Role of Economic Fundamentals, *OECD Economic Studies 26*, 157-76.

Karmann, A. (1993), Financial Deregulation and Macroeconomic Stabilization Rules, in: W.E. Diewert (ed.), Mathematical Modelling in Economics, Berlin, 622-31.

Karmann, A. (1998), Monetary Policy Strategies: From Rules to Central Bank Contracts under Contingent Target Agreements, this volume.

Laxton, D., G. Meredith and D. Rose (1993), Is the Canadian Phillips Curve Non-linear?, Bank of Canada, Working Paper No. 93-7.

McDonough, W. J. (1997), A Framework for the Pursuit of Price Stability, Federal Reserve Bank of New York, *Economic and Policy Review* 3, 3-7.

Mishkin, F. S. and S. Posen (1997), Inflation Targeting: Lessons from Four Countries, Federal Reserve Bank of New York, *Economic and Policy Review* 3, 9-110.

Svensson, L.E.O. (1997), Optimal Inflation Targets, "Conservative" Central Banks, and Linear Inflation Contracts, *American Economic Review* 87, 98-114.

Turner, D. (1995), Speed Limit and Asymmetric Inflation Effects from the Outputgap in the Major Seven Economies, *OECD Economic Studies* 24, 57-88.

Organisation for Economic Cooperation and Development (OECD) (1996), New Zealand, Country Survey 1996, Paris.

Wagner, H. (1997), Inflation Targeting, Diskussionsbeitrag der FernUniversität Hagen Nr. 245, Hagen.

4. Conceptual Problems of Monetary Policy

Central Bank Policy Rules: Conceptual Issues and Practical Considerations

Stephen G. Cecchetti
Federal Reserve Bank of New York, New York, NY 10045, USA

1 Introduction

Central bank policymakers are not primarily random number generators.[1] Reading both the financial press and the work of academics, however, one might get the opposite impression. Reporters (and the readers of their stories) seem to attach considerable importance to each Federal Open Market Committee policy decision. Academic work on the impact of central bank policy gives a similar impression, as empirical identification yields a series of white noise innovations that are labeled "policy shocks."[2] But central bankers expend substantial energy attempting to tailor their actions to current economic conditions. In other words, policymakers are reacting to the environment, not injecting noise.

But what is central bank policy anyway? As a problem in operations research, the answer seems trivial. Policy is, or should be, the solution to a stochastic, dynamic optimal control problem. Using a control variable (an interest rate) and knowledge of the evolution of the state (aggregate output and the price level), the policymaker minimizes a loss function (for example, the weighted sum of future variance of output and prices). This approach yields what most people would call a *policy rule*, that is, a rule for adjusting the control variable as a function of previous values of the state variable and of the control variable itself. In other words, the study of policy should focus on the systematic portion of policymakers' actions.

In this essay, I discuss a number of conceptual and practical issues associated with the procedure just described. What is the appropriate loss function? Where should it come from? What is the control variable? What is a policy target? Is there any justification for the adoption of what is typically called an intermediate target? What is the slope of the inflation-output variability frontier, and how should this affect policy decisions? How does

[1] Here I paraphrase a comment made by Bennett McCallum at a conference on monetary policy in January 1993.

[2] A naive reading of the recent work of Christiano, Eichenbaum, and Evans (1994a, 1994b) surely could lead to such an interpretation.

uncertainty influence the policy rule? What are the consequences for the optimal policy of the zero nominal interest rate floor? And how might we justify interest rate smoothing? For the most part, I will simply explore these questions rather than offer any definite answers.

The remainder of the essay addresses these issues in four sections. I begin in Section 2 with a discussion of the task facing policymakers, giving particular attention to the nature of the loss function that is to be minimized and the precise definition of policy. Section 3 provides a discussion of some of the conceptual and practical issues faced in the implementation of such a procedure, and Section 4 presents arguments for the adoption of policy rules. Section 5 summarizes the lessons for policy formulation with an emphasis on general issues of central bank independence, accountability, and policy transparency.

2 An Analytical Framework for Policy Formulation

What is central bank policy? As I suggested in the introduction, policy can be thought of as the solution to an optimal control problem. A truly complete description of the policymaker's problem begins with an intertemporal general equilibrium model based on a social welfare function (tastes), production functions (technology), and market imperfections that cause nominal shocks to have real effects (nominal rigidities). The goal would be welfare maximization.

I do not propose to delineate the fully specified problem. Instead, I begin with a commonly used quadratic loss function that might be a second-order approximation to the objective function in this more detailed problem.[3] Consider the following general form for the loss function the policymaker seeks to minimize:

$$(1) \qquad \mathcal{L} = E_t \left\{ \sum_{i=0}^{h} \beta^i \left\{ \alpha [p_{t+i} - p^*_{t+i}]^2 + (1-\alpha)[y_{t+i} - y^*_{t+i}]^2 \right\} \right) ,$$

where p_t is the (log) aggregate price level, y_t is the (log) aggregate output, p^* and y^* are the desired levels for p and y, β is the discount factor, h is the horizon, α is the relative weight given to squared price and output deviations from their desired paths, and E_t is the expectation conditional

[3]Throughout the discussion in this section, I will assume that the there is no dynamic consistency problem, and so policymakers can credibly commit to whatever rule they choose. Section 4 comments further on this issue.

on information at time t.[4] The loss function provides the policymaker with information about preferences over different paths for the variance of output and prices.

A complete formulation of $\mathcal{L}$ requires description of p^* and y^*. I will focus on the desired price path, ignoring issues concerning y^*.[5] Here we encounter the following question: Should the objective be a price-level path or an inflation rate? The first of these, *level targeting*, would dictate that

$$(2) \qquad p_t^* = p_{t-1}^* + \pi^* = \pi^* t \ .$$

That is, the optimal price level this period is the optimal level last period plus some optimal change (which may be zero). The alternative, *rate targeting*, is

$$(3) \qquad p_t^* = p_{t-1} + \pi^* \ ,$$

where the current target price level is just the last period's *realized* price level plus the optimal change.

The difference between price-level and inflation rate targeting is the path for the variance of prices. Level targeting implies more volatile short-horizon prices and less volatile long-horizon prices than does rate targeting. To see this, simply note that (3) implies that

$$p_t^* = \pi^* t + \sum_{i=0}^{\infty} (p_{t-i} - p_{t-i}^*) \ ,$$

which can be a random walk.

It is possible to nest these two objectives into a more general formulation. Consider a parameter δ representing the relative weight given to price-level and inflation targeting. Then

$$(4) \qquad p_t^* = \delta(\pi^* t) + (1 - \delta)(p_{t-1} + \pi^*) \ .$$

In (4) the percentage of the variance in p explained by its random walk component will be related to δ.

The description of the loss function is now complete. It is a function of

[4] In some formulations the loss function includes an additional term in the change in the control variable. That is, changes in interest rates are assumed to be explicitly costly. Inclusion of such a term here adds very little to the analysis.

[5] Specifying a process for y^* would be difficult because there is no agreement on a number of crucial issues. For example, should y^* have a random walk component or be a deterministic trend? Is the growth rate in y^* affected by the volatility of y?

the parameter vector $\theta = \{\alpha, \beta, \delta, h, \pi^*\}$. The values of each of these will depend on the underlying economic structure, that is, tastes and technology. The preference over different paths for inflation and output variability, as embodied in the loss function, depends on the fundamental reason that these things are costly. The same is true of the desired steady level of inflation, π^*.

The policymaker's problem cannot be solved without knowledge of the dynamics of the state variables y_t and p_t as functions of the policy control variable and the stochastic forcing process driving the economy. These relations, which are taken as constraints in the optimization problem, describe the structure of the economy. For the purposes of the current discussion, I will assume that the central bank policy is carried out in terms of an interest rate, r_t,[6] and that the innovations to the economy come from an n-variate process $\{\epsilon_t\}$, with expectation zero and variance-covariance matrix Σ. The reduced form for the evolution of the output and prices can then be written as

$$\begin{bmatrix} y_t \\ p_t \end{bmatrix} = A(L) \begin{bmatrix} \epsilon_t \\ r_t \end{bmatrix} , \tag{5}$$

where $A(L)$ is an $(n+1)$x2 matrix of (possibly infinite-order) lag polynomials in the lag operator L.[7] The coefficients in $A(L)$ describe a reduced form of the economy. For the moment, I will ignore the fact that $A(L)$ is likely to change when the policy rule changes.[8]

We can now characterize the policymaker's problem as choosing a path for r_t that minimizes the loss (1), with (4) substituted in for p^*, subject to (5). The result is a policy rule, which I will write as

$$r_t = \phi(L)\epsilon_t , \tag{6}$$

where $\phi(L)$ is a (possibly infinite-order) lag polynomial.[9] This path for interest rates as a function of the innovations to the economy (which could be written as differences in the observable quantities) is the policy rule. Importantly, $\phi(L)$ is a function of the parameters θ, as well as the coefficients in

[6] The use of an interest rate is not necessary. The control variable could be any quantity that is directly governed by the central bank. For example, the monetary base or some measure of reserves could be used as the control.

[7] Equation (5) is the vector moving-average form. The more common vector autoregressive (VAR) form is equivalent.

[8] This point is emphasized, for example, in Cecchetti (1995).

[9] The linear-quadratic structure of the problem described here will give rise to a linear policy rule. In general, this would not be the case. For example, if the loss function were nonlinear, or there were some additional constraints on the policymaker's behavior not considered here, then the policy rule would be nonlinear as well.

$A(L)$ and the covariance matrix of ϵ, Σ.

I would like to emphasize that the preferences over paths for the variability of output and prices, as well as the optimal steady inflation rate π^*, are *inputs* into the policymaker's problem.[10] In practice, I expect that these inputs are dictated by some legislative or executive body in the government. Given this objective and a model for the evolution of the state variables (the economy), the policymaker chooses a rule that governs the path of the control (the interest rate).[11]

3 Conceptual Issues and Practical Considerations

The framework of Section 2 helps clarify a number of issues inherent in the formulation of central bank policy. In this section, I will consider five such issues. I begin by exploring the nature of a target, with a particular focus on inflation targeting and nominal income targeting. Included is a discussion of the usefulness of what are commonly termed "intermediate targets." Why might we wish to focus attention on something other than either the interest rate (the instrument) or output and prices (the goals)?

In Subsection 3.2, I discuss the practical problems posed by the apparent steepness of the output-inflation variability trade-off and consider how it might influence decisions. This is followed in Subsection 3.3 with a general discussion of how uncertainty affects policymaking. I discuss the likely sources of uncertainty and how they might be incorporated in decision making. Next, I discuss how the nonlinearity created by the fact that the nominal interest rate cannot fall below zero influences the policy rule. And finally, I explore the issue of interest rate smoothing. While I am able to address directly a number of the issues raised, I often leave most of the questions unanswered.

3.1 What Is a Target?

Given the optimal control view of the policymaker's problem, how can we interpret the current debate over the proper choice of a policy target, or the

---

[10] Svensson (1996a) compares inflation and price-level targeting, arguing that one yields better performance than another depending on various properties of the economy. Such an exercise relies on a particular view of the costs of inflation that is not explicitly embodied in the loss function (1).

[11] Ball (1997) takes a different approach, focusing on the implications for the loss of adopting ad hoc rules that are not derived directly from the loss function. For example, after determining the minimized value of the loss $\mathcal{L}$, he then asks how close one can get by adopting a set of arbitrary rules that do not arise from the optimal control problem itself.

advisability of targeting in general? Commonly mentioned targets — for example, inflation and nominal income — are not control variables for the central bank, and so how might we approach this question? I will explore two ways of addressing the issue of targets. The first is purely technical, and the second has to do with the way in which policymakers might portray their intention to the public. Technically, the first-order conditions (or Euler equations) to the optimal control problem may be interpreted as producing a type of targeting regime. To see this, consider the case examined in detail by Svensson (1996b). He considers pure inflation rate targeting, $\delta = 0$, and a loss that is independent of output variation, $\alpha = 1$. The first-order condition of this problem implies setting the path for expected inflation, $E_t\pi_{t+i}$, as close to the optimal value, π^*, as possible. Svensson refers to this as "inflation forecast targeting."[12] More generally, any dynamic control problem implies a relationship among endogenous variables that holds along an optimal path — the equivalent to the statement that the expected intertemporal marginal rate of substitution in consumption equals the risk-free (real) interest rate.

Nominal income targeting does not naturally arise from the loss function (1). The reason is straightforward. Nominal income targeting would be an attempt to keep $(p_t + y_t)$ close to $(p_t^* + y_t^*)$. This suggests a loss function with terms of the form $[(p_t + y_t) - (p_t^* + y_t^*)]^2$. That is, the policymaker would be instructed to be averse to squared deviations of *nominal* income from its optimal path. If we expand this expression, it is easy to see that it includes a covariance term of the form $[(p_t - p_t^*)(y_t - y_t^*)]$ that does not appear in (1).[13]

Ball's (1997) analysis suggests another justification for targets. The argument is that the optimal control procedure I describe is too difficult to explain to the population at large (and possibly their elected representatives as well), and so will not lead to policy that is transparent enough to ensure the proper level of accountability.[14] But a pure inflation targeting rule is easy to explain and, more important, easy to understand and monitor. As a result, if the solution to the complex problem can be approximated by a simple rule, there may be substantial virtue in adopting the approximate solution.

Svensson's (1997) distinction between a *target rule* and an *instrument*

[12]Svensson (1997) notes that if $\alpha \neq 1$, and so weight is given to output variability in the loss function, then this can be interpreted as a form of inflation forecast targeting in which the path of the forecast moves gradually back to the optimal level.

[13]It is this covariance that is responsible for the poor performance of nominal income targeting noted by Ball (1997).

[14]See Section 4 for a further discussion.

rule is also useful here. As he defines it, an instrument rule is a relationship between the control variable and the observable state — equivalent to (6). So, an instrument rule is a statement that the federal funds rate will be raised or lowered by a specific amount following a forecast error in real output of a certain size. By contrast, the statement that the policymaker adjusts the instrument such that inflation and/or output will follow a certain specified path is a target rule. This is not a policy per se, but really just a statement about a relationship that is implied by the optimization.

It is worth digressing briefly to comment on where intermediate targets fit into this scheme. Over the last half-century or so, many monetary economists have advocated targeting various monetary aggregates. Consider the example of M2.[15] Researchers do not claim to care about M2 for its own sake, nor do they claim that central banks can control it exactly. Therefore, M2 is neither a direct objective nor an instrument. Instead, it is somewhere in between — an *intermediate* target — and the target path would again be akin to the first-order conditions of the optimal control problem.

I find it difficult to make an argument for intermediate targets. To see why, consider the case in which the policymaker controls an interest rate and cares about the price level ($\delta = 1$). To control the objective, the policymaker must know how prices respond to changes in the exogenous environment (the response of p_t to ϵ_t) and how the objective responds to changes in the instrument. But how does an intermediate target such as M2 help? Clearly, if the relationship between interest rates and M2 and that between M2 and prices are both stable and precisely estimable, then there is no advantage to looking at the two relationships separately. There may be some instances in which estimating the impact of interest rates on M2 and the impact of M2 on prices separately gives a more reliable estimate of the product of the two, but such instances would surely be rare. If M2 helps forecast prices, then it will be included in the model. But there is substantial evidence, some of which is in Cecchetti (1995), that reduced-form inflation forecasting relationships are very unstable even if they include M2, or any other potential intermediate target.[16]

As a result, the only case I can see for intermediate targeting is that it contributes to policy transparency. To quote Svensson (1996b), the ideal intermediate target "is highly correlated with the goal, easier to control than

[15]For a recent discussion of M2 targeting, see Feldstein and Stock (1994).

[16]This differs from the procedures of the Deutsche Bundesbank. As Mishkin and Posen (1997) note, since 1988 the German central bank has targeted growth in M3 in the belief that the demand for German M3 is stable.

the goal, easier to observe by both the central bank and the public than the goal, and transparent so that central bank communication with the public and public understanding and public prediction of monetary policy are facilitated" (pp.14-15). Monetary aggregates seem particularly poorly suited to such a task.

3.2 The Output-Inflation Variability Trade-off

Figure 1: Response of Output and Prices to Policy Innovations (With Two Standard Deviation Bands)

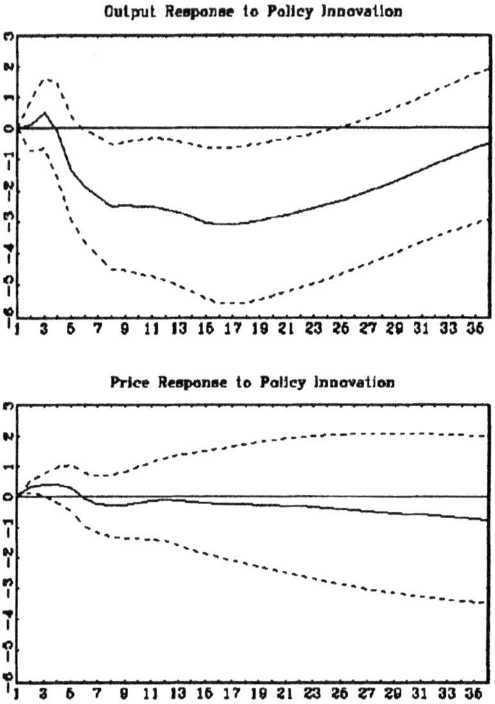

A number of practical issues arise in formulating policy rules. One of the most important concerns the output-inflation variability trade-off that policymakers actually face. To measure this trade-off, I turn to some empirical estimates developed in my earlier work, Cecchetti (1996). There, I present an estimate of the impact of central bank policy on output and prices. In effect, these are the lag polynomials in (5) associated with r_t.[17] Figure 1 plots these

[17]The methods used to produce these results are described in detail in that earlier work.

impulse response functions, or the dynamic reactions of prices and output to innovations (ϵ_t's), on the same vertical scale. The most important point to note is that the impact of policy innovations on output is both large and immediate. By contrast, policy affects prices only very slowly, and by much more modest amounts. Furthermore, the precision of the estimates is quite poor.

With the aid of a very simple model, these estimates can be used to give some sense of the shape and slope of the output-inflation variability trade-off. Consider the simple case in which $h = 0$ (and so δ and β are irrelevant), $\pi^* = 0$, $y^* = 0$, and $A(L)$ is such that

$$y_t = \gamma r_t + e_t, \quad \gamma < 0 \tag{7}$$

and

$$p_t = -r_t + u_t \ , \tag{8}$$

where, e_t and u_t are uncorrelated i.i.d. random variables with $E(e_t^2) = 1$ (a normalization) and $E(u_t^2) = \sigma_u^2$.[18] The parameter γ is a measure of the impact of policy innovations on output relative to their impact on prices. The example is meant to represent the medium-horizon impact of policy on the variables of interest. In this simple linear case, the policy rule will be

$$r_t = ae_t + bu_t \ . \tag{9}$$

Equation (9) implies that

$$\sigma_y^2 = (\gamma a + 1)^2 + (\gamma b)^2 \sigma_u^2 \tag{10}$$

and

$$\sigma_p^2 = a^2 + (1 - b)^2 \sigma_u^2 \ . \tag{11}$$

Minimizing the loss function $\mathcal{L} = \alpha\sigma_p^2 + (1 - \alpha)\sigma_y^2$ yields

$$a = -\frac{\gamma(1 - \alpha)}{\alpha + \gamma^2(1 - \alpha)} \tag{12}$$

Briefly, I estimate a four-variable vector autoregression including aggregate prices, commodity prices, industrial production, and the federal funds rate, using monthly data from 1984:01 to 1995:11. Central bank policy innovations are identified and used to estimate the impulse response functions under the assumption that no other variable beyond policy itself responds to policy shocks immediately.

[18] The fact that e and u are assumed to be uncorrelated is a simplification that has no substantive consequences.

and

$$b = \frac{\alpha}{\alpha + \gamma^2(1-\alpha)} . \tag{13}$$

Substituting these into the variance expressions (10) and (11) yields σ_p^2 and σ_y^2 as functions of α, γ, and σ_u^2.

Using the monthly data from Cecchetti (1996), I can now compute an approximate output-inflation variability frontier. From Figure 1, I estimate that γ is approximately -5. Once I determine σ_u^2, varying α allows construction of the frontier. Setting σ_u^2 such that the frontier passes through the value in the data (the ratio of output to price variability is approximately 3.72) and normalizing the variance of the detrended log price level in the data to be equal to one gives Figure 2. The arrow and the "X" mark the data.

Figure 2: The Inflation-Output Variability Trade-off

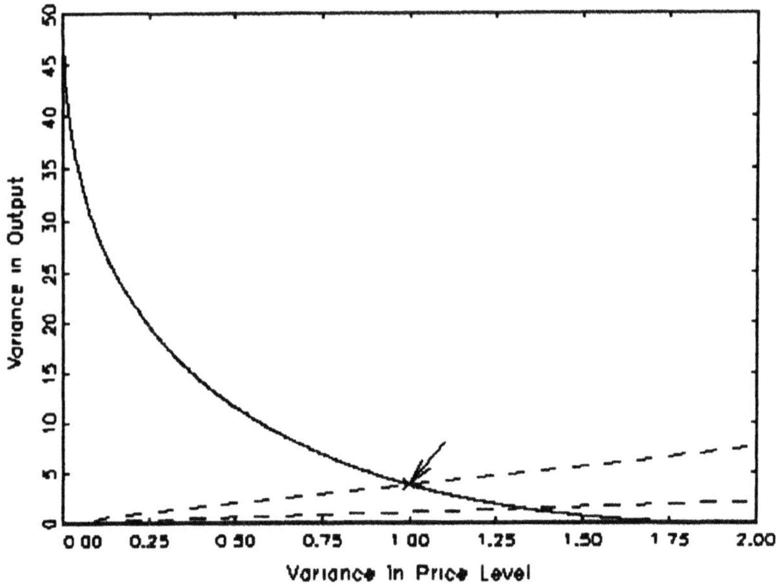

The figure includes two dashed lines. The lower one is a 45° line, at which $\alpha = 0.5$, while the upper line passes through the value from the data. As one rotates the ray from the origin in the counterclockwise direction, α falls. The historical value suggests that policymakers were operating as if α were approximately 0.21.

Importantly, Figure 2 shows that the trade-off is extremely steep. Reducing inflation variability entirely by setting $\alpha = 1$ creates an extremely high level of real variability. In fact, moving from the historically observed point where the ratio of output to inflation variability is 3.72, setting σ_p^2 to zero would increase the variability of output by a factor of nearly 13! By contrast, reducing real variability from 3.72 to 0 increases price variability from 1.0 to 1.92. This finding is not a consequence of the simplicity of the example, but rather of the fact that γ is so large. It is straightforward to show that the maximum value of σ_y^2, at $\alpha = 1$, is γ^2 times the maximum value of σ_y^2, at $\alpha = 0$, minus one. That is to say, the point of intersection of the line in Figure 2 with the x- and y-axes is solely determined by the size of the ratio of the impact of policy innovations on output to their impact on prices.[19]

This result has important implications for the current policy debate. As many central banks move toward some form of price-level or inflation targeting, they are implicitly changing the relative importance of output and inflation variability in their objective function, raising α toward one. From a purely pragmatic point of view, someone who cares about the aggregate price path loses little by allowing α to be less than one, but the reverse is emphatically not true. Someone who cares about output variability is made substantially worse off by moving to a price-level target. As a result, when considering policies based on prices alone, policymakers must ask whether they really care so little about output and other real quantities.

3.3 Uncertainty

How does uncertainty affect policy? Of the numerous types of uncertainty that might influence central bank policy decision making, two forms are examined here: Uncertainty about the likely impact of policy changes, and uncertainty about one's model of the economy.[20] The first of these has two parts, one that is straightforward to handle and another that is not. Intractable difficulties arise when one has to worry about shifts in regime. In particular, the underlying economic relationships, which policymakers had previously been able to exploit, may change. Such changes could be brought about by policy itself. It is this point, first noted by Lucas (1976), that has driven many macroeconomists to work on dynamic general equilibrium models with well-articulated microeconomic foundations. But these efforts are still at too early a stage to be of practical use.

It is straightforward to consider the sampling error from estimation of

[19] Cecchetti (1996) considers a substantially more complex case with the same results.

[20] There will also be uncertainty over the current state of the economy that arises from lags in the data. This has an impact similar to that of parameter uncertainty considered below.

the reaction of prices and output to changes in the policy instrument. In the simple example here, this is just the variance of the estimated γ, which I will call $\sigma^2_{\hat{\gamma}}$. Brainard (1967) originally noted that this type of uncertainty leads to caution in that policy rules imply smaller reactions.[21] In this simple example, inclusion of $\sigma^2_{\hat{\gamma}}$ implies that the policy parameters a and b become

$$(14) \qquad a = -\frac{\gamma(1-\alpha)}{\alpha + (\gamma^2 + \sigma^2_{\hat{\gamma}})(1-\alpha)}$$

and

$$(15) \qquad b = \frac{\alpha}{\alpha + (\gamma^2 + \sigma^2_{\hat{\gamma}})(1-\alpha)}.$$

Clearly, these imply smaller reactions to a given size shock.

Figure 3: Impact of Uncertainty on the Variability Trade-off

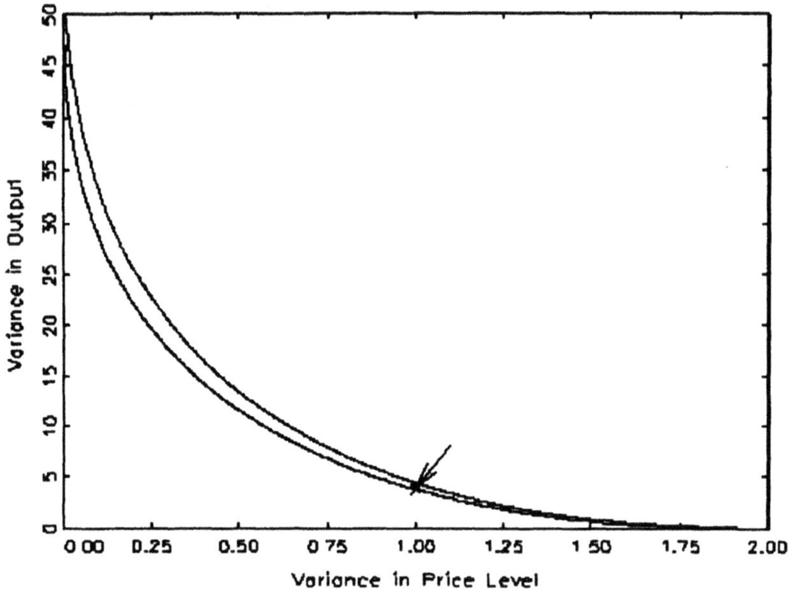

In a more realistic model, such as the one implied by Figure 1, accounting for parameter uncertainty can be very difficult. Is it likely to be worth the trouble? To get some sense of its impact, I have constructed an example in which γ is assumed to have variance equal to four (standard error equal to

[21] Blinder (1997) notes that in a multivariate model, things are not so simple, and the size and sign of covariances will determine whether policymakers exhibit more cautious or less cautious behavior.

two). The results are plotted in Figure 3. My impression is that the impact is minimal, as the variability frontier barely moves.

What about model uncertainty? McCallum (1997) argues convincingly that since there is little agreement over the true structural economic model, a policy rule should be robust to the possibility that numerous models are correct. In the context of the framework of Section 2, identifying such a rule would mean exploring the implications of various $A(L)$'s, each of which corresponds to a different model. The object would be to look for a rule that would perform well for a wide range of choices. One method for handling model uncertainty would be to treat it as variance in the estimate of the parameters in $A(L)$. This approach would be a generalization of the procedure used.[22] Unfortunately, I am forced to conclude that we know very little about how to solve this problem and that it is a worthwhile subject for future research.

3.4 The Zero Nominal Interest Rate Floor

What average inflation level should the policymaker target? There are two parts to this question. First, what is the optimal level of inflation, π^*? Second, should policy allow the average realized level of π to deviate from this?

I argued above that π^* should be dictated to the central bank by social welfare considerations. Here, there has been quite a bit of work. Most recently, Akerlof, Dickens, and Perry (1996) and Groshen and Schweitzer (1997) consider whether small positive levels of aggregate inflation can facilitate real adjustments in the presence of an aversion to nominal wage declines, suggesting π^* might be positive. But Feldstein (1996) contends that the tax distortions created by inflation reduce the level of output permanently, an argument that suggests π^* may even be negative.[23] Overall, we await further research for the definitive resolution of this issue.

There is one dominant argument for why policymakers might choose to allow average inflation to deviate systematically from the optimal level. The argument, raised in Summers (1991), concerns the case in which π^* is zero,

[22] A simple possibility would be to multiply the estimated covariance matrix of the estimated $A(L)$ by a positive constant.

[23] The problem of inflation bias is also relevant here, because measured inflation may systematically exceed true inflation. For example, Shapiro and Wilcox (1996) argue that the U.S. consumer price index may overstate inflation by 1 percentage point on average. Such a conclusion suggests that even if π^* is zero, the central bank should attempt to keep measured CPI inflation above zero.

and focuses on the fact that the nominal interest rate cannot fall below zero. In fact, any choice of π^* bounds the real interest rate. Summers goes on to note that in the historical record, the real interest rate (at least ex post) has often been negative. But if central bank policymakers successfully target zero inflation, then the fact that the nominal interest rate cannot be negative means that the real interest rate must always be positive as well. In essence, this restricts the ability of the policymaker to respond to certain shocks. The control problem as it is described above does not explicitly consider the fact that r_t is bounded at zero. As a result, there will be realizations of ϵ_t in which the policy rule (6) would imply negative values for the nominal interest rate. One interpretation of Summers's point is that the desirability of negative nominal interest rates in some instances should be taken into account, with the result that mean inflation may deviate from the optimal level in order to allow for a complete response to some larger set of shocks.

To see the point, consider the simple model of Section 3.2. Then, the restriction that $r_t \geq 0$ implies that the loss is minimized for target inflation equal to approximately $0.276\sigma_u$. That is, average inflation will be approximately one-quarter the standard deviation of the shocks to the price level. More complex forms of the model will have similar properties. In general, the greater the likelihood of a shock driving the desired nominal interest rate below zero, and the higher the loss associated with not being able to react to such a shock, the higher will be the average level of inflation that minimizes the policymaker's loss function.

A similar result would arise when the loss function is asymmetrical. It has been argued that there are potential costs associated with deflation rather than just realized inflation that is less than expected. These arise largely because the zero nominal interest rate floor implies that deflation beyond a certain level increases the real interest rate (ex ante and ex post), resulting in a lower steady-state capital stock.[24] This suggests that realized prices below target may be more costly than equivalent realizations above the target. This would naturally create a positive bias in the policy rule that would result in average inflation exceeding π^*.

To gauge the extent of this problem, Table 1 reports the frequency with which the ex post real interest rate has been below zero and below -1.0 percent. Note that the problem is clearly most severe for the United States and France. But for other countries it is relatively modest. In fact, assuming that inflation includes an upward bias of roughly 1 percentage point, the

[24]See the discussion in Cecchetti (1997).

Table 1: Frequency of Negative Ex Post Real Interest Rate

Country	Initial Observation	Less Than Zero	Less Than −1.0
France	1970.01	68%	82%
Japan	1978.11	82%	96%
Germany	1970.01	94%	99%
Italy	1979.11	94%	95%
United Kingdom	1974.06	77%	80%
United States	1970.01	69%	78%

Notes: Table reports the percentage of observations of the ex post real rate on three-month treasury securities, or equivalent, that are less than zero and less than −1.0 percent. Data are monthly.

realized real interest rates were negative less than 20 percent of the time in all countries except the United States.

3.5 Interest Rate Smoothing

Another important practical concern in the conduct of central bank policy is whether it is optimal to smooth the changes in the policy instrument. There are two issues here. First is the question of whether, following a shock, the optimal response is to have interest rates move immediately up (or down) and then return monotonically to the steady-state level. Second is the separate consideration of whether, given that the policymaker intends to change interest rates by some amount, the entire change should occur all at once.

The policy reaction function immediately yields the answer to the first question. Here the presumption must be that $\phi(L)$ is not monotone. To see this, consider Figure 4, which plots the optimal reaction of interest rates to an innovation in the aggregate price level implied by the impulse response functions plotted in Figure 1 (for the case where $h = 36$ and $\alpha = 1$).[25] The path is hump-shaped. That is, the optimal response to an innovation is to raise interest rates immediately, continue to raise them gradually, and then lower them slowly. This pattern could be further exaggerated if the loss function included an explicit cost to changing interest rates — a term of the form $k(r_t - r_{t-1})$.

The second question is more difficult. If the central bank were to decide that the interest rate should be increased by 100 basis points, should the change be in one large jump or in a series of smaller ones? If policy

[25] See Cecchetti (1996) for details on this computation.

Figure 4: Interest Rate Path following a Shock

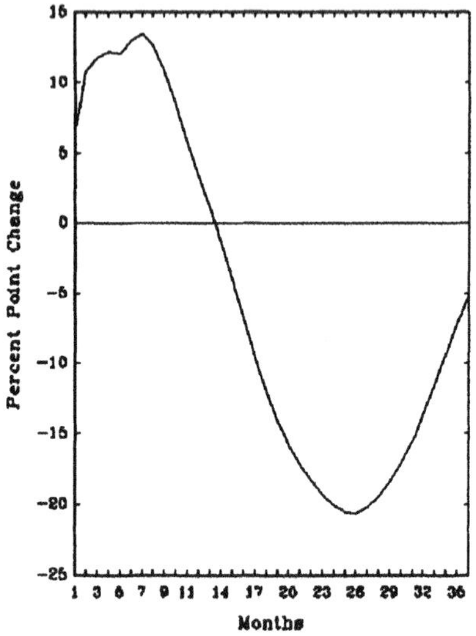

were sufficiently transparent that everyone knew that the interest rate would ultimately rise 100 basis points, so that the changes would be perfectly anticipated, then it is difficult to see why a series of smaller changes would be preferred over a single one. But often, I suspect, this question is asked with a different intention. In fact, the policymaker will start to change interest rates not really knowing what the final results are likely to be. This would be a form of experimentation.

4 Should Central Bankers Follow Rules?

The entire discussion thus far has been directed at the construction of a rule for central bank policy. But should we try to construct a set of systematic responses to external events? There are numerous reasons to support the adoption of rules by the central bank. The first is the well-known result that with pure discretion, the dynamic inconsistency problem leads to high steady inflation, and the second concerns the importance of policy transparency.

Over fifteen years ago, Barro and Gordon (1983) noted that if a policymaker cannot credibly commit to a zero inflation policy, then even if the policymaker announces that inflation will be zero and all private decisions are based on the assumption that inflation will in fact be zero, it is in the policymaker's interest to renege and induce inflation of some positive amount. The reason for this is that at zero inflation the value of the increase in output obtained from fooling private agents and creating a transitory increase in output (along a Phillips or Lucas supply curve) more than offsets the cost of the higher inflation, and so the claim of zero inflation in the absence of commitment is not credible. In the language of optimal control, a zero inflation policy is not dynamically consistent.

Since the problem is thought to be most severe when potentially shortsighted legislators are capable of influencing central bank policy directly, the most prominent solution has been to create independent central banks. It is commonly thought, and the data confirm, that policymakers who are more independent are better able to make more credible commitments to low-inflation policy.[26]

As Alan Blinder (1997) has recently pointed out, however, there is a potential conflict between central bank independence and representative democracy. Since one of the crucial elements of a democratic society is that the powerful policymakers are accountable to the people, how can we square these two apparently disparate goals of accountability and independence?

Blinder (1997) and Bernanke and Mishkin (1997) suggest that the solution is policy transparency. They argue that if policymakers announce targets and are forced to explain their actions in relation to these preannounced goals, then there is accountability. Put another way, transparency and accountability are enhanced if the elected officials announce the loss function the central bankers are charged with minimizing, and the central bankers in turn demonstrate how they are accomplishing this goal. Researchers have suggested that the publication of the target for prices and/or output along the optimal path would serve this purpose. In fact, not only would policymakers become more accountable, but their policies would become more transparent.[27]

Arguments such as these have led to the implementation of explicit targeting regimes in a number of countries. Prominent among these countries are Australia, Canada, Finland, Israel, New Zealand, Spain, Sweden, and the United Kingdom.[28] Because of their transparency, explicit targeting regimes are easily understood. As a result, potential policy actions are less likely to create uncertainty and instability.

[26]Alesina and Summers (1993) establish this empirically and raise the additional possibility that countries with independent central banks not only have lower steady inflation, but less variable output and higher growth. Cukierman, Kalaitzidakis, Summers, and Webb (1993) also investigate the impact of central bank independence on the growth rate of output.

[27]Mishkin and Posen (1997) argue that policy transparency and explicit targeting were important factors in the granting of operational independence to the Bank of England.

[28]See Haldane (1995) for a discussion.

5 Lessons for Policy Formulation

This analysis offers a number of lessons. First, and most important, if a policymaker were to focus on inflation alone, the likely result would be a very high level of real output variation. This factor seems to weigh heavily in favor of the way in which policy targeting is currently carried out around the world.

Consider the example of the countries that have adopted explicit inflation targeting. These include Australia, Canada, Finland, Israel, New Zealand, Spain, Sweden, and the United Kingdom. The central banks in most of these countries appear to take short- to medium-run real fluctuations into account when deciding on their policies. This is easiest to see in the banks' official statements. For example, the central banks in New Zealand, the United Kingdom, and a number of other countries announce target ranges — rather than point targets — for inflation. The Reserve Bank of Australia states that its goal is to have inflation average between 2 and 3 percent *over the business cycle.* By using this wording, trhe central bank retains the flexibility to stabilize in the face of short-run real shocks. Even countries with explicitly stated inflation targets behave as if they place some weight on output variability in their implicit loss function.

No country has adopted a zero inflation target, or even a range that is centered at zero. In fact, Haldane (1995) reports that only New Zealand's target range includes zero at the lower end. This suggests that there continues to be substantial aversion to the possibility of deflation and some sensitivity to the dangers inherent in bumping against the zero nominal interest rate floor.

Let me conclude by emphasizing that substantial work remains to be done before we can convincingly articulate a detailed and operational rule for central bank policy. The framework I have proposed requires crucial information on which there is simply no general agreement at this date. What is most needed is a set of stable numerical estimates of the impact of policy actions on output and prices — as well as the ability to estimate the impact of exogenous shocks on the goals of policy.

References

Akerlof, G. A., D.T. William and G. L. Perry (1996), The Macroeconomics of Low Inflation, *Brookings Papers on Economic Activity*, 1-59.

Alesina, A. and L. H. Summers (1993), Central Bank Independence and Macroeconomic Performance: Some Comparative Evidence, *Journal of Money, Credit, and Banking 25*, 151-62.

Ball, L. M.(1997), Efficient Monetary Policy Rules, NBER Working Paper No. 5952.

Barro, R. J. and D. Gordon (1983), A Positive Theory of Monetary Policy in a Natural Rate Model. *Journal of Political Economy* 91, 589-610.

Bernanke, B. S. and F. S. Mishkin (1997), Inflation Targeting: A New Framework for Monetary Policy?, NBER Working Paper No. 5893.

Blinder, A. S. (1997), Distinguished Lecture on Economics in Government: What Central Bankers Learn from Academics — and Vice Versa. *Journal of Economic Perspectives* 11, 3-19.

Brainard, W. C.(1967), Uncertainty and the Effectiveness of Policy. *American Economic Review* 57, 411-25.

Cecchetti, S. G.(1995), Inflation Indicators and Inflation Policy, in: B. Bernanke and J. Rotemberg, eds., *NBER Macroeconomics Annual*, Cambridge, MA., M.I.T. Press, 189–219.

______ ,Practical Issues in Monetary Policy Targeting, Federal Reserve Bank of Cleveland *Economic Review* 32, 2–15.

______ ,Understanding the Great Depression: Lessons for Current Policy. NBER Working Paper No. 6015.

Christiano, L. J., M. Eichenbaum and C. L. Evans (1994), The Effects of Monetary Policy Shocks: Evidence from the Flow of Funds, Federal Reserve Bank of Chicago Working Paper 94-2.

______ , Identification and the Effects of Monetary Policy Shocks, Federal Reserve Bank of Chicago Working Paper 94-2.

Cukierman, A., P. Kalaitzidakis, L. H. Summers and S. B. Webb (1993), Central Bank Independence, Growth, Investment, and Real Rates, *Carnegie Rochester Conference Series on Public Policy* 29, 95-140.

Feldstein, M. (1996), The Costs and Benefits of Going from Low Inflation to Price Stability, in: C. Romer and D. Romer (eds.), *Reducing Inflation*, Chicago, University of Chicago Press, 123-66.

Feldstein, M. and J. H. Stock (1994), The Use of Monetary Aggregates to Target Nominal GDP, in: N. G. Mankiw (ed.), *Monetary Policy*, Chicago,

University of Chicago Press for NBER, 7-70.

Groshen, E. and M. Schweitzer (1997), Identifying Inflation's Grease and Sand Effects in the Labor Market, NBER Working Paper No. 6061.

Haldane, A. G (1995), Introduction, in: A. G. Haldane (ed.), *Targeting Inflation*, Bank of England, 1-12.

Lucas, R. E., Jr (1976), Econometric Policy Evaluation: A Critique, *Carnegie-Rochester Conference Series on Public Policy* 2, 19-46.

McCallum, B. T.(1997), Issues in the Design of Monetary Policy Rules, NBER Working Paper No. 6016.

Mishkin, F. S., and A. Posen (1997), Inflation Targeting: Lessons from Four Countries, Federal Reserve Bank of New York *Economic Policy Review.*

Shapiro, M. D., and D. W. Wilcox (1996), Mismeasurement in the Consumer Price Index: An Evaluation, NBER Working Paper No. 5590.

Summers, L. H. (1991), How Should Long-Term Monetary Policy Be Determined? *Journal of Money, Credit, and Banking* 23, 625-31.

Svensson, L. E. O. (1996a), Price Level Targeting vs. Inflation Targeting: A Free Lunch?, NBER Working Paper No. 5719.

———, Inflation Forecast Targeting: Implementing and Monitoring Inflation Targets, NBER Working Paper No. 5797.

——— , Inflation Targeting: Some Extensions, NBER Working Paper No. 5962.

Implementation Problems of Monetary Policy Strategy

Gabriel P. Fagan[1]
European Monetary Institute, Postfach 10 20 31, D - 60020 Frankfurt/Main

1 Introduction

Monetary policy strategy may be defined, in broad terms, as the set of procedures according to which a central bank decides how to act in order to achieve its final objective. Since monetary policy faces a complex transmission process from policy actions to the final goals of interest to the central bank, it is now generally agreed that the monetary policy of the central bank should be both forward-looking and pre-emptive, with timely policy responses ensuring the achievement of the final objective. In addition, a clear framework, which guides the use of the central bank's monetary policy instruments so as to achieve it's final objective, is needed to establish credibility and consistency of the decision-making process over time. Against this background, the conduct of monetary policy poses formidable problems for central banks and raises a number of important practical issues in respect to implementation. These issues are the focus of this paper.

In terms of the final objective itself, there is now a consensus among central banks, academics and the policy-making community that the primary and overriding objective of monetary policy should be the pursuit of price stability (see, for example, Kahn (1996)). This increased emphasis on price stability in recent years stands, in the case of many countries, in sharp contrast to past practice, in which monetary policy was directed at a number of (often conflicting) objectives, including output stabilization (see, for example, Shigehara (1996)). The shift in focus is evident in recent changes in central bank legislation both in the EU and in other industrial countries (see, for example, Goodhart and Viñals (1995)and, for EU countries, EMI (1996)) where, in addition to enshrining formal independence, the statutes of central banks have been revised to include explicit references to price stability as the primary objective of monetary policy. In the case of the EU, this shift of focus towards price stability has received additional impetus from the move towards monetary union. Thus, as regards the future ESCB, the commitment to price stability is clearly set out in Article 105 of the Treaty: "The primary objective of the ESCB shall be to maintain price stability. Without prejudice to the objective of price stability, the ESCB shall support the

[1] Views expressed herein are those of the author and not necessarily those of the EMI. The author would like to thank colleagues at the EMI for helpful comments and suggestions.

general economic policies in the Community." The shift toward a price stability orientation is also evident in the inflation performance in OECD countries which, in the 1990s, has been running at levels well below those recorded in the inflationary 1970s and 1980s. This success to date in reducing inflation to low levels has even led some commentators to proclaim that inflation is 'dead' (Bootle (1996)).

This paper deals with the practical problems which arise in the context of the pursuit of a stability-orientated monetary strategy. In addressing this topic, we focus in particular on the case of two strategic options: intermediate monetary targeting (IMT) and direct inflation targeting (DIT), primarily because these strategies constitute the main strategic options for countries pursuing independent monetary policies. In this context, it is worth noting these two options have been identified as the main candidate strategies for the monetary policy of the ESCB in Stage Three.

The paper is structured as follows: Section 2 examines the fundamental question facing the central bank, namely the definition and elaboration of it's final objective of price stability. In Section 3 we examine a number of implementation issues which arise in the pursuit of either of the strategies under consideration, ranging from the choice of specific target variable to the supporting analytical infrastructure. Section 4 focuses specifically on the issue of monetary policy strategy in Stage Three and reviews the current state of the ongoing preparatory work. Section 5 concludes.

2 Specification of the Final Objective of Price Stability

The most fundamental practical problem facing a stability-orientated central bank, regardless of it's choice of specific strategy, is the definition of it's final goal, price stability. As evidenced by the frequency by which it is quoted in speeches of central bank governors and officials, the definition put forward by Chairman Greenspan - that price stability can be defined in qualitative terms as a rate of inflation by which does not materially influence economic behavior - would appear to enjoy widespread support among central bankers. However, moving from this broad concept to a specific quantitative counterpart is not without difficulties.

2.1 Level or Rate of Change

The first key issue to be addressed in this context is the issue of whether the central bank should formulate it's final objective of price stability in terms of the *level* [2] or the *rate of change* of the price index. In the first case, the final objective is specified in terms of a deterministic path for a particular price index (e.g. stabilization of the index at a particular level) while, in the second case, the objective is expressed in terms of the rate of change of the index, i.e. the inflation rate. While initially this issue may seem rather obscure, the choice has substantial implications for the time series properties of prices which may have major implications on economic behavior over longer horizons.

The difference between the two approaches is illustrated in Figure 1 (which follows Fischer (1996)). Starting at period 0, the central bank either aims for the price level to follow a deterministic path which involves an average rate of price increase of 2% or, in the second case, the objective is an inflation rate of 2% per annum. Ex-ante, before the realization of shocks, the paths for the price level implied by both approaches are identical. Now, suppose that in period 1 a shock occurs which drives the actual price level above the initially expected level to the point indicated as 'actual price level in period 1'. The response of the central bank to this development will depend crucially on whether it is focusing on the price level or on it's rate of change. If the price objective is set on the basis of rates of change, the central bank will accept the new level of the price index prevailing in period 1 as the new base (hence the term base drift) and will aim for an inflation rate of 2% in period 2, not attempting to reverse the overshoot of period 1. In contrast, if the central bank focuses on the price level rather than it's rate of change, it will attempt to reverse the overshoot of period 1 by aiming for a lower (in this case negative) inflation rate in order to ensure that the price level returns to the path originally planned.

Formulation of price stability in terms of rates of change has the effect of adding a unit-root to the price level. In this context, 'bygones are bygones' and the central bank would not necessarily aim to offset the effects of shocks on the price level, thereby allowing for base drift. As a consequence of such a specification, and the resulting unit-root property of prices, long-term uncertainty regarding the price level increases approximately linearly with the time horizon.[3] On the other hand, where the price stability is defined in terms of the level of a price index, long-term uncertainty is considerably reduced, since under this scheme the price level would be stationary.

A definition of price stability in terms of levels rather than rates of change could have a number of advantages. First, by reducing long-run uncertainty about the price level, it could facilitate longer term planning by agents and boost

[2] The simplest formulation of a price level target would be to stabilize a price index at a particular level. However, more general forms of price level targets could be envisaged in which particular deterministic paths for the price level are specified (e.g. a deterministic trend of say 2% per annum).

[3] In the simple case of a random walk in the price level, the variance of a forecast of the price level k periods ahead would then be $\sigma^2 k$, where σ^2 is the variance of a one-period ahead forecast.

investment, thereby promoting the long-term growth performance of the economy (Dugay (1994)). Secondly, such an approach could resolve the potential problem of nominal indeterminacy which could arise in the presence of a unit-root target. Since, in such a targeting framework, the long-run level of the price level (or the level of the money stock) is not predetermined by policy, it has been shown (see, Blake and Westaway (1994)and Andres et. al. (1996)) that in standard macro models of open economies with floating exchange rates and forward looking expectations, the *level* of the nominal exchange rate and of all nominal magnitudes in the economy become indeterminate. This is basically an extension of the nominal indeterminacy result obtained by Sargent and Wallace (1975) in the case of nominal interest rate pegging in a closed economy forward-looking framework. In contrast, a price level target, by providing a long-run anchor for the price level (or equivalently for the level of the money stock) serves to remove this indeterminacy for all nominal magnitudes.[4] Thus, to the extent that such indeterminacies play a role in financial market instabilities, it can be argued that financial markets would be more stable under price level targeting, which would reduce the scope for, e.g., the emergence of financial market bubbles.

However, these benefits do not come without costs. There seems to be a consensus that the need to offset shocks to the price level would imply that the short-run variability of inflation and of output would be higher under price level targeting. The rationale in this argument is straightforward. Any shock which drives the actual price level away from the target path, must under a price level formulation, be offset by policy actions in order to return the price level to the target path. Thus a positive shock to prices would need to be offset by subsequent periods of disinflation and possible deflation (as demonstrated in Figure 1). In the presence of sluggish price and wage adjustment, such policy actions would be expected to increase the volatility of real output. In the UK case, Haldane and Salmon (1995) demonstrate that output and short-term inflation variability are significantly higher under a price level targeting rule than under a rates of change formulation. However, Svensson (1996) argues that under certain circumstances (a discretionary central bank and some degree of persistence of shocks) a price level target could actually lead to lower short-term inflation and output variability than a target expressed in terms of rates of change. Finally, it should be noted that some considerations which are often put forward in the context of the optimal rate of inflation (e.g. measurement bias, the need for inflation to grease the wheels of the economy etc.) do not necessarily rule out price level targeting, since a positive trend of sufficient size could be incorporated into the deterministic price level target. The issue of the appropriate rate of inflation is addressed in the next Section.

---

[4] This would, of course, require that price level targets were in place in partner countries. For example, elimination of nominal indeterminacy in the US dollar-Yen exchange rate would require such frameworks to be in place in both the US and Japan.

2.2 The Appropriate Rate of Inflation

Regardless of whether a price level or rate of change formulation is adopted, a second key question which needs to be addressed is the issue of the appropriate level of inflation which constitutes price stability. Following the pioneering work of Friedman (1956), the basic literature on the optimal quantity of money would suggest a negative rate of inflation would be optimal (see, Woodford (1990)). A literal interpretation of the term 'price stability' as well as some of the literature on the costs of inflation (Briault (1995)) would suggest a zero rate of inflation. Nonetheless, there is a considerable body of opinion, which argues instead that a small positive rate of inflation would be preferable to a zero rate.

The first line of argument, which goes back to Tobin (1972), is that a small positive inflation rate can serve to grease the wheels of the economy. Since it is argued that workers would be unwilling to accept nominal wage cuts or that firms would be unwilling to reduce their prices in nominal terms, a small positive rate of inflation would enable real wage cuts to take place, if required, and/or facilitate changes in relative prices necessary for economic efficiency. In these circumstances, it is pointed out that, where the central bank aims for a zero inflation rate, adverse shocks may require that, from time-to-time, negative inflation rates would be required to restore the economy to equilibrium. In the face of significant downward nominal price and wage rigidity, this could result in substantial adverse effects on output and could lead to a dangerous deflationary spiral. The importance of this line of argument in practice, depends on the extent to which nominal wages and prices are downwardly rigid. In this respect, the empirical evidence on the importance of downward nominal rigidities is mixed (see Yates (1995), for a review). In addition, it should be noted that, as long as trend productivity growth is positive, zero nominal wage growth will enable reductions in unit labor costs to take place without explicit reductions in nominal wage rates. In addition, to the extent that earnings contain flexible elements, such as overtime payments, bonuses etc., wage costs may be reduced without reducing negotiated wage rates. Finally, the fact that, under a policy aiming at zero inflation on average, negative inflation rates will from time-to-time be recorded does not, however, imply that the economy would fall into a spiral of deflation. As Freedman (1996) notes: "the use of the term deflation to describe a small decrease in prices lasting a short period, rather than a period of sustained price declines, can be very misleading, particularly for the 'person on the street.' The term deflation is associated in the public mind with the depression of the 1930s, when prices fell more than 20 percent over a four-year period. Short periods in which the average level of prices fall 0.5 percent or 1 percent are not in any way similar to a situation with an ongoing decline of prices of a substantial amount over a number of years".

A second line of argument relates to the optimal taxation argument of Phelps (1973) who argues that in the presence of distortionary taxes, inflation (which represents a tax on currency and other nominal assets) is likely to form part of the optimal tax mix. However, as pointed out by Kimborough (1986), if money is viewed as an intermediate good, then optimal tax theory, which implies that taxing intermediate goods is less efficient than taxing final goods, would not necessarily favor a positive rate of inflation. Moreover, the Phelps argument is not an argument for a positive rate of inflation per se but only for a rate higher than optimal rate implied by the Friedman rule. Finally, as pointed out by Feldstein (1996), a positive rate of inflation may significantly magnify the welfare losses resulting from the distortions arising from insufficient indexation in existing tax systems.

The third argument relates to the so-called 'Summers effect' (Summers (1991)) which implies that since zero is the lower bound for nominal interest rates, a zero inflation target would imply that real interest rates could never become negative. Summers shows that, in practice, ex-post real interest rates have often been negative in the US and argues that in some circumstances, e.g. during severe recessions, negative real interest rate may be necessary to facilitate recovery and prevent the emergence of a deflationary spiral. The actual importance of this phenomenon is ultimately an empirical question. The fact that negative real interest rates have been observed in some countries in the past may simply reflect expectations errors on the part of investors and savers, in the face of rapidly rising inflation, rather than a genuine need for equilibrium interest rates to be negative. In addition, simulation exercises by Fuhrer and Madigan (1994) of the effects of imposing a zero bound on real interest rates in a forward-looking model of the US economy show that, while such a constraint does limit the ability of policy to react to shocks in the economy, the estimated welfare losses resulting from this constraint are small (0.1 to 0.2%) of GDP. Moreover, the possibility to use other instruments - e.g. fiscal policy - to offset the affects of adverse output shocks also diminishes the extent of the constraint posed by the Summers effect.

A fourth line of reasoning in favor of a small positive rate of measured inflation relates to biases in measured price indices. There exists a considerable body of evidence which points to the existence significant biases in the measurement of inflation, which imply that published indices may overstate the true rate of inflation (see Wynne and Sigalla (1996) for a survey). These biases reflect a number of factors. Firstly, traditional fixed-weight indices fail to adequately take into account the 'true cost of living' for consumers, implied by utility theory, since they do not adequately capture the fact that consumers will tend to shift purchases away from those goods whose prices have risen most rapidly; this effect is compounded in the case of infrequent updating of the weights employed in the construction of the price indices. Secondly, measured price indices do not adequately take into account improvements in the quality of existing goods or the availability of new goods, which again leads to an overstatement of the cost of living. Finally, other problems include biases arising from the formula employed in the construction of the indices. The problem of bias in measured price indices appears to be particularly severe in the case of the US CPI where with estimates of the bias being as high as 1.6% per annum (Senate Finance Committee (1996)). However, evidence for other countries points to the existence of smaller biases of around 0.5% per annum (see Cunningham (1995) for the UK and Crawford (1993) for Canada). However, as pointed out in Wynne and Sigalla (op cit.) estimating the extent of such biases poses formidable methodological problems and the results are subject to considerable uncertainties. Thus, it is difficult to draw strong policy conclusions on the basis of the existing evidence.

2.3 The 'Revealed' Preference of Central Banks

Summing up, it should be noted that issues of definition of price stability and the appropriate rate of inflation consistent with price stability have only recently begun to attract a high degree of interest from researchers. Thus it seems fair to say that, on the basis of our current knowledge, it would be unwise to make final judgments on either the issue of the price level stabilization or on whether central banks should aim for a zero rate of inflation.

On the basis of the observed behavior of central banks and their announced targets, there appears to be in practice a consensus that, at least for the time being, price stability is interpreted by central banks in terms the rate of change of prices rather than a price level and, to the author's knowledge, no central bank in the industrialized countries has specified its price stability objective in terms of a deterministic path for the price level. Within this framework, it is agreed that price stability should be defined as a small positive rate of inflation rather than a zero rate. Thus, for example, the Bundesbank has announced a price norm of 2% per annum since 1987; the goal recently set for the Bank of England is 2.5% and, of late, no central bank has announced a specific objective of zero measured inflation.

This preference seems to reflect concerns both to biases in measured price indices and the possible costs of reducing inflation towards zero referred to above. In addition, it is worth remembering that for many central banks, the achievement of an inflation rate of the order of 2% or less represents a considerable improvement over the performance of the 1970s and 1980s and, for these banks, consolidating this achievement is considered to the be the primary task of monetary policy, at least for the time being. However, given the growing interest among central bank and academic economists in the precise definition of price stability - a concern which would not have been assigned high weight in the previous inflationary era - it cannot be ruled out that, on the basis of the results of ongoing research, central banks will, in the future, give some consideration to more demanding objectives, such as stabilization of the price level (Kahn (1996)).

3 Implementation Aspects of Monetary Policy Strategy

In the pursuit of price stability, under either IMT or DIT, the central bank faces a number of implementation issues. The main practical issues which need to be addressed in this context may be summarized as follows:

1. The choice of the specific variables for the final and intermediate targets;
2. The length of the target horizon;
3. The choice of the central target path;
4. The precision (range) of the target;
5. The response of policy to deviations from the target;
6. Communication with the general public; and
7. Analysis of the economic environment, prospects and the impact of policy actions.

Of course, these issues need to be addressed jointly: for example, a decision on the width of the target range would be heavily dependent on the choice of target horizon.

3.1 Choice of Specific Variable for the Final and Intermediate Target

The fundamental issue arising in the case of either DIT or IMT is the choice of the particular variable or variables to be targeted by the central bank. In the case of DIT this involves the choice of a particular measure of the price level/inflation rate which will be focused on by the central bank. However, even in countries pursuing monetary targeting, some measure of prices must be selected as a basis for assessing performance in terms of the ultimate objective. In addition, in IMT, a monetary aggregate needs to be identified as a suitable target variable.

As regards the choice of price index, most central banks favor a measure based on the CPI. As argued by Freedman (1996), the emphasis on consumer prices is largely due to practical considerations. Firstly, the CPI is the price index which typically has the highest profile in terms of the public's perception of inflation. Secondly, in comparison with other price measures, it has desirable properties in terms of frequency and timelines. Thirdly, it is rarely revised. And, finally, it is argued that as the measure closest to the cost of living for households, the CPI is an appropriate measure for monetary policy. However, a number of arguments can be made against reliance on the CPI as a measure of inflation for monetary policy purposes. In particular, it has been argued that this index is too narrow in two respects. Firstly, since it focuses only on the price of current goods, it does not take into account the price of future goods and services, as reflected in asset prices, (Alchian and Klein (1973)) which should, in principle, be of concern to monetary policy. Secondly, since a major objective of a stability-orientated policy is to avoid distortions in investment and savings behavior, it could be argued that a more broadly based price indicator, such as the GDP deflator, would be more appropriate.

The choice of a particular price index would not be particularly problematic if it were the case that the various measures tended to move closely together. However, empirical evidence suggests that substantial divergence across different price measures can arise, even in the long run. This is confirmed in the US case by Lebow et al. (1994) although, evidence for the UK suggests that in the long-run different price indices are pairwise co-integrated (Yates (1995)). Nonetheless, as Freedman concludes "in the end, some variant of the CPI will continue to be the object of policy, largely because of its convenience and its usefulness for communicating with the public."

In any case, in analyzing inflation developments and prospects and, in some cases in formulating targets, central banks employ various core measures of consumer price inflation. Often this measure is calculated by excluding erratic items, such as food and energy prices, or items whose exclusion is considered appropriate for monetary policy purposes (e.g. indirect taxes, mortgage interest payments) in order to obtain a more accurate picture of underlying inflation. In addition, for the same reasons, various measures of underlying inflation, based on either on exclusion of outliers (Cecchetti (1996)) or time-series based measures such as the Quah-Vahey (1995), are used as indicators in some central banks. In addition, there is a general consensus among central banks that an understanding of the inflationary process requires a broad macroeconomic perspective. As a result, central banks routinely analyze and examine a whole range of price and cost indices, including trade prices, producer prices and various other price indicators.

In a strategy of monetary targeting the choice of a specific monetary aggregate to serve as an intermediate target is a crucial decision. In practice, this decision is influenced by a range of a-priori considerations and empirical properties. As regards a priori considerations, factors such as liquidity and use in transactions, substitutability for deposits have, inter alia, played a role as criteria for deciding which financial instruments can be considered as 'money' and be included in the monetary aggregate. On empirical aspects, there appears to be a consensus among central banks that two conditions are necessary for a particular aggregate to serve as a suitable intermediate variable: stability (or, at least, predictability) of the longer-term relationship between the aggregate and the price level and a sufficient degree of controllability of the chosen aggregate by the instruments available to the central bank (König (1996)). Of course, these necessary empirical properties - apart from being helpful in the choice of a particular aggregate - are also crucial to the continued success of a monetary targeting strategy. In a number of countries which have pursued monetary targets in the past - e.g. the US and UK - processes financial deregulation and liberalization resulted in significant distortions in the behavior chosen monetary aggregates, which impaired their usefulness for monetary purposes, and ultimately led to the abandonment or at least downgrading of the monetary targets. In contrast, where these conditions remained in place, the strategy itself was not called into question. Thus, for example, as König (op cit.) argues in the German case "the fact that the Bundesbank has been able to rely on an intermediate targeting strategy for more than 20 years now is, above all, due to the stability of financial relationships."

3.2 Length of the Target Horizon

Under either strategy, longer target horizons may in general[5] be expected to increase the likelihood of achieving the target, since the central bank has more time to assess the nature of, and choose an appropriate response to, apparent deviations from the target path. In the case of IMT, for example, it will be more difficult to hit a particular target, within a shorter time horizon, if protracted deviations from a stable long-run relation between money and prices occur. Similarly, given uncertainties and lags in the transmission mechanism, it is more difficult under DIT for the central bank to achieve an annual target rather than, say, an inflation target specified over the average of a few years. On the other hand, in has been argued that "extending the time horizon...almost inevitably results in a reduction of the disciplinary effects of monetary targeting" (Issing (1994)) and, in both cases, longer target horizons may reduce both the accountability and transparency of the monetary policy strategy if agents doubt the commitment of the central bank to reverse shorter term deviations.

3.3 Choice of Central Target Path

In either IMT or DIT, the chosen central target path depends strongly on initial conditions. If these are favorable, i.e. starting from an initial position of price stability, a specific time path of the target variable need not be specified in detail (e.g. a multi-year path for inflation or money would not need to be specified); instead, a fairly constant rate of growth of the money stock or of prices, consistent with price stability, could be sufficient. Thus, in these favorable circumstances, the central target for a DIT strategy would simply be a rate of increase in the targeted measure of prices over the target horizon consistent with the chosen definition of price stability. In an IMT strategy, the central path would be a rate of money growth over the target horizon consistent with price stability given potential output

[5] This will be true where the target growth of money or prices is relatively stable from planning period to planning period and where the target is expressed in terms of average growth over the target period rather than an end-point condition. Where these conditions are not fulfilled, there is no guarantee that longer horizons will reduce the probability of target misses.

growth and velocity trends, and allowing for any base drift or carry-over effects which might have to be taken into account.

If, however, the initial conditions are less favorable, the issue of the specification of an optimal transition path towards price stability arises. In this situation, the central bank has to strike a balance between the need to favorably impact on expectations and achieve its objective quickly against the possible costs in terms of foregone output which could arise, given inertia in price and wage formation, from a very rapid pace of disinflation. In a recent paper, King (1996) explores this issue and concludes that the expectations formation process exerts a crucial influence in this respect with a higher weight on the backward-looking component of expectations favoring a more gradualist approach. Except in cases in which expectations are fully rational and forward looking, the optimal rate of disinflation is a gradual approach, with the inflation objective always being below expected inflation and falling. In practice, central banks of the industrialized countries have tended to favor such a gradualist approach. Thus in a number of DIT countries (e.g. Canada) which started from a high initial inflation, a gradual reduction of inflation towards price stability was explicitly included in the announced inflation target. Similarly, the past, the Bundesbank has acknowledged that it may not be practical to restore price stability over a short horizon. Thus it has, on occasions, incorporated a price norm in the formulation of the monetary target which allowed for a level of unavoidable inflation higher than would be consistent with price stability, while at the same time aiming to restore price stability as soon as practicable.

3.4 Precision of Target (Range)

In either strategy the precision with which the target is expressed, for a given target horizon, influences the flexibility with which the central bank can respond to shocks and the likelihood of the target being hit. While wider ranges would tend to increase flexibility and, at the same time reduce, the chances of target misses, there is a danger that they may weaken transparency and accountability, implying, again, a need to achieve a balance between these objectives. On the other hand, while a narrow range may enhance the perception of the commitment of the central bank to the target and thereby promote transparency and provide a good basis for accountability initially, repeated target misses, which are more likely with narrower ranges, may weaken the public's confidence in the strategy. For either strategy, some empirical assessment of the probability of the target being hit or missed, depending on the width of the band, can be carried out. In essence, this would involve a comparison of the "standard errors" of money demand equations or inflation forecasts with the width of a target range (Haldane and Salmon (1995)) However, the precise impact of alternative target ranges on public perceptions of the strategy's performance is obviously more difficult to assess.

3.5 Response to Deviations from the Target

A fundamental issue in the implementation of either an IMT or a DIT strategy is the response of the central bank to actual (or expected) deviations from the target. In the face of such a deviation, the response of the central bank will depend on factors such as the nature, size and likely duration of the deviation. If the deviation is indeed perceived as signaling a threat to price stability over the medium term, then a monetary policy response is warranted. In this case, the issue of the extent and speed of the response arises, in particular whether the central bank should seek a rapid reversal of the deviation via a sharp change in interest rates as against a more gradual response.

If, on the other hand, the deviation is seen as being of a once-off transitory nature, then only a muted, or indeed no, response may be appropriate. For example, in the case of an IMT, once-off shifts in portfolio behavior of money holders (due to financial innovations, taxation or other factors) may lead to deviations of money growth from target. If such factors can be identified by the central bank and are not seen as likely to lead to inflationary pressure, the deviation of money stock from target may be tolerated under an IMT strategy. Similarly, in the case of both strategies, the first-round effects of once-off shifts in the price level (due to taxes or other supply factors) to the extent that these are not expected to lead to protracted increases in inflation and become embedded in inflationary expectations, may be tolerated by the central bank. Indeed, in some cases of countries pursuing DIT the type of shocks to which a response would not be considered appropriate are specified in some detail and pre-announced to the public, (e.g. New Zealand) in the form of "escape clauses" or caveats or else by defining the targeted price index with a view to excluding likely shocks from the targeted measure (e.g. exclusion of food and energy prices).

3.6 Communication with the General Public

Effective communication with the general public is a crucial element in either strategy. It can contribute to enhancing both the accountability of the central bank and building the credibility of the policy. As is common in most EU central banks, this communication strategy generally involves:

- publication of targets and the details of their derivation;
- regular publication of data and analysis relevant to the target; and
- explanations of deviations from the target and the policy response of central banks.

The means employed vary across central banks. All publish regular bulletins explaining monetary and economic developments with information supplemented by public statements by senior officials. In some central banks, newspaper and television interviews by senior officials also form part of the communications strategy.

3.7 Analysis of the Economic Environment, Prospects and the Impact of Policy Actions

As noted earlier, a fundamental requirement for the successful conduct of a forward-looking, stability-orientated, monetary policy is an adequate assessment by the central bank of current and prospective monetary and macroeconomic conditions and their implications for the final objective, price stability. Given the structure of the economy and the nature of the transmission mechanism, a proper understanding of inflation, which is essential for the conduct of policy, requires a comprehensive assessment of the general macroeconomic environment and, in particular, of the disparate forces acting on the price level. In addition, since the impact of monetary policy actions on prices does not occur instantaneously, but instead takes place through a transmission mechanism with long and varying lags, monetary policy decision making must perforce be *forward-looking* and, in consequence, an efficient monetary policy will require information of prospective future developments as well as current developments. Finally, the transmission mechanism of monetary policy is complex and many of its features are not well understood and not known with certainty. This implies the need for some degree of *methodological eclecticism*, in which information from a broad range of sources is taken into account in order to ensure that the assessment of the macroeconomic situation is valid, rather than strict mechanical adherence to a particular model of the economy.

This points to the need for the central banks to carry out extensive quantitative assessment of the economic, financial and monetary environment by monitoring, forecasting and modeling macroeconomic behavior and, especially, price developments. Most, if not all, central banks carry out this type of analysis in order to assist in the formulation of monetary policy.

Firstly, at present, all central banks carry out comprehensive assessment of the state of the economy and of price developments by monitoring a wide ranging set of indicators. This monitoring is typically based on the examination of a wide range of indicators. These include prices themselves, money and credit aggregates, income indicators, wage developments, demand pressure, profits, fiscal policy stance, and various monetary and financial indicators. The scope and type of analysis typically carried out can be seen in the published bulletins and reports of central banks. As well as being consumers of existing published data, central banks themselves are a key supplier of important data. In most cases, data on money stock and its counterparts are compiled by the central bank itself; central banks also have a major role in the field of balance of payments statistics. In addition, in a number of countries (e.g. the US, Japan and France) the central bank plays a major role in producing important cyclical indicators for its own use and for use by the general public.

Secondly, because of lags in the response to monetary policy, forecasts are central to policy setting in many central banks. Therefore, along with the use of indicators, most central banks employ forecasting methods to assess inflationary prospects. In inflation targeting countries, such forecasts, usually made conditional on the assumption of an unchanged policy stance, play a crucial role as an input into the monetary policy formation process. As a result, "an enormous weight of responsibility rests on the shoulders of the chief economic forecaster" (Goodhart and Viñals (1995)). In addition to point forecasts, there is a growing interest in the assessment of risks, alternative scenarios and probability distributions forecasts. In some cases, e.g. the UK, the published forecasts of the central bank play a crucial role in the communications policy of the central bank, although the majority of inflation targeting countries do not consider it appropriate to publish their forecasts which are produced for internal purposes only.

Thirdly, in nearly all central banks, econometric models make a valuable contribution to analysis of current conditions, forecasting and assessment of the impact of policy actions on the final variables. They help to understand the functioning of the macroeconomy and allow a systematic use of economic theory in explaining short- and long-run inflation dynamics. Furthermore, models capture historical regularities, identify key assumptions that must be made to condition the forecast, embody estimates of the effects of past and future policy actions on the economy, and provide a disciplined approach to learning from past errors. In this sense, models help to discipline the judgmental element which, to some extent, is always present in making the forecast. A model also helps to defend and communicate the forecast, by providing a coherent story that ties together the details of the forecast. Models used by central banks include both large-scale macroeconomic models and smaller structural macroeconomic models, although in some central banks more detailed and higher-frequency sectoral models are also used. In addition there seems to be an increasing tendency to use single equation estimations (e.g. auto regressive, Box-Jenkins type of methods), restricted VAR-models and small analytical models to forecast price movements - as a consistency check with larger size models.

4 Monetary Policy Strategy in Stage Three of EMU

In choosing and implementing its strategy in Stage Three, the ESCB will need to look closely at many of the issues examined in previous sections. Since final decisions on strategy in Stage Three will be taken by the Governing Council of the ECB itself, there is no need at this point for the EMI to make decisions on many of these issues. However, in 1996, in order to facilitate the preparation of ESCB' strategy, the EMI Council considered the issue of monetary policy strategy in

Stage Three and has recently published a special paper which presented it's thinking on this topic (EMI (1997)).

In this context, a number of major factors which will influence the ESCB's decisions regarding strategy have been identified. These include the normative guiding principles and key features of the economic and financial environment which will prevail at the time. Alternative strategies have been evaluated and a number of key elements and operational aspects common to the various strategies have also been elaborated. In addition, work on preparing the analytical infrastructure for monetary policy strategy commenced in 1996.

4.1 Factors Influencing the Choice of Strategy

In selecting the strategy for Stage Three, the ESCB will take into account a number of guiding principles. In particular, the strategy followed should be effective in the sense that its pursuit will put the ESCB in a position to achieve its final objective of price stability. In addition, there are a number of other principles, which contribute in some specific ways to the effectiveness of a strategy, for example, by helping to make announcements by the ESCB more credible, thereby anchoring the public's inflationary expectations and facilitating the maintenance of price stability. Such additional principles include accountability, transparency, medium-term orientation and compatibility with the independence of the ESCB.

In addition to these principles, the environment for monetary policy in Stage Three and the specific situation at the start of Stage Three also have to be taken into account. A key feature in this respect is the likely size and degree of openness to external trade of the euro area, both of which imply that exchange rate developments will most likely constitute less of a concern for the conduct of monetary policy than is currently the case for many NCBs. Other considerations include the characteristics of the monetary policy transmission process in the euro area, the fact that the ESCB will have no track record of it's own at the start of its operations, and the requirement to devise its strategy while taking into account the need to integrate new participants in the euro area over time.

4.2 Alternative Strategies

Discussions within the EMI have led to a consensus that two potential candidate strategies for Stage Three could be considered, namely monetary targeting and direct inflation targeting.

A detailed assessment of the two strategies in terms of the guiding principles mentioned above, and in the light of the environment expected at the start of, and during, Stage Three, indicates that it is neither possible nor necessary, at this stage, to determine precisely which strategy should be adopted by the ESCB. However, there is a consensus among EU central banks that, on the basis of experience, the following five key elements would be an indispensable part of any strategy adopted by the ESCB:

- Public announcement of a quantified definition of the final objective of price stability in order to enhance the transparency and credibility of the ESCB's strategy.
- Public announcement of specific targets against which the performance of the ESCB can be assessed on an ongoing basis by the general public, thereby enhancing accountability.
- The use of all available information relevant to the final target of monetary policy. In this sense the strategy is based on a broad set of monetary, financial and economic indicator variables which would help when assessing the risks to future price stability. The ESCB itself will decide on how to use these indicators, both internally and in its communication with the public, in the light of the specific circumstances prevailing.
- Within the set of indicators employed by the ESCB, monetary aggregates should be assigned a prominent role, with either targets or monitoring ranges set for their growth, provided that money demand has a sufficiently stable relationship to inflation in the long run.
- The ESCB should be in a position to make its own forecasts for inflation, potential growth, monetary aggregates and other economic variables.

In practice, these elements could be combined in different ways. They would afford the ESCB the choice of pursuing either a monetary or direct inflation targeting strategy, but could also be used in frameworks which place strong emphasis on monetary targets while using supplementary elements from direct inflation targeting strategies, or vice-versa. However, any specification of the options for combining key elements would be premature at this stage since their assessment will largely depend on the circumstances prevailing in Stage Three.

4.3 Implementation Issues and Preparatory Work

In order to implement its monetary policy strategy, there are many detailed technical issues on which the ECB will have to make decisions. The main choices, which have been discussed extensively above, concern the selection and precise identification of the target variable(s), the length of the target horizon etc.

Finally, it is agreed that the ESCB will need to be equipped with the statistical and analytical infrastructure to provide guidance for the conduct of the single monetary policy. In terms of data requirements, these have been identified and work is underway to ensure that the necessary data is in place by the start of Stage Three. In relation to the analytic infrastructure, a number of projects have been launched. This preparatory work concentrated on the development of tools to assist in the analysis and monitoring of area-wide monetary developments, to identify and quantify the likely features of the transmission mechanism in Stage Three and to produce forecasts of variables of interest. Included in this heading are detailed analysis of area-wide money and credit demand, the assessment of the leading indicator properties of various variables, the development of a range of forecasting tools. Work is also underway on the development of structural econometric models. These include an in-house multi-country model of the countries of the EU, which is being developed as a joint project by EMI and national central bank staff, as well as a number of area-wide models.

5 Conclusions

There now exists a broad consensus that the primary objective of monetary policy should be the pursuit of price stability, and this is increasingly reflected in both the legislative frameworks and in the behavior of central banks throughout the industrialized world. Against this background, the most fundamental issue facing central banks is how price stability should be defined, an issue which is attracting the increasing attention of researchers. In this respect, central banks, on the basis of their announced targets and observed behavior, appear to favor a concept of price stability which involves a very small positive rate of inflation. To date, central banks have not adopted more demanding definitions such as stabilization of the price level, although interest in this and other aspects of the definition of price stability is increasing.

Focusing on the two strategies of monetary and direct inflation targeting, this paper has identified and discussed seven key specific implementation issues on which decisions need to be made by the central bank. These issues are: the choice of the specific variables for the final and intermediate targets; the length of the target horizon; the central target path; the precision of the target; the response of policy to deviations from the target; communication with the general public; and, finally, the analysis of the economic environment, prospects and the impact of policy actions.

The move towards EMU has provided an occasion for European central banks, working within the framework of the EMI, to carry out a comprehensive review of the issues examined in this paper with a view to the choice of the strategy of the ESCB in Stage Three. This has led to extensive discussions among central banks, in which, though some divergence of views remain, a large measure of agreement has been reached on the key features of the monetary strategy in Stage Three. Needless to say, as EMU approaches, the implementation problems of monetary policy strategy will be very much in the forefront of discussions, both inside and outside the central banking community.

References

Alchian, A. A. and B. Klein (1973), On a Correct Measure of Inflation, *Journal of Money, Credit, and Banking* 5, 173-91.

Andres, J., R. Mestre and J. Valles (1996), Inflation Targeting and the Transition to Monetary Union: the Spanish Case, mimeo, Banco de España.

Blake, A. P. and P. F. Westaway (1994), Targeting Inflation with Nominal Interest Rates, National Institute of Economic and Social Research Discussion Paper No. 70.

Bootle, R. (1996), The Death of Inflation: Surviving and Thriving in the Zero Era, London.

Briault, C. (1995), The Costs of Inflation, *Bank of England Quarterly Bulletin* 35, 33-45.

Cecchetti, S. G. (1996), Measuring Short-Run Inflation for Central Bankers, mimeo, Cambridge, M.A.

Crawford, A. (1993), Measurement Biases in the Canadian CPI, Bank of Canada Technical Report No. 64, Ottawa.

Cunningham, A. W. F. (1996), Measurement Bias in Price Indices: an Application to the UK's RPI, Bank of England Working Paper Series, No. 47, London.

Dugay, P. (1994), Some Thoughts on Price Stability Versus Zero Inflation, in: F. Bruni (ed.), Central Bank Independence and Accountability.

EMI (1996), Progress towards Convergence, Frankfurt.

EMI (1997), The Single Monetary Policy in Stage Three: Elements of the Monetary Policy Strategy of the ESCB, Frankfurt.

Feldstein, M. (1996), The Costs and Benefits of Going from Low Inflation on to Price Stability, NBER Working Paper No. 5469, Cambridge,M.A.

Fischer, S. (1996), Why are Central Banks Pursuing Price Stability, in: Federal Reserve Bank of Kansas City (ed.), Achieving Price Stability, Kansas City, 7-35.

Freedman, C. (1996), What Operating Procedures Should Be Adopted to Maintain Price Stability? - Practical Issues, in: Federal Reserve Bank of Kansas City (ed.), Achieving Price Stability, Kansas City, 241-85.

Friedman, M. (1956), The Optimal Quantity of Money, in: Friedman, M. (ed.), The Optimal Quantity of Money and Other Essays, Chicago, 1969.

Fuhrer, J. and B. Madigan (1994), Monetary Policy When Interest Rates are Bounded at Zero, Federal Reserve Bank of Boston, Working Paper No. 94-1, Boston.

Goodhart, G. and J. Viñals (1994), Strategy and Tactics of Monetary Policy: Examples from Europe and the Antipodes, Bank of Spain Working Paper No. 9425, Madrid.

Haldane, A. G. and C. K. Salmon (1995), Three Issues on Inflation Targets, in: Haldane, A. G. (ed.), Targeting Inflation, London, 170-201.

Issing, O. (1994), Monetary Policy Strategy in the EMU, in: de Beaufort, J. O. Wijnholds, S.W. Eijffinger and L.H. Hoogduin (eds.), A Framework for Monetary Stability, Dordrecht, 135-48.

Kahn, G. A. (1996), Achieving Price Stability: A Summary of the Bank's 1996 Symposium, *Federal Reserve Bank of Kansas City Economic Review* 81, 53-59.

Kimborough, K. (1986), Inflation, Employment and Welfare in the Presence of Transactions Costs, *Journal of Money, Credit, and Banking* 18, 127-40.

King, M. (1996), How Should Central Banks Reduce Inflation? - Conceptual Issues, *Federal Reserve Bank of Kansas City Economic Review* 81, 26-52.

König, R. (1996), The Bundesbank's Experience of Monetary Targeting, in: Deutsche Bundesbank (ed.), Monetary Policy Strategies in Europe, München, 107-40.

Lebow, D. E., J. M. Roberts and D. J. Stockton (1992), Economic Performance Under Price Stability, Board of Governors of the Federal Reserve System, Working Paper No. 125, Washington, D.C.

Lebow, D. E., J. M. Roberts and D. J. Stockton (1994), Monetary Policy and the Price Level, mimeo, Board of Governors of the Federal Reserve System, Washington D.C.

Phelps, E. (1973), Inflation in the Theory of Public Finance, *Swedish Journal of Economics* 75, 67-82.

Quah, D. T. and S. Vahey (1995), Measuring Core Inflation, *Economic Journal* 105, 1130-44.

Sargent, T. J. and N. Wallace (1995) "Rational" Expectations, the Optimal Monetary Instrument and the Optimal Money Supply Rule, *Journal of Political Economy* 83, 241-54.

Shigehara, K. (1996), The Options Regarding the Concept of a Monetary Policy Strategy, in: Deutsche Bundesbank (ed.), Monetary Policy Strategies in Europe, München, 7-44.

Summers, L. (1991), How Should Long-Term Monetary Policy Be Determined? *Journal of Money, Credit, and Banking* 23, 625-31.

Svensson, L. E. O. (1996), Price Level Targeting Versus Inflation Targeting: A Free Lunch, CEPR Discussion Paper No. 1510, London.

Tobin, J. (1972), Inflation and Unemployment, *American Economic Review* 62, 1-18.

Woodford, M. (1990), The Optimum Quantity of Money, Chapter 20, in: Friedman, B. M. and F. Hahn (eds.), The Handbook of Monetary Economics, vol. II, Amsterdam, 1067-1152.

Wynne, M. A. and F. D. Sigalla (1996), A Survey of Measurement Biases in Price Indexes, *Journal of Economic Surveys* 10, 55-89.

Yates, A. (1995), On the Design of Inflation Targets, in: Haldane, A. G. (ed.), Targeting Inflation, London, 135-69.

Figure 1 Inflation versus price level targeting

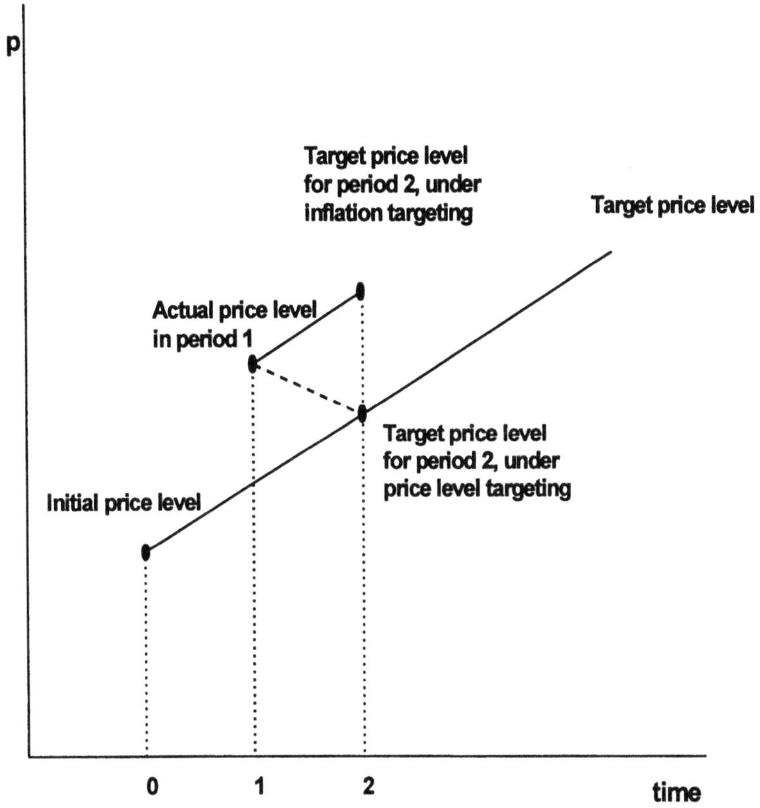

Comment (on *Stephen Cecchetti* and *Gabriel Fagan*)

Lukas Menkhoff
University of Aachen, Templergraben 64, D - 52056 Aachen

1 Introduction

Although there are few issues regarding monetary policy strategy that are completely undisputed among academics, central bankers cannot wait for final insights but have to act now. Thus it is interesting to see how they make judgments - at least implicitly - on the basis of competing theories and inconclusive empirical evidence. Since we even have two statements by competent authors from the Federal Reserve System (Fed) and the European Monetary Institute (EMI), we also have the chance to compare them.

Unfortunately, the European System of Central Banks (ESCB) has not yet commenced operations and many important decisions about monetary policy strategy have not yet been made. Therefore, one cannot expect that members of the EMI's staff to express clear preferences on disputed and often politically sensitive issues. Fagan's paper is indeed heavily based on official reports (EMI, 1997 and the "background analysis" EMI (1997a)), but it also offers a more in-depth analysis, since it is linked to the academic literature. These extensions make it comparable to Cecchetti's paper, regarding the issues addressed at all, the intensity given to them and the arguments having put forward.

This comparison is provided in the second section of the paper, after I concentrate on the most important open issue in this field, i.e. the choice to be made by the ESCB between the two strategies of monetary targeting (MT) and inflation targeting (IT). Section 3 addresses the communities and differences between these two strategies, while section 4 evaluates the practice of the Deutsche Bundesbank in relation to the previous discussion. Finally, a few minor implementation issues - i.e. policy objectives, price level targeting and the financial environment - are outlined in brief.

2 Comparing the Two Approaches Towards Strategy

Whenever two people give personal views on the same subject the outcome must necessarily be different. Nevertheless, it seems that something more than personal preference is behind the widely different treatments we have here. In summary, Fagan's papers reads as if dynamic consistency were the primary problem of the central bank, whereas Cecchetti explicitly starts his analysis by assuming that this issue has been solved already. This fundamental difference in approach is possibly influenced by the author's respective institutional environments: the ESCB does not exist yet and its credibility is already in doubt on the fringes. The Fed on the contrary, has already established a considerable reputation for fighting inflation and for its macroeconomic management ability.

These remarkably different approaches towards monetary policy strategy explain much about the formulation of the policy goals, and how alternative strategies are evaluated. It is also at the roots of most dissent regarding detailed aspects of strategy. A list of issues addressed in the papers by Cecchetti and Fagan and a comparison of their respective approaches is given in Table 1 (unfortunately, Fagan's earlier section on "main features of monetary and inflation targeting" has been eliminated in the final version).

Table 1: Comparison of contents

Subject	Cecchetti (Fed)	Fagan (EMI)	Consensus + Dissent -
policy goal	inflation control; subordinated: minimization of loss function (price level and output level variability)	price stability	-
framework of the paper	explicit analytical framework based on loss function (see above)	implicit overriding aspect of credibility	-
strategies considered	nominal income targeting (NT), inflation targeting (IT) and present practice (PP) (3.1)	monetary targeting (MT) and inflation targeting (IT) (section in the version presented)	-
evaluation:			
▪ NT	-	n.a.	n.a.
▪ IT	- neglect of output variability possible	+/- continuity	-
▪ MT	-- poor contribution to transparency	+/- controllability	-
▪ PP	+ implicitly positive	n.a.	n.a.

Table 1: Continued

Strategy aspects:			
▪ output-inflation variability trade-off	numerical estimations (3.2)	few conditions (3.5)	-
▪ uncertainty	impact uncertainty: low; model uncertainty: unknown (3.3)	n.a.	n.a.
▪ price level targeting	exogenous optimizing problem (2)	favors privce level targeting (2.1)	+
▪ optimum inflation rate	favors positive inflation rate (3.4)	favors zero inflation (2.2)	-
▪ interest rate smoothing	open (3.5)	open (central target path 3.3)	n.a.
▪ transparency	conflict between independence and democracy -> transparency (4)	communication (3.6)	-
▪ length of target horizon	e.g. over the business cycle (5)	open (3.2) (flexibility vs. credibility)	-
▪ range of the target	target range rather than point target (5)	width of traget range (3.4)	+
▪ target variable	n.a.	CPI deflator, core inflation etc. (3.1)	n.a.
▪ econonmic environment	n.a.	e.g. transmission mechanism (3.7)	n.a

Note: numbers in brackets refer to sections in the respective papers

Of particular interest in my opinion is Cecchetti's clear negative verdict on MT, since this is in sharp contrast to the balanced evaluation in Fagan's paper. Basically no single aspect MT is spread by the author. A summary of this discussion is given in Table 2. Cecchetti's view is directly opposed to the mainstream German view, which tends towards a more friendly evaluation. The reasons for this difference are probably that Cecchetti reflects US experience to a greater extent, and that he is analytically very strict.

Another divergence to be highlighted is the numerical treatment of the output-inflation variability trade-off provided by Cecchetti. The fact that output is greater than the price reaction to interest rate innovations is the basis for the central policy message that authorities should also address output variability and should not solely concentrate on fighting inflation. The question then arises as to how stable these impulse response functions are and to what degree they might be exploited by monetary policy. Nevertheless, the successful anti-inflation policies of the past as well as the pragmatic approach of model central banks, such as the Deutsche Bundesbank or the Federal Reserve (see also below), strongly suggest an explicit consideration of real variables in monetary policy strategy.

Table 2: The contribution of an intermediate money target to the transparency of policy

Characteristics of an ideal intermediate target	Strict interpretation (Cecchetti?)	German experience
high correlation with final target	no	longer term: yes shorter term: no
easier to control than final target	velocity instability: no	see above
easier to observe than final target		
• by the central bank	?	yes
• by the public	no	} not important as long as the public trusts the central bank
facilitates public understanding	no	
summary conclusion	negative	relatively positive

Source: interpretation according to Cecchetti (1998), section 3.1, and e.g. Issing (1996)

3 The Relationship between Monetary and Inflation Targeting

The European central bank's discussion of a number of potential monetary policy strategies has led to a preference for either MT or IT. The formulation of direct inflation targeting only evolved in the last few years. As the latter has replaced other monetary policy targets, such as money or exchange rate targets, in the respective countries it seems natural to regard monetary and inflation targeting as clearly competing approaches. However, recent analysis also stresses common elements in both strategies (emphasized in Fagan's presentation).

At the level of its most obvious characteristics, Leiderman and Svensson (1995) define IT as essentially having "an explicit inflation target" and possibly "the absence of an explicit intermediate target for monetary aggregates or exchange rates". Although an intermediate target does not have to exist, it may do; however if it does it should not have priority in case of conflict.

An attempt to define MT using the same elements would stress the dominance of monetary aggregates in implementing the strategy. In this case the final target is a matter of choice. In reality, however, there is a broad consensus now that monetary policy should aim primarily for price stability, which translates into an inflation target as a final (explicit or implicit) objective. Therefore, both strategies look very similar, if not practically identical, at an aggregated level of analysis.

In a more detailed approach, EMI has formulated six "guiding principles" for assessing the competing strategies (EMI (1997a)). In my evaluation of the pros and cons of the competing strategies with regard to these six principles, no clear winner emerges (regarding principles of "transparency", "medium-term orientation" and "consistency with independence"). Only three arguments seem to be unrivaled: the principle of "accountability" favors monetary targeting, since money volume is subject to closer control by the central bank than inflation development. "Continuity" , on the other hand, favors inflation targeting, as more EU central banks pursue this strategy than monetary targeting. Finally, the most important aspect of "effectiveness" depends on the stability of money demand.

Thus the whole body of arguments boils down to the decisive question of whether a stable relationship between money and prices will exist following monetary union. A major factor influencing the answer to this is the level of ambition: the longer the horizon and the more appropriate the definition of money, the easier stability will be. In the shorter term, however, the process of financial innovation and liberalization will affect money demand and the start of a monetary union may be regarded as a change in regime, the effects of which are still unknown. Again: Would anybody recommend a strict k-percent rule under these circumstances, or neglect the longer-term change of money volumes?

Therefore, the distinction between MT and IT may be intellectually appealing but be an exaggeration when it is applied to effective policy making. Indeed, a study of best practices rather gives the impression that an integration of MT and IT may be taking place and desirable (Mishkin and Posen (1997)). Hence Bernanke and Mishkin (1997) proposed the term "inflation targeting framework" to describe this integrated approach (with reference to King (1996))who advanced similar ideas).

The term "inflation targeting framework" already indicates a certain closeness to the strategy of IT, being backed up by King´s (1996) competent interpretation of IT. It is MT that seems to be more alien to the framework outlined above. However, recent interpretations of the Bundesbank´s monetary policy weaken the superficial antagonism of MT and IT.

4 The Practice of the Deutsche Bundesbank

Since the Deutsche Bundesbank introduced a monetary aggregate as its intermediate target in 1974, this has become a kind of role model for monetary targeting. In the late 1970s and early 1980s this approach was popular because monetarism and MT dominated. Today, the Bundesbank's strategy looks old-fashioned because IT has evolved as the modern approach. Although this classification is obvious from the Bundesbank's M3 target, it probably does not do justice to the Bundesbank's effective policy, which is strictly anti-inflationist in the longer term but basically pragmatic in the shorter term (cf. Issing (1996)).

The anti-inflationist stance is obvious from the D-Mark's record of price stability. The short-term pragmatism, i.e. the subordinated targeting of further goals such as the exchange rate, was recognizable from the beginning. The fact that the Bundesbank did not care too much about short-term deviations of money growth from the announced target was merely a consequence of this approach. Figure 1 clearly demonstrates deviations from money targets and close adherence to the "announced" inflation rate (unavoidable or normative).

Thus, it is appropriate to say that the Bundesbank practices "disciplined discretion" (Laubach and Posen (1997)) and follows an "implicit inflation target" (Bernanke and Mishkin (1997), cf. Menkhoff (1988)). This implies "... that the Bank's credibility should not be judged on the basis of its performance in reaching the monetary target" (von Hagen (1995) and in a similar rein Kool (1996)). So why did the Bundesbank not introduce an inflation target in 1974, but rather a monetary target? First, the theoretical environment emphasized the importance of MT and velocity was quite stable at the time. Second, money can be more directly controlled by the central bank than inflation. Third, the Bundesbank was most probably reluctant to announce either realistic inflation targets of 4.5% p.a. or unrealistic lower targets. From this perspective, MT was a way to give the central bank credibility even in a higher inflation environment.

Figure 1: Monetary and Inflation Targeting in Germany

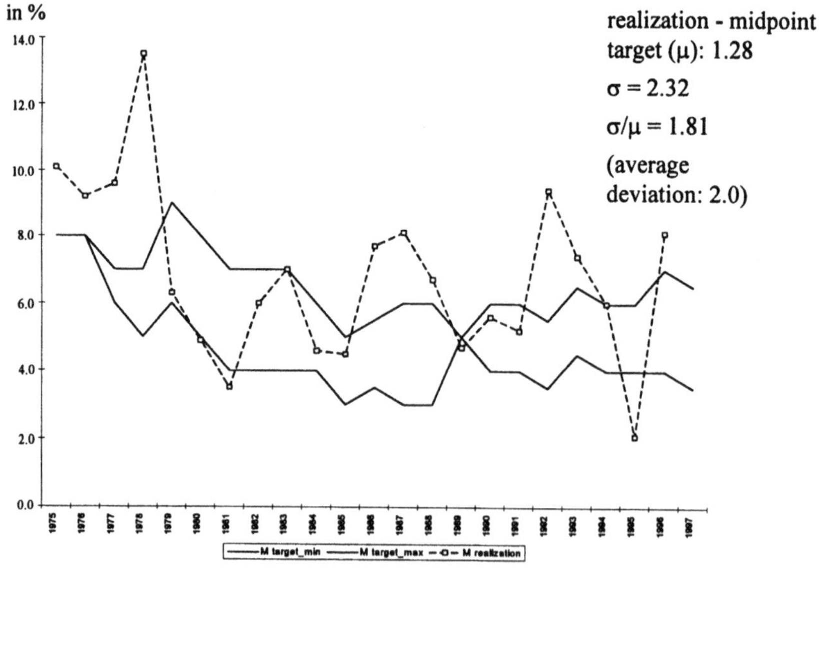

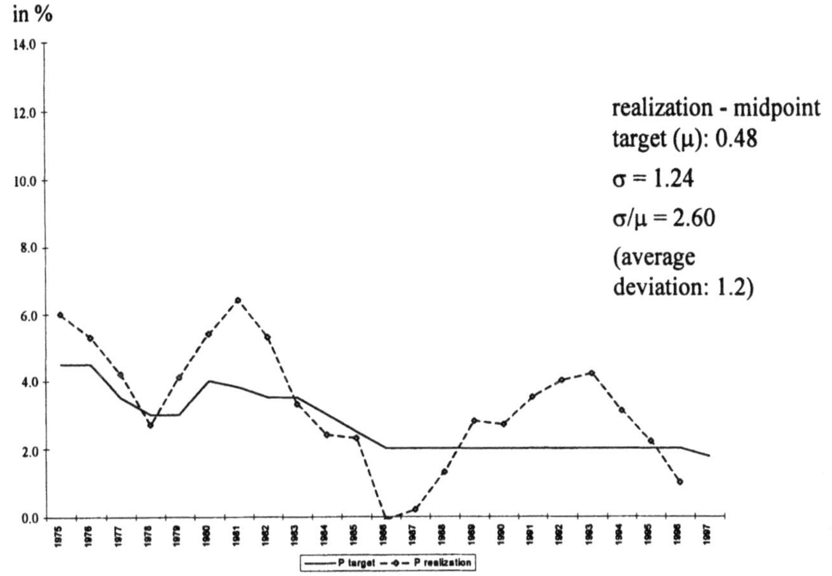

Note: Data 1975 - 1994: von Hagen (1995), data 1995 - 1997: various reports of Deutsche Bundesbank

5 Other Implementation Issues in Monetary Policy Strategy

Of the many other implementation issues addressed by Cecchetti and Fagan I would like to choose three particularly relevant ones for further discussion:

(1) Policy objectives: Price stability is the "primary objective" of the ESCB's monetary policy, but not its only one. Thus it would be interesting to learn the way in which subordinated goals may be treated. What is more, the acceptance of further objectives has consequences for implementation specifics: a target range is then probably preferable, inflation may be measured as a kind of core inflation, and escape clauses should be explicitly or implicitly integrated (see Bernanke and Mishkin (1997)).

(2) Price level targeting: Fagan's analysis provides numerous arguments as to why it may be interesting to target the absolute price level instead of the inflation rate and why the level may be held constant over time (the inflation rate zero). When compared to reality, this sounds like an even more ambitious program than that realized by successful central banks in the past. For example, the Bundesbank's policy was dominated by an inflation target and merely supplemented by a certain degree of price level targeting, and the inflation target was formulated as about 2% p.a. (von Hagen (1995)).

Fagan correctly points out that the optimum policy in this respect is regime-dependent (p. 147). Because of this dependency and because empirical evidence does not clearly support the hypothesis for a change in regime during the last few years, it seems to be even more appropriate to remain modest (see also Bernanke and Mishkin (1997)).

(3) Financial environment: Finally, the EMI reports mention the dependence of optimum monetary policy on the financial environment. This issue is not debated either in these reports or in Fagan's paper, of course nor, in Cechetti's. As the financial environment influences the transmission process (EMI, 1997a, p.4), it must be expected that, given the prevailing country-specific circumstances, the conduct of monetary policy will affect the EMU members in different ways (e.g. Menkhoff (1997)).

From a policy perspective one may therefore expect a certain degree of argument about the course of monetary policy, and even alternative actions. In anticipation of such a debate and possible infighting it is very important to clarify analytically and empirically the possible impact of financial structures on the transmission mechanisms (according to EMI (1997a) this is under review).

6 Conclusion

In keeping with the role of EMI to prepare the operation of the ESCB but not to decide on critical issues, the central question of whether to implement a MT or IT strategy is as yet unanswered. The evidence from official statements (e.g. EMI (1997a)) tends to suggest a compromise in which inflation and intermediate monetary aggregates both play prominent roles. The central banks best practices confirm such a kind of inflation targeting framework (for a concrete proposal see e.g. Filc (1996)).

The ESCB should rely on the experience of presently successful central banks regarding further aspects of monetary policy, too. This implies that there are in effect several policy objectives rather than only one, that the design should leave room for choice and that a low inflation target is ambitious enough to aim for at the beginning.

References

Bernanke, B. S. and F. S. Mishkin (1997), Inflation Targeting: A New Framework for Monetary Policy?, *Journal of Economic Perspectives* 11, 97-116.

Cecchetti, S. G. (1998), Central Bank Policy Rules: Conceptual Issues and Practical Considerations, in this volume.

EMI (1997) [European Monetary Institute], The Single Monetary Policy in Stage Three, Specification of the operational framework, Frankfurt.

---- (1997a), The Single Monetary Policy in Stage Three, Elements of the monetary policy strategy of the ESCB, Frankfurt.

Fagan, G. P. (1998), Implementation Problems of Monetary Policy Strategy, in this volume.

Filc, W. (1996), Geldmengenziel versus Inflationsziel in der Europäischen Währungsunion, *Wirtschaftsdienst* 76, 208-16.

Hagen, J. von (1995), Inflation and Monetary Targeting in Germany, in: Leiderman L. and L. E. O. Svensson (eds.), Inflation Targets, London, 107-21.

Issing, O. (1996), Is Monetary Targeting in Germany Still Adequate?, in: Horst Siebert (ed.), Monetary Policy in an Integrated World Economy, Tübingen, 117-30.

King, M. (1996), Direct Inflation Targets, in: Deutsche Bundesbank (ed.), Monetary Policy Strategies in Europe, München, 45-75.

Kool, C. J. M. (1996), Comment on Otmar Issing Is Monetary Targeting in Germany Still Adequate?, in: Horst Siebert (ed.), Monetary Policy in an Integrated World Economy, Tübingen, 131-36.

Laubach, T. and A. S. Posen (1997), Disciplined Discretion: The German and Swiss Monetary Targeting Frameworks in Operation, Federal Reserve Bank of New York Research Paper No. 9707, New York.

Leiderman, L. and L. E. O. Svensson (1995), Introduction, in: Leiderman L. and L. E. O. Svensson (eds.), Inflation Targets, London, 1-18.

Menkhoff, L. (1988), Mehr Handlungsspielraum durch besseres "Marketing" der Geldpolitik, *Wirtschaftsdienst* 68, 484-88.

---- (1997), Monetary Policy Instruments for European Monetary Union, Berlin et al.

Mishkin, F. S. and A. S. Posen (1997), Inflation Targeting: Lessons from Four Countries, Federal Reserve Bank of New York Economic Policy Review No.3, 9-110.

Part III:

Theoretical Aspects of Exchange Rate Policy and Monetary Union

5. Problems of Flexible and Fixed Exchange Rates

Controversies on Exchange Rate Systems

Michael Frenkel
Otto Beisheim Graduate School of Management, Burgplatz 2, D - 56179 Vallendar

1 Introduction

The vigorous debate between proponents of a fixed exchange rate system and proponents of a flexible exchange rate system has not decreased over the past 30 years. New theoretical and empirical research and new reform proposals have continued to fuel the dispute which regime is the best for an individual country and which serves best the task of an international monetary system, which is to provide a stable environment for international trade and investment. The experience with fixed exchange rates under the Bretton Woods system, in which the adjustment process to external imbalances was too slow in many countries and in which the central banks were eventually unable and unwilling to defend the fixed rates, most economists in the late 1960s and the 1970s advocated flexible exchange rates. The decision to let the Bretton Woods system collapse and to implement a flexible exchange rate regime between major international currencies reflected the firm belief in the superiority of flexible exchange rates at the time. However, with the strong rise in the value of the U.S. dollar in the early 1980s and its subsequent decline, doubts arose about the advantages of flexible rates. As a result, the 1980s were characterized by a growing disenchantment with flexible exchange rates, which led to an increasing support for limitations on the flexibility of exchange rates. The creation of the European Monetary System (EMS) in 1979 and its expansion in the 1980s as well as the evolution of the nominal anchor argument are among the developments that marked this rising support for fixed exchange rates. But in the early 1990s, with the emergence of several currency crises, notably within the EMS, the pendulum began swinging back again from fixed exchange rates to more flexibility.

The dispute on the advantages of fixed versus flexible exchange rates has not been without an effect on policymakers. As shown in Figure 1, the share of IMF member countries that had flexible exchange rate arrangements increased steadily from a relatively small base in the 1970s. However, this trend was halted in the early 1980s with the sharp change in the value of the U.S. dollar. The stagnation of the share of countries that had flexible exchange rates rose again significantly in the 1990s. It is worthwhile noting that this was only partly due to the fact that a sizable amount of new member countries of the IMF in the early 1990s chose a flexible exchange rate regime.

Figure 1: Exchange Rate Arrangements of IMF Member Countries

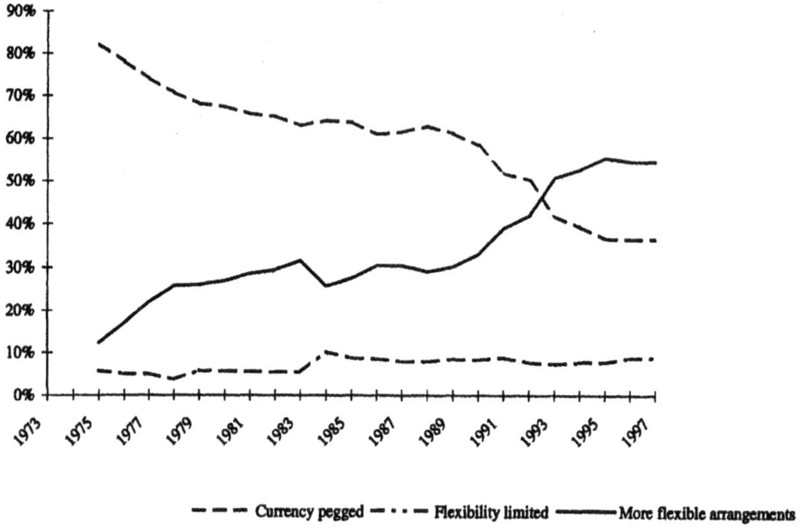

This paper gives a selective survey on the recent discussion of fixed and flexible exchange rate regimes. Given the variety of aspects of exchange rate regimes several topics are not subject to the discussion in this paper. These topics include the determinance of the choice of the exchange rate regime, specific developing country problems, real exchange rate rules, currency boards, and a number of policy proposals on how to reform the international monetary system. The paper is structured as follows: Section 2 examines the validity of the criticism about flexible exchange rates. The discussion focuses on exchange rate volatility and its implications, on the question of destabilizing speculation, the insulation properties of flexible exchange rates and the effectiveness of central bank interventions in the foreign exchange market. Section 3 investigates the problems of fixed exchange rates in light of recent developments. Here the discussion first addresses the argument that a peg induces more monetary and fiscal discipline. Subsequently, the credibility problem, the nominal anchor argument, and the target zone proposal are examined. Section 4 presents a brief summary and some conclusions.

2 Controversies on Flexible Exchange Rates

After more than 25 years of experience with flexible exchange rates among major currencies of industrial countries, it is often argued that such a system does not work well. Comparing the experience with flexible exchange rates with the hopes of the strongest proponents of a float already expressed quite some time before the

Bretton Woods system collapsed, many argue that flexible exchange rates work very differently than expected and do not yield the expected benefits. The works of Friedman (1953) and Johnson (1970) suggested that flexible exchange rates would generate small and continuous changes in exchange rates rather than large discretionary changes, discourage destabilizing speculation, lead to more autonomy of national policies and, thus, allow countries, for example, to choose their own long-term inflation rate, and insulate an economy from foreign economic shocks. The following sections survey the controversies over these alleged advantages of flexible exchange rates.

2.1 Exchange Rate Volatility

2.1.1 Higher and Excessive Volatility under Flexible Exchange Rates?

A major criticism about the flexible exchange rates system as experienced during the post Bretton Woods era is that exchange rates fluctuated significantly more than justified by price differentials. One way to demonstrate exchange rate volatility is to examine short-term changes in bilateral exchange rates. Figure 2 illustrates the empirical evidence for some exchange rates between major currencies. The series show percentage changes of monthly real exchange rates. As the diagrams show, monthly changes of five or more percent have not been uncommon during the flexible exchange rate period.

Figure 2: Short-Term Volatility of Bilateral Real Exchange Rates 1968-1997

Deutschmark/Dollar

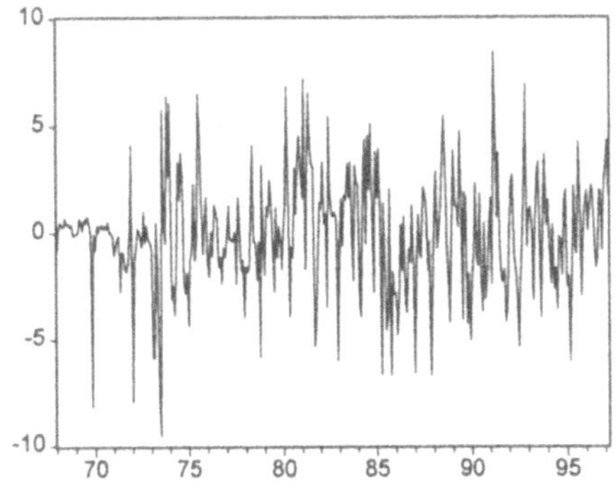

Yen/Dollar

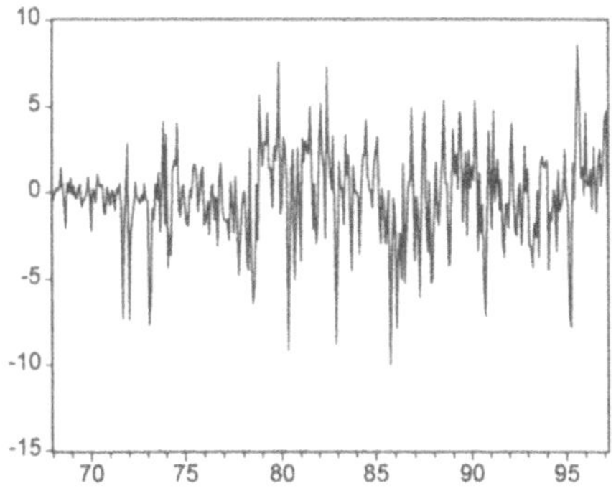

Figure 2: Continued

Pound/Dollar Deutschmark/Yen

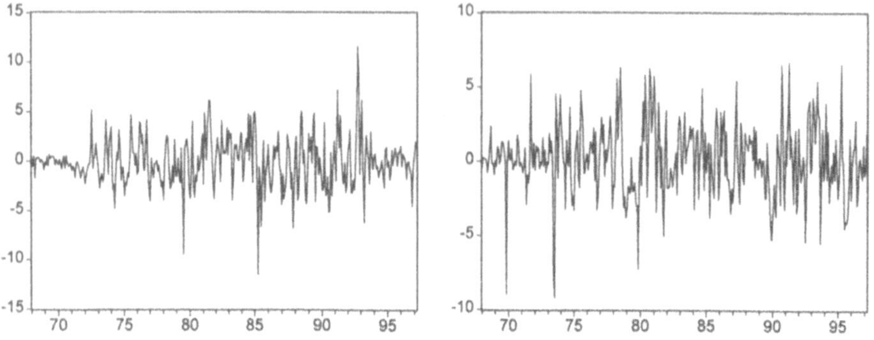

Source: IMF, International Financial Statistics

Table 1 contains calculations of different volatility measures for monthly bilateral exchange rates during the last five years of the Bretton Woods system and for the period since 1975.[1] Appendix Table I reports details on the extent of volatility over different subperiods. With the exception of the less volatile deutschmark-pound exchange rate, the average absolute monthly percentage change between the major currencies amounted to about two percent. The values suggest that, for example, the average absolute monthly percentage change has increased from about one percent to about two percent. However, if one uses a measure of volatility that takes into account average quadratic changes the difference between the two periods gets smaller. This suggests that exchange rate changes in the Bretton Woods system were fewer but on average more pronounced.

Although it is generally argued that the higher volatility since 1973 is attributable to the flexible exchange rate system, some reject this argument by emphasizing that a fair comparison of the periods is not possible, because the world economy was not exposed to so many structural changes during the Bretton Woods era as it did afterwards.

An interesting comparison, therefore, is between the volatility of major flexible exchange rates with the more fixed rates of the EMS. This allows a comparison of exchange rate volatility of different exchange rate regimes during the same period. As Table 1 shows, the short-term volatility of bilateral exchange rates between the deutschmark and other major international currencies vis-à-vis which exchange

[1] The period from the collapse of the Bretton Woods system in March 1973 through end-1974 is not taken into account because it can be argued that exchange rates had to adjust to the regime shift during this period.

more details). This supports the view that flexible exchange rates induce higher real exchange rate volatility. Again, this result is not without caveats, because, by evaluating exchange rate volatility within the EMS, exchange rates between relatively small and similar economies are compared.

Table 1: Changes in Monthly Bilateral Real Exchange Rates 1968-1997

	Average Absolute Monthly Percentage Changes	Standard Deviation of Monthly Percentage Changes
1968.01 - 1973.03		
Pound/US Dollar	0.73	1.06
Yen/US Dollar	1.05	1.91
Mark/US Dollar	1.02	1.90
Yen/Mark	0.88	1.68
Mark/Pound	1.02	1.87
1975.01 - 1997.03		
Pound/US Dollar	2.15	2.81
Yen/US Dollar	2.25	2.94
Mark/US Dollar	2.18	2.73
Yen/Mark	2.04	2.51
Mark/Pound	1.74	2.26
1979.04 - 1997.03		
Mark/French Franc	0.52	0.76
Mark/Lira	1.00	1.57
Mark/Peseta	1.08	1.54
Mark/Port. Escudo	1.16	1.55

Source: IMF, International Financial Statistics, and own calculations.

In order to study changes in the overall value of currencies associated with exchange rate changes, bilateral rates can sometimes be misleading. This is so because the currency of a country may fluctuate heavily only vis-à-vis one other currency but may remain fairly stable against the currencies of its other trading partners. In this case, the overall value of the domestic currency and, thus, international trade are not significantly affected. In order to examine the short-term volatility of the overall value of major currencies, we investigate the changes in the real effective exchange rate of major international currencies. We use monthly as well as quarterly data for the U.S. dollar, the Japanese yen, the British pound, and the deutschmark since 1975, which is the first year the IMF published these data. Table 2 reports calculations of volatility measures for the period 1975-1996. The results indicate that volatility was relatively high over the period with average absolute changes in effective exchange rates after taking into account inflation differentials amounting to around two percent on a monthly basis and three percent on a quarterly basis for all currencies taken together. The appendix includes additional calculations for several subperiods.

Table 2: Short-Term Volatility in Real Effective Exchange Rates 1975-1996

Real Effective Exchange Rate	Average Absolute Quarterly Percentage Changes	Standard Deviation of Quarterly Percentage Changes
Monthly data*		
US Dollar	1.56	1.93
British Pound	1.50	2.00
Japanese Yen	2.00	2.70
Deutschmark	0.83	1.05
Quarterly data		
US Dollar	2.70	3.32
British Pound	3.02	4.01
Japanese Yen	4.08	5.14
Deutschmark	1.72	2.11

* As monthly data were not published before 1979, series cover the period 1979-1996.
Source: IMF, International Financial Statistics, and own calculations.

It is sometimes believed that volatility was a particular strong phenomenon during the 1980s because of the heavy fluctuations in the value of the dollar during that period. However, more detailed data shown in Appendix Tables III and IV demonstrate that volatility, although varying over time, was not a phenomenon of the 1980s only. In fact, volatility stayed high during the period 1990-1996 with, for example, average absolute quarterly changes of around 2.5 percent for the U.S. dollar and 4.7 percent for the Japanese yen. In order to more precisely compare the short-term volatility of real effective exchange rates in the 1980s with the one in the 1990s (1990-1996), tests are performed on various null hypotheses. The results shown in Table 3 indicate that the null hypothesis of equal volatility in both periods cannot be rejected at the five percent significance level for any of the four major international currencies.

Table 3: Test of a Change in Short-Term Volatility of the Real Effective Exchange Rate Volatility in the 1990s Compared to the 1980s

	Test value on null hypothesis of equal short-term volatility in the period 1980-1989 and 1990-1996*
U.S. Dollar	1.90 (H0 cannot be rejected)
British pound	0.67 (H0 cannot be rejected)
Japanese yen	-1.91 (H0 cannot be rejected)
Deutschmark	-1.03 (H0 cannot be rejected)

Tests are based on average quadratic quarterly percentage changes. The null hypothesis is rejected if the test value in absolute terms exceeds 1.96 (5% significance level).

Short-term volatility is only one aspect of exchange rate changes experienced since the collapse of the Bretton Woods era. Longer-term fluctuations represent another and more serious aspect of the flexible exchange rate experience. They involve periods of partly several years, during which the exchange rate seems to deviate from its trend. It is often argued that such misalignments are particularly harmful for trade and investment decisions, because standardized hedging instruments do not exist for longer horizons.

Figure 3 shows developments of the real effective exchange rate of the U.S. dollar, the Japanese yen, the British pound, and the deutschmark since 1975. It illustrates that medium-term changes in effective exchange rates, after taking into account inflation differentials, have been significant over the entire period 1975-1997, although deviations from the long-run trend have not been constant over time. The most significant longer-term movements were the rise and the fall of the U.S. dollar in the 1980s and the rise and the fall of the Japanese yen in the 1990s. There can be no doubt that these changes had a sizable impact on the profitability of industries involved in international trade.

A comparison with data from the EMS suggests that medium-term fluctuations of exchange rates were also smaller in this system than in the float. Table 5 shows that, despite the crises in the EMS, the maximum variation of real exchange rates in the EMS was significantly lower than among the major floating currencies. As shown by Table 4, the maximum medium term spread of the listed European currencies was still smaller than the smallest difference of the calculated differences for major exchange rates under the float. This suggests that EMS has also seen less medium-term fluctuations of real exchange rates.

Figure 3: Medium-Term Fluctuations of Real Effective Exchange Rates

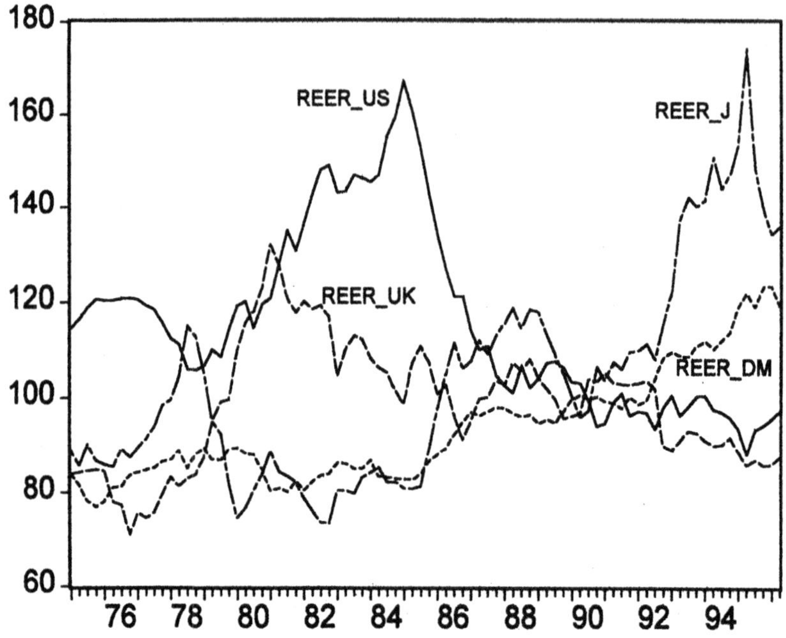

Source: IMF, International Financial Statistics.

An evaluation of exchange rate fluctuations under flexible exchange rates, that is based on a comparison of nominal exchange rate and price developments, does not take into account that the exchange rate is a financial variable, i. e., an asset price. This suggests to compare exchange rate fluctuations with price developments in other asset markets. Data presented in Table 5 indicate that nominal exchange rates, while fluctuating significantly more than consumer prices, exhibit considerably less volatility than stock prices. The results of more formal tests on the differences in volatility are included in Appendix Table V. These also suggest that there is no significant difference between the volatility of nominal effective exchange rates and real effective exchange rates.[2]

[2] This is consistent with earlier findings of Mussa (1986, 1990).

Table 4: Medium-Term Spread of Various Bilateral Real Exchange Rates 1979-1996

Bilateral Real Exchange Rate	Maximum Difference of the Real Exchange Rate (1990=100) over the Period 1979-1996
Flexible Exchange Rates	
Deutschmark/U.S.Dollar	91.89
Deutschmark/Yen	67.71
Deutschmark/Pound	47.98
Pound/Dollar	84.13
Yen/Dollar	95.44
European Monetary System	
Deutschmark/French Franc	18.25
Deutschmark/Lira	40.36
Deutschmark/Peseta	31.52
Deutschmark/Port. Escudo	41.71

Source: IMF, International Financial Statistics, and own calculations.

Table 5: Short-Term Volatility of Consumer Prices, Exchange Rates, and Stock Prices 1975-1997[1)]

	United States	Japan	United Kingdom	Germany
Consumer prices	a) 0.41 b) 0.34	a) 0.42 b) 0.52	a) 0.57 b) 0.64	a) 0.29 b) 0.30
Nominal effective exchange rates	a) 1.41 b) 1.81	a) 1.83 b) 2.44	a) 1.35 b) 1.86	a) 0.71 b) 0.93
Real effective exchange rates	a) 1.56 b) 1.93	a) 2.00 b) 2.70	a) 1.50 b) 2.00	a) 0.83 b) 1.05
Stock prices[2)]	a) 3.21 b) 4.19	a) 4.02 b) 5.39	a) 3.76 b) 4.85	a) 3.99 b) 4.90

1) Numbers shown under a) are average absolute monthly percentage changes, under b) standard deviation of average monthly percentage changes.

2) Calculations are based on the Dow Jones index for the U.S., the Nikkei index for Japan, the FTSE for the U.K. (only 1978.2-1997.8) and the DAX index for Germany (only 1988.01-1997.-08).

Source: IMF, International Financial Statistics.

The observation of higher volatility of flexible exchange rates compared to the Bretton Woods era and compared to the EMS has led to the frequent criticism that flexible exchange rates are excessively volatile. This, in turn, would add undesirable risk to international transactions. This conclusion is drawn from studies which found that exchange rates change more than is implied by the change in the fundamentals related to specific exchange rate models. However, some have argued that this conclusion is not convincing because it is dependent on the exchange rate models used and is, therefore, only as reliable as the exchange rate models applied. Empirical research on exchange rate models show very poor results for virtually all prominent exchange rate models.[3] The numerous testing efforts on empirical exchange rate models have not changed this impression. Studies that presented more hopeful empirical results, often seem to be rather fragile to the specification of the time period used. This even led Frankel and Rose (1995) to conclude "... we, like much of the profession, are doubtful of the value of further time-series modelling of exchange rates at high or medium frequencies using macroeconomic models."

A consequence of the poor empirical results of exchange rate models for in-sample fitting is the poor out-of-sample forecast precision of all structural exchange rate models. Meese and Rogoff (1983) demonstrate in their seminal paper that prominent structural exchange rate models have very poor out-of-sample forecast precision and cannot beat a simple martingale process. Later studies could not reject these findings at shorter horizons.[4]

This has not been the only grounds on which the hypothesis of excessive volatility of flexible exchange rates has been rejected. Frenkel and Goldstein (1986) and a number of authors emphasized that exchange rates should be regarded as asset prices and, hence, one should expect them to fluctuate more than the traditionally used fundamentals, such as output prices, wages, and income. Moreover, since these variables are subject to rigidities, one may even argue that it is desirable to allow flexible exchange rates to be more volatile.

Some literature has studied the empirical evidence of exchange rate models across fixed and floating regimes. They often investigate not only nominal exchange rate volatility but also the relationship between nominal and real exchange rate volatility. For virtually all major currencies, nominal exchange rate variability during the post Bretton Woods era has translated into real exchange rate variability. From a theoretical perspective, this observation would result from a flexible-price model when most shocks originate in the real sector of the economy. Since the experience suggests that real shocks must have been greater during the flexible exchange rate era since 1973, Obstfeld (1995) holds the view that the flexible-price model is unable to explain why real shocks rise when

---

[3] For surveys, see MacDonald (1990), MacDonald and Taylor (1992), and Frankel and Rose (1995). For recent work, see MacDonald (1997).

[4] Only at longer horizons, structural models performed better; see, for example, Chinn and Meese (1995) and Mark (1994).

nominal exchange rates can fluctuate more. However, this implication may not be true. It could well be that real shocks increased after 1973 for purely exogenous reasons and that exchange rate regimes have to be considered endogenous. The view of more pronounced real shocks is supported by the fact that, since 1973, the world economy has experienced stronger raw material price changes, faster structural changes, and greater swings in government policies, which are likely to have contributed to more pronounced real shocks in the 25 years following the collapse of the Bretton Woods system than during the 25 years before. One problem in associating the observation of high nominal and high real exchange rate fluctuations with dynamics described by the monetary flex-price model is that the basic assumption, i.e., price flexibility, is in contrast to empirical evidence. Very detailed and thorough studies by Engel (1993) and Engel and Rogers (1995) on consumer price dynamics in the United States and Canada find that price movements are consistent with the assumption of sticky consumer prices.

Flood and Rose (1993) present an interesting study in this context. Examining monetary exchange rate models, the authors find that volatility of money, output, and prices is not significantly different between fixed and flexible exchange rate regimes, but the exchange rate variability is several times higher under a float than in a fixed exchange rate system.[5] This suggests that standard macroeconomic variables of this approach have little influence on the exchange rate volatility and that the exchange rate regime itself affects exchange rate volatility. As a consequence, this raises serious doubts about the „nominal exchange rate neutrality" implied by a number of models. However, several authors debate this view. For example, Stockman (1988) emphasizes that real exchange rate variability is induced by innovations in tastes and technologies. In addition, he argues that these changes have been more pronounced after the collapse of the Bretton Woods system so that real exchange rate changes would have been larger in any case. The drawback of this hypothesis is that changes in taste and technology cannot be observed by econometricians.

Another reason why structural exchange rate models have shown unsatisfactory results could have been gradual expectation adjustments due to uncertainty in financial markets. An example for the latter case is uncertainty resulting from the difficulty in identifying the changes in policy strategies in observable data. For instance, money supply, in addition to reflecting monetary policy, is also affected by random influences. As a result, agents may find it difficult to attribute observed deviations of money supply from the trend to random or to policy influences. As Lewis (1989a, b) and Frenkel (1995) show, agents may apply learning procedures like Bayesian updating or least square learning in order to find out over time, which the true process of economic policy is. This can lead to exchange rate dynamics not to be explained by observed

---

[5] More specifically, the authors rearrange the equation for the monetary approach to get $s_t-\alpha(i_t-i_t^*)= (m_t-m_t^*)-\beta(y_t-y_t^*)-(\varepsilon_t-\varepsilon_t^*)$. When calculating the volatility of exchange rates, they look at the whole left-hand side of the equation.

macroeconomic variables. However, the difficulty with this approach is that it is confined to major policy changes and can, thus, only explain part of the medium-term exchange rate volatility.

In sum, the hypothesis that flexible exchange rates have been excessively volatile is still disputed. One of the open questions is whether the fact that nominal and real exchange rates have been more volatile after 1973 than before is attributable to flexible exchange rates as such or whether it reflects more pronounced economic shocks during the era after Bretton Woods. Some indication may be derived from the investigation of speculation in a flexible exchange rate system.

2.1.2 Destabilizing Speculation through Bubbles and Noise Traders?

Given the finding of empirical studies that exchange rate volatility has been higher in flexible exchange rate regimes than under fixed rates and given the unsatisfactory results of empirical exchange rate models, the question arises what the possible explanations for the unexplained exchange rate dynamics are. The literature provides three approaches to answer this question. The first emphasizes that the foreign exchange market is efficient and some variables that determine exchange rates cannot be observed directly. A second approach is based on the possibility that rational speculative bubbles can occur. The third approach argues that increased volatility under flexible exchange rates is due to bandwagon effects, which are important characteristics of foreign exchange markets. By implication, this approach stresses that the assumption of rational expectations does not hold in currency markets in the short run. As a consequence, bandwagon effects can drive exchange rates away from their fundamental values. The previous section addressed the first explanation. In this section, we focus on the second and third approach.

The development of rational speculative bubbles has been suggested by proponents of the rational expectations hypothesis as an explanation of exchange rate movements unrelated to macroeconomic variables. In monetary models that yield a reduced form as the solution of a differential or difference equation, the bubble term is the indeterminate term of the solution. When focusing on the influence of macroeconomic variables, this term is set equal to zero. However, as pointed out by, for example, Singleton (1987), this term can arise in foreign exchange markets. Unfortunately, we cannot say anything about what causes such rational speculative bubbles to develop and burst because these factors are exogenous. In addition, one would have to explain why these bubbles seem to be more frequent under flexible exchange rates. Empirical evidence on rational speculative bubbles has been relatively limited and mixed. In assessing the literature to date on this topic, it seems difficult to imagine that this represents a strong explanation of exchange rate volatility.

The third category of explanations for flexible exchange rate volatility starts from the microstructure of foreign exchange markets. A number of studies raise doubts about the validity of rational expectations assumption for the foreign exchange market. A number of studies on the formation of exchange rate expectations, for example by Frankel and Froot (1987), Froot and Ito (1989), Taylor, Allen and Menkhoff (1992), and Ito (1994), study survey data collected by survey services as The Economist and American Express. Most of them highlight that foreign exchange traders extrapolate recent exchange rate changes for their short-run projections. One of the reasons can be seen in the widespread use of technical analyses for short-term purchases and sales of foreign exchange. Studies on the microstructure of the foreign exchange market also suggest that these short-term traders dominate the daily turnover in the foreign exchange markets.[6] Since most of them have to close any open position they generate during the day within the same working day, their horizon is mostly only a few hours. Since they are extrapolative in the short run, they generate bandwagon effects and are, thus, destabilizing, which is in contrast to the hopes of Friedman (1953). In addition, survey studies demonstrate that believes in the foreign exchange market are heterogenous. This is an important reason for the trading volumes.

Traders with very short-term horizons are often referred to as chartists or noise traders. The bandwagon effect induced by them frequently translates into exchange rate dynamics which exhibit bubble characteristics. Several recent papers analyze foreign exchange dynamics under the assumption that the market includes chartists and other traders, e.g., traders with rational expectations and traders with regressive expectations (often called fundamentalists). As shown by DeLong et al. (1990), Cutler et al. (1991), and Frenkel (1997), this leads to dynamics which can take very different forms and which can also look like runs or frequent bubbles. However, they can be expected to be very irregular. Frankel and Froot (1988) and Goldberg and Frydman (1993) show that the share of chartists and fundamentalists may vary over time depending on the accuracy of their forecasts. De Grauwe and Dewachter (1990) show that the interaction of noise traders and fundamentalists can create chaotic exchange rate dynamics.

Additional studies on the microstructure of the foreign exchange market examine reasons for variations in volatility over time, the relationship of volatility and trading volumes, and the behavior of market-makers. Frankel and Rose (1995) present a survey on the recent literature in this area.

In sum, the results of the research of the microstructure of currency markets has generated a number of important results in understanding flexible exchange rates. Although a number of economists prefer to analyze currency markets using equilibrium theory and rational expectations, the overwhelming evidence from the microstructure of foreign exchange markets is that noise traders or chartists have an important market share. There can be little doubt that noise trading is one of the

---

[6] For studies that examine the relationship between turnover and volatility, see the survey of Frankel and Rose (1995).

driving forces behind deviations of exchange rates from the levels explained by fundamentals. Since the results of some exchange rate models which are based on macroeconomic variables already suggest some overshooting of exchange rates, noise trading adds further volatility to the exchange rates. Therefore, this effect has sometimes been called „overshooting the overshooting equilibrium". In this sense, the microstructure seems to be able to explain short-run volatility and possibly some of the misalignment. The study of the foreign exchange market structure has contributed to explain why exchange rates may be off the fundamentally determined equilibrium path in the short run and why the empirical evidence of structural models is so poor. The dominance of short-term oriented participants in the currency markets may also be a reason why longer-term policy changes often take quite some time to translate into exchange rate effects. Clarida and Gali (1994) find considerable lags between policy changes and the full reflection in the exchange rate. This suggests that we may indeed have to adopt a longer-term perspective when we use structural exchange rate models to explain currency market developments. However, the research in this area is still fairly new and questions about how heterogeneity evolves over time, how the shorter-term and the longer-term can be integrated and what causes speculative movements still need to be investigated in more detail.

The results of this research also have important implications for the evaluation of exchange rate regimes. As noise trading seems to be destabilizing in the short run, this behavior can be seen as a disadvantage of a flexible exchange rate regime. In the controversy over the better exchange rate system, critics of a float can be expected to point to this characteristic of flexible exchange rates.

Given the fact that flexible exchange rates have been more volatile than the underlying fundamentals and given the research reviewed in this section, one controversy is whether or not higher volatility has had harmful effects on trade, investment, and financial integration. The next sections investigate whether volatility was associated with such economic costs.

2.1.3 Is Exchange Rate Volatility Harmful?

2.1.3.1 The Impact on International Trade

One of the most important criticisms about exchange rate fluctuations is that it allegedly impedes international trade. Over the past five decades, world trade has virtually always grown faster than world output, but the difference declined after the end of the Bretton Woods era (Table 6). However, one needs to take into account that the growth rates of both world trade and world output declined. As Table 6 shows this ratio only changed dramatically in the early 1980s, but this is a reflection of the impact of the second oil price shock. Later on, this ratio increased again and in the 1990s it has even been at a somewhat higher level than during the time of fixed exchange rates under the Bretton Woods system.

Table 6: Growth of World Trade and World Output

Growth Rates (in percent)	1950 bis 1954	1955 bis 1959	1960 bis 1964	1965 bis 1972	1973 bis 1979	1980 bis 1984	1985 bis 1989	1990 bis 1994	1995 bis 1998
World Trade (1)	7.5	6.7	9.6	8.4	5	2	5.6	5.1	7.2
World Output (2)	4.7	4.2	5.1	4.8	3.5	2.2	3.8	2.4	4.1
Difference (1)-(2)	2.8	2.5	4.5	3.6	1.5	-0.2	1.8	2.7	3.1
Ratio (1)/(2)	1.60	1.59	1.88	1.75	1.43	0.91	1.47	2.13	1.76

Source: International Monetary Fund, World Economic Outlook (data for 1997 and 1998 are estimates of the IMF).

Although the hypothesis that higher exchange rate volatility reduces trade because of the increased risk associated with international trade may be intuitive at first glance, economic theory shows that the impact of more pronounced exchange rate fluctuations on the volume of international trade is ambiguous. This is so because the total effect comprises a substitution and an income effect. The substitution effect reflects the decline in export incentives when exchange rates involve more uncertainty and, thus, exports become more risky. The income effect arises because lower utility derived from risk-related lower expected export earnings could increase efforts to compensate this effect through more exports (Goldstein (1995), De Grauwe (1988)).

One could argue that exchange rate uncertainty can be eliminated through hedging. However, since hedging implies costs, this argument only points to the monetary equivalent of the exchange risk. The question is, what difference do flexible rates make? After all, hedging may be used even in a fixed exchange rate system because, if the fixed rate is changed, losses can be quite substantial, amounting, for example, from five to ten percent on the very day of the change of the peg. In this case, the change in the exchange rate may be quite disruptive. Even in the Bretton Woods system, exporters and importers could not exclude exchange rate changes, although those changes hardly occurred before the mid-1960s. In the European Monetary System, realignments have also included substantial changes in the fixed exchange rates. The question, therefore, is whether the higher exchange rate volatility after 1973 shown in the previous section can indeed be set equal to higher exchange rate uncertainty. On the basis of the preceding argument, the answer is far from being clear. However, for simplicity and in order to further explore the implications, volatility and uncertainty are treated as synonymous.

There is a vast number of empirical studies on the effects of exchange rate volatility on international trade. Goldstein (1995), Sapir et al. (1994), Edison and Melvin (1990), and an IMF study (1984) present surveys on the evidence from time-series analyses. These studies typically regress the total export volume of a country on the short-run volatility of the exchange rate and on other variables which, according to economic theory, influence export volumes (in particular, the level of real output or income, the relative price of traded goods). The majority of these studies focus on industrial countries. Taking the various empirical studies together, the results on whether there is a significant influence of exchange rate volatility on international trade are very mixed. The studies either find a negative effect or no effect. As a whole, they cannot be used to support the view that trade was impeded by exchange rate volatility.

Another empirical approach pursued in the literature in order to test the influence of exchange rate uncertainty on trade is the examination of bilateral trade flows in the framework of cross-sectional studies. Using a comprehensive pool of data, they typically try to estimate an imperfect substitutes trade model or a gravity model.[7] In the end the regressions try to explain export and import volumes between pairs of countries mainly through real exchange rate volatility, non-economic variables (like proximity to a trading partner and common language), and dummy variables reflecting nonparametric factors (like common membership in a preferential trading arrangement or adjacency). Earlier work includes the studies of De Grauwe (1988) and Brada and Mendez (1988). As Frankel and Wei (1995a, b) note in their more recent and very comprehensive studies, such an approach involves the problem of simultaneous causality: an estimated negative effect of exchange rate volatility on bilateral trade flows could arise from the fact that a government tries to stabilize the exchange rate, in particular, vis-à-vis the most important trading partners. Without taking into account this problem, the authors find a negative effect of exchange rate volatility on trade flows, which, however, is extremely small and even declining in the 1970s and 1980s.[8] They conclude that by the mid-1980s this effect has even disappeared and, indeed turns positive. It is interesting that Frenkel and Wei (1995b), when taking into account the problem or simultaneity in the regressions by using an instrumental variable approach, find that the negative effect is statistically significant only before 1970, i.e., during a period of the Bretton Woods era.

---

[7] According to the gravity model bilateral trade depends positively on the product of the two countries' GNPs and negatively on the distance between the two countries.

[8] Their estimates imply that the elimination of exchange rate volatility worldwide would have increased the volume of world trade in 1980 by less 0.01 percent. Eliminating exchange rate volatility altogether within the EU, the effect would have been even smaller.

Since other cross-sectional studies also yield mixed evidence, it is fair to say that the hypothesis of a negative impact of exchange rate volatility on international trade has no solid empirical basis or, at least, this is not the case anymore. However, it is interesting to ask why the negative effect, which some studies find, has diminished over time. Goldstein (1995) sees the most plausible explanation in the greater availability of hedging instruments. Indeed, data on the variety of these instruments (e.g., forward market operations, currency futures, currency options, and currency swaps) and their volumes suggest that hedging is more widely spread today than two decades ago. Due to technological progress, it has also become less expensive to use these instruments, as, for example, the costs of closely monitoring their price developments and purchasing them has declined. This also indicates that, contrary to claims of Kenen (1994b), firms are fairly familiar with the hedging opportunities which various instruments offer. A problem with data on forward market operations and derivatives is that the rise in their volume also reflects an increase in their use for currency speculation. However, it seems implausible that the increase in their use is exclusively attributable to more speculation.

Despite the intuition of the argument according to which the increase in derivative trading has reduced the negative impact of volatility on trade, other reasons also seem to play a role for this change. First, the growth of multinational corporations with their possibility to diversify production and use of transfer pricing could have reduced the impact of exchange rate fluctuations on the volume of trade. After all, according to an estimate of UNCTAD (1994), intrafirm trade of multinationals account for about a third of world trade.[9] Second, firms are aware of increased sunk costs involved in penetrating a market and, thus, have increasingly adopted a pricing to market strategy (Hooper and Marquey (1993)). Third, firms have learned over the years that exchange rate changes are often transitory, which has led to a smaller response to exchange rate changes. This decline in price elasticities of demand is confirmed by the study of Hooper and Marquez (1993).

2.1.3.2 The Impact on Investment and Growth

It has sometimes been argued that the decline in growth rates of industrial countries, which can be observed comparing the flexible exchange rate era with the Bretton Woods system, is related to lower investment ratios, which, in turn, are a reflection of higher short-run exchange rate variability (Bretton Woods Commission (1994)). However, neither economic theory nor the results of empirical findings yield strong support for this hypothesis. Economic theory is ambiguous about the effect of exchange rate volatility on investment. If we use exchange rate volatility and exchange rate uncertainty again as synonyms, we can

[9] This order of magnitude is consistent with the study of Grant et al. (1993).

take recourse to the theory of the firm. The latter tells us that increased uncertainty does not necessarily lead to lower profit opportunities. On the contrary, it can well lead to higher investment if profit convexity in prices is assumed and risk aversion is not too high.[10]

Among the few existing empirical studies of the investment response to exchange rate fluctuations, the analysis of Pindyck and Solimano (1993) is the most comprehensive. They examine 14 OECD countries and 16 developing countries for the period 1960-1990. They present several sets of regression analyses. The more comprehensive regressions try to identify the quantitative effects of different possible sources affecting the variability of the marginal profitability of capital. The sources considered are, among others, the mean rate of inflation, the variability of inflation, and the variability of the real exchange rate. All explanatory variables other than the mean inflation rate are consistently insignificant as a determinant of profitability fluctuations. Only when inflation or inflation variability are left out in the regressions, the volatility variable comes out as statistically significant with a negative sign. In another study, Goldberg (1993) investigates the investment behavior of U.S. industries during the period 1970-1989. She finds ambiguous results with respect to the influence of real exchange rate volatility on investment activity. The results differ both in magnitude and significance levels for different industries and different subperiods.

In sum, the different empirical studies, taken as a whole, cannot be seen as supporting the hypothesis of a negative impact of exchange rate volatility on investment. This applies in particular to industrial countries.[11] The evidence seems to support the hypothesis somewhat more for developing countries (see also Goldstein (1995)). However, my own reading of the results of the empirical work to date is that, in developing countries, exchange rate volatility reflects general economic instability, which, in turn, often leads to price instability and affects investment through this channel. In addition, for risk averse firms, financial markets in developing countries offer less hedging possibilities against short-term uncertainty than in advanced economies. In contrast, as mentioned before, in advanced economies, hedging instruments against exchange rate risk have increased both in volume and in diversity, so that hedging has become less expensive and can better meet a firm's needs. In these countries, routinely available currency swaps now offer the possibility to even hedge risks related to maturities of up to ten years. Fischer (1993) points out that international trade of

[10] This follows, for example, from the analysis of Abel (1983).

[11] In more recent studies on the factors that caused the decline in growth and productivity in industrial countries beginning in the 1970s, exchange rate volatility is hardly even mentioned anymore as a cause. By contrast, the reasons that have emerged as the most important and commonly agreed upon are the sharp increases in oil prices and other raw material prices in the 1970s, the increase in inflation, a slowdown in R&D expenditure, and measurement problems of productivity in the services sector, which may have led to an underestimation of the true productivity growth (Goldstein (1995)).

developing countries is more negatively affected by inflation than by exchange rate fluctuations. He points out that high levels of inflation and inflation volatility in developing countries often reflect the inability of governments to control the macroeconomy, which, in turn, is likely to represent an impediment for investment.

2.1.3.3 The Impact on Foreign Direct Investment and Integration

An important hypothesis about the effects of exchange rate fluctuations is that it exerts a positive impact on foreign direct investment. This is mainly because foreign direct investment allows firms to diversify and increase their production flexibility. It isolates part of their profitability from the effects of exchange rate fluctuations. Although it has often been argued that, for example, Japanese car manufacturers engaged in foreign direct investment in the U.S. exactly because of the fluctuations in the dollar-yen exchange rate, more systematic empirical studies have not yet yielded a solid basis for the hypotheses of a positive impact of exchange rate volatility of foreign direct investment. Cushman (1988) found some support for the hypothesis for U.S. foreign direct investment inflows and outflows between 1963 and 1986 and Goldberg and Kolstad (1994) confirmed this result for bilateral flows between the U.S. on the one hand and the U.K., Canada, and Japan on the other hand. However, the hypothesis was rejected by Bayley and Tavlas (1991) and Morsink and Molle (1991), whose results even suggest that exchange rate volatility may have negative effects on foreign direct investment flows.

As with most studies related to foreign direct investment, the results always have to be interpreted with caution, since the measurement of foreign direct investment only captures the direct capital transfer in a given period. However, this only yields a partial picture. For example, gradual capital formation undertaken by the firm which once was a regular foreign direct investment of multinational, does not enter the balance of payments as such anymore and is, therefore, not accounted as foreign direct investment.

The welfare effects of changes in foreign direct investment induced by exchange rate volatility cannot be directly derived from the volume effects. As Cooper (1988) and Goldstein (1995) point out, any globalization of production activities attributable to higher exchange rate fluctuations involves diseconomies, because the dispersion of production leads to a loss in economies of scale.

One could also argue that high volatility of exchange rates adds additional risk on international capital flows and, thus, a negative effect on capital market integration can be expected. However, it seems to be difficult to find evidence that could support this hypothesis. Capital market integration has grown steadily over the past 30 years. Table 7 shows that cross-border financial transactions have increased significantly more than GDP. With the elimination of capital controls in most industrial countries, capital markets are now more integrated than ever. Thus, it seems that investors do not have a clear preference for fixed exchange rates.

Table 7: Cross-Border Financial Transactions with Nonresidents as Percentage of GDP[1]

	1965	1975	1985	1995
Canada	1.9%	4.3%	3.4%	8.8%[2]
Germany	-	6.5%	8.8%	11.8%
United Kingdom	-	2.3%	26.6%	28%
USA	-	1.9%	3.6%	5.8%
France	-	5.6%	3.9%	4.7%

Source: IMF, International Financial Statistics, and own calculations.

[1] Data include transactions with nonresidents in financial assets, such as corporate securities, bonds, money market instruments, and financial derivatives.

[2] Data refer to 1994.

Taking the evidence on the effects of volatility of trade, investment, and financial integration together, there is hardly any evidence that the short-term volatility of flexible exchange rates has had a damaging effect on macroeconomic performance. Both trade and investment seem to be better able today to deal with exchange rate fluctuation than at the end of the Bretton Woods system. Although longer-term deviations from fundamental equilibrium values are more harmful, they seem to have led to efficiency-increasing strategies of firms by diversifying production and distribution. The increased number of multinational enterprises, together with the widening and deepening of financial markets offering a broad spectrum of hedging instruments, can explain why firms have become better prepared to cope even with medium-term exchange rate swings.

2.2 The Insulating Effects of Flexible Exchange Rates

A major advantage of a flexible exchange rate system suggested by early proponents of a float was the claim that it generates an insulating effect against foreign disturbances. Experience to date shows that these hopes were too optimistic. On the one hand there is widespread agreement that flexible exchange rates have indeed been able to insulate individual economies from foreign inflation trends over the long-run (see, for example, Obstfeld (1995)). On the other hand, the experience suggests that flexible exchange rates do not eliminate the transmission of business cycles. Table 8 shows the correlation of unemployment rates in the United States, Japan, Germany, and France and shows that international business cycle synchronization, while diminishing after the collapse of the Bretton Woods system, remained significant under flexible exchange rates. One factor which may have contributed to this result could have been the occurrence of common shocks (oil price shocks in 1973, 1979/80, and 1995/6) that impacted on the business cycles in all four countries.

The theoretical controversy on the insulating effects of flexible exchange rates can be investigated using, for example, the model originally developed by Obstfeld (1985). In this Keynesian two-country model, asset markets adjust faster than goods markets and the exchange rate ensures continuous portfolio balance. A key feature of the model is that expectations take into account that the exchange rate determines the equilibrium terms of trade between economies in the long run. The model allows to examine short- and medium-term dynamics of output, prices, interest rates, and exchange rates following a monetary or a real shock and can explain the early exaggeration of the insulating properties of flexible exchange rates.[12] If a positive demand shock occurs in one economy, either through the private sector or through expansionary fiscal policies, the domestic currency appreciates in real terms and the real interest rate as well as prices in both economies rise. Thus, there is no insulation against a demand shock from abroad.

Table 8: Correlation Matrix of Annual Unemployment Rates

Country	United States	Japan	Germany	France
1960 - 1972:				
United States	1.00	0.57	0.35	0.48
Japan	...	1.00	0.91	0.93
Germany	...	...	1.00	0.94
France	...	...	...	1.00

[12] For some criticism of the structure of the model see Cooper (1985) and Krugman (1985).

Table 8: Continued

1975 - 1996:				
United States	1.00	0.22	0.38	0.11
Japan	...	1.00	0.78	0.59
Germany	...	...	1.00	0.72
France	...	...	...	1.00

However, the model demonstrates that medium-term insulation is provided by a flexible exchange rate system if the shocks originating abroad are purely monetary. In this case, due to assumed monetary neutrality, the world real interest rate and the real exchange rate are not affected. Spillovers from foreign monetary shocks in form of domestic price effects, thus, do not occur. This also implies that each country can indeed choose its own long-run inflation rate. It confirms the early hopes associated with flexible exchange rates. The model can easily be extended by including changes in expected money growth and expected demand shifts. However, the thrust of the results remains unchanged.

There are several conclusions for the controversy over flexible exchange rates that can be derived from this analysis. First, the exchange rate depends on both monetary and real factors because it is a variable which, together with other factors, determines both goods market and asset market equilibrium. Second, if the shocks are real shocks, one can expect the nominal and the real exchange rate to be highly correlated. Over the flexible exchange rate period since 1973, nominal and real effective exchange rates and their fluctuations have been highly correlated. We present supportive tests for the similarity in volatility in Appendix Table V. Third, inasmuch as foreign monetary shocks have short-term real effects, flexible exchange rates do not even insulate against monetary disturbances in the short run. For example, a permanent unanticipated decline in the foreign money growth rate reduces foreign output and prices and, hence, induces a real appreciation of the foreign currency. The domestic economy benefits from the real depreciation and, hence, experiences an increase in output and prices, if this effect dominates the direct demand effect of lower exports to the foreign economy associated with the output decline abroad.

2.3 Can Central Banks Manage the Float through Intervention?

In the 1980s as well as in the 1990s, central banks of the main industrial countries have intervened at a relatively large scale in the foreign exchange markets in order to "manage the float." This has created interest in both economic theory and empirical studies in the effectiveness of these interventions. Almekinders and Eijffinger (1991) and Edison (1993) provide surveys of studies in this area.

Pilbeam (1991) discusses the question of desirability of central bank intervention in the foreign exchange market. This section briefly reviews the results of recent theoretical and empirical work.

When analyzing through which channels foreign exchange market intervention affects the dynamics of exchange rates, the way intervention is modelled is crucial. However, common to all approaches developed in the literature is the distinction between sterilized and unsterilized intervention. Usually, sterilized intervention is seen as having only a limited direct effect on the exchange rate. One channel through which sterilized intervention could affect the exchange rate is through its effect on the relative supply of foreign and domestic assets if these two asset types are imperfect substitutes. For example, if the central bank sells foreign exchange to stabilize the domestic currency against a depreciation, international reserves of the central bank decline and domestic assets in circulation decrease. Since the private sector now holds relatively more foreign assets, the risk premium associated with holding domestic assets can be expected to decline. This can be shown in a portfolio model or even in a flow model. For example, Black (1985) demonstrates in an extended Mundell-Fleming model that sterilized foreign exchange sales of the central bank reduces the uncertainty of speculators about future exchange rate changes, which, in turn, increases their willingness to purchase domestic currency in the foreign exchange market. However, this would probably require sizable amounts of intervention to affect the uncertainty perceived by the private sector. Thus, whether the effect on risk and uncertainty resulting from sterilized intervention is strong enough to significantly affect the course of the exchange rate is a disputed and ultimately an empirical question.

A second channel through which sterilized intervention could affect the exchange rate is through a signalling effect, which was first introduced by Mussa (1981). This effect arises if the private sector derives new information about future monetary policy even from sterilized intervention and changes its expectation about the future exchange rate. For example, a central bank sale of foreign exchange could be interpreted as signalling a more restrictive future monetary policy. However, this effect may be questionable. As long as the private sector has no clear indication of changes in the monetary policy stance, it may not alter its portfolio decisions. On the contrary, the signalling effect could well go in the opposite direction: sterilized intervention not followed by other policy decisions may indicate to financial markets that no major effect on the exchange rate can be exerted by the central bank. In such case, a strengthening of the currency does not follow central bank sales of foreign exchange.

Unsterilized intervention is in essence not different from monetary policy. Therefore, it can be seen as conducting monetary policy through the foreign exchange market. Almekinders (1994) studies a number of structural exchange rate models and shows that all of them imply that unsterilized intervention is effective, although the channels through which foreign exchange market intervention affects the exchange rate as well as the implications for money supply and interest rates are partly different.

Koedijk et al. (1995) develop a model similar to Krugman (1991) in which they show that the instantaneous effectiveness of central bank intervention in the foreign exchange market tends to be larger the more implicit the width of the band of fluctuation is, which the monetary authorities are willing to tolerate. In their approach, uncertainty of market participants about the extent of tolerated exchange rate fluctuations leads to a lower probability, with which financial markets expect the central bank to abandon the initial band of fluctuation. By contrast, if this band is more explicit, as is the case in a formal target zone arrangement, a movement of the exchange rate towards the margin increases the immediate realignment probability. They find empirical support for their hypothesis from a study of the Belgian intervention during 1979-92 in the EMS and U.S. intervention after the Louvre Accord in 1987. However, their results should be interpreted with caution, because their empirical study focuses on a relatively short period of both the EMS and the float.

One problem in the investigation of foreign exchange market intervention arises form the fact that its effects are typically studied within structural exchange rate models. However, as discussed earlier, these models do not perform well empirically. Hardly any work has been done to examine whether intervention is a powerful instrument in alternative models such as those that are based on microstructure analyses of foreign exchange markets. Exceptions are DeGrauwe (1989) and Hung (1991a, b). De Grauwe (1989) doubts that even unsterilized intervention can change the perception of the financial markets about the appropriate exchange rate. He argues that, due to the lack of a commonly accepted exchange rate model, financial markets may not take into account fiscal and monetary changes properly. Therefore, deviations of exchange rates from fundamental values cannot be reduced by unsterilized intervention. By contrast, Hung (1991a, b) shows that noise traders offer the central bank a possibility for successful interventions. This is the case if the central bank can stay anonymous in the foreign exchange market and if it can affect the trendline used by noise traders in the direction it wants the exchange rate to move. Then, short-run oriented traders would reverse their foreign exchange positions and the intended exchange rate effect results.

Another problem of studies of foreign exchange market interventions is the data availability. Complete and detailed series on foreign exchange market interventions are usually not published by central banks. This makes it difficult to estimate the reaction function of individual central banks or the effects of different types of interventions satisfactorily.

In sum, the question of the effectiveness of central bank intervention in the foreign exchange market is still a debated question. Sterilized intervention seems to have at most a short-lived effect on the course of exchange rates. Unsterilized intervention may not necessarily be successful depending on which factors drive the exchange rate.

3 Controversies on Fixed Exchange Rates

3.1 More Monetary and Fiscal Discipline under Fixed Exchange Rates?

It has often been argued that fixed exchange rates exert a disciplinary effect on both monetary and fiscal policy (Obstfeld (1985)). This would serve to bring about price stability and low government indebtedness. By contrast, under flexible exchange rates, governments may have an incentive to adopt overexpansionary policies because they are not anymore bound by a peg. Such expansion could ultimately be harmful to both the domestic economy and its trading partners. This suggests that there can be a trade-off between monetary autonomy and discipline. However, this conclusion is not undisputed.

We first examine the discipline argument for monetary policy. The alleged disciplinary mechanism of fixed exchange rate regimes is straightforward. If the domestic economy has a higher inflation rate than the country to which its currency is pegged a real appreciation evolves, which reduces demand for domestically produced goods and increases demand for imports. This leads to recessionary effects in the domestic economy and puts downward pressure on the price level. Ultimately, the economy has to adopt the same low inflation rate as the partner country. In addition, negative effects on the balance of payments may force the government to intervene in the foreign exchange market, which, assuming unsterilized intervention, reduces the money supply and adds to the downward pressure on the domestic price level.

However, the possibility that a fixed exchange rate system exerts more disciplinary pressure requires that the access to international reserves is highly limited. This is, for example, the case under a gold standard or a currency board system. However, in a fixed exchange rate system, monetary expansion can still occur without creating economic tensions if it takes the form of internationally coordinated monetary expansion. In this case, fixed exchange rates would not be able to automatically exert discipline on individual countries. Moreover, a flexible exchange rate system could also exert monetary discipline if a government associates unfavorable effects with a depreciation of its currency.

Svensson (1994) examines whether fixed exchange rates induce more price stability through monetary discipline and derives the result that fixed exchange rates are less efficient in achieving price stability through monetary discipline than the profession thought several years ago. He argues that the process through which price stability is brought about is too slow because fixed exchange rates are often not credible enough to modify wage and price setting. He uses the EMS as an example and points to several countries, for which such discipline was sought through the means of fixed nominal exchange rates during the period 1987-92 when virtually no realignment occurred in the EMS. These countries experienced a period of several years of continuing real appreciations of their currencies.

In addition, fixed exchange rates may induce procyclical and, thus, destabilizing monetary policy. The intuition is as follows. A country that gets hit by a recession experiences a decline in inflation. Since the peg implies a given interest rate from abroad, the real interest rate rises, which makes monetary policy contractionary and, thus, procyclical. If financial markets subsequently expect the currency to be devaluated, the monetary authorities have to increase the interest rate, which raises the real interest rate even further and makes monetary policy even more contractionary or procyclical. This argument has been put forward first by Walters (1986) and has been developed more formally by Giavazzi and Spaventa (1990) as well as Miller and Sutherland (1991).

Obstfeld (1995) provides an interesting empirical study which can shed some light on the question of monetary discipline and price stability. He uses an ARIMA approach in order to study price persistence during fixed and floating exchange rate periods. If fixed exchange rates exert more monetary discipline one would expect that lower freedom for monetary policy results in less persistence of inflation. However, the Obstfeld's results cast doubt on this hypothesis. Comparing the coefficients of the lagged autocorrelations of consumer price indices he finds basically no difference for the United States between the two periods. For most other countries, his results show somewhat smaller inflation persistence under fixed rates but the differences to the float are statistically not significant.

We now turn to the disciplinary effect or fixed exchange rates on fiscal policy. The common argument is that, in a fixed exchange rate system, expansionary fiscal policies induce a balance of payments deficit which will eventually force the government to abandon the peg. Since it is assumed that this leads to high costs for the government, this would deter the government from pursuing lax fiscal policies in the first place (Frenkel et al. (1991)). Hence, fixed exchange rates induce fiscal policies that are consistent with the peg.

Buiter et al. (1993) as well as Svensson (1994) interpret the EMS experience of fiscal divergence as empirical evidence against this view. Tornell and Velasco (1995) see the recent experience with the French Franc zone countries in West Africa also at odds with the hypothesis of fiscal discipline resulting from fixed exchange rates. In addition, they stress that many exchange rate-based stabilization programs in Latin America have also been extremely unsuccessful in reducing fiscal deficits.

How can these observations be explained? With fixed exchange rates, higher bond-financed government expenditure induces an increase in the interest rate and in capital inflows, which can even improve the net foreign asset position. As long as there is confidence in the government finances, there is no automatic disciplinary effect on fiscal policy in a fixed exchange rate system. Only when confidence declines, governments will find it increasingly difficult to run high fiscal deficits. However, this is also the case under a flexible exchange rate system.

It could even be argued that flexible exchange rates may generate more fiscal discipline. If the government, for example, considerably loosens the fiscal stance the induced rise in the budget deficit leads to a significant appreciation. As a consequence, exporters are likely to get hurt. Depending on the size of the resulting unemployment effect, this may well force political pressure upon the government to reduce the budget deficit.

Tornell and Velasco (1995) develop a modern and interesting analysis of the effects of different exchange rate systems on fiscal discipline. They present an intertemporal model in which the stance of fiscal policy is determined endogenously by an optimizing fiscal authority. The government's objective function depends positively on transfers to the private sector and the utility of private agents stemming from present and future consumption. There are two key features of the model. First, transfers yield positive utility because it increases the popularity and reelection chances of the government. This causes the 'political distortion' which leads to positive transfers in the optimum. Second, the internalization of the utility of private agents is not necessarily based on the same discount rate as in the private agents' objective function.

The crucial question to analyze in this model is under which exchange rate regime the fiscal authority opts for a stronger political distortion. Maximizing its objective function, the government weighs the benefit against the cost of these expenditures. The benefit is its increased popularity, the cost is the higher inflation rate induced by higher transfers, because taxes are given and the only way to balance the budget is through inflation tax. The difference between the two regimes in the model of Tornell and Velasco is in the intertemporal allocation of the higher inflation tax. With fixed exchange rates, there is no immediate effect on inflation, but inflation in the future rises. With flexible exchange rates, both the exchange rate and the inflation rate are affected immediately. Thus, flexible exchange rates imply that the government can spread the inflation tax more evenly between the present and the future, while fixed exchange rates imply that the burden of the inflation tax is completely shifted into the future. Depending on the time preference rate of the government relative to private agents, flexible or fixed exchange rates create a higher incentive for a lax fiscal policy stance. For example, if the government is relatively patient, future costs are relatively more deterrent and the government would therefore show more fiscal discipline under a fixed exchange rate regime, because it implies relatively high future costs. By contrast, if the government is impatient, fixed exchange rates exert less fiscal discipline than flexible rates. This is the case, because the government welcomes the possibility of a peg to avoid incurring any costs in the present and to be able to shift the entire burden into the future.

The result of the model of Tornell and Velasco (1995) is that it is ambiguous which exchange rate regime exerts more fiscal discipline. If one accepts their framework, one is tempted to conclude that due to frequently assumed impatient governments flexible exchange rate regimes are more suited to generate fiscal discipline. This is not inconsistent with the observation of late fiscal adjustment in the EMS in the 1990s. Although governments were aware of the fiscal convergence criteria for EMU already in 1991, fiscal adjustment in most EMS countries was delayed until the mid-1990s.

Despite the elegant nature of the analysis in the model of Tornell and Velasco (1995), their approach is not without problems. The most critical point is related to the political distortion of transfers, which is a key feature of the model. Such distortion seems somewhat strange in a world with totally rational agents. After all, would a government not lose against a competitor with the same objective function as private agents?

The experience within the EMS in the early 1990s seems to demonstrate an additional new lesson on the disciplinary effect. Given the asymmetric shock on EMS countries triggered by German unification, a number of countries found it difficult to cope with overcontractionary policies imposed by fixed exchange rates. Italy and the U.K., by leaving the ERM in 1992, demonstrated impressively that they could pursue less costly adjustment policies under a flexible exchange rate regime.

In sum, the disciplinary effect of fixed exchange rates remains ambiguous. The controversy over this effect with its recent experience in Europe suggests that, while fixed exchange rates impose monetary discipline, if no coordinated monetary expansion takes place, the difference between fixed and flexible exchange rates with respect to automatic disciplinary effects is smaller than often thought. In both cases, the ultimate objective of price stability can only be achieved through credible economic policies. These, in turn, are a function of long term fiscal policies, that are compatible with the inflation target and institutional factors related to monetary policy (i.e., central bank autonomy) and wage policies (i.e., labor market flexibility).

3.2 Sustainability of a Peg: the Problems of Credibility and Speculative Attacks

The crises in the EMS in 1992 and 1993 and the Mexican peso in 1994 have recently increased the interest of economists in the sustainability of fixed exchange rates. They showed how difficult it can be to defend a peg even at high costs. For example, when the Bank of England tried to prevent the collapse of its peg in the EMS in September 1992, it is said to have incurred more than $5 billion in capital losses within half a day. The crisis of Asian currencies in mid-1997, in which several Asian countries lost sizable amounts of their reserves has also reiterated that one of the weaknesses of exchange rate arrangements with limited flexibility is the possibility that a balance of payments crisis can occur, during which financial markets attack the peg and possibly force the government to completely abandon the fixed exchange rate system and to adopt a free float. In the turmoil of such a crisis the financial sector can also experience a general bank run and significant disintermediation.

A sizable literature on currency crises has been developed over the past decade. Following Velasco (1996), two lines of research approaching this topic can be distinguished. The first one, which has generated by far the most publications in this area, is the literature, in which the collapse of a system is determined by a minimum level of international reserves of the central bank. Typically these papers start from the Krugman (1979) model and investigate various aspects of the conditions, under which such a crisis unfolds, and what the timing of the crisis is. One of the questions that result from the analyses is whether or not an early warning system can be developed in order to prevent such crises. The formal framework of the speculative attack analyses, which has some similarities with the target zone approach, is based on the concept that, in the absence of unanticipated shocks, no discontinuities of asset prices can occur. The second line of research on currency crises uses an optimization approach to examine the cost-benefit analysis of the government to determine the conditions, under which the government chooses to devalue the currency and to renege on previous commitments. These papers are usually based on a Barro-Gordon model for the open economy. In this section, we briefly review both directions of research.

The idea of the speculative attack literature goes back to work of Salant and Henderson (1978), who originally analyze a buffer stock to stabilize the price for gold. Krugman (1979) applies this principle to the foreign exchange reserves of the central bank. The idea behind his model is the starting point of basically all papers on the topic of speculative attacks on a fixed exchange rate system. Crucial assumptions of the analysis are that capital is perfectly mobile, credit is available for speculation, prices are flexible, real variables are exogenous, and the collapse of the exchange rate system is ultimately induced by domestic policies that are inconsistent with a fixed exchange rate system. It is assumed that there is a continuous increase in domestic credit, which, given the fixed exchange rate, leads to a gradual decline in international reserves and ends in the breakdown of the fixed exchange rate regime.

The intuition behind the basic idea of the speculative attack approach can be illustrated by using Figure 4. It is assumed that domestic credit D grows at a constant rate (shown in Fig. 4 with logarithmic scaling). This is accompanied by an equal decline in central bank reserves R so that money supply M (=R+D) remains unchanged. When financial markets realize that reserves will soon reach the minimum level of foreign exchange reserves, which may be a positive, zero, or negative level, they anticipate that a regime switch to a flexible exchange system is inevitable. For simplicity, it is assumed in Figure 4 that the minimum reserve level is zero. However, they also know that, after such a crisis, money supply will increase as credit expansion is not offset anymore by the decline in reserves. Thus, agents anticipate a rise in inflation and a decline in their desired money holdings. Therefore, they will exchange domestic currency for foreign exchange exactly at the time, when the reserves of the central bank exceed the minimum level precisely by the equivalent of the desired reduction in the money holdings. At this point in time (t_0), reserves jump downward to the minimum reserve level, which, in turn, triggers the collapse of the fixed exchange rate system. However, no jump in the exchange rate occurs.

Figure 4: The Basic Model of Speculative Attacks

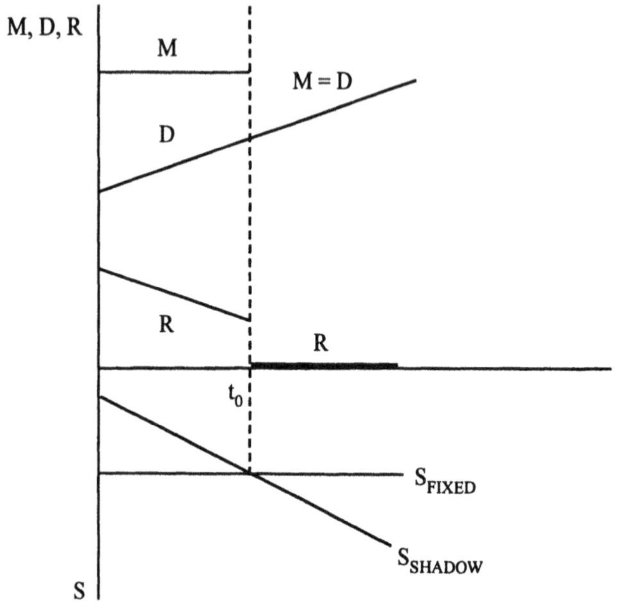

The rate of credit expansion, together with parameters of the money demand function and the minimum level of reserves determine the time of the collapse. The minimum reserve level is negative, if the central bank abandons the fixed rate regime only after having borrowed foreign exchange. A positive minimum reserve level reflects the desire of the central bank to safeguard a minimum balance in order not to endanger its future creditworthiness in international markets too much. In any case, the initial level of reserves does not matter. The collapse is inevitable as long as macroeconomic policies are inconsistent with a fixed exchange rate system.

The time of the speculative attack can also be determined by comparing the initial exchange rate (S_{FIXED}) with a shadow exchange rate (S_{SHADOW}). The latter is the exchange rate that would prevail under a free float if reserves were at the minimum level.

The question arises whether the model gives a realistic picture of how speculative attacks or balance of payments crises develop and how they are characterized. The answer is that the standard model developed by Krugman (1979) describes significant features of such extraordinary situations but simplifies a number of important characteristics. The development of a balance of payments crisis is often more difficult to detect than the standard model suggests and the crisis itself is accompanied by some government actions to maintain the peg.

These include the imposition of capital controls and interest rate increases to attract capital. In addition, the development from a fixed exchange rate system to a free float may often not describe reality. Governments may try to rescue the fixed exchange rate system by introducing some flexibility like adding or widening a band of fluctuation or devaluating the domestic currency. Governments may also try to reduce the turbulence arising during the development of a balance of payments crisis by adopting some adjustment measures and additional borrowing abroad.

The limitations of the basic model of balance of payments crises led to a number of extensions of the model. For example, a critical component in the development of a balance of payments crisis is the knowledge of the minimum reserve level. Krugman (1979) already indicates that uncertainty about the minimum reserve level may lead to repeated attacks. Flood and Garber (1984) and Grilli (1986) investigate effects of uncertain domestic credit expansion on the timing of the balance of payments crisis. This eliminates the uniqueness of the timing of the speculative attack that triggers the collapse of the fixed exchange rate regime. Several papers take into account changes in the real economy (Flood and Hodrick (1986), Willman (1989)). Capital controls as a means to sustain a fixed exchange rate system are examined by Wyplosz (1986), Bacchetta (1990) and Dellas and Stockman (1993). Frenkel and Klein (1991) analyze whether, in order to prevent a balance of payments crisis, announcements of adjustment programs help reduce the required adjustment efforts. Ozkan and Sutherland (1995) also study possibilities to prevent a currency crisis. Optimizing behavior of governments rather than simple rules of credit expansion are examined in Obstfeld (1986), Penati and Penacchi (1989), and Claessens (1991). Connolly and Taylor (1984) show alternatives to a flexible exchange rate system after the speculative attack. Obstfeld (1986), Goldstein et al. (1993), and Svensson (1994) discuss multiple equilibria exchange rate dynamics, that may exist under certain conditions. Their existence affects the speculator's believe that a regime switch is close. Finally, Ozkan and Sutherland (1994) present a model, in which the development of a balance or payments crisis cannot be identified in the data. Their approach emphasizes that a government can abandon a peg if sticking to a fixed exchange rate involves a strong rise in unemployment and if this endangers the survival of the government. This implies that it would be useful to study unemployment data in order to examine the possible occupance of a balance of payments crisis.[13]

Studies on the empirical evidence of speculative attacks are fairly limited. A major reason for this is the fact that speculative attacks are fairly limited in numbers for each currency during a certain exchange rate regime. Thus, they are more event analyses. They try to find out whether the timing of attacks and the development of the exchange rate after the crisis are in line with the predictions of

---

[13] Agénor, Bhandari, and Flood (1992), Garber and Svensson (1995), and Eichengreen et al. (1995) include more detailed reviews of the literature on balance of payments crises.

the models developed in this area. Blanco and Garber (1986) examine the Mexican strong devaluations in 1976 and 1982. They find good predictive power of the approach for the timing of the devaluations in these years. Goldberg (1994) investigates the Mexican case for the period 1980-86 and identifies fiscal and monetary shocks contributing to speculative attacks on the peso. The Mexican experience is also examined by Ötker and Pazarbasioglu(1997). Conolly (1986) and Cumby and Wijnbergen (1989) apply the approach to examine the Argentinean crawling peg regime during the period 1979-81. They find evidence for major implications of the speculative attack approach. In a less quantitative approach Goldstein et al. (1993), Svensson (1994), and Eichengreen and Wyplosz (1993) discuss speculative attacks on currencies of the EMS. Eichengreen and Wyplosz strongly argue that the EMS is an example for the existence of multiple equilibria and that speculative attacks are not necessarily a reflection of exogenous shocks. They also find that recessions make governments more vulnerable to speculative attacks. Ötker and Pazarbasioglu (1997) also examine European countries and find that macro policies are necessary but not sufficient to ensure the maintenance of a fixed exchange rate system.

The second and until now smaller line of research on currency crises focuses on the credibility problem of a peg. Most economists agree that permanent shocks originating in the goods market may require a change in the exchange rate. However, as markets are aware of this necessity, questions about the credibility of a peg are likely to arise. When markets realize that discretionary exchange rate changes may occur, rapid changes in international capital flows are likely to develop causing volatility in the balance of payments transactions that a fixed exchange rate system aims to avoid. In this case, the advantages of a fixed exchange rate may be compromised. Ultimately, as the peg appears to be unsustainable, one-way speculation and a balance of payments crisis result.

Theoretical analyses investigate this problem by examining the conditions, under which governments choose to devalue the currency and thereby renege on the promised peg. In these analyses, the government weighs possible advantages of a surprise devaluation against the losses associated with changing the peg. Advantages could be the inflation tax revenue or a reduction in the real stock of debt. Disadvantages include the dissatisfaction of voters or loss of pride. If the benefits of a surprise devaluation are higher than the perceived costs the government has an incentive to renege on the commitment to peg. In this case, the peg is not credible and rational agents will trigger a speculative attack. In a recent study, Velasco (1996) shows that government debt may be a crucial factor in the cost-benefit analysis of governments and, thus, for the sustainability of a fixed exchange rate regime. His analysis confirms previous findings of a trade-off between credibility and flexibility of an exchange rate system: credibility is high if the government has no incentive to make use of the exchange rate instrument.

A powerful argument against the credibility and, thus, sustainability of a fixed exchange rates is the fact that structural changes in the economies require real exchange rate changes. Such structural changes may not arise on a regular basis and are not predictable. However, they can sometimes develop rather rapidly. As they cannot be anticipated and their effects on the long-run equilibrium exchange rate level is difficult to quantify, discretionary exchange rate changes in a fixed rate regime may not come in time and, therefore, credibility of the regime may be jeopardized. If the peg is eventually changed, the change may reduce the credibility and, in addition, the new nominal exchange rate may not immediately be consistent with the equilibrium real exchange rate level. In this case, the peg only remains credible if the real exchange rate effect comes about through wage and price changes. In case of a required real devaluation, wages and prices have to decline relative to the world market, which may involve a long and painful adjustment process. In case of a required real appreciation, the adjustment would have to come about through higher inflation. Hence, the macroeconomic costs of a lack of exchange rate flexibility can be high in such situations. This suggests a trade-off between credibility and flexibility. A peg is particularly ill-suited when significant and abrupt real exchange rate changes are required for macroeconomic equilibrium. In this case, flexible exchange rates facilitate the adjustment process. Italy and the United Kingdom in 1992 can serve as examples for the ability of flexible rates to better achieve a necessary adjustment rapidly.

The results of the analyses on credibility and speculative attacks suggest that there is a variety of factors that affect the credibility of a fixed exchange rate system and, thereby, the occurrence and timing of a currency crisis. Controversies over the relevant factors demonstrate that it may be difficult to foresee a balance of payments crisis. This implies that developing an early warning system in a fixed exchange rate regime may be a strenuous task. However, considering the fact that there is only a fairly small number of long-lived fixed exchange rate arrangements today, this may nevertheless of utmost importance.

The results developed so far still leave plenty of room for future theoretical and empirical work. There also seems to be some research necessary to combine analyses of short-term behavior of exchange rates under a float, which is dominated by noise traders, with the speculative attack arguments presented thus far. However, the various studies underline how vulnerable a fixed exchange rate system can be to speculative attacks. This is consistent, for example, with the experience in the EMS, which provides some of the best examples for balance of payments crises. The EMS also shows how governments try to defend the peg and that this has been mostly unsuccessful. Since these crises create more turmoil than most of the volatility of exchange rates observed under a free float, the possibility that such crises occur is a strong limitation of a fixed exchange rate system. It also highlights that governments have fewer degrees of freedom under a peg. More specifically, they have to take into account constraints imposed by a fixed exchange rate regime when designing macroeconomic policies.

3.3 Fixed Exchange Rates as a Nominal Anchor

In the 1980s and 1990s, a number of countries, in particular in the developing world, have tried to use a fixed exchange rate system to bring down inflation. By fixing the nominal exchange rate price increases of tradables are reduced to the world market inflation rate. Thus, a nominal peg implies that the inflation rate of tradables becomes exogenous, for which reason the term „nominal anchor" is used for this approach. The hypothesis that fixing the exchange rate can stabilize inflation in the long run implicitly claims that tying down the price increases of tradables will exert a stabilizing effect on price increases of nontradables too. Price stabilization is achieved if the price increase for nontradables can indeed be tight to the inflation rate of tradables. Bruno and Meridor (1991) give a detailed exposition of this strategy and compare the exchange rate anchor to alternative anchors.

Theoretical work on fixed exchange rates as nominal anchors has been advanced over the past few years by Calvo and Végh (1991, 1992, 1993, 1994a) and Kiguel and Liviatan (1992). This work relies on the casual empirics of several chronic inflation countries which demonstrates that exchange-rate based disinflation programs are, contrary to conventional wisdom, not always contractionary but often induce a temporary economic expansion during the first years of the stabilization efforts. The recessionary costs of disinflation appear later in the programs.[14] In rationalizing the business cycle observed in exchange rate led stabilization programs, Calvo and Végh (1991) assume that the lack of credibility in temporary stabilization policies represents a key in explaining the boom-recession puzzle. Therefore, they develop a two sector cash-in-advance model, assuming Ramsey-type consumers within a perfect capital mobility world. The representative consumer maximizes discounted lifetime utility given by

$$(1) \qquad \int_0^{\infty} \left[\log\left(c_t^T\right) + \log\left(c_t^N\right) \right] + \exp(-rt)dt$$

where c_t^T and c_t^N denote consumption of traded and nontraded goods, respectively, and r is a positive and constant subjective discount rate, which is, for simplicity, assumed to equal the international real interest rate. Consumption is constrained by the requirement to use money for purchasing goods, given by

$$(2) \qquad \alpha\left(c_t^N / e_t + c_t^T\right) \le m_t , \qquad \alpha > 0$$

The real exchange rate e $(=EP^*/P)$ is defined as the relative price of traded goods in terms of home goods, where E stands for the nominal exchange rate, P^* is the

[14] The Tablita-programs of the late 1970s in Chile, Argentina, and Uruguay as well as the heterodox stabilization programs of the mid 1980s in Mexico and Israel did show the so-called pattern of a 'boom-recession-cycle'.

(constant) price of the traded good in units of foreign currency, and P is the domestic price of nontraded goods, respectively. Given a positive nominal interest rate, equilibrium consumption must equal real money balances in terms of traded goods, m_t $(=M/EP^*)$. The intertemporal budget constraint equates discounted lifetime expenditures to discounted lifetime resources

(3)
$$a_0 + \int_0^\infty \left(y_t^N / e + y_t^T + \tau \right) \exp(-rt)dt = \int_0^\infty \left(c_t^N / e_t + c_t^T + i_t m_t \right) \exp(-rt)dt.$$

Here, a_t denotes real financial wealth that can be held either in domestic money or international bonds; τ_t stands for real government lump-sum transfers, y^N and y^T represent output of home and traded goods, and i is the domestic nominal interest rate. The representative household chooses optimal paths of c_t^T, c_t^N, and m_t subject to equations (2) and (3). The first-order conditions of this optimization problem are given by

(4)
$$1/c_t^T = \lambda(1+\alpha i_t)$$

and

(5)
$$c_t^N = e_t c_t^T$$

where λ is the constant Lagrange multiplier, which can be interpreted as the marginal utility of wealth. Condition (4) indicates that the real effective price of traded goods consists of the market price, which is equal to unity, plus the opportunity cost αi_t of holding α units of domestic currency units required to carry out purchases. Furthermore, optimal consumption implies that the marginal rate of substitution between home goods and traded goods equates the relative price (see condition (5)).

For the supply side, the model assumes that output of traded goods is exogenously given while production of home goods is demand determined. Since individual price setters act in a nonsynchronous manner, taking into account their expectations about the future paths of both the average price and excess demand of home goods, the rate of change in the inflation rate of nontraded goods is a negative function of excess demand in that market given by

(6)
$$\dot{\pi}_t^N = -\phi\left(y_t^N - \bar{y}^N \right)$$

where $\bar{y}^N$ is the full-employment level of output in the sector of nontradables, while y^N represents the demand level. Hence, despite the rigidity of the domestic price level, inflation could change because of forward-looking expectations.

Typically, exchange-rate based stabilization programs focus on setting a (preannounced) path for ε, which is the expected and actual rate of devaluation. Assuming that uncovered interest parity condition

(7) $$i_t = i^* + \varepsilon_t$$

holds, where i^* denotes the foreign nominal interest rate, one can easily show how Calvo and Végh attribute the boom-recession cycle phenomenon to the expectation that stabilization policy is perceived by the representative agent as an only temporary policy: at time t=0, policymakers may announce a permanent reduction in ε from ε^h to ε^l ($\varepsilon^l < \varepsilon^h$), which would imply a one-to-one decrease in the domestic nominal interest rate, given the uncovered interest parity condition. But since the public expects the program to be abandoned with certainty at some time t=T in the future, condition (7) implies that the nominal interest rate is expected to be lower just for the time interval [0,T] of stabilization. After the stabilization phase (i.e. t≥T), the domestic nominal interest rate rises back to its initial level. Hence, the transitory decrease in the nominal interest rate lowers the effective cost of consumption of traded goods because of the declining opportunity costs of holding money (see equation (4)). This effect, in turn, induces individuals to shift forward the timing of purchasing (durable) goods. Since the real exchange rate does not change on impact because of the presence of staggered prices, equation (5) indicates that the higher consumption of traded goods has to be accompanied by a corresponding rise in the demand for home goods. Therefore, intertemporal substitution effects induce a temporary consumption boom in the nontradables sector, which generates a rise in domestic production as well as a deterioration in the current account.

Furthermore, there are two qualitatively different effects on the domestic inflation rate: while the lower rate of devaluation dampens domestic inflation on impact, the rise in aggregate demand fuels the inflation rate for nontradables over time. Consequently, the domestic inflation rate declines by less than the pre-announced devaluation rate, leading to a real appreciation of the domestic currency until the stabilization program is abandoned. Moreover, the less credible the program is the more pronounced is the effect of intertemporal substitution in consumption, the lower is the initial fall in the inflation rate. Thus, due to the assumption of imperfect credibility, the model exhibits an expectation-induced inflation inertia. As the relative price of home goods in terms of traded goods increases during the stabilization interval, aggregate demand and therefore domestic output begins to decline (see equation (5)). Depending on the length of the time interval, a recession appears later on when the disinflation program is discontinued or even before the policy is reversed. Therefore, on the one hand the model predicts a U-shaped time path of both the domestic inflation rate and the real exchange rate. On the other hand, the model provides a quite intuitive explanation of the so-called 'boom-recession cycle'. Thus, the Calvo and Végh model is consistent with most of the key stylized facts of exchange-rate based disinflation programs in chronic inflation countries.

Nevertheless, since empirical studies (Reinhart and Végh (1995), Ostry and Reinhart (1992)) did only find significant support for the intertemporal subsitution channel in case of the heterodox programs of the mid 1980s, the recent literature has examined some different approaches to explain the empirical regularity of a boom-recession-cycle within exchange-rate based stabilization programs. Assuming, for example, backward-looking indexation mechanisms (Calvo and Végh (1993), Ambler and Cardia (1992)), pegging the exchange rate leads to a rise in real wages on impact and, therefore, fuels aggregate demand. Furthermore, a decline in the rate of inflation induced by a lower devaluation rate causes the inflation tax to decrease, which, in turn, generates a positive wealth effect (Calvo and Végh (1994a), Bruno and Meridor (1991)) and stimulates aggregate demand. The resulting real appreciation of the domestic currency implies a loss of competitiveness in the tradeable goods sector and a possible loss in foreign reserves. Both effects can eventually create a credibility problem. When financial markets become convinced that the peg cannot be sustained anymore, a currency crisis develops. A forced devaluation or abandoning of the fixed exchange rate system may subsequently trigger exactly what the nominal anchor idea tried to prevent.

Since a real appreciation of the domestic currency has been observed in most countries adopting an exchange rate anchor strategy, the recent literature has examined other channels through which this effect provides could be induced. One other explanation states that capital-account liberalization combined with microeconomic and trade reforms lead to capital inflows which necessitates a real appreciation (Obstfeld (1995)). However, there seems to be very little empirical support for this hypothesis. Another cause of the real appreciation could be the backward-looking indexation carried over from the preceding high inflation period. This could make it difficult to reduce wage and price inertia.[15]

Edwards (1996) recently suggested an optimization framework to model the credibility problem of the use of a fixed rate as a nominal anchor. In his set-up, the government loss function reflects that the authorities dislike both inflation and real-exchange-rate misalignment. The real exchange rate is assumed to be subject to terms of trade shocks. In addition, wage increases, which are set in each period in advance, depend on forward-looking inflation expectations. He shows that in this framework the inflation dynamics depend on the degree of credibility of the policies under the stabilization program. If the public assigns a probability of greater than zero but less than one to the possibility of a failure of the new policies, price inertia will disappear over time, but a real appreciation nevertheless develops. Since this can lead to significant misalignment of the exchange rate, credibility indirectly determines the optimal policy of the government.

Several authors examine recent cases of exchange rate-base stabilization programs. Calvo and Végh (1994b) investigate eleven major programs in Latin

---

[15] Other explanations are provided by Dornbusch and Werner (1994) and Giovannini (1990).

America and Israel between 1960 and 1991. Edwards (1996) presents estimates of inflation dynamics for Mexico and Chile (1974-1982) and Mexico (1980-1994) and tests for structural breaks caused by exchange rate-based stabilization programs. Mecagni (1995) studies the experience of 15 countries which used a fixed exchange rate as a nominal anchor during the period 1988-92. He also compares their experience with stabilization efforts in other countries or other periods. Several results of the study are particularly interesting. First, in order to protect the external sector from a sharp deterioration during the period of real appreciation, most countries which adopted an exchange rate based stabilization program, devalued their currency drastically before they implemented the exchange rate anchor. Second, in countries with a fixed exchange rate as a nominal anchor, the initial inflation performance was considerably better than in other countries. However, the experience after the initial progress varied significantly. In a number of countries, it was followed by a resurgence of inflation. Third, in countries, in which the exchange rate anchor failed, financial policies were generally inconsistent with a pegged exchange rate. A loss of credibility and a sizable decline in international reserves were the resulting effects. Fourth, where the exchange rate successfully worked as a nominal anchor, the policy was accompanied by a decisive and front-loaded fiscal adjustment program. Fifth, exchange rate-based stabilization programs were in general more successful in removing backward-looking indexation than other stabilization programs. Sixth, in all exchange rate-based stabilization programs examined, countries could not keep initial money growth within targets set at the beginning of the programs.

A more difficult question the Mecagni (1995) study tries to answer is, whether, in successful exchange rate based stabilization programs, the success is attributable also to the nominal anchor or just to the fiscal adjustment. He finds indications that the exchange rate anchor has complemented the effects of the fiscal adjustment on inflation. This is derived from a comparison of the inflation performance of countries with and without an exchange rate anchor. The latter countries did not achieve as much an inflation decline for a given fiscal deficit reduction as countries with an exchange rate anchor. However, these results mainly refer to the short-run effects. A medium-term comparison demonstrates that fiscal performance was very different among the countries with an exchange rate anchor.

The overall experience of developing countries with the nominal anchor strategy is mixed and, therefore, the strategy is not undisputed. The clear conclusion is that a fixed exchange rate does not guarantee a lasting decline of inflationary pressures. In particular, if financial policies are inconsistent with the peg, an initial success is short-lived. Credibility of the exchange rate anchor is a key element for its success. Lack of credibility create disruptions which can be stronger under an exchange rate anchor than under a float.

3.4 Fixed Exchange Rates Reformed: The Target Zone Approach

Before Krugman (1988, 1991) developed his ingenious model on target zones, which has become the standard model on the subject, initial work on the target zone proposal was presented by Frenkel and Goldstein (1986), Williamson (1985, 1987), and Williamson and Miller (1987). In the more policy-oriented contributions of Williamson (1985) and Williamson and Miller (1987), which has become known as the "blueprint" of a target zone approach, the target zone approach is seen as a compromise between fixed and flexible exchange rates. Since the authors focus on a target zone for real rather than nominal exchange rates, their proposal is somewhat different from what is examined in most of the theoretical literature. In addition, their policy proposal includes a fairly wide band of fluctuation (±10 percent around the central parity). In general, a target zone is seen today as a variant of a fixed exchange rate system that includes some flexibility.

The target zone literature deals with several questions: The first question is one of positive economics and explains exchange rate dynamics under a target zone arrangement. The second questions is on what the empirical evidence of either the assumptions of the theoretical work or the implications of it are. Frequently, the conclusions have led to extensions of the theory related to the first question. The third question is normative and deals with the advantages of this regime over a fixed or a flexible exchange rate system. This section addresses these three questions and looks at the policy impact.

Work on the first question, which deals with positive economics, generally starts from the model presented by Krugman (1988, 1991). The framework of the model builds on the monetary model of exchange rate determination and can be described in the following three equations:

(8) $$s_t = f_t + \alpha \frac{E_t(ds_t)}{dt}$$

(9) $$f_t = v_t + m_t$$

(10) $$dv_t = \sigma dW_t$$

Equation (8) describes the logarithm of the exchange rate at time t, s_t, expressed as the price of the foreign currency in domestic currency units, as a function of fundamental factors f_t, and the instantaneous expected change in the exchange rate. Fundamentals include, for example, relative money, price, and output developments.

Equation (9) defines fundamentals as the sum of a stochastic component v_t and the money supply m_t, which the central bank is assumed to be able to control. Foreign exchange market interventions, which are necessary to keep the exchange rate within the band of fluctuation, take the form of changing m_t. When the domestic currency depreciates and reaches the margin of the band, i. e., s_t rises to the upper ceiling, the central bank intervenes by reducing money supply. Equation (10) specifies the stochastic part of the fundamental as a Brownian motion that has an instantaneous variance σ^2 and is based on the increment of a standard Wiener process dW_t with $E_t(dW)=0$ and $E_t(dW^2)=dt$.

The structure of the model implies that the exchange rate under a float is $s_t=f_t$. This is shown by the FF line in Figure 5 where the exchange rate is depicted as a function of the value of the fundamentals. Under a float, monetary policy is independent of the exchange rate system and, therefore, $E_t(dv_t)=E_t(df_t)=0$, which, in turn, implies $E_t(ds_t)=0$.

Figure 5: Exchange Rate Function in the Krugman Model

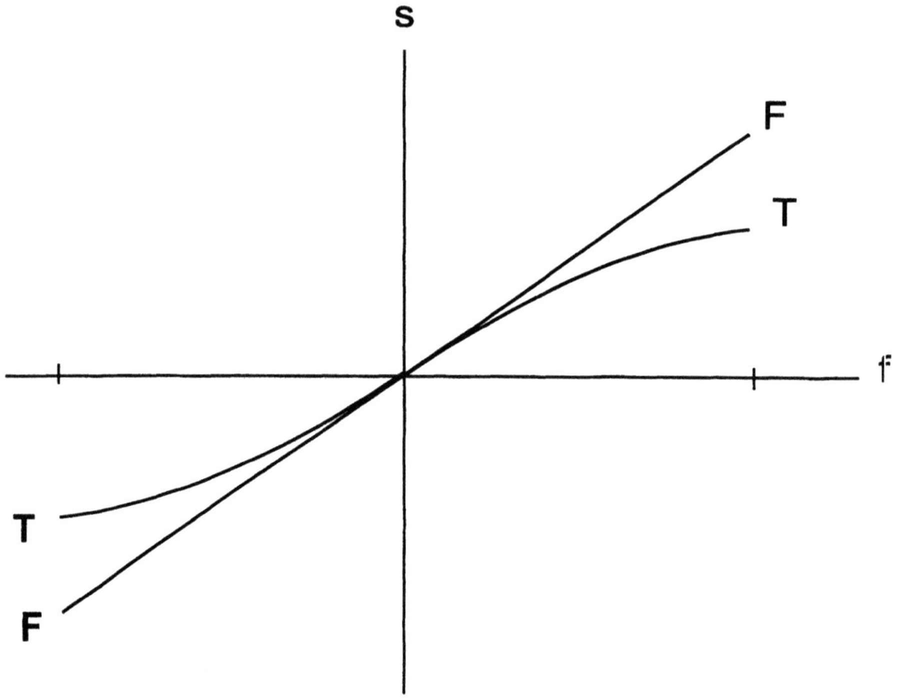

For the target zone regime, Krugman assumes that only marginal interventions take place and that the central bank policy is perfectly credible. This rules out the possibility that speculation can drive the exchange rate beyond the upper margin s_u or the lower margin s_l. Since the fundamentals determine the exchange rate, the margins for the band of fluctuation for the exchange rate imply a band of fluctuation for the fundamentals. As can be shown, the exchange rate function in a target zone describes an S-shaped line TT. This can be derived by using Ito's Lemma to specify the term for the expected exchange rate change in equation (8). Together with $dv_t = df_t = \sigma dW_t$, this yields the solution

$$s_t = f_t + A_1 e^{\lambda_1 f_t} + A_2^{\lambda_2 f_1} \tag{11}$$

where $\lambda_{1,2} = \pm \{2/(\alpha\sigma^2)\}^{1/2}$ and A_1 and A_2 are constants. The latter are determined by the fact that the exchange rate line TT is horizontal at the margins of the band for the fundamentals, which is referred to as the "smooth pasting" conditions.

The explanation of the S-shaped exchange rate function (i.e., the form of the TT curve) is fairly complex. It can intuitively be explained as follows. If the exchange rate could jump at the margin there would be opportunities for arbitrage, which, in turn, would ultimately eliminate the jump. Since the exchange rate function is linear in the fundamentals and in the expected exchange rate change, this implies that, at the margin, the expected exchange rate change cannot jump either and the exchange rate is completely insensitive to the value of the fundamentals. Krugman referred to the implications of these considerations therefore as "tying down the ends of the S". Bertola (1994) includes an excellent formal exposition of this effect.[16]

The S-shaped exchange rate function implies a so-called "honeymoon effect": since foreign exchange market participants are assumed to know how the exchange rate is determined, they will, once the exchange rate moves beyond the central parity towards the margin, assign a decreasing probability to a continuation of the exchange rate movement. The closer the exchange rate gets to the margin, the more likely they will find a reversal of this movement. In addition, since the exchange rate basically does not respond to changes in the value of the fundamentals when it is very close to the margin, the margins are consistent with different values of the fundamentals. By contrast, the exchange rate responds more intensely to changes in the value of the fundamentals when it is close to the central parity rate. These considerations imply a U-shaped density function of the exchange rate as shown by Svensson (1991a, b). This, by itself, reduces exchange rate fluctuations and the necessity of interventions. However, it crucially hinges upon the credibility assumption.

As Svensson (1991a, b) demonstrates, the Krugman model also implies that, assuming uncovered interest parity, there is a negative deterministic relationship between the level of the exchange rate and the interest rate differential. When a currency weakens and reaches the margin, full credibility ensures that financial markets do not expect a realignment, but either that the currency remains at the margin or appreciates again. Thus the conditional expectation value is an appreciation. Since uncovered interest parity implies that the difference between the domestic and the foreign interest rate is equal to the expected exchange rate change, the expected appreciation means that the interest differential becomes

[16] For a detailed formal exposition see also Froot and Obstfeld (1991).

negative. Thus, a high exchange rate level (i.e., a weak currency) is associated with a negative expected exchange rate change or, put differently, with a negative interest differential.[17]

The empirical evidence on the implications of the Krugman model have been relatively poor. While Meese and Rose (1990) study the exchange rate of the dollar vis-à-vis several currencies of industrial countries under the Bretton Woods system, Flood, Rose and Mathieson (1991) focus their empirical study on the EMS, and Lindberg and Söderlind (1994) examine the exchange rate of the Swedish krona in the 1980s vis-à-vis EMS currencies. In virtually all analyses, the authors were unable to find support for a U-shaped density function of exchange rates. Instead, these studies often find a hump-shaped density function or rejected nonlinearity of the exchange rate function altogether. In addition, the results of Svensson (1991b) and Flood, Rose and Mathieson (1991) suggest that there is very little indication for a negative correlation between the value of the domestic currency and the interest rate spread. Often, there is a positive or no correlation between the level of the exchange rate and the interest rate differential. Finally, Food, Rose and Mathieson (1991) also reject the hypothesis of an S-shaped exchange rate function. Other tests can be found in Smith and Spencer (1991) and Pessach and Razin (1994).

Several rather restrictive assumptions of the Krugman model cause its inability to explain, for example, exchange rate developments within the European Monetary System (EMS). A first critical assumption is perfect credibility, i.e., financial markets are sure that the margin will be defended by the central bank under any circumstances. This implies that financial markets do not take into account any realignment risk. Svensson (1992) examined the realignments within the EMS before the crises in 1992 and 1993 and found that virtually all realignments were anticipated by financial markets. For example, the interest rate differential between France and Germany regularly increased when the French franc reached the lower margin against the deutschmark. By contrast, the Krugman model would suggest that the interest differential becomes negative due to the expectation that the French franc would strengthen again, which, of course, hinges on the full credibility of the target zone margins. Hence, the jump in the interest differential observed in the data must reflect the anticipation of a realignment. Rose and Svensson (1995) use a drift adjustment method to estimate the expected rate of exchange rate realignment. According to their results, the margins of the exchange rate bands in the EMS were not perfectly credible. This also explains why the exchange rate cannot have been an S-shaped function of the fundamentals.

Although Krugman (1991) already addresses the issue of imperfect credibility, several other papers have elaborated on the credibility problem and realignment

[17] Further implications of the Krugman approach are examined by Delgado and Dumas (1992), who apply computer simulations to examine the influence of the width of the band on exchange rate dynamics and the interest differential in Krugman's model.

risk. Bertola and Svensson (1993) introduce a time-varying realignment risk. Svensson (1992) and Garber and Svensson (1995) also include realignment risk into the standard model and show that any pattern between interest rate differentials and exchange rates can result from this extension.

A second restrictive assumption of the Krugman model is the absence of any intra-marginal interventions. However, as shown in Svensson (1992) and in Garber and Svensson (1995), incorporating such intervention into the approach can lead to a linear rather than an S-shaped exchange rate function within most of the band of fluctuation. This is the case if the expected rate of appreciation (depreciation) is proportional to the increase (decline) in the exchange rate resulting from changes in fundamentals. In general, expected exchange rate changes in a target zone system with intra-marginal interventions are a function of the expected marginal and the expected intra-marginal interventions, with the former becoming dominating expectations around the margins and the latter dominating expectations more within the band. A simple way to introduce intra-marginal interventions is given by Garber and Svensson (1995). The consequence of introducing intra-marginal interventions into the target zone model is that the exchange rate function (the TT curve in Figure 4) is now only slightly S-shaped, as it retains the smooth pasting at the margins of the band. The result of a less pronounced S-shape results from the fact that financial markets assign some probability to central bank interventions already when the exchange rate deviates somewhat from the central parity. As a consequence, the exchange rate function is more linear than in the case with only marginal interventions. Compared to the free float the exchange rate function is flatter, indicating that a honeymoon effect carries over to this modification. However, it can be shown that the entire regime now becomes very similar to a managed float, with the exception that in a target zone speculators anticipate higher intervention as the exchange rate approaches the margin. Incorporating intra-marginal interventions also implies that the density function is not as U-shaped anymore as in the Krugman model and, thus, it is more in line with observed data.[18] Moreover, the exchange rate exhibits mean reverting property.

The fact, that the Krugman model is based on the monetary exchange rate model represents a further restriction. However, various studies have shown that exchange rate developments do not support this approach well. Moreover, the monetary model implies perfect price flexibility and, thus, continuous market clearing. In this case, exchange rate fluctuations only involve costs, so that any limitation of exchange rate flexibility is beneficial and totally fixed rates would be even better than a target zone. Several extensions develop a target zone approach in the context of a different exchange rate model. For example, Miller and Weller (1991) use a Dornbusch-type overshooting model and stochastic price movements

[18] Several other extensions deal with issues related to realignment risk, which include the risk of a collapse of the target zone, a regime shift, and learning about the shifts. For a brief listing see Garber and Svensson (1995).

to show the qualitative implications of a real and a nominal target zone. They derive the result that exchange rates are mean reverting. Assuming a positive price shock, the real exchange rate declines, which, given short-run price rigidity, reduces output demand and employment. In the medium term, this puts downward pressure on domestic prices so that the real exchange rate and output demand rise again.[19]

The third and normative question posed at the beginning of this section addresses the issue of superiority of a target zone over fixed rates and flexible rates. The analysis of Miller and Weller (1991) suggests that stochastic price shocks could make a real target zone an optimal strategy. A price increase, which would otherwise lead to a real appreciation and unemployment, is to be offset by expansionary monetary policy to keep employment at its long-run level. Thus, monetary policy and the proposed target zone approach are policy instruments that aim at offsetting the unpleasant effects of price stickiness. However, since the described shock leads to a permanent price increase, which is accompanied by a nominal depreciation, a trade-off between employment and price stability arises. This poses a conflict that cannot be solved on theoretical grounds.

Sutherland (1995) analyzes the advantages and disadvantages of a nominal target zone compared with a fixed exchange rate system and a flexible exchange rate system. He uses a Keynesian model with fixed nominal wages, which implies that output and prices are positively correlated. He confirms the result known from the discussions of fixed versus flexible exchange rates according to which fixed exchange rates are optimal when monetary shocks occur, while flexible exchange rates are optimal when real shocks hit the economy. Since it is likely that economies experience both types of shocks, Sutherland considers a target zone approach as an intermediate solution. Implicitly, he uses a welfare argument, which makes the intermediate case of a target zone superior to the „corner solutions“.[20]

In their „blueprint,“ Williamson and Miller (1987) see the advantages of the target zone approach in the combination of some exchange rate flexibility and the avoidance of any harmful effect of misalignment on trade and investment, which, in their view, cannot be ruled out under a free float.[21] They suggest a target zone for the real exchange rate and assign monetary policy to the exchange rate objective and fiscal policy to the objective of achieving internal equilibrium. The authors suggest that the central parity of the target zone should be determined on

---

[19] Sutherland (1995) develops a more formal solution of the exchange rate dynamics for the framework used by Miller and Weller (1991). Beetsma (1994) also uses an overshooting model and examines, in addition to stochastic price shocks, which represent supply shocks, stochastic monetary shocks, and real demand shocks. He also finds a mean-reverting process.

[20] Genberg (1989) as well as Persson and Tabellini (1990) discuss additional aspects of the normative question.

[21] See also Bergsten and Williamson (1994).

the basis of Williamson's (1985) proposal of the fundamental equilibrium exchange rate (FEER). The latter is derived from a target for the current account balance, which is determined by an assessment of medium term capital flows. Problems with this proposal include the determination of the FEER and the problem of achieving through fiscal policy both price stability and labor market equilibrium as the two features of internal equilibrium.

Svensson (1992) and Garber and Svensson (1995) discuss the question of how wide the zone should be and approach this question by asking whether there are arguments against a zero band. Most of the reasons they discuss have to do with higher degrees of freedom for a central bank under a nonzero band. This freedom may allow the central bank to change the domestic interest rate in response to changes in national economic conditions, e.g., in times of a recession. However, these arguments do not seem to be convincing since such policies could induce changes in the credibility of the target zone. A textbook example was the attempt of the French central bank in the summer of 1993 to reduce the interest rate in order to stimulate the domestic economy. This led to high capital outflows and, ultimately, forced the EMS to give up the narrow bands in the ERM.

In a recent paper, Werner (1996) discusses target zones as a possibility to reduce interest rate variability compared to a fixed exchange rate. He uses a framework similar to Bertola and Svensson (1993) and derives the expected exchange rate as determined by the expected change in the exchange rate towards the central parity and the expected realignment rate. The latter follows in Werner's approach a Brownian motion. This yields exchange rate expectations, which depend on the variances of the two Brownian motions in the model, i.e., of the realignment rate and of the fundamentals. An expected realignment rate depreciates the currency, which, in turn, increases the probability of an exchange rate change towards the central parity. As a consequence, rising realignment expectations increase the expected exchange rate change and the interest rate differential less than proportionally. By contrast, in a fixed exchange rate system, the expected exchange rate change and, thereby, the interest rate differential is equal to the expected realignment rate. This implies that, under fixed rates, interest differentials are more variable than in the target zone regime. The target zone arrangement in Israel versus the end of the 1980s and in Mexico in the early 1990s are seen as empirical evidence for the interest rate differential diminishing effect resulting from this exchange rate regime.

Despite the extensive academic work on the target zone approach, it seems fair to state that it had no significant impact on economic policy. Sometimes, the attempts among the G-7 countries to coordinate foreign exchange market interventions in the context of the 1985 Plaza accord and the 1987 Louvre accord are seen as an implicit target zone for the international monetary system (McKinnon (1993)). However, this coordination was rather short-lived and was far from representing an agreed-upon target zone arrangement.

Why has there not been a stronger impact of this reform proposal on exchange rate policy? Six major factors seem to have played a role. First, the theoretical and empirical work has not brought forward enough convincing arguments in favor of a target zone. Still too few papers compare the advantages and the disadvantages of a target zone with alternative exchange rate systems.

Second, in Europe, where the target zone approach could be regarded as the implemented within the EMS, the currency crises in 1992 and 1993 have shed serious doubts about the viability of such a system. In particular, is highlighted that, in the absence of capital controls, central banks may not be able to defend the band, which reduces the credibility of arrangements of this type. Since the focus in this region is now on monetary unification, little time is spent to consider target zones a realistic alternative.

Third, the theoretical work on target zones regularly assumes efficiency of the foreign exchange market and rational behavior of market participants. As work on the short-term determination of exchange rates shows this is a rather problematic assumption. However, dropping this assumption would make it even more difficult to determine exchange rate dynamics under a target zone arrangement. Nevertheless, it suggests, for example, that bandwagon effects could make it difficult or very costly for central banks to defend a target zone even if policymakers were willing to coordinate interventions internationally.

Fourth, in order to implement the target zone approach as an international monetary system, a set of equilibrium exchange rates and an appropriate mechanism of how to adjust the zones over time would have to be agreed upon. The determination of the equilibrium exchange rates is difficult because there is no commonly accepted equilibrium exchange rate model.[22] It is unlikely that this could be done without publication of the zones. The adjustment mechanism for the margins could consist of either discretionary adjustments as in the EMS or an automatic adjustment rule as proposed by the "blueprint" of Williamson and Miller (1987) and Williamson (1987). Both adjustment mechanisms would have to take into account differences in inflation developments and changes in economic conditions that affect the long-run equilibrium level of the real exchange rate. The latter often appears to be difficult to quantify. While the disadvantage of an automatic mechanism is that the optimal rule may not remain constant over time, the disadvantage of discretionary adjustments can be seen in the possibility to delay the adjustment of the economy through intervention.

Fifth, if the target zone approach is to be implemented among major international currencies, the right timing of the implementation of a target zone system between these currencies becomes crucial. Since most international transactions are made in these currencies, the timing is more important for the world economy than the implementation of a target zone between smaller countries. The timing problem led the Bretton Woods Commission (1994) to suggest that exchange rate bands should be introduced only after the governments of major industrial countries have strengthened their macropolicies and, thus, after

[22] This topic is covered by a number of very good papers in Williamson (1994).

their economies have converged more.[23]

Finally, a critical and sixth problem for the target zone approach as an international monetary regime stems from the fact that policymakers, in designing their macroeconomic policies, are not willing to give the external equilibrium priority or to agree on international coordination of macroeconomic policies. By contrast, whenever policymakers find a target zone appealing, it seems that this is the case, because they misperceive this system as a possibility to combine stability of exchange rates, open markets, and autonomy of national economic policies. This inconsistency is the traditional problem brought forward against any limitation of the flexibility of exchange rates.

Unlike the Bretton Woods Commission (1994) and Kenen (1994a), who favor macro convergence before the implementation of a target zone, Bergsten (1994) states that it is unlikely that major economies agree on and successfully implement coordinated macro policies. He therefore supports the implementation of a target zone arrangement, which, in his view, would exert enough pressure to force government policies to converge. However, this appears to be an overoptimistic view. While some disciplinary effect can be expected from the commitment to limited exchange rate flexibility, the EMS experience teaches us that such a strategy can easily lead to speculative attacks and balance of payments crises.[24]

In sum, in light of the results of the theoretical work, the empirical evidence, and the experience about the political economy of exchange rate policy, it is difficult to imagine that the target zone model represents a serious reform alternative for the international monetary system. Too strict are the rules that such a system would impose on big industrial economies. However, it may play a more important rule for a small economy considering a link of its currency to another currency without implementing a purely fixed exchange rate regime. In addition, it seems that still more theoretical work is required to establish a solid basis for the target zone approach. For example, the models to date include fairly simple types of intervention policies and very simple assumptions about exchange rate uncertainty as well as the behavior of financial market participants.

4 Summary and Conclusions

The discussion in this paper shows that the dispute on fixed versus flexible exchange rates continues. For the major trading blocs, there seems to be hardly any alternative to the float in the near future. The experience since the collapse of the Bretton Woods system shows that, contrary to the hopes prevailing in the early 1970s, the optimism about the advantages of a float was exaggerated.

---

[23] Kenen (1994a), who is a prominent proponent of the target zone proposal, argues in the same direction.

[24] Therefore, the combination of a target zone with sanctions, as suggested by Larosiere (1994), also seems relatively unrealistic.

Nevertheless, for major industrial countries, the experience supports the flexible exchange rate system, because it suggests that flexible exchange rates have made the rough ride through economic changes over the past 25 years just a little bit smoother. Both theoretical contributions and empirical studies have taught us that, whenever national policies of major economies go in different directions, the flexible exchange rate system cannot function well.

Exchange rate volatility of flexible exchange rates has often been the focus of the critics of a float. Although volatility continues to be higher than in fixed exchange rate regimes, the claim of induced misalignment is not undisputed, since there is no accepted model to estimate the equilibrium exchange rate. An exchange rate level that some economists may interpret as misalignment, others may regard as an equilibrium level. Recent theoretical contributions on floating rates emphasize the microstructure of the foreign exchange market as a determinant of the short-run behavior of flexible exchange rates.

The experience of several currency crises in the EMS, Mexico, and Asia during the period since 1992 has highlighted the problems of more limited exchange rate flexibility. Recent theoretical contributions emphasize, in particular, aspects of credibility and sustainability of a peg as well as the government incentives to either stay with a peg or change it. There can be no doubt that these contributions have advanced our understanding of the working of currency crises and the conditions for a successful peg.

In comparing fixed with flexible exchange rate regimes, theoretical considerations teach us that the choice of an optimal exchange rate regime depends on a several criteria as nature of shocks and behavior in asset markets. The choice is difficult because these criteria may well change over time.

References

Abel, A. (1983), Optimal Investment Under Uncertainty, *American Economic Review* 73, 228-33.

Agénor, P.-R, J. S. Bhandari and R. P. Flood (1992), Speculative Attacks and Models of Balance of Payments Crises, *IMF Staff Papers* 39, 357-94.

Almekinders, G. J. (1994), Theory on the Scope for Foreign Exchange Market Intervention, *Kredit und Kapital* 25, 363-95.

Almekinders, G. J. and S. C. W. Eijffinger (1991), Empirical Evidence on Foreign Exchange Market Intervention: Where Do We Stand?, *Weltwirtschaftliches Archiv* 127, 645-77.

Ambler, S. J. and E. Cardia (1992), Optimal anti-inflation programs in semi-industrialized economies: orthodox versus heterodox policies, *Journal of Development Economics* 38, 41-61.

Bacchetta, P. (1990), Temporary Capital Controls in a Balance of Payments Crisis, *Journal of International Money and Finance* 9, 246-57.

Bayley, M. and G. Tavlas (1991), Exchange Rate Variability and Direct Investment, *The Annals AAPSS* 516, 106-16.

Bertola, G. (1994), Continuous-Time Models of Exchange Rates and Intervention, in: van der Ploek (ed.), The Handbook of International Macroeconomics, Oxford, 251-98.

Bertola, G. and L. E. O. Svensson (1993), Stochastic Devaluation Risk and the Empirical Fit of Target Zone Models, *Review of Economic Studies* 60, 689-712.

Beetsma, R. M. W. J. (1994), Macroeconomic Stabilization and Intervention Policy under an Exchange Rate Band, Seminar Paper No. 562, Institute for International Economic Studies, Stockholm.

Bergsten, C. F. (1994), An International Monetary Fund for the 21st Century, Paper presented at IMF/World Bank conference „Fifty Years After Bretton Woods“, Madrid.

Bergsten, F. and J. Williamson (1994), Is the Time Ripe for Target Zones or the Blueprint?, in: Bretton Woods Commission, Bretton Woods: Looking to the Future, Conference Proceedings, Bretton Woods Commission, Washington, D.C.

Black, S. W. (1985), The Effect of Alternative Intervention Policies on the Variability of Exchange Rates: The Harrod Effect, in: Bhandari, J. S. (ed.), Exchange Rate Management under Uncertainty, MIT Press.

Blanco, H. and P. M. Garber (1986), Recurrent Devaluation and Speculative Attacks on the Mexican Peso, *Journal of Political Economy* 94, 148-66.

Brada, J. and J. Mendez (1988), Exchange Rate Risk, Exchange Rate Regimes and the Level of International Trade, *Kyklos* 41, 198- 210.

Bretton Woods Commission (1994), Bretton Woods: Looking to the Future, Commission Report, Staff Review, Background Papers, Bretton Woods Commission, Washington, D.C.

Bruno, M. and L. Meridor (1991), High Inflation and the Nominal Anchors of an Open Economy, Essays in International Finance No. 183, International Finance Section, Princeton University, June.

Buiter, W., G. Corsetti and N. Roubini (1993), Excessive Deficits: Sense and Non-Sense in the Treaty of Maastricht, *Economic Policy* 16, 57-100.

Calvo, G. A. and C. A. Végh (1994a), Credibility and the Dynamics of Stabilisation Policy: A Basic Framework, in: Sims, C. A. (ed.), Advances in Econometrics: Sixth World Congress, Cambridge.

Calvo, G. A. and C. A. Végh (1994b), Inflation Stabilization and Nominal Anchors, in: Barth (ed.) Approaches to Exchange Rate Policy, 90-102.

Calvo, G. A. and C. A. Végh (1993), Stabilization Dynamics and Backward-Looking Contracts, IMF Working Paper No. WP/93/29, International Monetary Fund, Washington, D.C.

Calvo, G. A. and C. A. Végh (1992), Inflation Stabilization and Nominal Anchors, IMF Paper on Policy Analysis and Assessment No. PPA A/92/4, International Monetary Fund, Washington, D.C.

Calvo, G. A. and C. A. Végh (1991), Exchange Rate-Based Stabilization Under Imperfect Credibility, IMF Working Paper No. WP/91/77, International Monetary Fund, Washington, D. C.

Chinn, M. and R. A. Meese (1995), Banking on Currency Forecasts, *Journal of International Economics* 38, 161-78.

Claessens, S. (1991), Balance of Payments Crises in an Optimal Portfolio Model, *European Economic Review*, 35, 81-101.

Clarida, R. and J. Galli (1994), Sources of Real Exchange Rate Fluctuations: How Important are Nominal Shocks?, NBER Working Paper No. 4658, Cambridge.

Connolly, M. B. and D. Taylor (1984), The Exact Timing of the Collapse of an Exchange Rate Regime and its Impact on the Relative Price of Traded Goods, *Journal of Money, Credit, and Banking* 16, 194-207.

Cooper, R.N. (1985), Comment, *Brookings Papers on Economic Activity,* 451-56.

Cooper, R.N. (1988), Toward an International Commodity Standard, *Cato-Journal* 8, 315-338.

Cumby, R. E. and S. van Wijnbergen (1989), Financial Policy and Speculative Runs with a Crawling Peg: Argentina 1979-81, *Journal of International Economics* 27, 111-27.

Cushman, D. (1988), Exchange Rate Uncertainty and Foreign Direct Investment in the United States, *Weltwirtschaftliches Archiv* 124, 322-34.

Cutler, D. J. (1991), Speculative Dynamics, *Review of Economics Studies* 58, 529-46.

De Grauwe, P. (1988), Exchange Rate Variability and the Slowdown in the Growth of International Trade, *IMF Staff Papers* 35, 63-84.

De Grauwe, P. (1989), International Money, Post-War Trends and Theories, Oxford.

De Grauwe, P. and H. Dewachter (1990), A Chaotic Monetary Model of the Exchange Rate, CEPR Discussion Paper No. 466, London.

Delgado, F. and B. Dumas (1992), Target Zones, Broad and Narrow, in: Krugman, P., and Miller, M. (eds.), Exchange Rate Target Zones and Currency Bands, Cambridge, MA.

Dellas, H. and A. Stockman (1993), Self-fulfilling Expectations, Speculative Attacks, and Capital Controls, *Journal of Money, Credit, and Banking* 25, 657-73.

DeLong, J. B., A. Shleifer, L. H. Summers and R. J. Waldmann (1990), Noise Trade Risk in Financial Markets, *Journal of Political Economy* 98, 703-38.

Dornbusch, R. and A. Werner (1994), Mexico: Stabilization, Reform, and No Growth, *Brookings Papers on Economic Activity*, 253-07.

Edison, H.(1993), The Effectiveness of Central Bank Intervention: A Survey of the Literature after 1982, Special Papers in International Economics, No. 18, Princeton University.

Edison, H. and M. Melvin (1990), The Determinants and Implications of the Choice of an Exchange Rate System, in: Haraf, W., and T. Willett (eds.), Monetary Policy for a Volatile Global Economy, Washington, D.C.

Edwards, S. (1996), Exchange-Rate Anchors, Credibility, and Inertia: A Tale of Two Crises, Chile and Mexico, *American Economic Review* 86, Papers and Proceedings, 159-63.

Eichengreen, B. and C. Wyplosz (1993), The Unstable EMS, *Brookings Papers on Economic Analysis,* 51-124.

Eichengreen, B., A. K. Rose and C. Wyplosz (1995), Exchange Market Mayhem - The Antecedents and Aftermath of Speculative Attacks, *Economic Policy* 18, 249-96.

Engel, C. (1993), Real Exchange Rates and Relative Prices: An Empirical Investigation, *Journal of Monetary Economics* 32(1), 35-50.

Engel, C., and J. H. Rogers (1995), How Wide is the Border?, International Finance Discussion Paper No. 498, Board of Governors of the Federal Reserve System, Washington, D.C., February.

Fischer, S. (1993), Overview, in: Federal Reserve Bank of Kansas City, Policies for Long-Run Economic Growth, Federal Reserve Bank of Kansas City, Kansas City.

Flood, R.P. and P. M. Garber (1984), Gold Monetization and Gold Discipline, *Journal of Political Economy* 92, 90-107.

Flood, R. P. and R. Hodrick (1986), Real Aspects of Exchange Rate Regime Choice with Collapsing Fixed Rates, *Journal of International Economics* 21, 215-32.

Flood, R. P. and A.K. Rose (1993), Fixing Exchange Rates, NBER Working Paper No. 4503, Cambridge, M.A.

Flood, R. P., A. K. Rose and D. J. Mathieson (1991), An Empirical Exploration of Exchange Rate Target Zone, *Carnegie-Rochester Conference Series on Public Policy* 35, 7-35.

Frankel, J. A. and K. Froot (1987), Using Survey Data to Test Standard Proportions Regarding Exchange Rate Expectations, *American Economic Review* 77, 133-53.

Frankel, J. A. and K. Froot (1988), Chartists, Fundamentalists, and the Demand for Dollars, *Greek Economic Review* 10, 49-102.

Frankel, J. A. and A. K. Rose (1995), Empirical Research on Nominal Exchange Rates, in: Grossman, G., and Rogoff, K. (eds.), Handbook of International Economics, 3, 1689-1729.

Frankel, J. A. and S. Wei (1995a), European Integration and the Regionalization of World Trade and Currencies, in: Eichengreen, B., Fieden, J., and von Hagen, J., Monetary and Fiscal Policy in an Integrated Europe, New York.

Frankel, J. and S. Wei (1995b), Emerging Currency Blocks, in: Genberg, H. (ed.), The International Monetary System: Its Institutions and its Future, Berlin.

Frenkel, J. and M. Goldstein (1986), A Guide to Target Zones, *IMF Staff Papers* 33, 633-73.

Frenkel, M. and M. Klein (1991), Balance of Payments Crises and Fiscal Adjustment Measures, *Journal of Macroeconomics* 13, 657-73.

Frenkel, M. (1995), Learning and Exchange Rate Dynamics: A Theoretical Analysis, *Studies in Economics and Econometrics* 19, 1-17.

Frenkel, M. (1997), Chartist, Fundamentalists and Rational Speculators in the Foreign Exchange Market, *Journal of International Business* 2, 1-24.

Friedman, M. (1953), The Case of Flexible Exchange Rates, in: Friedman, M. (ed.), Essays in Positive Economics, Chicago, 157-203.

Froot, K. and M. Obstfeld (1991), Stochastic Process Switching: Some Simple Solutions, *Econometrica* 59, 241-50.

Froot, K. and T. Ito (1989), On the Consistency of Short-Run and Long-Run Exchange Rate Expectations, *Journal of International Money and Finance* 8, 487-510.

Garber, P. M. and L. E. O. Svensson (1995) The Operation and Collapse of Fixed Exchange Rate Regimes, in: Grossman, G. and Rogoff, K.,`Handbook of International Economics, 3, 1865-1911.

Genberg, H. (1989), Exchange Rate Management and Macroeconomic Policy: A National Perspective, *Scandinavian Journal of Economics* 91, 439-69.

Giavazzi, F. and L. Spaventa (1990), The 'New' EMS, in: DeGrauwe, P., and Papademos, L. (eds.), The European Monetary System in the 1990s, London.

Giovannini, A. (1990), European Monetary Reform: Progress and Prospects, *Brookings Papers on Economic Activity* 2:1990, 217-74.

Goldberg, L. (1993), Exchange Rates and Investment in U.S. Industry, *Review of Economics and Statistics* 75, 575-89.

Goldberg, L. (1994), Predicting Exchange Rate Crises: Mexico Revisited, *Journal of International Economics* 36, 413-30.

Goldberg, L. and R. Frydman (1993), Theories, Consistent Expectations and Exchange Rate Dynamics, in: Frisch, H., and Wörgoötter, A. (eds.), Open-Economy Macroeconomics, London.

Goldberg, L. and C. Kolstad (1994), Foreign Direct Investment, Exchange Rate Variability, and Demand Uncertainty, NBER Working Paper No. 4815, National Bureau of Economic Research, Cambridge, MA.

Goldstein, M., D. Folkerts-Landau, P. Garber, L. Rojas-Suarez and M. Spencer (1993), Exchange Rate Management and International Capital Flows, International Capital Markets, Part I , International Monetary Fund, Washington, D.C.

Goldstein, M. (1995), The Exchange Rate System and the IMF: A Modest Agenda, Institute for International Economics, Washington, D.C.

Grant, R., M. Papadakis and D. Richardson (1993), Global Trade Flows: Old Structures, New Issues, Empirical Evidence, in: Bergsten, C.F., and M. Noland (eds.), Pacific Dynamism and the International Economic System, Institute for International Economics, Washington, D.C.

Grilli, V. (1986), Buying and Selling Attacks on Fixed Exchange Rate Systems, *Journal in International Economics* 20, 143-156.

Hooper, P. and J. Marquez (1993), Exchange Rates, Prices, and External Adjustment in the United States and Japan, International Finance Discussion Paper No. 456, Board of Governors of the Federal Reserve System, Washington, D.C.

Hung, J. H. (1991a), Noise Trading and the Effectiveness of Sterilized Foreign Exchange Intervention, Federal Reserve Bank of New York Research Paper No. 9111.

Hung, J. H. (1991b), The Effectiveness of Sterilized U.S. Foreign Exchange Intervention: An Empirical Study Based on the Noise Trading Approach, Federal Reserve Bank of New York Research Paper No. 9118.

International Monetary Fund (1984), Exchange Rate Volatility and the Level of International Trade, *IMF Occasional Paper No. 28*, International Monetary Fund, Washington, D.C.

Ito, T. (1994), Short-Run and Long-Run Expectations of the Yen/Dollar Exchange Rate, *Journal of the Japanese and International Economics* 8, 119-43.

Johnson, H. (1970), The Case for Flexible Exchange Rates, 1969, in: Halm, G.N. (ed.), Approaches to Greater Flexibility of Exchange Rates: The Bürgenstock Papers, Princeton, N.J.

Kenen, P. (1994a), Ways to Reform Exchange Rate Arrangements, in: Bretton Woods Commission, Bretton Woods: Looking to the Future, Conference Proceedings, Bretton Woods Commission, Washington, D.C.

Kenen, P. (1994b), The Agenda for the Bretton Woods Institutions, Paper presented at IMF/World Bank Conference on „Fifty Years after Bretton Woods,“ Madrid.

Kiguel, M. and N. Liviatan (1992), The Business Cycle Associated with Exchange-Rate-Based Stabilization, *World Bank Economic Review* 6, 279-305

Koedijk, K. G., B. Mizrach, P. A. Stork and C. G. de Vries (1995), New Evidence on the Effectiveness of Foreign Exchange Market Intervention, *European Economic Review* 39, 501-8.

Krugman, P. (1979), A Model of Balance of Payments Crises, *Journal of Money, Credit, and Banking* 11, 311-325.

Krugman, P. (1985), Comment, *Brookings Papers on Economic Activity,* 456-459.

Krugman, P. (1988), Target Zones and Exchange Rate Dynamics, NBER Working Paper No. 2481, January.

Krugman, P. (1991), Target Zones and Exchange Rate Dynamics, *Quarterly Journal of Economics* 106, 669-82.

Larosiere, J. (1994), the International Monetary System Fifty Years after Bretton Woods: in: Bretton Woods Commission, Bretton Woods: Looking to the Future, Conference Proceedings, Bretton Woods Commission, Washington, D.C.

Lewis, K. K. (1989a), Can Learning Affect Exchange-Rate Behavior? The Case of the Dollar in the Early 1980s, *Journal of Monetary Economics* 23, 79-100.

Lewis, K. K. (1989b), Changing Beliefs and Systematic Rational Forecast Errors with Evidence from Foreign Exchange, *American Economic Review* 79, 621-36.

Lindberg, H. and P. Söderlind (1994), Testing the basic target zone model on Swedish data 1982-1990, *European Economic Review* 38, 1441-69.

MacDonald, R. (1990), Exchange Rate Economics: An Empirical Perspective, in: Bird, G. (ed.), The International Financial Regime, London and San Diego, 91-144.

MacDonald, R. (1997), What Determines Real Exchange Rates? The Long and Short of It, IMF Working Paper WP/97/21, International Monetary Fund, Washington, D.C.

MacDonald, R. and M. P. Taylor (1992), Exchange Rate Economics, *IMF Staff Papers* 39, 1-57.

Mark, N. C. (1994), Exchange Rates and Fundamentals: Evidence on Long-Horizon Predictability, *American Economic Review* 84, 201-18.

McKinnon, R. I. (1993), The Rules of the Game: International Money from a Historical Perspective, *Journal of Economic Literature* 31, 1-44.

Mecagni, M. (1995), Experience with Nominal Anchors, International Monetary Fund Occasional Paper No. 129, 65-106.

Meese, R. A. and K. Rogoff (1983), Empirical Exchange Rate Models of the Seventies, *Journal of International Economics* 14, 3-24.

Meese, R. A. and A. K. Rose (1990), Nonlinear, Nonparameter Nonessential Exchange Rate Estimation, *American Economic Review* 80, 192-96.

Miller, M. and A. Sutherland (1991), The 'Walters Critique' of the EMS - A Case of Inconsistent Expectations?, *The Manchester School* 59, Supplement, 23-37.

Miller, M. and P. Weller (1991), Exchange Rate Bands with Price Inertia, *The Economic Journal* 101, 1380-99.

Morsink, R. L. and W. T. Molle (1991), Direct Investment and Monetary Integration, in: Commission of the European Communities, The Economics of EMU, Commission of the European Communities, Brussels.

Mussa, M. (1981), The Role of Official Intervention, Group of Thirty Occasional Papers No. 30, New York.

Mussa, M. (1986), Nominal Exchange Rate Regimes and the Behavior of the Real Exchange Rate, in: Brunner, K. and Meltzer, A. H. (eds.), Real Business Cycles, Real Exchange Rates and Actual Policies, New York, 117-213.

Mussa, M. (1990), Exchange Rates in Theory and in Reality, Essays in International Finance, No. 179, Princeton.

Obstfeld, M. (1985), Floating Exchange Rates: Experience and Prospects, *Brookings Papers on Economic Activity,* 2, 369-450.

Obstfeld, M. (1986), Rational and Self-Fulfilling Balance of Payments Crises, *American Economic Review* 76, 72-81.

Obstfeld, M. (1995), International Currency Experience: New Lessons and Lessons Relearned, *Brookings Papers on Economic Activity,* 1, 119-196.

Obstfeld, M. and K. Rogoff (1995), The Mirage of Fixed Exchange Rates, *Journal of Economic Perspectives* 9 (4), 73-96.

Ostry, J. D. and C. M. Reinhart (1992), Private Saving and Terms of Trade Shocks: Evidence from Developing Countries, *IMF Staff Papers 39*, 495-517.

Ozkan, F. G. and A. Sutherland (1994), A Model of the ERM Crisis, CEPR Discussion Paper No. 879, London.

Ozkan, F. G. and A. Sutherland (1995), Policy Measures to Avoid a Currency Crisis, *The Economic Journal* 105, 510-19.

Pazarbasioglu, C. and I. Ötker (1997), Likelihood versus Timing of Speculative Attacks: A Case Study of Mexico, *European Economic Review* 41, 837-845.

Penati, A. and G. Penacchi (1989), Optimal Portfolio Choice and the Collapse of a Fixed Exchange Rate Regime, *Journal of International Economics* 27, 1-14.

Persson, T. and G. Tabellini (1990) Macroeconomic Policy, Credibility and Politics, London.

Pessach, S. and A. Razin (1994), Targeting the Exchange Rate Under Uncertainty, *Review of International Economics* 2, 40-49.

Pilbeam, K. (1991), Exchange Rate Management: Theory and Evidence, Basingstoke.

Pindyck, R. and A. Solimano (1993), Economic Instability and Aggregate Investment, Policy Research Working Paper No. 1148, World Bank, Washington, D.C.

Reinhart, C. M. and C. A. Vegh (1995), Nominal Interest rates, Consumption Booms, and Lack of Credibility: a Quantitative Examination, *Journal of Development Economics* 46, 357-78.

Rose, A. K. and L. E. O. Svensson (1995), Expected and Predicted Realignments: The FF/DM Exchange Rate during the EMS, 1979-93, *Scandinavian Journal of Economics* 97, 173-200.

Salant, S. W. and D. W. Henderson (1978), Market Anticipation of Government Gold Policies and the Price of Gold, *Journal of Political Economy* 86, 627-48.

Sapir, A., K. Sekkat and A. Weber (1994), The Impact of Exchange Rate Fluctuations on European Union Trade, CEPR Discussion Paper No. 1041, Centre for Economic Policy Research, London.

Singleton, K. (1987), Speculation and the Volatility of Foreign Currency Exchange Rates, in: Brunner, K. and H. Meltzer (eds.), Bubbles and Other Essays, *Carnegie-Rochester Conference Series on Public Policy* 26, 9-56.

Smith, G. W. and M. G. Spencer (1991), Estimation and Testing in Models of Exchange Rate Target Zones and Process Switching, in: Krugman, P. and M. Miller (eds.), Exchange Rate Targets and Currency Bands, Cambridge, U.K., 211-39.

Stockman, A. (1988), Real Exchange-Rate Flexibility under Pegged and Floating Exchange-Rate Systems, *Carnegie-Rochester Conference Series on Public Policy* 29, 259-94.

Sutherland, A. (1995), Monetary and Real Shocks and the Optimal Target Zone, *European Economic Review* 39, 162-72.

Svensson, L. E. O. (1991a), Target Zones and Interest Rate Variability, *Journal of International Economics* 31, 27-54.

Svensson, L. E. O. (1991b), The Term Structure of Interest Rate Differentials in a Target Zone: Theory and Swedish Data, *Journal of Monetary Economics* 28, 87-116.

Svensson, L. E. O. (1992), An Interpretation of Recent Research on Exchange Rate Target Zones, *Journal of Economic Perspectives* 6, 119-44.

Svensson, L. E. O. (1994), Fixed Exchange Rates as a Means to Price Stability: What Have we Learned, *European Economic Review* 38, 447-68.

Taylor, M. P., H. Allen and L. Menkhoff (1992), The Use of Technical Analysis in the Foreign Exchange Market, *Journal of International Money and Finance* 11, 303-14.

Tornell, A. and A. Velasco (1995), Fiscal Discipline and the Choice of Exchange Rate Regimes, *European Economic Review* 39, 759-70.

UNCTAD (1994), World Investment Report, United Nations, Geneva.

Velasco, A. (1996), Fixed Exchange Rates: Credibility, Flexibility and Miltiplicity, *European Economic Review* 40, 1023-35.

Walters, A. (1986), Britain's Economic Renaissance, Oxford.

Werner, A. M. (1996), Target Zones and Realignment Expectations: The Israeli and Mexican Experiences, *IMF Staff Papers* 43, 571-86.

Williamson, J. (1985), The Exchange Rate System, Policy Analyses in International Economics, 5, Institute for International Economics, Washington, D.C.

Williamson, J. (1987), Exchange Rate Management: The Role of Target Zones, *American Economic Review* 77, Papers and Proceedings, 200-4.

Williamson, J. (1994), Estimating Equilibrium Exchange Rates, Institute for International Economics, Washington D.C.

Williamson, J. and M. H. Miller (1987), Targets and Indicators: A Blueprint for the International Coordination of Economic Policy, Policy Analyses in International Economics, 22, Institute for International Economics, Washington, D.C.

Willman, A. (1989), The Collapse of the Fixed Exchange Rate Regime with Sticky Wages and Imperfect Substitutability between Domestic and Foreign Bonds, *European Economic Review* 32, 1817-38.

Wyplosz, C. (1986), Capital Controls and Balance of Payments Crises, *Journal of International Money and Finance* 5, 167-79.

Appendix

Appendix Table I: Changes in Monthly Bilateral Real Exchange Rates 1968-1997

	Average Absolute Monthly Percentage Changes	Standard Deviation of Monthly Percentage Changes
1968.01 - 1973.03		
Pound/US Dollar	0.73	1.06
Yen/US Dollar	1.05	1.91
Mark/US Dollar	1.02	1.90
Yen/Mark	0.88	1.68
Mark/Pound	1.02	1.87
1975.01 - 1997.03		
Pound/US Dollar	2.15	2.81
Yen/US Dollar	2.25	2.94
Mark/US Dollar	2.18	2.73
Yen/Mark	2.04	2.51
Mark/Pound	1.74	2.26
1975.01 - 1981.12		
Pound/US Dollar	2.11	2.65
Yen/US Dollar	2.21	2.79
Mark/US Dollar	1.99	2.59
Yen/Mark	2.31	2.78
Mark/Pound	1.96	2.45
1982.01 - 1989.12		
Pound/US Dollar	2.31	2.91
Yen/US Dollar	2.37	3.12
Mark/US Dollar	2.42	2.94
Yen/Mark	1.71	2.05
Mark/Pound	1.67	2.25
1990.01 - 1997.03		
Pound/US Dollar	2.01	2.84
Yen/US Dollar	2.14	2.86
Mark/US Dollar	2.09	2.60
Yen/Mark	2.13	2.68
Mark/Pound	1.60	2.03

Source: IMF, International Financial Statistics and own calculations.

Appendix Table II:Changes in Monthly Bilateral Real Exchange Rates in Europe 1975-1997

	Average Absolute Monthly Percentage Changes	Standard Deviation of Monthly Percentage Changes
1975.01 - 1979.03		
Mark/French Franc	1.27	1.64
Mark/Lira	1.49	2.24
Mark/Peseta	1.80	2.87
Mark/Swed.Krona	1.05	1.53
Mark/Austrian Sch.	0.35	0.45
Mark/Belgian Fr.	0.53	0.64
Mark/Port. Escudo	1.84	2.44
1979.04 - 1986.12		
Mark/French Franc	0.62	0.92
Mark/Lira	0.75	0.95
Mark/Peseta	1.14	1.66
Mark/Swed.Krona	1.41	2.12
Mark/Austrian Sch.	0.34	0.45
Mark/Belgian Fr.	0.53	0.93
Mark/Port. Escudo	1.48	1.96
1987.01 - 1997.03		
Mark/French Franc	0.46	0.62
Mark/Lira	1.19	1.88
Mark/Peseta	1.04	1.45
Mark/Swed.Krona	1.39	1.91
Mark/Austrian Sch.	0.35	0.46
Mark/Belgian Fr.	0.33	0.55
Mark/Port. Escudo	0.92	1.29
1979.04 - 1997.03		
Mark/French Franc	0.52	0.76
Mark/Lira	1.00	1.57
Mark/Peseta	1.08	1.54
Mark/Swed.Krona	1.40	2.01
Mark/Austrian Sch.	0.35	0.45
Mark/Belgian Fr.	0.42	0.73
Mark/Port. Escudo	1.16	1.55

Source: IMF, International Financial Statistics, and own calculations.

Appendix Table III: Changes in Quarterly Real Effective Exchange Rates 1975-1996

	Average Absolute Quarterly Percentage Changes	Standard Deviation of Quarterly Percentage Changes
1975.1 - 1996.2		
US dollar	2.70	3.32
British Pound	3.02	4.01
Japanes Yen	4.08	5.14
Deutschmark	1.72	2.11
1975.1 - 1981.4		
US dollar	2.24	2.87
British Pound	3.74	4.49
Japanes Yen	4.30	5.17
Deutschmark	2.00	2.48
1982.1 - 1989.4		
US dollar	3.18	3.72
British Pound	3.33	3.99
Japanes Yen	3.38	4.22
Deutschmark	1.42	1.68
1990.1 - 1996.2		
US dollar	2.58	3.10
British Pound	1.89	3.09
Japanes Yen	4.73	5.98
Deutschmark	1.81	2.08

Source: IMF, International Financial Statistics, and own calculations.

Appendix Table IV.: Changes in Monthly Real Effective Exchange Rates 1979-1997

	Average Absolute Monthly Percentage Changes	Standard Deviation of Monthly Percentage Changes
1979.01 - 1997.02		
US dollar	1.56	1.93
British Pound	1.50	2.00
Japanes Yen	2.00	2.70
Deutschmark	0.83	1.05
1979.01 - 1981.12		
US dollar	1.82	2.07
British Pound	1.95	2.22
Japanes Yen	2.43	2.97
Deutschmark	1.04	1.25
1982.01 - 1989.124		
US dollar	1.65	2.04
British Pound	1.56	1.98
Japanes Yen	1.65	2.26
Deutschmark	0.72	0.93
1990.01 - 1997.02		
US dollar	1.35	1.68
British Pound	1.25	1.79
Japanes Yen	2.22	2.96
Deutschmark	0.86	1.07

Source: IMF, International Financial Statistics, and own calculations.

Appendix Table V: Test on Volatility Differences between Prices, Exchange Rates, and Stock Indices 1975-1997

Null Hypothesis	Test value
Nominal effective exchange rates more volatile than consumer prices*	
United States	9.94 (H0 not rejected)
Japan	8.63 (H0 not rejected)
United Kingdom	6.40 (H0 not rejected)
Germany	6.98 (H0 not rejected)
Stock prices more volatile than nominal effective exchange rates*	
United States	5.66 (H0 not rejected)
Japan	6.66 (H0 not rejected)
United Kingdom	5.50 (H0 not rejected)
Germany	9.56 (H0 not rejected)
Stock prices more volatile than real effective exchange rates*	
United States	5.43 (H0 not rejected)
Japan	6.18 (H0 not rejected)
United Kingdom	5.38 (H0 not rejected)
Germany	6.60 (H0 not rejected)
Real effective exchange rate and nominal effective exchange rate are equally volatile**	
United States	1.22 (H0 not rejected)
Japan	0.76 (H0 not rejected)
United Kingdom	1.14 (H0 not rejected)
Germany	1.32 (H0 not rejected)

Tests are based on average quadratic quarterly percentage changes and a 5% significance level.

*H0 rejected for test value < 1.65,

**H0 rejected for test value < -1.96 or > 1.96.

Comment

Manfred Willms
University of Kiel, Olshauserstr. 50-60, D - 24098 Kiel

All exchange rate systems ever implemented are imperfect. Fixed exchange rate systems typically lead to delayed adjustments while flexible systems can produce highly volatile and misaligned exchange rates. Therefore, both systems might cause economic losses. Numerous economists have tried to measure these effects and to make suggestions for more stable and more efficient systems.

In his paper, Frenkel exploits and evaluates the more recent theoretical and empirical literature on exchange rate regimes. It should already be mentioned here that he has done an extremely good job. All basic aspects are covered and the conclusions are well developed.

The paper is structured in two basic chapters, one on flexible and the other on fixed exchange rates. At the beginning of the first chapter, Frenkel presents some own calculations on exchange rate volatility of selected currencies since 1975. Some interesting results are:

- the short-term volatility of bilateral real exchange rates of the major floating currencies of the world has been higher than the volatility among the EMS-currencies;
- the maximum variation of real exchange rates of the major currencies of the world was significantly higher than among the EMS-currencies;
- short-term exchange rate volatility is substantially lower than the volatility of stock prices in the corresponding countries.

Frenkel does not give a clear answer to the question whether the higher volatility under flexible exchange rates compared to the Bretton Woods System or the EMS is an excessive volatility, disconnected from fundamentals, or whether it is the result of more pronounced real shocks or destabilizing speculation through bubbles or bandwagon effects.

According to more recent studies the dominance of bandwagon effects is widely accepted. A just completed study at the University of Kiel on the microstructure of foreign exchange markets shows that on the spot market intrabank trade is by far the largest market segment.[1] In Germany, it counts for 92.2% of the daily turnover, while trade between banks and nonbanks only covers 7.8%. Most of the intrabank transactions are open positions which have to be

---

[1] Wolgast (1997).

closed at the same day. The decisions of the traders in the banks are mainly based on charts and on the exchange of information between the traders themselves. This generates extrapolative expectations and creates the observed short-run and medium-run volatility via bandwagon effects. The question is why do banks speculate in the exchange market despite of a zero-sum-game. The study mentioned above concludes that there is asymmetric information between the bank management and the traders. As a result, the profitability of speculative exchange market trading is not sufficiently controlled by the management.

Investigating the effects of the high short-run volatility of exchange rates, Frenkel comes to the conclusion that international trade, investment, and growth, after the compensations for the oil price shocks, have not negatively been affected. In addition, misalignments have done no significant harm to the integration of the world economy. Companies have adjusted to such misalignments by international diversification of investments and by a greater availability and a better handling of hedging instruments.

With respect to the insulation effect of a flexible exchange rate system, empirical research indicates that in the long-run an import of inflation can be prevented while the domestic economy cannot be neutralized against cyclical impacts from the world market.

At the end of the first basic chapter Frenkel studies the question whether exchange rate volatility can be reduced or eliminated by central bank intervention. It seems to be true that sterilization interventions only have very short-run effects and that even the impact of unsterilized interventions is ambiguous.

The chapter on fixed exchange rates begins with the discussion on the higher monetary and fiscal discipline attributed to this system. Frenkel utilizes some recent theoretical and empirical papers which question this widely accepted statement. However, the new models, especially the one by Tornell and Velasco (1995) are very limited with respect to their applicability to the real world. And the empirical studies are mainly carried out for the EMS which certainly is not a good example for a fixed exchange rate system. A better example is the Bretton Woods System in its first twenty years of existence. During this time monetary and fiscal discipline prevailed until the United States as the anchor country started an excessive macroeconomic policy.

As a next step Frenkel gives a very good presentation of the models of currency crises, especially on the standard model of Krugman (1979). Open questions are the precise causes of a balance-of-payments crisis and the adequate strategies for its prevention. The occurrence of such crises indicates that fixed exchange rate systems are vulnerable institutions and endangered when countries do not consequently stick to the rules of the game.

Especially developing countries try to bring down high inflation rates by pegging their exchange rate to the currency of a low inflation country. The idea behind this approach is to break inflationary expectations via the import of credibility and, thus, to prevent the negative impact of a reduction of the inflation rate on employment. By exploring the relevant literature Frenkel shows that a number of problems are associated with this approach. One of the most important undesired effects is a real appreciation of the domestic currency due to wage and price pressure stemming from past experience.

One possibility to increase credibility and to reduce the wage pressure is the establishment of a currency board system. Unfortunately, this system and its implications are not discussed in the paper.

Finally, Frenkel puts great effort into the analysis of the target zone approach, especially to the presentation of the Krugman model (1991) and its extension by other researchers as well as its empirical testing. Frenkel detects three critical assumptions of the Krugman model which are - according to his view - in conflict with reality:

1. Perfect credibility for a defense of the exchange rate at the margin.
2. Absence of intramarginal interventions.
3. Utilization of the monetary model of the exchange rate.

With respect to the third point, Frenkel claims that the monetary model has empirically not been confirmed. According to some recent research this statement is not correct anymore. Applying a vector error correction model for cointegration between purchasing power parity and the mark/dollar exchange rate the monetary theory of the exchange rate cannot be rejected.[2] Hansen comes to this conclusion by testing the monetary theory of the exchange rate via money demand functions for Germany and the United States.

The target zone approach requires the determination of some kind of equilibrium exchange rate. Correctly, Frenkel criticizes the concept of the Fundamental Equilibrium Exchange Rate (FEER) proposal by Williamson (1985), which principally is based on the current account and on medium term capital flows. However, he does not consider the much more advanced Natural Real Exchange Rate Approach (NATREX) developed by Stein (1992)[3] and recently applied for Germany by Stein and Sauernheimer (1996).[4]

Frenkel tries to explain by six arguments why the target zone approach has not been implemented in the past. Three arguments are concerned with typical problems of fixed exchange rate systems. Only the other three are clearly connected to target zone problems like shortcomings in the theoretical foundation, the adequate determination of the equilibrium exchange rate and the right timing for the implementation of the target zone.

In summarizing, Frenkel's paper gives an excellent survey on the discussion of flexible versus fixed exchange rates. The paper underlines the problems associated

---

[2] Hansen (1996).

[3] Stein (1992).

[4] Stein and Sauernheimer (1996).

with both systems and, therefore, makes clear that it is extremely difficult to decide under what conditions a flexible or a fixed exchange rate system is superior to the other.

References

Hansen, Gerd, (1996), The Mark-Dollar Exchange Rate and Purchasing Power Parity. Some Empirical Evidence. Arbeiten aus dem Institut für Statistik und Ökonometrie der Universität Kiel, No. 89, Kiel.

Krugman, P. (1979), A Modell of Balance of Payments Crises, *Journal of Money, Credit, and Banking* 11, 311-25.

Krugman, P. (1991), Target Zones and Exchange Rate Dynamics, *Quarterly Journal of Economics* 106, 669-82.

Stein, J. L.(1992), Fundamental Determinants of Exchange Rates, *Journal of International and Comparative Economics* 1, 125-62.

Stein, J. L. and K. Sauernheimer (1996), The Equilibrium Real Exchange rate of Germany, *Journal of International and Comparative Economics* 4, 97-131.

Tornell, A. and A. Velasco (1995), Fiscal Discipline and the Choice of Exchange Rate Regimes, *European Economic Review* 39, 759-70.

Williamson, J. (1985), The Exchange Rate System, Policy Analyses in International Economics, 5, Institute for International Economics, Washington, D.C.

Wolgast, M. (1997), Deviseneigenhandel der Geschäftsbanken, Devisenspekulationen und nichtfundamentale Wechselkursbewegungen. *Untersuchungen über das Spar-, Giro- und Kreditwesen* 161, Berlin.

6. Approaching European Monetary Union: On Conversion Rates

The Indeterminacy of the Euro Conversion Rates. Why It Matters and How It Can Be Solved

Paul De Grauwe
University of Leuven, Naamsestraat 69, B - 3000 Leuven

1 Introduction

On January 1, 1999 the conversion rates of the euro into the national currencies of the EMU-countries will be fixed irrevocably. Two conditions have been attached to this conversion process. First, the Maastricht Treaty stipulates that the adoption of the irrevocably fixed conversion rates should not modify the external value of the ecu. Second, at the Madrid Summit Meeting of December 1995 it was decided that at conversion time one euro should be equal to one ecu. These two conditions severely constrain the choices about how to set these conversion rates for stage three. In a nutshell, the constraint is that the euro conversion rates used on January 1, 1999 will have to be the market rates of the ecu observed at the end of the previous day. In addition, it will not be possible to announce in advance the euro conversion rates that will be applied on January 1, 1999. The reason is that the ecu rates of the participating currencies will continue to fluctuate until the last day because the ecu contains non-participating currencies (e.g. the pound sterling). This will create problems. In particular, if the authorities rely on the market to decide about these conversion rates an indeterminacy problem will arise (see Begg, et al. (1997) and De Grauwe & Spaventa (1997)). This can be described as follows. The ecu rate of say the DM before conversion time will be determined by the expectations the market has about the future euro conversion rate of the DM. The latter, however, will be equal to the last day's ecu rate of the DM. As a result, any movement of the ecu rate will be self-validating since it determines the choice of the euro conversion rate. The market has nothing to anchor its beliefs on.

This problem can only partially be avoided if it is decided to set the euro conversion rates indirectly, by first determining the bilateral rates and then deriving the implied eurorates. In that case it is possible to announce bilateral conversion rates in advance. If the commitment towards these bilateral conversion rates is credible, market rates will converge to the bilateral conversion rates before the latter are irrevocably set (see Begg, et al. (1997) and De Grauwe & Spaventa (1997)). This solution, however, does not eliminate the problem of indeterminacy of the euro conversion rates. In addition, the indeterminacy of the euro conversion rates spills-over into the exchange markets of the in-currencies with outside currencies.

In section 2 we analyze the nature of this indeterminacy. In the next sections we propose solutions to the problem.

2 The Fundamental Indeterminacy of the Euro Conversion Rates

We illustrate the indeterminacy problem involving the euro conversion rates as follows. Suppose that of the N currencies belonging to the ecu basket I are of in-countries while N-I are of out-countries, not joining the single currency at the outset.

From the basket definition of the ecu we know that:

$$(1) \qquad Ecu_i = \sum_{j=1}^{I} a_j S_{ji} + \sum_{k=I+1}^{N} a_k S_{ki}$$

where Ecu_i = the value of the ecu in terms of currency i (i = 1...I); a_j, a_k = the amounts of currency j (j = 1...I) and of currency k (k = I+1...N) in the ecu basket; S_{ji}, S_{ki} = the exchange rate of currency j (j = 1...I) and of currency k (k = I+1...N) in terms of currency i (units of currency i per unit of currency j and of currency k).

Let us now assume that the bilateral conversion rates S_{ji}^* are fixed in advance. This has been proposed by Begg, et al. (1997) and De Grauwe & Spaventa (1997) to solve the indeterminacy problem involving the **bilateral** conversion rates. We want to show that fixing bilateral rates still keeps the euro rates indeterminate. In addition, this indeterminacy problem spills over into an indeterminacy in the determination of the exchange rates between the in-currencies and the outside currencies.

We rewrite equation (1) as follows:

$$(2) \qquad Ecu_i^t = \sum_{j=1}^{I} a_j S_{ji}^* + \sum_{k=I+1}^{N} a_k S_{ki}^t$$

where S_{ji}^* are the fixed bilateral conversion rates that the authorities have announced; the superscript t refers to time.

Let us take the dollar as the prototype external currency, we can rewrite (2) in the following way:

$$(3) \qquad Ecu_i^t = \sum_{j=1}^{I} a_j S_{ji}^* + S_{\$i}^t \left(\sum_{k=I+1}^{N} a_k S_{k\$}^t \right)$$

where $S_{\$i}^{t}$ is the price of the dollar in units of currency i (an inside currency) and $S_{k\$}^{t}$ is the price of currency k (an outside currency) in units of dollars. Note that in (3) we have used the triangular arbitrage condition $S_{ki}^{t} = S_{k\$}^{t} S_{\$i}^{t}$.

Equation (3) can also be rewritten as follows

$$(4) \qquad Ecu_i^t = A + S_{\$i}^t \bar{S}_{\$0}^t$$

The first term on the right hand side is a constant and is determined by the chosen fixed bilateral conversion rates. The second term consists of the product of the dollar rate of currency i (an inside currency) and a weighted sum of dollar rates of the currencies not participating in EMU (the out-currencies). The latter can be considered as an exogenous variable.

Let us apply equation (4) to the last day before the start of EMU. We call this day *T-1*. To focus the attention suppose currency i is the DM. We then have

$$(5) \qquad Ecu_{DM}^{T-1} = A + S_{\$DM}^{T-1} \bar{S}_{\$0}^{T-1}$$

In order to determine the value of the ecu in terms of the DM on day *T-1* agents need to know the dollar rates of the outside currencies and of the DM. We concentrate our attention on the determination of the latter. (The former are exogenous from the point of view of the euro conversion process). We use a well-known model of exchange rate determination which allows us to write the dollar/DM exchange rate in period *T-1* as follows

$$(6) \qquad S_{\$DM}^{T-1} = (1-\beta) Z^{T-1} + \beta E_{T-1} S_{\$DM}^{T}$$

where Z^{T-1} is the fundamental variable driving the exchange rate in period *T-1*, and β is a discount factor. The closer we come to period T (conversion time) the closer β approaches 1.

On day T the euro will be introduced and the euro conversion rates will be fixed. This will affect the dollar/DM rate. This can be seen from the following triangular arbitrage condition

$$(7) \qquad S_{\$DM}^{T} = S_{\$E}^{T} S_{E,DM}^{T}$$

where $S_{E,DM}^{T}$ is the euro conversion rate of the DM, and $S_{\$E}^{T}$ is the exchange rate of the dollar in units of euro that will prevail at time T. Thus, in order to be able to forecast the future dollar/DM rate the agents must forecast the future euro conversion rate of the DM and the euro/dollar exchange rate. Given the constraint imposed by the Treaty and the Madrid Council decision both the euro/DM conversion rate and the euro/dollar exchange rate at time T will be determined by the market ecu rate of these currencies at the end of period *T-1*. Thus

$$S^{T}_{E,DM} = Ecu^{T-1}_{DM}$$

(8) and

$$S^{T}_{\$E} = \frac{1}{Ecu^{T-1}_{\$}}$$

where we have made the period *T-1* small enough (e.g. the last second before closing time) so as to move arbitrarily close to period *T* (e.g. the first second after the opening of the market on day T). Substituting (7) into (6), using (8) and taking into account that as we move closer to *T*, β approaches 1, we obtain

$$(9) \quad Ecu^{T-1}_{DM} = A + \frac{Ecu^{T-1}_{DM}}{Ecu^{T-1}_{\$}} S^{T-1}_{\$0}$$

The solution is given by the following expression

$$(10) \quad Ecu^{T-1}_{DM} = A\left[\frac{Ecu^{T-1}_{\$}}{Ecu^{T-1}_{\$} - S^{T-1}_{\$0}}\right]$$

Graphically, the solutions lie on the hyperbole represented in figure 1.[1]

Equation (10) makes clear the nature of the indeterminacy problems: there are infinitely many solutions to this (non-linear) equation. Any choice made by the market will be self-validating. There is nothing that will tie down this choice. This feature can lead to turbulence in the exchange markets. In particular, it will necessarily spill over into the dollar/DM market. This can be shown as follows.

Triangular arbitrage ensures that

$$(11) \quad \frac{Ecu^{T-1}_{DM}}{Ecu^{T-1}_{\$}} = S^{T-1}_{\$DM}$$

Dividing (10) by $Ecu^{T-1}_{\$}$ and using (11) yields the solution for the dollar/DM rate at time *T-1*.

$$(12) \quad S^{T-1}_{\$DM} = A\left[\frac{1}{Ecu^{T-1}_{\$} - S^{T-1}_{\$0}}\right]$$

[1] Note that we restrict the solution to lie in the positive quadrant.

The infinitely many solutions for $S_{\$DM}^{T-1}$ and $Ecu_{\$}^{T-1}$ must lie on the hyperbole shown in figure 2.

Figure 1:

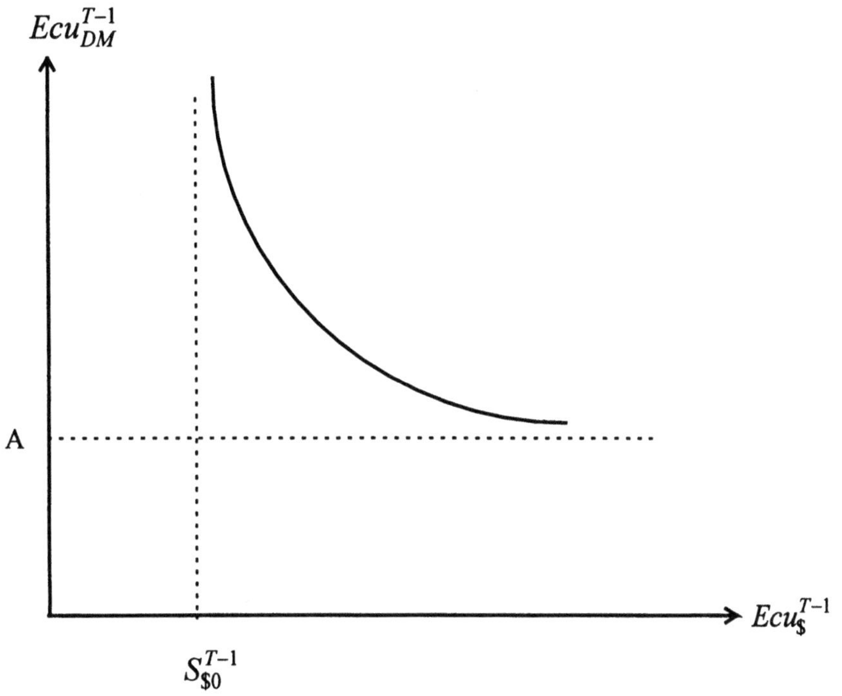

Figure 2:

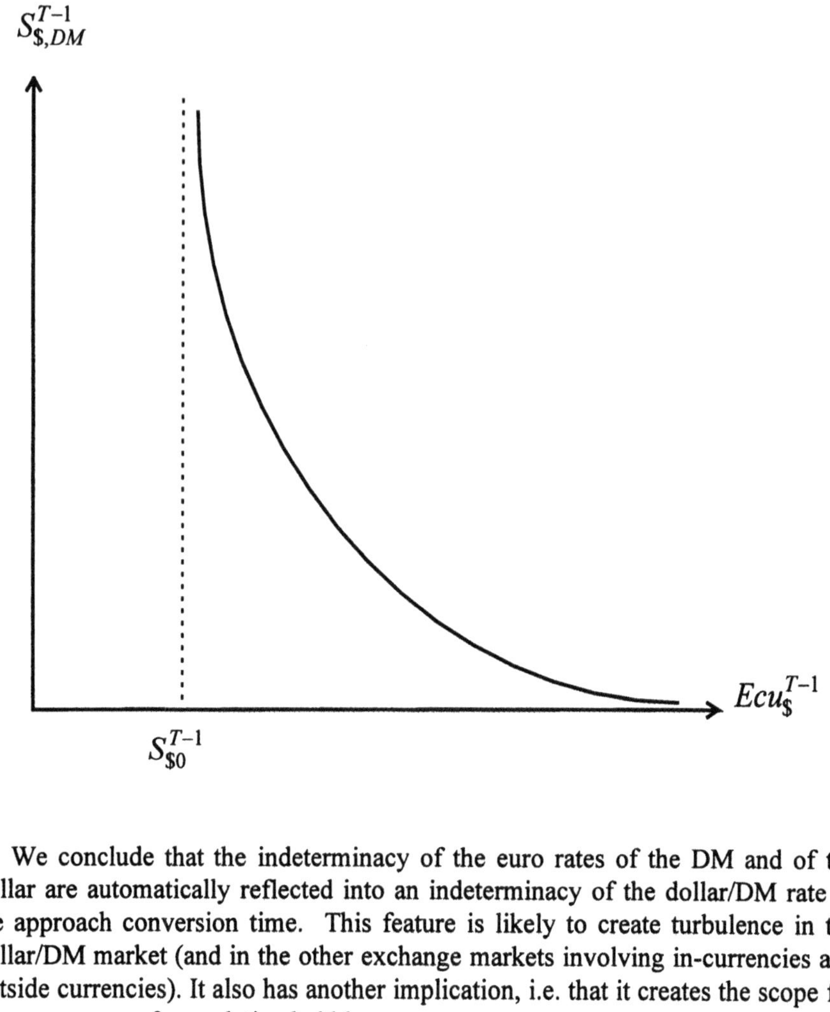

We conclude that the indeterminacy of the euro rates of the DM and of the dollar are automatically reflected into an indeterminacy of the dollar/DM rate as we approach conversion time. This feature is likely to create turbulence in the dollar/DM market (and in the other exchange markets involving in-currencies and outside currencies). It also has another implication, i.e. that it creates the scope for the occurrence of speculative bubbles.

3 Euro Indeterminacy and Speculative Bubbles

In the previous section we showed that on the last day before the start of EMU there are infinitely many solutions for the ecu rates that can be used as euro conversion rates on the next day. This means that before the start of EMU there will be no fixed point to tie down expectations. When speculators will be aware that every move in the market is self-validating the conditions for the development of speculative bubbles are met. A speculative bubble may therefore start during the interim period which guarantees substantial profits for the speculators jumping on the speculative bubble path. Whatever the point reached by the speculative bubble on December 31, 1998 it will be validated by the authorities.

In order to illustrate how self-fulfilling speculative bubbles can arise we performed the following simulations. We allowed the dollar/DM rate to move along many different speculative bubble paths. On each such path speculators expect the next period's dollar/DM rate to increase (decrease) at a constant rate. By varying that rate we obtain a multiplicity of speculative bubble paths. We then plugged the values of the dollar/DM rates into the definition of the ecu rate of the DM according to formula (4). We assumed that the dollar rates vis-à-vis the outside currencies follow a random walk.[2] We show some examples of these simulations in figures 3 and 4. The end values we obtain are all consistent with the conversion rules as specified in the Treaty and in the Madrid Council decision.

The question that arises then is how likely the development of such speculative bubbles is. The fact that they can occur does not mean that they will necessarily develop. There is a co-ordination problem that must be solved for a bubble to arise, i.e. speculators must jointly be expecting, say, an increase of the dollar of x% each period to generate an incentive for speculators to join the bandwagon. In order to answer the question of whether a speculative bubble is likely we have to solve an interpretation problem of the Treaty. Article 109 1 4 says that "at the starting date of the third stage, the Council shall (...) adopt the conversion rates at which their currencies shall be irrevocably fixed and at which irrevocably fixed rate the ecu (the euro) shall be substituted for these currencies, and the ecu (the euro) will become a currency in its own right. This measure shall by itself not modify the external value of the ecu". How should this last sentence be interpreted? The problem can be analyzed by starting from the triangular arbitrage condition (11). On day T the Council adopts the euro conversion rates. This should not change the external value of the ecu. Let us assume first that this sentence implies that the ecu rates of the DM and the dollar should not change. (This is the assumption we have used up to now). Thus, the euro conversion rate of the DM is set equal to Ecu_{DM}^{T-1} (the numerator in (11)), and the euro/dollar rate is set equal to the ecu/dollar rate of the previous day. But suppose that at that very moment of announcing the euro conversion rate of the DM, the dollar/DM rate drops in the market. We can see from (11) that this must also lead to an immediate increase in the euro/dollar rate. Thus, at that very moment the external value of the ecu is not maintained. What should the ECB do? Does the Treaty imply that it should prevent the increase of the euro/dollar rate? And if so, for how long? Just a few minutes, or just during the first day? All this is quite important because it can influence the risk of speculative bubbles. If the ECB guarantees a fixed euro/dollar rate during, say, the first day, it will have to intervene in the foreign exchange

[2] It was assumed that Denmark, Greece, Italy and the UK are out-currencies.

market. The ECB could then become a "money machine" making the occurrence of a speculative bubble very likely.

To see this, consider the following example. Take the bubble in figure 3 where the dollar/DM increases from 1.7 to 2.8 on day T-1. The corresponding dollar/ecu rate on day T-1 is 2.4. Speculators who have bought the dollar at a rate of, say, 2 DM will be able to sell dollars on day T against the euro at the rate of 2.4 euro per dollar. (This is the rate the ECB is guaranteeing on day T based on the ecu rate achieved on the previous day). Speculators will then be able to sell these euros for DM at the irrevocably fixed exchange rate, allowing them to cash in 2.8 DM. The implication of this is that the ECB will function as a "money machine" selling euros to speculators at an inflated price so that the latter can cash in their profit. If this happens, speculators know that there can be no crash on the day of conversion. This by itself will increase the probability of the occurrence of a speculative bubble.

We conclude that the ECB has a rather uncomfortable choice. Either it does not intervene to guarantee the external value of the ecu (in terms of dollars) on day T. In that case the probability that speculative bubbles arise is reduced, but then the Treaty provision that the external value of the ecu must be maintained is a theoretical one. Alternatively, the ECB backs up this provision by interventions (say, on the first day of EMU) but then it increases the likelihood that speculative bubbles arise.

There is another possible interpretation of the Treaty provision, however. In this interpretation "external" means non-EMU currencies. This means that on conversion day, the Council would be free to select any euro conversion rate of the in-currencies independent from the previous day ecu market rates. The practical implication can again be seen from the triangular arbitrage condition (11). It would mean that on day T the euro conversion rate of the DM could be devalued relative to the previous day's ecu rate of the DM. Given that the denominator is fixed, this would imply that the dollar/DM rate is devalued in the same proportion. This would be equivalent to organizing a crash, if the dollar/DM had experienced an upward bubble before. Therefore, this interpretation of the Treaty would reduce the risk of a bubble. We return to this interpretation in the last section.

We conclude that the likelihood of speculative bubbles very much depends on how the treaty provision about the conversion is organized in practice. In any case, something should be done to prevent the occurrence of such speculative bubbles. The need to do something is made more intense because at the start of EMU the national currencies will still be in existence. If this were not the case, one could argue that these speculative bubbles don't really matter. For, in that case, all that would happen is that on conversion time a different euro conversion rate would exist, the choice of which is arbitrary any way.

The trouble arises because the DM will continue to exist for three years after conversion time. Thus, if an upward bubble of the dollar/DM rate has developed prior to the start of EMU, a strong upward pressure on the DM-prices will be set in motion, leading to a situation where the EMU would start with strong inflationary pressures. Since the euro and the DM will be tightly linked, this upward pressure would be felt both on the euro and the DM price levels[3]. Of course, if a bubble has occurred prior to the start of EMU, it is likely that a correction will be set in motion after the start of EMU. In that case the euro would appreciate. This would then put downward pressure of the euro price level. In any case the strong volatility of the dollar rates prior and after the start of EMU would make the stabilization of the euro price level more difficult.

From the preceding analysis we conclude that the euro conversion process has serious flaws. Even if large scale speculative bubbles can be prevented, the fundamental indeterminacy of the euro conversion rates can generate exchange rate volatility prior to the start of EMU and to price level instability afterwards.

Figure 3:

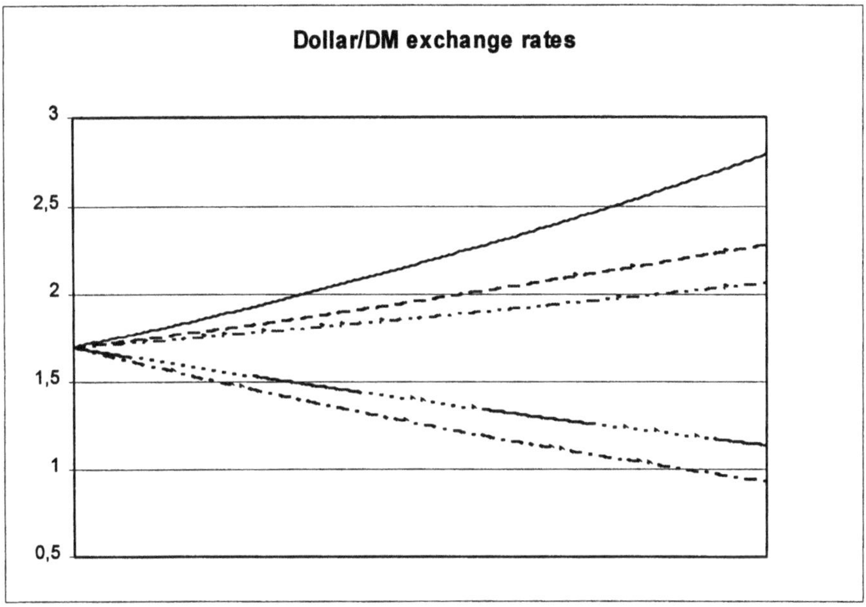

The question we analyze in the next sections is how these problems can be solved. All the proposals we formulate involve providing an anchor in the exchange markets. In sections 3 and 4 we discuss a solution which involves fixing

[3] Conversely, if the speculative bubble that occurs prior to conversion time leads to a decline of the dollar against the DM, it would generate a downward pressure on the price level expressed in euro and in DM after the start of EMU. This would not be a good way to start EMU.

euro rates in advance and we analyze the condition under which this can be done. In section 5 we discuss a solution involving fixing the dollar/DM exchange rates. Finally, in section 6 we propose the simplest possible solution which implies interpreting the Treaty in such a way that on conversion time the euro/DM conversion rate can be arbitrarily reset.

Figure 4:

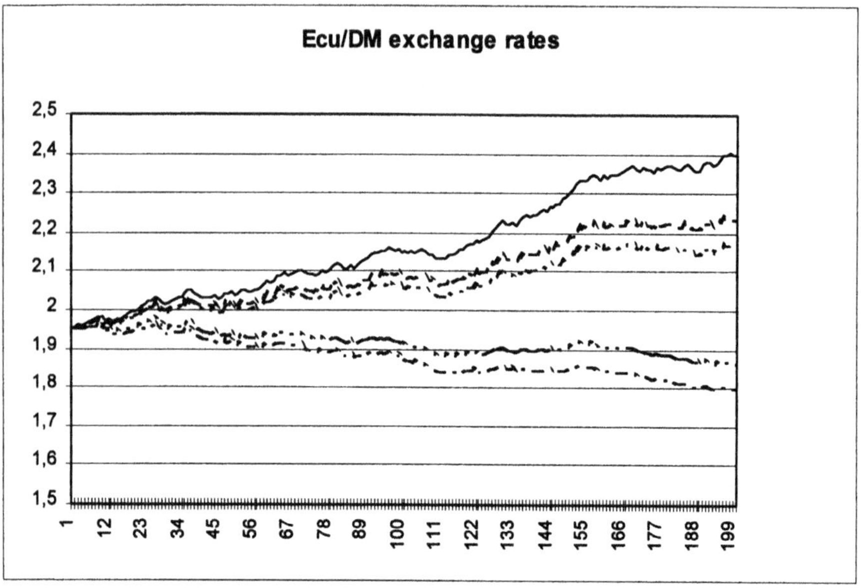

4 Fixing Euro Coneversion Rates in Advance

Suppose the authorities announce in advance fixed euro rates to be applied at the start of stage three (time *T*). Under what conditions can this be done? Call these pre-announced euro-rates $Euro_i^*$. The Madrid Council resolution now implies that on January 1, 1999 $Ecu_i^T = Euro_i^*$. In addition the Treaty requires that $Ecu_i^T = Ecu_i^{T-1}$. Triangular arbitrage ensures that, by fixing the euro/ecu rates, the bilateral exchange rates for the in-currencies are also fixed, i.e.:

$$(13) \quad S_{ji}^* = \frac{Euro_i^*}{Euro_j^*}$$

We rewrite equation (1) filling in these announced conversion rates (euro and bilateral rates). We set the values of the bilateral rates of the outside currencies equal to S_{ki}^t. These could be the central rates of these currencies or any other value (e.g. the market value of these currencies at time t).

$$(14)\quad Euro_i^* = \sum_{j=1}^{I} a_j S_{ji}^* + \sum_{k=I+1}^{N} a_k S_{ki}^t$$

It can immediately be seen that the euro conversion rates cannot be kept fixed because the bilateral exchange rates of the outside currencies will continuously change. Put differently, from the moment of the announcement, the market ecu rates will tend to diverge from these euro conversion rates because the currencies of the non-participating countries will fluctuate continuously. The difference between the euro conversion rates and the market ecu rates on day *T-1* will be given by the following expression.

$$(15)\quad Ecu_i^{T-1} - Euro_i^* = \sum_{j=1}^{I} a_j \left(S_{ji}^{T-1} - S_{ji}^*\right) + \sum_{k=I+1}^{N} a_k \left(S_{ki}^{T-1} - S_{ki}^t\right)$$

If the market is confident that the bilateral conversion rates will be applied the bilateral market rates will converge to these values on day *T-1*, i.e. $S_{ji}^{T-1} = S_{ji}^*$. We obtain

$$(16)\quad Ecu_i^{T-1} - Euro_i^* = \sum_{k=I+1}^{N} a_k \left(S_{ki}^{T-1} - S_{ki}^t\right)$$

Under what conditions can we make sure that the market rates of the ecu on day
T-1 also converge towards the conversion rates, i.e. $Ecu_i^{T-1} = Euro_i^*$? At first sight this seems impossible to achieve since on day *T-1* there is no reason why $S_{ki}^{T-1} = S_{ki}^t$. One can, however, achieve this result if one is willing to adjust the amounts of the currencies in the basket. This can be done in the following way. We return to equation (14) but we now consider the amounts a_j as variables changing over time. This yields

$$(17)\quad Euro_i^* = \sum_{j=1}^{I} a_j^t S_{ji}^* + \sum_{k=I+1}^{N} a_k S_{ki}^t$$

It can now be seen that we can allow a_j^t to vary so as to compensate the variations of S_{ki}^t. The following expression tells us how these a_j^t must vary (given that $\Delta Euro_i^* = 0$).

(18) $$\sum_{j=1}^{I} \Delta a_j^t S_{ji}^* = - \sum_{k=I+1}^{N} a_k \Delta S_{ki}^t \qquad \text{for } i = 1, \dots I$$

In words, all we have to do is to adjust the amounts a_j of the in-currencies in such a way that these changes equal the weighted average of the changes of the out-currencies exchange rates. Note that although there are I equations in (18) these are not independent. In fact it can be shown that there is only one independent equation in (18) (see appendix). As a result, one equation suffices to determine the necessary adjustments in the a_j's. Since there is only one equation to determine the a_j's there is plenty of choice. We could for example, choose one in-currency (say the DM) to be adjusted in the basket, keeping all the other a_j's constant. Alternatively, one could impose that all the a_j's be adjusted in the same proportion. This is the choice we make here. This then yields the following solution.

(19) $$x_I^t = - \sum_{k=I+1}^{N} \frac{b_k}{b_I} y_{ki}^t$$

where x_I^t is the (common) rate of change of the amounts a_j's of the in-currencies; y_{ki}^t is the rate of change of the exchange rate of out-currency k vis-à-vis the in-currency i (note that $y_{ki}^t = y_k^t$ for all i); b_k is the share of the out-currency k in the ecu basket and b_I is the total share of the in-currencies in the basket. (In appendix this formula is derived explicitly).

An example will clarify the formula. Suppose the only outside currency is the pound sterling. (In any case it will be the most important one). If on day *T-1* the pound has appreciated by say 20% against the initial value used to compute the euro conversion rates, the required adjustment in the amounts a_j of the in-currencies is equal to - (b_{UK}/b_I) 20%. The term between brackets is likely to be small as the share of the pound in the ecu is small relative to the total share of the prospective in-currencies.

This result can also be interpreted as follows. When the out-currencies appreciate relative to the in-currencies this tends to increase the value of the ecu against the in-currencies. In order to keep the ecu rates equal to the announced euro rates the value of the ecu must be reduced. This is achieved by reducing the amounts a_j in the basket. The opposite occurs when the out-currencies depreciate against the in-currencies. It should be stressed, however, that these adjustments are likely to be small because the shares of the out-currencies are most likely going to be a small fraction of the shares of the in-currencies in the basket.

Note also that the adjustments in the a_j's could be done on a continuous (say daily basis) instead of doing this at the last day before EMU starts.

We conclude that it is technically possible to announce fixed euro conversion rates before the start of the third stage of EMU without coming into conflict with the external value constraint and the requirement that on January 1, 1999 one ecu must be exchanged for one euro. Such an announcement, if credible, would also make it possible to avoid the indeterminacy problem and the ensuing risk for speculative bubbles.

5 The Legal Problem

The proposal formulated in the previous section to change the composition of the ecu basket in response to fluctuations of the exchange rates of the out-currencies may lead to a legal problem. According to article 109g of the Treaty "The currency composition of the ecu basket shall not be changed". This article was introduced into the Treaty because it was felt that the five year adjustments of the currency composition of the ecu which existed prior to 1991, introduced too much uncertainty about the value of the ecu. Paradoxically, the freezing of the currency composition decided at Maastricht, may exacerbate volatility in the exchange markets in the run-up towards stage three of EMU. The question that arises is then whether this Treaty provision can be circumvented so as to achieve the goal of greater exchange rate stability during the transition towards EMU. In this section we formulate a proposal that achieves this.

The proposal consists in stripping the ecu into two components, an "insider" ecu defined as the sum of the amounts a_j of the insider currencies and an "outsider" ecu defined as the sum of the amounts a_k of the outsider currencies. The sum of these two new ecus is equal to the old ecu, i.e.

$$Ecu = EcuI + EcuO \tag{20}$$

The authorities now commit themselves to always convert *1 EcuI + 1 EcuO* into 1 ecu. At the same time they announce that they will fix the euro conversion rates in the way defined by equation (14). Given the constraints imposed by the Treaty (external value constraints on the ecu) and the one to one conversion requirement of the ecu into the euro this announcement amounts to fixing the ecu rates of the insider currencies. We obtain

$$Ecu_i^* = EcuI_i + EcuO_i \qquad \text{for i} = 1, \dots \text{I} \tag{21}$$

where $EcuI_i = \sum_{j=1}^{I} a_j S_{ji}$

$$EcuO_i = \sum_{k=I+1}^{N} a_k S_{ki}$$

The fixing of the euro conversion rates, however, also means that the bilateral conversion rates are fixed. This implies

$$(22) \quad EcuI_i^* = \sum_{j=1}^{I} a_j S_{ji}^*$$

and is to be interpreted as the officially fixed price of the insider ecu. Since Ecu_i^* is fixed (by the announcement) and since $EcuO_i$ is fluctuating continuously the market value of $EcuI_i^*$ must be able to fluctuate. Arbitrage will make sure that this happens. Call P_i the market value of $EcuI_i^*$, one obtains

$$(23) \quad Ecu_i^* = P_i EcuI_i^* + EcuO_i$$

Taking first differences yields

$$(24) \quad \Delta P_i = -\frac{1}{Ecu_i^*} \Delta EcuO_i$$

The market value of the inside ecu adjusts so as to offset the fluctuations of the exchange rates of the out-currencies. Thus, for example, if sterling appreciates the market value of the inside ecu declines. This decline achieves the same result as the reduction of the amounts a_j in the basket which we analyzed in the previous section. In fact it can be shown that the proportional change in the amounts a_j is the same as the proportional change in the market price P_i. It implies that this change in the market price of the inside ecu following movements of the exchange rates of the out currencies are likely to be small.

In the previous paragraphs we have argued that arbitrage can be relied upon to create the same effects as changing the currency composition of the ecu. There is another arbitrage activity that could operate in the scheme we propose here. This can be described as follows. When the market price of the inside ecu, P_i, deviates from 1 there will be an incentive to bundle or unbundle the inside ecu. For example, suppose P_i is less than 1. In that case it will be profitable to buy the inside ecu cheaply in the market and then to unbundle it so as to sell the different constituent currencies. If this arbitrage works perfectly, P_i will always be equal to 1. This is very unlikely to happen, however. There is a lot of evidence that arbitrage through bundling and unbundling the ecu has not worked well, producing relatively large deviations between the market value of the ecu and its theoretical value (see Gros and Thygesen (1992), and Gonzales-Pacheco and Steinherr (1996)).

6 Fixing the Dollar/DM Exchange Rate

In the previous sections we argued that it is technically possible to fix euro conversion rates in advance. The legal problem may, however, necessitate creating new sub-units of the ecu, which in turn requires the creation of new markets for these new currencies. It is not clear whether this can be done in such a short period of time.

There is another solution to the indeterminacy problem, however, requiring no technical or institutional changes. This consists in an agreement between the European and the American authorities to fix the dollar/DM exchange rate during the transition period to EMU. From an analytical point of view this is the most obvious solution. It can immediately be seen from equation (12) that if $S_{\$DM}^{T-1}$ is fixed, this ties down $Ecu_{\$}^{T-1}$. By equation (10) this also ties down Ecu_{DM}^{T-1}. Thus by fixing the dollar/DM exchange rate an external anchor is provided so that the Ecu_{DM}^{T-1} is also safely anchored.

Several points should be stressed. First, the fixing of the dollar/DM does not mean that the ecu/DM rate will not vary prior to conversion time. It will, as can be seen from equation (12), because the outside currencies will continue to vary against the dollar. However, the indeterminacy problem (i.e. the existence of infinitely may solutions for the ecu rates) will disappear. At the same time the scope for great turbulence is also reduced. Second, the fixing of the dollar/DM exchange rate may take the form of defining a band of fluctuation within which the exchange rate floats freely. All the markets need is some anchor to fix their beliefs. Third, the agreement would only hold for the interim period between May and December 1998, so as to provide an anchor for this crucial exchange rate during the approach into EMU. After the start of EMU, the dollar/DM exchange rate would again be left free.

Although this solution is technically easy, the question remains whether such an agreement is politically feasible between the US and Europe. If unfeasible, an alternative solution would consist in an agreement between the EMU participants and the UK to fix the pound/DM exchange rate. This would provide for an equivalent anchor allowing the market to find a fixed point in their forecasts of the future euro rates.

7 Interpreting the External Value Constraint

The final solution we consider involves giving a particular interpretation to the external value constraint. As will be remembered, the Treaty stipulates that the conversion process should not change the external value of the ecu. Up to now we have interpreted this to mean that the ecu value of all currencies (i.e. in- and out-currencies) should not jump from the close of the market on December 31, 1998 to

January 1, 1999. There is another interpretation possible, however (see Kenen (1995), and Arrowsmith (1996) on this). The Treaty provision can also be interpreted to mean that only out-currencies' exchange rates (e.g. sterling, dollar) vis-à-vis the ecu should not jump from T-1 to T. There could still be a discrete adjustment in the ecu and thus euro rates of the in-currencies. We propose that this would be the interpretation given to the external value constraint. This would make it possible to avoid the occurrence of speculative bubbles from arising. In order to show this consider the triangular arbitrage condition (11) which we repeat here:

$$(11) \qquad \frac{Ecu_{DM}^{T-1}}{Ecu_{\$}^{T-1}} = S_{\$DM}^{T-1}$$

Suppose that a speculative bubble has brought the dollar/DM exchange rate to, say, 2.8 and the ecu/DM rate to 2.4 (These are the numbers generated by one of the speculative bubbles simulated in figures 3 and 4). By (11) this implies an ecu/dollar rate of 1.167. The authorities now only guarantee that the latter will not change on January 1, 1999. In this interpretation of the Treaty provision, nothing prevents the authorities from choosing a euro conversion rate for the DM different from 2.4. They can set this conversion rates at, say, 1.5 (or any other number). This implies by (11) that the dollar/DM rate on January 1, 1999 is reduced in the same proportion compared to its level reached on the previous day.

If the authorities make clear in advance that this is what they intend to do, speculative bubbles will not start off. Speculators know then with great certainty that the bubble must crash on day T. Since they know the exact time of the crash we can apply a reasoning developed to show that a deterministic bubble can never start off. The reasoning is as follows. Since everybody knows when the crash will occur, everybody has an incentive to jump off the bubble an instant before the crash, say the day before. Since this is common knowledge, speculators have an incentive to jump off still earlier. We can repeat the argument until we come to the conclusion that the bubble will never get off the ground.

One way the authorities could make their announcement is by promising that the euro/DM conversion rate will be such as to keep the dollar/DM rate between a given band of fluctuation. Equation (11) shows us that the authorities can do this. This announcement, therefore, is very similar to the fixing of the dollar/DM rate discussed in the previous section. The difference, however, is that the European authorities can do this without American co-operation. All they need to do is to choose the appropriate euro/DM conversion rate that will keep the dollar/DM rate within the pre-announced band.

There is a problem with this solution, however.[4] Every adjustment in the euro/DM rate which leads to a change in the dollar/DM rate on day T implies a

[4] The problem was pointed out to me by Luigi Spaventa.

similar change in the exchange rate of the DM against all outside currencies, including those that are in the basket. Thus, if say the dollar has moved up against the DM prior to conversion time, and the authorities therefore devalue the dollar on day T, they will also devalue the pound sterling and the lira (if that currency stays out of EMU). This would be quite awkward since day T coincides with the start of ERM II. Thus, this new exchange rate regime would start with realignments of all the currencies not participating in EMU. In addition, these realignments may have nothing to do with fundamental developments of these currencies.

8 Conclusion

In this paper we have analyzed issues relating to the procedure for setting euro conversion rates at the start of EMU. The constraints imposed by the Maastricht Treaty and by the Madrid Council decision lead to two problems. One is that the euro conversion rates will only be known at the closing of the markets on December 31, 1998. Second, and more importantly, there will be an indeterminacy problem in the selection of these euro conversion rates. Because the euro conversion rates selected on January 1, 1999 must be equal to the ecu rates reached the previous day, there will be infinitely many possible euro rates that the market may select. In other words, the market will lack an anchor for determining the ecu rates that will be used as euro conversion rates. This problem is not solved by announcing fixed bilateral conversion rates in advance of the start of EMU. The indeterminacy problem involving the euro conversion rates will also spill over into the foreign exchange markets involving outside currencies and the in-currencies. Because the market has no way to forecast the euro conversion rate of, say, the DM, it cannot forecast the dollar/DM exchange rate beyond conversion time either. This indeterminacy can create turbulence in these foreign exchange markets. In particular, as speculators are aware that every move in the market is self-validating the conditions for the development of speculative bubbles in for example the dollar/DM market will be met. Put differently, since on the last day before the start of EMU there are infinitely many solutions, there is no fixed point to tie down expectations. A speculative bubble may therefore start during the interim period which guarantees substantial profits for all the speculators jumping on the speculative bubble path.

This feature of the euro conversion process creates risks. First, if a speculative bubble arises, it may destabilize the price level in the euro-area during the early phase of EMU. But even if the occurrence of speculative bubbles can be prevented, the indeterminacy of the euro conversion rates can create turbulence in the foreign exchange markets. It is therefore imperative that the flaws in the euro conversion process be corrected.

In this paper we have proposed several possible solutions aiming at providing an anchor in the markets. A first solution consists in announcing fixed euro rates in advance of the start of EMU. This solution necessitates changing the currency composition of the ecu in response to exchange rate movements of the currencies not participating in EMU (e.g. sterling). This solution may create legal problems since the Treaty forbids changing the currency composition of the ecu. We discussed a scheme that can circumvent this legal problem. It would imply that the ecu is stripped into two parts so that the market can price them differently.

A second solution consists in fixing the dollar/DM exchange rate during the interim period (May-December 1998), or alternatively to keep that exchange rate within some band of fluctuation. This solution would be facilitated by a (temporary) agreement between the US and the German monetary authorities. It is not clear that this can be done politically. The American monetary authorities, however, could be convinced to do so when they realize that in the absence of such an agreement the dollar exchange rates with important European currencies could become quite turbulent.

A third solution does not require an agreement with the US authorities. It consists in interpreting the Maastricht Treaty provision that the ecu should not change its external value at the start of EMU to mean that only the outside currencies (e.g. dollar, sterling) should not change their value against the ecu. This would allow the European authorities to announce that they will choose the euro conversion rate of, say, the DM in such a way that the dollar/DM rate remains within a given band of fluctuation at conversion time. This announcement would have the effect of providing an anchor and to stabilize expectations. The problem with this solution is that it may require realignments between the currencies in the EMU and the outside currencies that have decided to join the ERM II.

One of the previously formulated solutions will have to be chosen if one wants to avoid the risk that the start of EMU runs into great difficulties because of excessive turbulence of the exchange rates of EMU-currencies with outside currencies.

Appendix

In this appendix we first show that the system of I equations (18) has only 1 independent equation. Rewrite (18) in matrix form as follows:

$$\text{(A1)}\quad \begin{bmatrix} 1 & S_{21}^{*} & \cdots & S_{I1}^{*} \\ S_{12}^{*} & 1 & \cdots & S_{I2}^{*} \\ \vdots & \vdots & & \vdots \\ S_{1I}^{*} & S_{2I}^{*} & \cdots & 1 \end{bmatrix} \begin{bmatrix} \Delta a_1^t \\ \Delta a_2^t \\ \vdots \\ \Delta a_I^t \end{bmatrix} = -a_{I+1} \begin{bmatrix} \Delta S_{I+1,1}^t \\ \Delta S_{I+1,2}^t \\ \cdots \\ \Delta S_{I+1,I}^t \end{bmatrix} + \cdots - a_N \begin{bmatrix} \Delta S_{N1}^t \\ \Delta S_{N2}^t \\ \cdots \\ \Delta S_{NI}^t \end{bmatrix}$$

It can now be shown that the matrix of the cross rates has rank 1. We first note that triangular arbitrage ensures that

$$\text{(A2)}\quad S_{ij}^{*} = \frac{1}{S_{ji}^{*}} \qquad \text{or} \qquad S_{ij}^{*} S_{ji}^{*} = 1$$

Next, we multiply the 2nd row by S_{21}^{*}, the 3th row by S_{31}^{*}, ... the Ith row by S_{I}^{*}, and use (A2). This yields the following matrix

$$\text{(A3)}\quad \begin{bmatrix} 1 & S_{21}^{*} & \cdots & S_{I1}^{*} \\ 1 & S_{21}^{*} & \cdots & S_{I1}^{*} \\ \vdots & \vdots & & \vdots \\ 1 & S_{21}^{*} & \cdots & S_{I1}^{*} \end{bmatrix}$$

This implies that there is only one independent equation in (A1).
In addition, the right hand side variables in (A1) are identical for each equation. This can also be shown by multiplying the second entry in each vector by S_{21}^{*}, the third entry by S_{31}^{*}, etc. ... This yields

$$\text{(A4)}\quad -a_{I+1}\begin{bmatrix}\Delta S_{I+1,1}^t\\ \Delta S_{I+1,1}^t\\ \vdots\\ \Delta S_{I+1,1}^t\end{bmatrix}\cdots - a_N\begin{bmatrix}\Delta S_{N1}^t\\ \Delta S_{N1}^t\\ \vdots\\ \Delta S_{N1}^t\end{bmatrix}$$

Thus one equation, say, the first one describes the whole system (A1).

We can now derive formula (19). Take the first equation in (A1)

$$\text{(A5)}\quad \Delta a_1^t + S_{21}^*\Delta a_2^t + \cdots S_{I1}^*\Delta a_I^t = -a_{I+1}\Delta S_{I+1,1}^t \cdots - a_N\Delta S_{N1}^t$$

This can also we rewritten as

(A6)

$$a_1^t\left(\frac{\Delta a_1^t}{a_1^t}\right) + S_{21}^* a_2^t\left(\frac{\Delta a_2^t}{a_2^t}\right)\cdots + S_{I1}^* a_I^t\left(\frac{\Delta a_I^t}{a_I^t}\right) =$$

$$- a_{I+1}S_{I+1,1}\left(\frac{\Delta S_{I+1,1}^t}{S_{I+1,1}^t}\right)\cdots - a_N S_{N1}^t\left(\frac{\Delta S_{N1}^t}{S_{N1}^t}\right)$$

We now assume that the rates of change in the amounts a_j are the same for all in-currencies. Thus

$$\text{(A7)}\quad \frac{\Delta a_i^t}{a_i^t} = x^t \qquad \text{for all i = 1, ... I}$$

Substituting (A7) into (A6) yields

(A8) $$\left(a_1^t + S_{21}^* a_2^t \cdots S_{I1}^* a_I^t\right) x^t = -a_{I+1} S_{I+1,1}^t y_{I+1}^t \cdots - a_N S_{N1}^t y_N^t$$

where $y^t{}_k$ is the rate of change of the exchange rate of currency k against the in-currencies.

This yields the expression (19) in the text where

$$b_I^t = a_1^t + S_{21}^* a_2^t \cdots S_{I1}^* a_I^t$$

and $b_k^t = a_k S_{k,1}^t$

b_I^t is to be interpreted as the share of the I in-currencies in the ecu basket, and b_k^t as the share of the out-currency k in the ecu basket.

References

Arrowsmith, J. (1996), The Role of Exchange-Rate Arrangements in Preparing for EMU, in: Kenen, P. (ed.), Making EMU Happen. Problems and Proposals, Essays in International Finance No. 199, Princeton.

Begg, D., F. Giavazzi, J. von Hagen and C. Wyplosz (1997), EMU. Getting the End-game Right, Monitoring European Integration 7, CEPR, London.

De Grauwe, P. and L. Spaventa (1997), Setting Conversion Rates for the Third Stage of EMU, CEPR Discussion Paper No.1638, London.

Folkerts-Landau, D. and P. Garber (1995), Determining the Value of a Financial Unit of Account Based on Composite Currencies: The Case of the Private ECU, *IMF Staff Papers* 42.

Gonzalez-Pacheco, L. and A. Steinherr (1996), A proposal to stabilise the value of the ECU, *EIB Papers*, Special Issue on EMU No.1, European Investment Bank.

Gros, D. and K. Lannoo (1996), The Passage to the Euro, Report of a CEPS Working Party, Working Party Report No. 16, Brussels.

Gros, D. and N. Thygesen (1992), European Monetary Integration, London.

Kenen, P. (1995), Economic and Monetary Union in Europe, Cambridge.

Comment

Ansgar Belke
University of Bochum, Universitätsstr. 150, D - 44780 Bochum

1 Introduction

At their Mondorf (Luxembourg)-meeting on 14 September 1997, the EU ministers of finance and heads of central banks agreed upon fixing bilateral exchange rates of their currencies in May 1998, that is to say, in advance of stage three of European Monetary Union (EMU). In a recent strand of papers, De Grauwe and coauthors turn their focus on problems of different proposals of *how to set* these *conversion rates* for the third stage of EMU. Different proposals take EMS central rates, market rates at the date of announcement or on the last day of stage two, an average of past or past and future market rates (which is frequently called the Lamfalussy rule though the latter mentioned it only a few times) and forward rates as their basis. By his current paper, De Grauwe *convincingly* contributes to a significant *reduction* in this large number of possible options how to set the irrevocable conversion rates of the currencies of the EMU member states.[1] Moreover, he is *absolutely right* in paying special attention to *credibility-enhancing* announcement solutions, as setting the final conversion factors no sooner than the last trading moments in 1998 will probably lead to serious problems after EMU will have been started. Since he deserves great merits for both jobs, critical comments should only concern some *minor* points. These points are actually intended to be possible suggestions for further discussions.

As it is well-known, controversies about the locking of exchange rates at the beginning of EMU are to a large extent due to *different interpretations* of the Treaty on European Union. These different interpretations mainly concern the 'external value of the ecu' clause in Article 109l(4) -a *first* requirement- and the Madrid Council's '1 euro = 1 ecu rule' decreed in December 1995 -a *second* requirement.[2] Both constraints, however, are generally said to have no persuasive economic rationale. Moreover, they say little on the *exact* conversion procedure,

[1] At the Mondorf-meeting there was no agreement made on the exact method of conversion. Instead, the latter shall be treated confidentially in the near future.

[2] Cf. Gros and Lannoo (1996). It is important to note that the external value constraint must hold *at a moment in time* as an accounting requirement but *not across* time. As the ecu basket will cease to exist at the start of the third stage, the treaty in a strict sense *does not require* that there will be *no change in the external value* of the basket ecu during the shift to the euro. Cf. Kenen (1997).

though the requirement of Article 109l(4) originally aimed at assuring confidence in the private ecu market (Gros and Thygesen (1992)). Nonetheless, as De Grauwe (1998) correctly states, *both* requirements are *the key to any discussion* about final conversion rates since they heavily *constrain the choices* of euro conversion factors. Moreover, De Grauwe emphasizes that the exact interpretation of the first requirement determines the probability of speculative bubbles under the Maastricht setting. The relevant distinction here is between a strict interpretation - i.e. ecu/euro vis-à-vis *any* currency- and a relaxed interpretation of the 'external value' clause -i.e. ecu/euro vis-à-vis *non-composing* currencies (Gros and Lannoo (1996)).

2 Impacts of Institutional Constraints on the Choice of Euro Conversion Rates

2.1 Absence of Credible Commitments on Bilateral Rates

One interpretation is that the *first* requirement *alone* forces the European Council to choose on 1 January 1999 bilateral conversion factors such that they correspond to the respective *market* rates observed at the foreign market's close on 31 December 1998 (Gros and Lannoo (1996), Obstfeld (1997)). At the same time, *earlier commitments* on bilateral rates -as at least implicitly proposed by De Grauwe (1998) and De Grauwe and Spaventa (1997) and propagated at the Luxemburg-meeting on 14 September 1997- do *not* seem to be *credible* in a game-theoretic sense. Since Article 109l(4) of the Maastricht Treaty obliges the ECB to ratify ex-post end-of-Stage 2 rates, whatever their magnitude might be, any preannounced conversion factors actually are noncredible threats (Obstfeld (1997)).[3] When end-1998 market exchange rates thus do *not move towards* the preannounced start-1999 conversion values -a case which will actually be difficult to rule out in practice since i.e. trading is not continuous from 31 December 1998 and 4 January 1999- markets will test their doubts about the steadfastness of the Council. Since in the case of confirmation of the earlier announcement -even if market rates will deviate from the announced rates- markets anticipate legal action and the political reaction of loser groups and, by this, the possibility of a *reversal* of the Council' decision. A further reason might be that, from a strictly legal point of view according to Article 109l(4), any preannouncement of conversion rates has to be characterized as *a mere declaration of intent* and, from a game-theoretic perspective, as a threat *without any legally binding commitment* (Gros and Lannoo

---

[3] Moreover, a binding commitment of e.g. the European council locking 31 December 1998 exchange rates in advance seems to be rather unlikely in political practice. However, the Mondorf-summit on 14 September 1997 tried to convey the impression of a credible commitment with respect to fixing exchange rates in advance in order to avoid speculative bubbles towards the end of stage two of EMU.

(1996)). Even if one does not agree with Obstfeld's and Gros' and Lannoo's arguments one has to concede that it will be very *difficult* for central banks to engage in nonsterilized intervention in order to credibly peg each exchange rate at its preannounced value (De Grauwe and Spaventa (1997), Kenen (1997)).[4] One commitment technology to solve the above problems is proposed by De Grauwe (1996) himself. It consists of an *'institutional frontloading'* of monetary cooperation or even of the ECB itself in advance of the start of stage 3. However, authors like e.g. Obstfeld (1997) refer to the risk of serious opposition of dominant players like the Deutsche Bundesbank and to troublesome legal aspects (indivisibility doctrine, i.e. independent national banks until the end of stage 2) in the case of implementation of this kind of 'frontloading' (Obstfeld (1997)). Both aspects will render such a 'frontloading scenario' quite unrealistic.

This infeasibility of earlier commitments on conversion rates has been derived solely *from the first* requirement. As stated by De Grauwe (1998), *both* requirements, taken as a whole, lead to *uncertainty* of the euro's value until 31 December 1998 and to *indeterminacy* with respect to the *euro* conversion rates. The latter is the central focus of De Grauwe's (1998) paper and, thus, of the following comments too.

2.2 Uncertainty about Euro Conversion Factors

It is *not disputed* in the literature that there can be *no way to know or even to fix in advance* the conversion rates between *the euro* (!) and the participants' national currencies if an out-country, as e.g. the U.K., does not join EMU. The main reason is that the value of the ecu basket in terms of an in-currency, e.g. the DM, at the last moment of foreign-exchange trading on 31 December 1998 $B_{DM}(t)$ will be determined by that trading via the mark price of the currency of out-countries (which still is included in the ecu basket), say e.g. the pound, $S_{UK}(t)$ at that moment in time. The currencies of the Outs will most likely fluctuate unforecastably in the meantime. Moreover, intervention schemes that theoretically might allow pre-fixing of the euro conversion rates are very unlikely. Neither would out-countries have an obvious incentive to peg to in-currencies nor would the Bundesbank feel inclined to make its monetary policy dependent on non-qualifying out-countries (Obstfeld (1997)). Thus, the '1 euro = 1 ecu rule' not only has all the disadvantages of the Maastricht Treaty's external value constraint -as e.g. the enhancement of shocks of intermediate persistence and the resulting

[4] However, confidence in the central banks' ability to engage credibly in interventions might arise from the fact that the closer the date of the third stage the less the probability of jeopardizing price stability will be. The reason is that overall European money supply will be unchanged by a shift of assets between EMU member countries from the beginning of stage 3 on. Cf. Gros and Lannoo (1996).

higher exchange rate variability- but will additionally lead to *random* ultimate euro *conversion factors*. (Arrowsmith (1996), De Grauwe and Spaventa (1997), Kenen (1997)). In contrast to De Grauwe and Spaventa (1997), De Grauwe (1998) states throughout his paper: it is the conversion rates set *in euros and not* the bilateral conversion rates between the Ins which cannot be specified in advance. The unpredictability of ultimate euro conversion factors will have *impacts on the real sector*. Uncertainty over the relationship between the euro and national in-currencies will increase the present value of the option to prolong the attachment to national currencies and of the option to delay investment. Thus, it might make the introduction of the euro *more costly* at least at the retail level (Belke and Gros (1997), Obstfeld (1997)).

2.3 Indeterminacy of Euro Conversion Factors

While uncertainty about euro conversion factors is *not disputed* in the literature, however, *a debate* has evolved about the implications of this insight for (among other matters) the interpretation and the implementation of the external-value clause. Consequently, De Grauwe (1998) focuses his analysis on one still open central question: Does Article 109l lead to the *indeterminacy of euro conversion rates* on the eve of the third stage? As for example also Begg et al. (1997) and De Grauwe and Spaventa (1997) he implicitly allows for the fact that the treaty may actually make the *bilateral* conversion rates indeterminate if the Council does not credibly choose them in advance. De Grauwe (1998) and De Grauwe and Spaventa (1997), therefore, assume that *bilateral* conversion rates of in-currencies have to be *credibly fixed* in advance in order to exclude indeterminacy problems of bilateral rates from the beginning. According to De Grauwe (1998), however, this solution does not rule out indeterminacy of *euro* conversion rates. In the respective literature, indeterminacy is generally derived from monetary exchange rate theory. The latter states, to get to the heart of it, that a bilateral exchange rate that will be pegged from a given date onwards is compatible with *several different* relative money supply paths starting on that date, and hence with *several different* equilibrium (fixed) exchange rates (Begg et al. (1997), Obstfeld (1997)).

De Grauwe (1998) is even more specific on the nature of the indeterminacy of euro conversion rates. In order to demonstrate the properties of this indeterminacy, he starts from the usual definition of in-currencies in terms of the ecu basket. He then applies a technique of stepwise substitution and different types of triangular arbitrage conditions. His main result is that in the end a kind of 'anchor' to stabilize expectations is missing. Any, let's say, DM/ecu rate at the eve of stage 3 (T-1) necessarily validates itself at the time of conversion (T). The market DM rate of the ecu in T-1 determines the euro conversion rate of the DM in T due to the Maastricht Treaty provision (requirement one) and the Madrid agreement (requirement two). At the same time, however, the euro conversion rate of the DM in T determines the market DM rate of the ecu in T-1.[5]

Just to summarize both explanations for indeterminacy (the first actually being implicitly included in the second) in De Grauwe's words, due to *both* institutional requirements described already at the beginning of these comments, 'any choice of the market with respect to conversion rates will be *self-validating*'.[6]

3 The Relevance of Exchange Rate Indeterminacy

3.1 Does Exchange Rate Indeterminacy Matter in Theory?

De Grauwe's indeterminacy claim with respect to (at least the) bilateral conversion rates might appear *intuitively odd* against the background of *standard* monetary models in which prices are (at least for the necessary few days from 31 December 1998 on) sticky and exchange rates are determined by expectations on future prices and the monetary policy stance relative to foreign countries. It seems to be overall plausible that political authorities will avoid large jumps in prices at the beginning of stage three. Price stickiness will thus also be ensured indirectly by the authorities.[7]

Additionally and more important, there might also exist *game-theoretic reasons* to disagree with De Grauwe in that respect. That is, in a standard monetary model of the Mussa-Obstfeld type it can be shown that this additional constraint might be *unnecessary*. The crucial aspect here is that market participants will expect the bilateral conversion factor to equal the 31 December 1998 fundamental, i.e. relative monetary policy, *regardless of any supplementary pronouncements* the participating authorities might make. The reason is that, under interest parity, individual traders would defect from any other equilibrium. In each of these other potential equilibria a sort of a *nominal return advantage* for one of the currencies would theoretically arise. This would induce traders to move away from this constellation which therefore cannot be labeled an 'equilibrium'. (see in all detail Obstfeld (1997), Kenen (1997)). The ending level of the fundamental, i.e. monetary policy, on 31 December 1998 (which actually is controllable, incentive-

[5] The corresponding strain of technical arguments is the following. In order to determine the DM-market rate of the ecu in T-1 one needs the empirical realization of the DM/$ rate in T-1. According to models of the Obstfeld-Mussa-type (Mussa (1976), Obstfeld (1997a)) the latter is (infinitesimally even solely) determined by expectations on the $ rate of the DM in T. The $ rate of the DM in T, however, is a function of the DM- and $-conversion rates of the euro and, thus, via the two Maastricht and Madrid requirements finally of the DM- and $-market rates of the ecu in T-1.

[6] Cf. De Grauwe (1998).

[7] I owe this point to Daniel Gros. See also Gros and Lannoo (1996).

constrained and therefore not indeterminate) will thus have an outstanding large influence on the stage 3 conversion factors specified on 1 January 1999. If one regards e.g. the incentives for competitive devaluation in the last trading moments on 31 December 1998, the relative money supply path as driving variable seems to be unique: Would for example the Deutsche Bundesbank would have an incentive to contract in the case of a sharp devaluation of the French Franc to accommodate the latter? No! These constraints thus *do not exclude* an equilibrium of bilateral conversion rates which is *unique* and, thus, *not indeterminate* as proposed at least implicitly by De Grauwe.[8]

That is to say, a commitment to peg nominal exchange rates to their levels at the close of business on 31 December 1998 *does not*, in itself, *rule out* a monetary policy stance that leaves *bilateral* exchange rates *exactly determined.* Moreover, as Obstfeld (1997) notices, an ex ante non-accommodating monetary policy stance is overall consistent with the time profile of monetary policy implied by the pegging requirement of the Maastricht Treaty. The ECB will, if necessary, accommodate *ex post* the (fundamentally determined) conversion values of bilateral exchange rates which result at the close of business on 31 December 1998 by adjusting national money stocks on 4 January 1999.

It is, however, important to note in defense of De Grauwe that Obstfeld (1997) *admits* the possibility of *indeterminacy* in cases where *forward* instead of spot (same-day settlement) exchange rates are the benchmarks for pegging. Seen on the whole, thus, exchange-rate indeterminacy seems to be a problem in practice at most partially. Two central questions for further discussion will therefore arise: Is De Grauwe's and Spaventa's (1997) indeterminacy claim with respect to *bilateral* conversion factors and De Grauwe's (1998) indeterminacy result with respect to the *euro* conversion rates of in-currencies compatible with *well determined bi*lateral conversion rates? If it is compatible, how detrimental would it be in view of the fact that it cannot be ruled out totally that it only concerns *the level but not the ratio* of *euro* conversion rates (which actually corresponds to the bilateral rate of in-currencies)?

3.2 Does Euro Conversion Rate Indeterminacy Matter in Practice?

In an earlier paper together with Luigi Spaventa (1997) De Grauwe concedes that fixing bilateral parities between the in-currencies in advance (in May 1998) might eliminate the uncertainty prevailing with respect to the ratio of euro conversion rates but *not* with respect to the *levels* of these rates (De Grauwe and Spaventa

[8] All these arguments might also be transferred from bilateral to *euro* conversion rates, if there will be some spillovers from indeterminacy in bilateral to indeterminacy in euro conversion rates. De Grauwe, however, claims that euro rates might still be indetermined if bilateral rates are determined (i.e. fixed).

(1997)). Interestingly enough, he states: 'the uncertainty as to the levels (of euro conversion rates) has *little economic relevance*, as the choice of euro rates has an element of arbitrariness anyway: dividing or multiplying those rates by any arbitrary number would leave the bilateral rates unaffected'. In his 1998 paper, however, De Grauwe sort of changes his perspective and concludes that the indeterminacy of *euro* conversion rates of the in-currencies might lead to *serious economic consequences*. In this sense, De Grauwe's 1998 paper is the legitimate successor of the De Grauwe and Spaventa (1997) contribution. On the one hand, this indeterminacy enhances the possibility of *turbulences in exchange markets* of the in-currencies with outside currencies. On the other hand, it leads to a certain scope for self-fulfilling *speculative bubbles* before the start of the third stage of EMU and a correction of these bubbles after the start. The resulting strong volatility of dollar rates around the beginning of EMU will render a *stabilization of euro price level difficult* and might have *negative real impacts*. These real impacts are in many cases prolonged by certain persistence mechanisms. This renders the argument even more important (Belke and Gros (1997), Obstfeld (1997)).

4 The De Grauwe-Proposals: Legal and Political Implementation Problems

Aiming at providing an anchor in the markets and at the same time taking into account both requirements specified by the Maastricht Treaty and the Madrid Council, De Grauwe (1998) proposes *three solutions*. First, he propagates *the announcement of (indirectly) fixed euro rates* in advance of the start of EMU (De Grauwe (1998)). This solution bears an *indirect* character since it necessitates a *change in the currency composition* of the ecu responding to movements in the exchange rates of out-currencies (feedback-rule). De Grauwe's main idea is the following. If e.g. out-currencies revalue vis-à-vis the in-currencies, the same happens with the ecu vis-à-vis the in-currencies, by definition. It follows directly that, in this case, the ecu has to be devalued vis-à-vis the in-currencies to align the ecu rates of the in-currencies with the preannounced euro rates of the in-currencies (two requirements of the Maastricht Treaty and the Madrid Summit). There is only one degree of freedom available for the necessary counter-adjustment: the weights of in-currencies in the ecu basket can be lowered.

In technical terms, De Grauwe (1998) propagates a change of the weight of in-currencies which is chosen to be proportional to the weighted average of bilateral exchange rate changes of in-currencies vis-à-vis out-currencies. As already set out, the latter carry on fluctuating even after a preannouncement of euro conversion rates of and bilateral rates of in-currencies at about the midst of 1998.

Although the necessary adjustment of in-currency weights might be technically possible it is *questionable* whether the relevant countries *manage to cooperate* on that aspect in practice. As De Grauwe himself admits, this solution will also lead to *legal* problems since the Maastricht Treaty (Art. 109g) states that the *currency composition* of the ecu basket *shall not be changed.* De Grauwe argues that this legal problem might be circumvented by *stripping the ecu in two components*, an 'inside' and an 'outside' ecu, and at the same time imposing a commitment of the monetary authorities always to convert both components together into one ecu. De Grauwe's proposal actually boils down to substitute the necessary change of the currency substitution by a *proportional* change in the market price of the inside ecu.

However, some counter-arguments against the feasibility of this proposal might be brought forward. First, *arbitrage* through bundling and unbundling the ecu -a mechanism on which the De Grauwe proposal implicitly relies- has *not* generally worked successfully already in the past (Gros and Thygesen (1992)). Second, the necessary *new markets* for inside and outside ecus *cannot* be established as *quickly* as necessary. If it would prove to be impossible to circumvent the treaty provisions by stripping the ecu in two components, the first De Grauwe-strategy would require ratification by *15* national electorates. On the one hand, the latter would involve *domestic political challenges.* On the other hand, revising any aspect of the treaty would represent an incentive for the signatories to *open a Pandora's box* of second thoughts. Thus, *any* treaty revision, including a change in the currency composition of the ecu, will most probably *be resisted* in EU political reality (Obstfeld (1997)). All in all and apart of its theoretical appeal, the first De Grauwe proposal seems to be the most complex one and to be fraught with some legal and political problems.

The *second* solution De Grauwe proposes is the fixing of the dollar/DM exchange rate during the transition period from May to December 1998 in order to provide markets with an external 'anchor'.[9] It is not at all clear according to de Grauwe himself that this proposal will be politically feasible since it obviously *depends on an agreement between the Bundesbank and the Fed.*

Solution *number three* goes on from a relaxed interpretation of the wording of the 'external value of the ecu' clause, i.e. it reads Art. 109l(4) of the treaty as referring only to the *non*-composing currencies (e.g. the dollar) as external currencies. This proposal actually boils down to indirectly steering the DM/$ rate by credible announcements with respect to the euro/DM conversion rate. As cooperation with U.S. authorities does not seem to be necessary with respect to the latter political feasibility might be the advantage of the third De Grauwe-proposal.

[9] De Grauwe (1998), demonstrates on the basis of his central 'indeterminacy equations' that a fixing of the DM/$ rate implies a fixed $/ecu rate and, by this, also a pegged DM/ecu rate at the eve of the third stage of EMU.

5 Conclusion

Seen on the whole, the De Grauwe proposals are technically and theoretically very appealing *given that* the indeterminacy problem exists in theory and practice. Paying tribute to the above theoretical considerations, however, one could in further discussions focus on the question whether De Grauwe develops *too complex solutions* (solutions 1 and 3) for an indeterminacy problem which is probably *not as relevant in practice* as estimated by De Grauwe himself.

References

Arrowsmith, J.A.A. (1996), Economic and Monetary Union: Economic, Financial and Legal Aspects of the Transition to a Single European Currency, Written Evidence Submitted to the Treasury Committee of the House of Commons, in: Treasury Committee, the Prognosis for Stage 3 of Economic and Monetary Union, HC 283, London, HSO.

Begg, D. et al. (1997), EMU. Getting the End-Game Right, Monitoring European Integration 7, CEPR,London.

Belke, A. and D. Gros (1997), Evidence on the Costs of Intra-European Exchange Rate Variability, Paper Presented at the International Seminar on Macroeconomics (National Bureau of Economic Research inc. European Economic Association), Gerzensee, Switzerland, June 15-17.

De Grauwe, P. (1996), How to Fix Conversion Rates at the Start of EMU, *EIB Papers* 1, Special Issue on EMU, 97-118.

De Grauwe, P. (1998), The Indeterminacy of the Euro Conversion Rates: Why It Matters and How It Can Be Solved, in this volume.

De Grauwe, P. and L. Spaventa (1997), Setting Conversion Rates for the Third Stage of EMU, CEPR Discussion Paper No. 1638, London.

Gros, D. and N. Thygesen (1992), European Monetary Integration, London.

Gros, D. and K. Lannoo (1996), The Passage to the Euro, Report of a CEPS Working Party, Working Party Report 16, Brussels.

Kenen, P. (1997), A Note on the Introduction of the Euro, Memo to Participants at the International Seminar on Macroeconomics (National Bureau of Economic Research inc. European Economic Association), Gerzensee, Switzerland, June 15-17.

Mussa, M. (1976), The Exchange Rate, the Balance of Payments and Monetary and Fiscal Policy under a Regime of Controlled Floating, *Scandinavian Journal of Economics* 78, 229-48.

Obstfeld, M. (1997), A Strategy for Launching the Euro, Paper Presented at the International Seminar on Macroeconomics (National Bureau of Economic Research inc. European Economic Association), Gerzensee, Switzerland, June 15-17.

Obstfeld, M. (1997a), Lectures, Summer School on International Macroeconomics, ZEI - Zentrum für Europäische Integrationsforschung, July 28 - August 8, Bonn.

Part IV:

Monetary and Exchange Rate Policy in Developing and Transition Countries: Selected Issues

7. Some Explanation on Recent Currency Crises

Issues in Monetary and Exchange Rate Policy of Developing Countries

Friedrich L. Sell
University of Dresden, Mommsenstr. 13, D - 01062 Dresden

1 Introduction[1]

The aim of this paper is to discuss issues that relate to the recent exchange rate and capital market crises in developing countries. The body of existing literature on the basics of money and exchange rate reform in developing countries - and increasingly transformation economies as well - is extremely large. I believe, however, that by now it is possible to find a certain number of essentials, i.e. elements that are conditions of sine qua non character for monetary and exchange rate reform in those countries. About the essentials there is either a wide-spread consensus or the differences in opinion have already been comprehensively identified.[2] Little value would be added if one was to try to list these essentials again. I consider it a much more rewarding task to analyze those developments that despite extensive existing research „routinely" surprise national as well as international policymakers, in spite of the dramatic experience with Mexico in 1994/95. As a matter of fact, these developments have shakened a group of newly industrializing countries in East and Southeast Asia which were treated before as the most challenging competitors for the OECD group. By now, it is less than clear what their growth prospects in the future really are.

Reading the papers during the past weeks and months one was frequently confronted with reports about capital market and exchange rate turbulences in the ASEAN countries in general and Thailand in particular.[3] I had the chance to visit the five founding member countries of this rather loose supra-national organisation as part of the field work for my habilitation thesis (Sell (1988)). The thesis analyzed the progress the ASEAN countries made in removing the effects of "financial repression" - a term that had just been coined by E. S. Shaw and R. I. McKinnon in the seventies. As many of my colleagues I then read the famous contribution "Goodbye Financial repression - Hello Financial Crash" by Carlos Díaz-Alejandro (1985, 1991). The author died too early (a neostructuralist would add: especially for his intellectual adversaries). I also forgot about his contribution

[1] I am indebted to Axel Jochem and to Markus Mende for comments and suggestions.

[2] This applies for example to the „timing and sequencing of reform programs" issue.

[3] Our analysis will not cover other affected countries like South Korea, Taiwan or Hongkong.

too early - too early because, as we will see later on, many of the issues raised in his seminal contribution are still of relevance today. As a result of the baht crisis even the show-case country for the export-led growth strategy in the ASEAN group, Thailand, has lost some of its shine. In a well positioned newspaper article Paul Krugman recently proposed that the East Asian economic miracle was occasioned more by transpiration than inspiration.

At least since the Mexico crisis in December 1994 we know that speculative attacks are not only directed against established capital market currencies, e.g. the British pound in the ERM crisis in 1992, or against more or less "soft" currencies that belong to an established exchange rate mechanism, e.g. the Italian Lira and the Spanish Peseta during the ERM crisis in 1992 and 1993 (Sell (1993)). Currencies of the so-called "emerging markets" - a term that is assumed to include developing and transformation countries as well as the ASEAN countries and the OECD economy of Mexico - are also prime targets for speculative currency attacks.

In the following I will try to provide an analysis of the recent crisis in Thailand that is preliminary in nature given the scarcity of up-to-date data and literature. The analysis of the 1994 crisis in Mexico will be more thorough against a background of an ample academic discussion of this event. The focus is on a diagnosis of the currency crises and the specific role that monetary and exchange rate policy played. As far as I know there are no comparable cases of exchange rate crisis in transformation countries with the possible exception of the Czech Republic depending on further economic developments. Nevertheless I think that the results from the analysis of Mexico's and Thailand's crises could be very helpful for the transformation countries in the future.

2 Recent Examples of Monetary and Foreign Exchange Rate Crises in Developing Countries

2.1 The Case of Thailand[4]

The Thai currency crisis has been imminent for over one year. In 1996 GDP and export growth dropped significantly. In June 1997 a budget deficit began to emerge for the fiscal year 1996/97 for the first time. After the resignation of the minister of finance and trade the exchange rate for the baht rose to the upper boundary of its target zone during the same month. The stock exchange continued its tendency - known for almost two years - to produce sudden gyrations downwards. At this stage the government still ruled out a devaluation. However, in the face of continued speculative activity against the baht - there had already been two attacks earlier in the year - the government was forced to abandon the

[4] Data and information were considered until mid of September, 1997.

peg to the US dollar on July 2nd. As a consequence the Thai exchange rate fell by 30 percent against the dollar, massive capital outflows ensued and equity prices on the Bangkok stock exchange continued their downward trend. Between January and September 1997 total capitalisation on the Bangkok stock exchange fell by 41 percent.

What had happened? Most observers emphasised the collapse of the Thai real estate sector in their analysis of the crash. The sector had previously enjoyed a boom that by many critics had been identified very early on as a speculative bubble supported by mostly non-performing loans from domestic banks and so-called finance companies (Sell (1988)). An estimate puts the total of non-performing loans to the real estate sector at 36 billion US dollars. During the last five years Thai banks advertised growth rates of 25 percent annually for their lending activities. But these loans - principally funded through capital borrowed abroad in US currency - were not supported by an adequate risk assessment. Towards the end of last year 29 percent of all loans by commercial banks went to the real estate sector. At first the government refused to let financial institutions declare bankruptcy and tried to shore up their operation through subsidies. The second problem are Thailand's finance companies. As part of the IMF stabilisation program an additional 42 finance companies in trouble are to be closed for at least 60 days. This comes on top of the closure of 16 finance companies in June and the loss of licence by about half of the registered banks in Thailand. This increases the proportion of finance companies closed by the authorities to 51 out of a total of 91, i.e. 64 percent. Sources in Bangkok put the proportion of lending by finance companies that went to the construction and real estate sector at about one fourth of total assets.

Last year the total capital inflow into Thailand was 10 percent of GDP. The flood of foreign capital was directed primarily at the real estate sector causing rapidly rising prices. When the bubble nature of theses price increases became more and more obvious given limited fundamental demand, confidence in the baht collapsed and speculative attacks against the currency followed. Thailand has a gross foreign debt of around 43 percent of GDP or 89 billion US dollars. At the middle of the year the net value of these foreign liabilities was reduced by foreign exchange reserves of 32.4 billion US dollars. Half of the gross outstanding loans are owed to Japanese banks and 82 percent of these loans are owed by Thai nationals or companies. The devaluation of the Baht has increased the vulnerability of Thai banks and companies further since the nominal value of outstanding liabilities in domestic currency has gone up.

We can identify the following stylised facts: Foreign capital was absorbed principally by the non-tradable sector. The Central Bank showed extreme neglect in its duty to supervise the lending activities of Thai banks. It is very likely that the speculative activity by financial institutions was fed significantly by sources in the informal capital market. These sources routinely require very high rates of return combined with an extremely short-term investment horizon. This confronts banks almost automatically with problems of term matching and provides a strong incentive to invest in high risk-high return projects in the spirit of the Stiglitz-Weiss hypothesis (Stiglitz and Weiss (1981)).

On August 11th a multi-lateral emergency package giving Thailand access to 17.2 billion US dollars - of which the IMF funds 4 billion US dollars - was agreed in Washington, D.C. After the financial rescue operation of 1995 for Mexico amounting to 50 billion US dollars, the emergency support for Thailand is the second package prepared by the IMF to avoid major disturbances in global capital markets. In the case of Thailand, Japan has assumed a leading role by providing 4 billion of the 17.2 billion US dollars in non-conditional loans. This engagement comes as no surprise given that Japan is Thailand's largest single creditor and has a strong interest in the stabilisation of the countries' capital markets and economy. But particularly in Japan there are doubts as to whether the rescue package is sufficient: Through interest payments and repayments on mostly short-term foreign debt and additional needs to support the baht in the near future a capital outflow of about 25 billion until the end of 1997 is probable. Japan's banks now find themselves in the dilemma situation well known from previous debt crises: should good money be thrown after bad money or is it necessary to provide fresh loans to maintain the value of outstanding loans?

It is remarkable that in its emphasis the IMF rescue package does not follow the capital market approach to currency crises (Sachs et al. (1996); Calvo and Mendoza (1996)) but rather the goods market/balance of payments approach proposed by Dornbusch and Werner (1994). In addition to higher government revenue (through value added tax) and a reduction in expenditure, it is the aim of the IMF programme to reduce the current account deficit from currently 8 percent of GDP to 5 percent this year and to 3 percent next year. Foreign exchange reserves are to be stabilised at a level that covers four months worth of imports. Even after the magnitude and the content of the IMF package was announced at the end of August/beginning of September, pressure on the baht remained. This is because problems of credibility persist: on the one hand the domestic value of Thailand's foreign debt continues to increase on the other hand the terms of trade between tradables and non-tradables have not reached a level that renders the necessary real outward transfers on the foreign debt sustainable in the long term.

It should be kept in mind that as a knock-on effect of the crisis in Thailand the currencies of other ASEAN countries have come under pressure since August: the Malaysian ringgit, the Singaporean dollar (the Central Bank defended the exchange rate with particular vigour) the Indonesian rupee (the authorities decided very early on to stop their intervention in the exchange rate markets and let the currency float), the Philippine peso (the authorities decided on a float already on July 11th) and even the Hong Kong dollar since the end of August. However, in contrast to the South Korean won whose value declined significantly against the US dollar since the end of August, the Hong Kong dollar managed to retain its previous rate on international capital markets.

Currently (that is early of September, 1997), all currencies in the ASEAN group continue their decline against major capital market currencies. Obviously investors have downgraded the growth prospects of the ASEAN countries and, as a logical extension, their companies. Drastic increases in interest rates aimed at shoring up the value of the respective currencies have so far been met with little success.

2.2 The Case of Mexico

An Outline of the Exchange Rate Crisis

In the case of Mexico the United States assumed, similarly to Japan in the case of Thailand, the role of foster parent contributing a lion share of 12 billion dollar to the rescue package.

In the following a brief outline of the development culminating in the crisis is provided.[5] In 1993 Mexico's economic prospects appeared to be excellent given its imminent accession to NAFTA. In the period from 1990 to 1994 Mexico attracted 95 billion US dollars of foreign capital of which the main component were 43 billion US dollars of portfolio investment into high-yielding teso bonos. Foreign direct investment and equity investment only attracted respectively 24 billion and 28 billion US dollars. Before the exchange rate crisis, Mexico's government debt consisted mainly of short-term, peso-denominated bonds (Cetes), most of which were held by foreign investors. However, after the assassination of the most probable presidential candidate Colosio in spring of 1994, foreigners began to withdraw invested capital for the first time. The government reacted through an expansionary sterilisation of capital outflows on the monetary side, and through an increasing substitution of peso-denominated Cetes bonds through dollar-denominated teso bonos on the fiscal side. This had an ambiguous effect on investor confidence. On the one hand, the teso bonos insured investors against capital losses from a possible devaluation of the peso. On the other hand, the increasing use of teso bonos eroded confidence as investors saw that the outstanding total was not covered by foreign exchange reserves and there seemed to be little opportunity for a roll-over of the liabilities.

Among experts analysing the peso crisis since the beginning of 1995 a consensus on the causes can be identified. These causes bear a remarkable resemblance to the causes responsible for the current crisis in Thailand. Of relevance are three domestic and one global factor:

(i) Not a fiscal deficit, as described in the standard analysis of balance of payments crisis, but a past lending boom "caused by poorly managed capital inflows leads to a banking-system bail out“ (Calvo and Mendoza (1996)). It is important to understand not only how the Central Bank manages capital inflows but also how commercial banks invest these funds on the micro-level, e.g.

[5] See also the chronicle in the appendix.

increased lending as a result of abolished minimum reserve requirements, accelerated privatisation, insufficient supervision of banks[6], etc.

In fact Mexico's crisis is seen in part of the relevant literature as deriving from a liquidity crisis in the banking system. It is argued that, as in the case of Thailand, there was a severe problem of term mis-match in Mexico: "the banks' increased reliance on short-term financing such as certificates of deposits from non-residents" (Griffith-Jones (1996)). Comparisons are made with the banking crisis in the US at the end of the 19th century. The approach emphasises the liability side of the banks' balance sheets. Even mildly negative news, let alone the assassination of Colosio, led to a significant withdrawal of funds from banks. This train of thought is compatible with the sterilisation policy of the Central Bank. In addition, aspects pertaining to the asset side of banks' balance sheets are considered. In the period from the end of 1992 to the end of 1994, the proportion of non-performing loans in the commercial banking sector rose from 5.6 percent to 8.3 percent. The proportion of assets classified as "risky" rose from 51 percent to 70 percent in the same period (Gruben (1996)).

Another perspective on the pivotal role of the banking sector for the Mexican crisis is developed by Sachs, Tornell and Velasco (1996). Financial market reform in Mexico was accompanied by an aggressive borrowing and lending policy. To attract deposits banks offered high interest rates that were invested in high-yielding but risky investment projects to finance the return on liabilities. The larger capital inflows during the reform programme, the more likely are lower interest rates on the one hand as long as the Central Bank refrains from sterilising measures. But this is precisely what the Banco Central de Mexico did not do. On the other hand, with increasing capital inflows the danger of a lending boom manifesting itself in explosive credit growth coupled with a deteriorating average risk assessment rises. The ability and also the willingness of banks to screen for marginal projects is reduced. In the end banks administer portfolios with a high proportion of underperforming assets (but not necessarily riskier assets in the sense of Stiglitz and Weiss (1981) (Sachs et al. (1996)).

(ii) Even before the crisis actually broke the financial vulnerability of Mexico was visible. The vulnerability derived from the discrepancy between the amount of foreign exchange reserves on one side and the on other side a) the outstanding total of government debt (in particular the dollar denominated proportion) and b) the quantity of money in circulation e.g. M2. The money aggregate M2 is of importance because it relates to the problems of the banking system on the liability side. It includes sight and savings deposits by non-residents that can be quickly exchanged into foreign currency. In times of crisis not only the high-powered monetary base but total money supply M2 becomes the liability of the Central Bank (Sachs et al. (1996)). In this context, the sterilisation attempts of the Central Bank as a reaction to capital outflows after the assassination of Colosio also play

[6] The seignorage aspect of minimum reserve requirements will be analysed below.

an important role. This is because with fixed or quasi-fixed exchange rates, continued capital outflows (outflows that were wrongly deemed temporary) are reflected in a one-to-one reduction of the money supply. The effect was compensated through an expansive discounting policy to commercial banks. Importantly, this funding helped the banks to survive the withdrawal of deposits by foreign investors (Sachs et al. (1996)). Chances for a devaluation rise with a lower relation of foreign exchange reserves to M2.

(iii) The crawling peg policy agreed with the unions in the so-called "pacto" with the purpose of limiting the effect of imported inflation on domestic wages led to a massive real appreciation of the peso (there are estimates of 20 to 40 percent). In the framework of the Australian dependent economy model, this should have reduced the demand for non-tradables and led to lower prices or at least to a lower rate of price increases in the sector under normal circumstances. However, prices in the real estate and construction sector continued to move upward reducing profit margins in the tradable sector that uses non-tradable output as an input. This adverse effect was enhanced by the fact that because of higher output prices employers in the non-tradable sector were able to offer higher wages than employers in the tradable sector in the competition for skilled workers.

(iv) Similarly to Thailand that is also considered an emerging markets from a capital market perspective, Mexico experienced the effects of globalisation during the crisis. There are two important effects. Firstly, there is a trade-off for investors between the gains from diversification and the cost of information gathering. Consequently, the more diversified a portfolio is, the less a representative investor will collect and process information on an individual asset. But even "small" negative news will then provoke a radical reaction by the investor, i.e. a "fire-sale" of the asset. This first effect is magnified by the tendency of investors to mimic the behaviour of other investors, so that sales by individual investors will quickly translate into a stampede of sales giving rise to speculative attacks (Griffith-Jones (1996)).

Sachs et al. (1996) stress the role of domestic factors in the case of Mexico's crisis. Bad fundamentals in the form of an exchange rate over-valued in real terms, a weak banking system and a low level of foreign exchange reserves made the country a prime target for speculative attacks.

2.3 Early Hints from Díaz-Alejandro

Carlos Díaz-Alejandro (1985, 1991) described the Chilean exchange rate crisis twelve years ago. Re-capitulating the stylised facts presented by him begs the question why the case of Mexico has been received as such a surprise. In the Chilean lending boom domestic credit rose by 41 percent between December of 1981 and June of 1992 (Díaz-Alejandro (1985)). Similarly to Mexico, the domestic financial system had funded a significant part of the credit expansion through foreign borrowing. In June of 1981 the Chilean peso was devalued drastically and - as in the case of Thailand - a period of widespread destruction of asset values followed. In the second half of 1982 the authorities sought to avert the bankruptcy of numerous financial institutions, so that the end of the year they had assumed the responsibility for almost the entire foreign debt. This confirms the rule of thumb - said to have been identified by the Japanese - that for developing countries a distinction between private sector and public sector external debt is irrelevant (Díaz-Alejandro (1985)). But a "nationalization" of private debt can never be a substitute for a proper supervision and regulation of the banking sector. This is especially true when the private sector anticipates the government acceptance of private debt. Then the problem of moral hazard in private borrowing will be particularly accentuated.

3 A Simple Model of Speculative Attacks in the Framework of Sachs, Tornell and Velasco (1996)

In the following we analyze a government that pegs the nominal value of its currency to a foreign anchor currency. The nominal exchange rate is E_0 and the real exchange rate is E_0/P. Here P represents the ratio of the domestic to the foreign price level. For the short-term this ratio is assumed to be equal to one and constant. The nominal peg is maintained by the government as long as foreign exchange reserves, R, are sufficient to finance capital outflows, K. Hence as long as the condition

$$K \le R$$

is fulfilled there is no devaluation or floating of the exchange rate. If

$$K > R$$

there is always a devaluation. In this case the government establishes a new peg rate

$$E^T,$$

to achieve a target real exchange rate. Consequently, the exchange rate of the following period is

$$E_1 = E_0 \quad \text{for} \quad K \le R$$

$$E_1 = E^T \quad \text{for} \quad K > R$$

The extent of devaluation is measured by D so that

$$D = \frac{E_1}{E_0} - 1$$

$$D = \begin{cases} 0 & \text{for} \quad K \le R \\ \dfrac{(E^T - E_0)}{E_0} & \text{for} \quad K > R \end{cases}$$

The target exchange rate E^T reflects a large number of structural variables, e.g. the terms of trade, the extent of current and capital account liberalisation, expectations about long-term capital flows etc.. In addition the target exchange rate must take into account the "health" of the banking system. If the banking system is in "good health" then the government chooses the target exchange rate of

$$E^T = e,$$

where e represents the long-term real exchange rate. If there is a crisis in the banking sector then the government will choose an exchange rate that is lower then e. This is because the government will try to avoid high interest rates that are necessary to defend a higher exchange rate but increase the chances of bankruptcies in the financial system. The vulnerability should be assessed on the basis of whether there was a lending boom with a high proportion of banking portfolios suffering from non-performing loans immediately before the period analysed. Hence for the target exchange rate we have:

(1) $$E^T = ef(LB); \quad f'(LB) > 0; \quad f(0) = 1$$

The options for devaluation are

(2) $$D = \begin{cases} \dfrac{e}{E_0} f(LB) - 1 & \text{for} \quad K > R \\ 0 & \text{for} \quad K \le R \end{cases}$$

This implies the following. The devaluation is larger the larger the extent of over-valuation of the exchange rate in relation to its long-term equilibrium value. Consequently, e/E_0 is larger the larger the previous lending boom, i.e. the larger $f(LB)$. This is as far as the analysis by Sachs, Tornell and Velasco (1996) goes. Against the background of the crisis in Thailand, the following extension of the model appears reasonable. The extent of the lending boom becomes a function of the proportion of non-performing loans *(NKr)* in total loans outstanding *(Kr)*:

(3) $$LB = g\left(\frac{NKr}{Kr}\right)$$

It is also useful to differentiate between non-performing loans, i.e. claims (*F*) on the tradable and on the non-tradable sector:

(4) $NKr = aF_{NT} + (1-a)F_T \quad \text{where} \quad a \geq 1/2$

The reason for this distinction is that the market for claims *(F)* on the non-tradable sector is less liquid than the market for claims on the tradable sector. Hence non-performing loans to the non-tradable sector trade with a bigger discount, especially since they cannot contribute to the solution of the transfer problem after the crisis. The expression for *D* then becomes

(2a) $$D = \begin{cases} \frac{e}{E_0} f\left[g(\frac{aF_{NT} + (1-a)F_T}{Kr})\right] - 1 & \text{for} \quad K > R \\ 0 & \text{for} \quad K \leq R \end{cases}$$

Next we look at the *N* small investors who each hold assets amounting to *k* in the domestic banking system. If in a speculative attack all investors withdraw their assets, then there will be a capital outflow of magnitude

(5) $K = Nk$

As long as the expected devaluation is smaller than/equal to θ *(=i-i*)*, hence as long as the advantage in terms of return of holding domestic assets exists, investors will not withdraw their assets. Thus

(6) $$k_j = \begin{cases} 0 & \text{if} \quad D \leq \theta \\ k & \text{if} \quad D > \theta \end{cases}$$

Because of symmetry we also have

(7) $$K = \begin{cases} 0 & \text{if} \quad D \leq \theta \\ Nk & \text{if} \quad D > \theta \end{cases}$$

For *scenario 1* we assume that fundamentals are pointing in the right direction

(8) $$(\frac{e}{E_0})f(LB) - 1 \leq \theta$$

Under theses circumstances every possible devaluation is smaller than the threshold that needs to be exceeded for capital flight to set in. Condition (8) can be fulfilled for an exchange rate that is only mildly overvalued and a moderate lending boom if θ is very small. Even if a devaluation does take place, *K* remains equal to zero. But if this is true then by equation (2) and (2a) no devaluation will take place.

For *scenario 2* it is assumed that the fundamental variables suffer from a crisis situation, so that

(9) $$(\frac{e}{E_0})f(LB) - 1 > \theta$$

In this case the threshold for capital flight is passed and for a devaluation K equals Nk. But would a devaluation actually take place? As long as $K = Nk < R$ it would not take place since the authorities would be able to defend the peg even with large capital outflows. However, if $K = Nk > R$ then a devaluation is possible but not inevitable. As long as every investor expects exchange rate stability, i.e. $D = 0$, the value of k will be zero and no devaluation is realised. If every investor expects a devaluation then in addition to $K = Nk > R$ the condition $D > \theta$ holds. Summarising we can say that a balance of payments crisis and a consequent devaluation ($D > 0$) are only possible for

$$(10) \qquad (\frac{e}{E_0})f(LB) - 1 > \theta \quad \textit{and at the same time} \quad R < Nk.$$

The model predicts that a country with bad fundamentals and a low level of international reserves is a prime target for speculative attacks.

4 Differences and Similarities between Developing and Transformation Countries

Differences between transformation and developing countries clearly do not only exist with respect to the fact that the former still have to grow into their role as emerging markets. Transformation countries generally suffered from a significant monetary overhang that they sought to reduce through price liberalisation. With accommodating monetary policy inflation increases sharply and the authorities are soon under pressure to reduce inflation without being able to limit the budget deficit to ensure that the recently gained signalling effect of the price system is not destroyed. Importantly, transformation countries are frequently rationed partially on international capital markets. This provides an incentive for the authorities to increase seignorage through the introduction/increase of minimum reserve requirements in the banking system. With constant money supply this increases the share of the Central Bank in total credit expansion at the cost of reducing the lending possibilities of commercial banks. The drawback of this strategy is that while a limited success in terms of stabilisation is achieved an additional distortion in terms of interest rates is introduced or increased. The costs of this distortion and the seignorage revenue obtained by the authorities is born by the users of the commercial banking system, on the liability as well as asset side.

Parallel to this point, Pinto (1991) argued several years ago that the removal of a distortion in the foreign exchange market, e.g. the unification of exchange rates after a regime of multiple exchange rates, can have a dual effect. On the one hand, the efficiency of the economy is increased. However, as long as the revenue needs of the government remain unchanged the authorities will after the abolition of the implicit export tax seek out new sources of income and will decide frequently on seignorage. In practice, this implies higher demand for Central Bank loans and

consequently a higher inflation rate. Depending on the money demand function, this can also lead to higher income from inflation tax.
When the time has come for capital market liberalisation in transformation countries then minimum reserve requirements can be reduced if previously the budget deficit has been reduced as well. Transformation countries can learn from the "new tigers" like Mexico that liberalization of the banking system must be accompanied by strict banking supervision and that large capital inflows can quickly reverse their direction.

Among the transformation countries, China and Russia are each very interesting cases, not in spite but rather because of their strong differences. For the period between 1994 and 1996, China's authorities enjoyed a seignorage revenue of 6 percent of GDP while Russia's authorities had to content themselves with a revenue of 4 percent of GDP. Importantly, in China 58.5 percent of this revenue derived from minimum reserve requirements for the banking system while the comparable figure for Russia was only 36 percent (IMF (1997)).

The two emerging markets economies whose exchange rates crises were analyzed above relied to a much smaller extent on seignorage income during the period from 1989 to 1996. In Mexico and Thailand government income from that source amounted to 0.76 percent and 1.28 percent of GDP respectively (IMF, 1997). But here too the relationship held that the country with the higher average inflation rate of 21.4 percent, Mexico (the rate for Thailand's was 5.2 percent) relied to a smaller extent, 11.8 percent against 34.4 percent for Thailand, on seignorage from minimum reserve requirements (IMF (1997)).

5 Conclusions for Exchange Rate and Monetary Policy

What conclusions should policymakers in emerging markets draw with respect to monetary and exchange rate policy from the experiences in Mexico and Thailand? As concerns monetary policy, the authorities have to extend their policy coverage to monitoring and supervision of the banking system. A strong lending boom is - as illustrated well by the examples analysed - rarely accompanied by solid asset portfolios in the banking sector.

Moreover, attention should be paid to the monetary aggregate M2 as an important early warning indicator of an impending speculative attack. If private agents are assumed to hold domestic currency more or less voluntarily then the reduction in the real value of the currency will be dramatic following a fall in foreign exchange reserves. Sterilization policy that causes a strong expansion of M2 is highly problematic in fixed or quasi-fixed exchange rate systems since non-sterilization provides the anchor for this type of exchange rate regime.

How early and how much Mexico should have devalued its exchange rate in discretionary manner (Dornbusch and Werner have discussed these questions extensively and publicly in 1994) to avoid or reduce the risk of a speculative attack is probably not the core issue of exchange rate policy. The principal question seems to be whether any form of fixed exchange rate system is only optimal for a while and needs to be replaced by a floating exchange rate. As Sachs, Tornell und Velasco (1996a) argue pegging regimes might by very sensible at the beginning of a reform programme, e.g. to stabilise inflationary expectations and to remonetise the economy, "but just as important is to get out of the fixed exchange rate system in time" (ibid.).

On the other hand, it should be borne in mind that the commitment of the Mexican authorities convinced private investors that there was no plan to devalue the currency. But dwindling currency reserves and a fast growing government debt must have made it clear to the public that if a devaluation was to take place it would have been large (ibid.).

From the experience of Thailand and the other ASEAN countries during the past weeks and months some analysts have concluded that not only the policy of exchange rate pegging but also the choice of anchor currency needs to be re-examined. This line of argument evolves against the background of the common dollar peg in contrast to a growing importance of the yen, e.g. for trade factoring, in the ASEAN region.

One last point is worth considering. If the accounting identity approach that regards savings deficits/surpluses as the force determining the direction of medium- to long-run capital flows is correct then the countries that fell victim to exchange rate crises would be justified in suspecting that the rescue packages in their favour only re-patriated capital that had left the country in haste some weeks before. The only difference being that the return of the capital is achieved at a much higher cost from the perspective of the recipient country. This somewhat depressing insight begs the question how speculative attacks can be rendered loss-making and stabilising at the same time. This, however, is contrary to Keynes' famous credo. To have the fundamental data is a necessary but not a sufficient condition.

References

Calvo, G. A. and E. G. Mendoza (1996), Mexico's Balance-of-Payments Crisis: A Chronicle of a Death Foretold, *Journal of International Economics* 41, 235-64.

Díaz-Alejandro, C. (1991), Goodbye Financial Repression, Hello Financial Crash. Reprinted in: L. Bendesky (ed.), El Papel de la Banca Central en la Actualidad, Banco de Espana, Madrid, 215-42.

Dornbusch, R. and A. Werner (1994), Mexiko, Stabilization, Reform, and No Growth, *Brookings Papers on Economic Activity* 25(1), 253-97.

El País (1997), various issues.

Espinosa, M. and R. Russell (1996), The Mexican Economic Crisis: Alternative Views, *Federal Reserve Bank of Atlanta Economic Review* 81, 21-43.

Frankfurter Allgemeine Zeitung (1997), various issues.

Griffith-Jones, S. (1996), The Mexican Peso Crisis, Insitute of Development Studies, Discussion Paper No. 354, Mexiko.

Gruben, W. C. (1996), Policy Priorities and the Mexican Exchange Rate Crisis, *Federal Reserve Bank of Dallas Economic Review*, 19-29.

Handelsblatt (1997), various issues.

Horne, J. (1996), External Sustainability: The Mexican Peso Crisis, Macquarie Economics Research Papers, November.

Internatonal Monetary Fund (1997), International Financial Statistics, various issues.

McKinnon, R. I. (1991), The Order of Economic Liberalization - Financial Control in the Transition to a Market Economy, Baltimore, John Hopkins University.

Neue Zürcher Zeitung (1997), various issues.

Ötker, I. and C. Pazarbasioglu (1996), Speculative Attacks and Currency Crises: The Mexican Experience, *Open Economies Review* 7, 535-52.

Pinto, B. (1991), Unification of Official and Black Market Exchange Rates in Sub-Saharan Africa, in: Emil Maria Claassen (ed.), Exchange Rate Policies in Developing and Post-Socialist Countries, San Francisco, 327-51.

Reichmann, T. (1992), Case-Study of Mexico (1982-91). Approaches to Exchange Rate Policy: Choices for Developing and Transition Economies, edited by R. C. Barth and C. H. Wong, Washington D.C., 157-71.

Sachs, J., A. Tornell and A. Velasco (1996), Financial Crises in Emerging Markets: The Lessons from 1995, *Brookings Papers on Economic Activity* 26(1), 147-215.

Sachs, J., A. Tornell, and A. Velasco (1996a), The Mexican Peso Crisis: Sudden Death or Death Foretold? *Journal of International Economics* 41, 265-83.

Sell, F. L. (1988), Geld- und Währungspolitik in Schwellenländern, am Beispiel der ASEAN-Staaten, Berlin.

Sell, F. L. (1993), Liberalisierung des Kapitalverkehrs und makroökonomische Stabilisierung, *List Forum für Wirtschafts- und Finanzpolitik* 19, 64-75.

Stiglitz, J. A. and A. Weiss (1981), Credit Rationing in Markets with Imperfect Information, *The American Economic Review* 71, 393-410.

Whitt, J. A. (1996), The Mexican Peso Crisis, *Federal Reserve Bank of Atlanta Economic Review* 81, 1-20.

Appendix A: Chronicle of Mexico's Recent Economic Past (1982 - 1994)

Period	Exchange rate system	Policy changes	Comments
February 1982	Free floating exchange rate	Devaluation of the peso. Subsequent switch float	Devaluation = more than 75 percent in February
August 5, 1982	Fixed but adjustable exchange rates in a dual exchange rate system	Introduction of the dual exchange system	Exchange rate in the controlled market determined by the Bank of Mexico Excchange rate in the free market determined by commercial banks
December 20, 1982	Preannounced crawling peg	Introduction of a preannounced crawling peg against the dollar Establishment of exchange controls as part of the economic Program	Value of the controlled exchánge rate announced daily Rate of crawl: 13 cents per day
December 6, 1984	Preannounced crawling peg	An increase in the rate of crawl	Rate of crawl: 17 cents per day (32.2 percent annual implied depreciation)
March 6, 1985	Preannounced crawling peg	An increase in the rate of crawl	Rate of crawl: 21 cents per day (38.0 percent annual implied depreciation)
July 25, 1985	Preannounced crawling peg	Devalution of the peso	Devalution = 20 percent
August 5, 1995	Managed float	Abandonment of preannounced crawling peg subsequent switch to managed floating in the controlled market	The value of the peso adjusted daily by unspecifed amounts (effectively a crawling peg)
November 18, 1987	Free floating exchange rate	Withdrawal of Bank of Mexico support from the foreign exchange market	The flexible exchange rate depreciated 32.8 percent in one day Differential between preferential and flexible rate reached 35.1 percent

Appendix A: Continued

Period	Exchange rate system	Policy changes	Comments
December 14, 1987	Free floating exchange rate	Devaluation of the peso	Devaluation = 21.8 percent
December 15, 1987	Preannounced fixed peg	Announcement of preannounced fixed peg	Fixed rate: Mex$2,209.7/US$
January 31, 1988	Preannounced fixed peg	Increase in preannounced fixed peg	Fixed rate: Mex$2,221/US$
February 1988	Preannounced crawling peg	Abandonment of preannounced fixed peg Switch to preannounced crawling peg Devalution of the peso	Fixed rate: Mex$ 2,221/US$ Rate of crawl: 2 pesos per day Devalution = 2.7 percent
March 1988	Fixed exchange rate system	The peso fixed against the U.S. dollar	Fixed rate: Mex$2,28/US$
January 1989	Preannounced crawling peg	Switch to preannounced crawling peg	Rate of crawl: 1 peso per day (1.3 percent per mounth, 16.5 percent annual implied depreciation)
May 27, 1990	Preannounced crawling peg	Reduction in the crawl rate	Rate of crawl: 80 cents per day
November 12, 1990	Preannounced crawling peg	Reduction in the crawl rate	Rate of crawl: 40 cents per day
November 11, 1991	Exchange rate intervention band	Abolition of dual exchange rate system and exchange controls Introduction of exchange rate bands	Band floor: fixed at Mex$3,05/US$ Band ceiling: depreciate daily against the U.S. dollar Rate of Crawl of the ceiling: 20 cent per day (2.36 percent per year) No official announcement of central rate, daily announcement of lower and upper bounds

Appendix A: Continued

Period	Exchange rate system	Policy changes	Comments
October 21, 1992	Exchange rate intervention band	Increase of the crawl rate of the upper band	Band floor: fixed at Mex$3,051/US$ Band ceiling: depreciate daily against the U.S. dollar Rate of Crawl of the ceiling: 40 cent per day (4.63 percent per year)
January 1, 1993	Exchange rate intervention band	Introduction of new peso	MexN$1 = Mex$1,000
December 20, 1994	Exchange rate intervention band	Devaluation of the new peso's band ceiling	Devaluation = 15 percent Exchange rate rose from MexN$3.46/US$ to MexN$3.99/US$
December 22, 1994	Free floating exchange rate	Abolition of intervention bands and Switch to free floating	Peso depreciated by 71 percent for 1994 as a whole

8. Monetary System Design: On Currency Boards

Towards a General Theory of a Currency Board System

Wilfried Fuhrmann
University of Potsdam, August-Bebel-Str.89, D - 14482 Potsdam

1 Introduction

1.1 Concept of a Currency Board

There is no such thing as a general theory of the currency board (CB). Hitherto, there is no generally accepted definition of a currency board. Additionally the term is increasingly being used in political discussions, and thereby it is becoming increasingly meaningless.

To help with the understanding of a currency board, one can look to a discussion on a particular form or design of a central bank. And with respect to the treatment of inside-money or the domestic component of the money supply, economists distinguish between a pure or narrow CB on the one hand and a modified or broad CB on the other. But a discussion on whether the establishment of a currency board is meaningful, on its advantages and disadvantages or on its stability is always a discussion on a totally interdependent market system with all its monetary and real sectors. In other words, it has to be a discussion about a market system with a currency board (CBS).

1.2 The Economical Embedding

There are many reasons for dealing with a CB.[1]

---

[1] In 1920 Silvio Gesell already proposed the introduction of an international currency unit "Iva" as well as the foundation of an "International Valuta-Association" (Iva) and a currency department in every member state. Each member has to hold an Iva-currency-reserve of at least 20 percent of its national banknote circulation and it has to guarantee a fixed rate between the unit of its national currency and the international unit Iva (especially within the clearing between the national currency departments). The national money supply rule is fixed. These are the essential features of a CB which can, however, be autonomously institutionalized by every country with reference to another existent national currency.
Gesell's proposal was more far reaching. He was looking for a symmetric solution for all member countries (within a dynamic macroeconomic global system). In accordance with the Iva-concept there could have been a much more flexible frame for a European Central Bank and a currency unit "euro" to which all members peg their currencies in a fixed

Firstly Estonia, the most successful transformation country of the three Baltic states, has positive experiences with a CB. The three Baltic states took part in a type of field experiment, in which they used three different ways of monetary transformation. Immediately, and against the advice of many external economists, Estonia established a CB, and ambitiously introduced a new national currency into the international markets with a fixed tie to the German Mark. Latvia chose a system of free, but dirty floating exchange rates. Lithuania experienced nearly every possibility and then under increasing pressure from abroad introduced a CB with a fixed tie to the US-Dollar (as Poland formerly had).

As we know from the theories of optimal currency areas, a fixed exchange rate seems to be an optimal solution for a small and only partly diversified country. Then this country will, according to international trade theory, get the highest possible welfare gain from international trade by adjusting its relative prices to those of its main trading partner(s) and thus to its most important foreign currency community. This way of adjustment reduces the currency risk to its foreign direct investors. This decision and announcement comes very close to a kind of relational international contract, which in return needs to be backed by a high degree of credibility of the CB. However, by doing this the small country imports the same type of market system („Ordnungspolitik“) that the anchor currency community has.

The second reason for dealing with the theory of a CBS is the possibility of using the establishment of a CB as an economically strategic decision of a country, which finds itself as an emerging national market system within the phase of transition and transformation. It is a sort of strategical investment. According to the newly developed theory of transformation this institutionalization, if it is credible, is the fastest route to

- security for the publics` expectations concerning the intended general economic framework and market system („Ordnungsrahmen“) and the isolation of the monetary system from day-to-day politics,
- perfect (domestic and foreign) convertibility and full integration within the global capital markets,
- an efficient domestic monetary sector which minimizes the bottlenecks in (available) human capital and know-how about foreign exchange and financial markets as well as about the risk management of banks etc.,
- a (ex- or implicitly) cooperative behavior of the central bank in the anchor currency country,
- international confidence in the countries monetary stability to foreign capital exporters (attracting direct investments),[2]

relation; the volume and the annual expansion of this reserve currency could have been commonly determined by all members.

[2] With a CB there is no possibility for monetary expansion, as a means of adjusting uncompetitive high nominal wages. A CB excludes all types of balancing (base-)money

- finance the expected current account deficit and to
- a reduction of the countries risk premium and thus its capital costs.

Benefits from a CB are to be expected from

a. a rapidly gained international reputation for the (generally through a currency reform newly introduced) domestic currency,
b. its permanent pressure on the bargaining partners in labor markets and on a consolidated federal budget (by the exclusion of a monetary extension induced from a deficit budget and the intrinsic pressure to privatize) and thus pressing for optimal factor allocation, and
c. the growing national consensus and culture for stability in the course of time.

Costs from a CB are to be expected especially in three cases:

a. national disturbances make a discrete monetary policy optimal,
b. the CBS credibility is cut back by (mainly nationalistic) politicians in treating the CB as a necessary evil and thus a temporarily limited institution prior to an (ultimately to be) institutionalized national central bank with discretion,
c. politicians evade the disciplining pressure of the CB and bypass the limitations set for their elbow room and economical interventions. This is possible if the CB is a single and dichotomized institution, with counteracting institutions (such as a publicly owned investment and reconstruction bank, which has direct or indirect access to the creation of high-powered money) and if the CB is neither a part of an effective banking supervision nor a part of a general institutional framework of a market system (Fuhrmann (1994)).
   This means without
   - an adequate monetary policy for the fixed exchange rate with the anchor currency,
   - a sound („weight-conservative") banking supervision and effective rules of competition,
   - a consensual general acceptance of the economic structure, which grows endogenously with deepening integration with the anchor currency country and the anchor currency community,
   - the abandonment of national autonomous industrial and structural politics all the well known disadvantages and costs of a revaluation of a non market equilibrium exchange rate will be expected to arise sooner or later.[3]

---

creation, for social programs, the budget (including of the existing public enterprises) or demand stabilization.

[3] Perfect examples are the Mexican Peso crisis, as well as the current currency crisis of developing Asian countries with their newly dissolved exchange rate ties to the US-Dollar. Their problems have been caused by their (ambitious) national growth-, military- and structural policies. These policies as well as their non compliance with the monetary rules

The third reason for observing a CB is the approach of some central banks in industrial countries towards a certain type of CB. This can be observed in countries with a fixed exchange rate, which is publicly announced, supported by the government and all social parties (in Austria for instance they call it „Sozialpartnerschaft") and making it thus credible. It works permanently as a measure of driving structural adjustment and increasing productivity. It can be also observed in countries, which successively reduce their exchange rate band and generate an ever more stable narrow exchange rate target zone (as for example The Netherlands).

2 On Optimization

2.1 The Approach

Contrary to an independent central bank with an unrestricted discretional power over the national currency (in the foreign exchange and domestic money markets), a CB is generally seen as a non-state-contingent rule. Thus the analysis links directly to the broad discussion, initiated by Kydland and Prescott (1977) as well as Barro and Gordon (1983), about rules versus discretion, time inconsistencies, surprise inflation with higher rates of the natural unemployment (u*) and higher variances of the real income in the long run, and about first-, second-, third- and fourth-best solutions.

A CB can be understood as a specific form of delegation with a defined inflationary target. Thus the usual minimization of the social loss (V), the capital value of all, with a given time preference rate discounted, social period losses (L) seems to be applicable in demonstrating differences between a central bank with discretion and a CB. The given targets for a CB may deviate from the first-best solution. But here delegation means that preferred and well defined stability targets and weighting parameters are prefixed or that the board is recruited in such a way, that enforced by their contacts it sets these weights itself.[4]

The following is given:

(1) $$L = ((p-p^*)^2 + a\,(y-y^*)^2)/2$$

of their fixed exchange-rates have led in those countries to very different economical developments compared to the U.S.A..

[4] In the case of a CB there is only a small difference between an independent solution (Rogoff (1985)) with a constitutional backing of "weight- conservative" central bankers and the contract solution (Walsh (1995), Persson and Tabellini (1993)). Interesting are the possibilities of orientating of the board towards stability by putting foreigners on the board (Hanke, Jonung, Schuler (1993)), attaining the second-best solution by adding a linear inflation contract (Svensson (1995)) or by adding specific costs for the board's members, and the institutionalization of the CB with only a few measurement, supervision and accountability problems.

The relationship between income and unemployment is assumed to be linear, the net factor income is given, the time index t has been neglected. The income equation with an in t-1 determinated nominal wage rate is added:

(2) $y = ß (p-p^{e}) + v$

and the expected inflation-rate for period t is a conditional expectation on all in period t -1 available information:

(3) $_{t}p^{e} = {}_{t-1}E(p)$

with:

E	expectation operator,
a	weight given to the employment target,
ß	price elasticity of output,
v	(supply-) shock, disturbance term (mean 0, var. given),
p, y	(log) inflation-rate, output,
p*, y*	optimal levels of inflation, output (politicians normally aim at higher levels than the natural ones) (by normalization equal to zero).

2.2 Additional Assumptions

In order to reduce the intertemporal analysis to an one period model (Svensson (1995), Persson and Tabellini (1994)) we assume that:

1. the parliament (and not the government) determines and delegates the objective function and targets,
2. the central bank is able to control p,
3. neither (ouput-) effects of persistence nor of hysteresis exist.

Ad 1.:
The parliament determines the anchor currency and the parity to the anchor currency which are then handed over to the CB. It thus sets targets according to the purchasing-power-parity (expected for the long run) the inflation rate of the anchor currency country and according to the interest rate parity the interest rate of the anchor currency community. There has to be an escape clause, but to prevent a fall in credibility only the parliament is (constitutionally) allowed to change both intermediate targets. It can decide on a revaluation and another anchor currency with qualified majority.[5] The parliament establishes thus a specific monetary constitution and monetary order.

[5] A currency anchor in the form of a composed currency basket, like the SDR, does not correspond to the CB framework.

The importance of the purchasing-power-parity-theory (even in the long run) for a national price target is limited because of the internationally non-traded goods (even in a small open economy) and because of lots of administrated prices (especially in a country in transformation). This encourages us to use the L-function with a parameter $a > 0$. To fill this gap and to be in accordance with a target independence (of a central bank and even a CB), the national price target is assumed to be identical to the price target for tradeables. The CB aims for a constant real exchange rate. Higher inflation rates for the non-tradeables, which would enforce a depreciation in the medium-run, and terms-of-trade effects in the commodity supply function are excluded. Ignored are all such situations and phenomena as high price rigidities or speculative price bubbles in the „domestic" sector.

Ad 2.:
The abandonment of a national discretionary monetary policy is supposed to prevent national (or domestically created) nominal shocks and to prevent the inflation rate exceeding that of the anchor currency country.

This is proved in the long run, as a transforming country wants to avoid or to eliminate inflation as soon as possible. This inflation is often concurrent with a change of the system. Price releases with a view to adjust the price structure should be achieved during the preparation for the regime shift and hence still in the old monetary regime (this happened in Estonia whilst Roubel was still legal tender) or immediately in the short transitional phase. As inflation can very often be attributed to the adjustment of administrated prices and the introduction of social security contributions as well as taxes (especially a VAT) the yearly inflation rates in a country in transition will be higher than those in the anchor country for many years. The fixed parity will not necessarily be endangered. The adjustment of the inflation rate is striven for by the imposition of a coverage of 100 percent anchor-currency[6] reserves for the monetary base in the CB.

A CB differs in this coverage from a central bank in the Bretton Woods system and with a type of central bank in the Friedman rule. It is more comparable with a central bank in the international gold-standard.

In the CB- and in the anchor country the terms of payments, financial innovations (as electronical cash) can develop differently. The CB has to react to this relative variation of the national nominal money demand. This requires a central bank and moreover a modified CB with monetary measures to be able to control the whole monetary aggregate and thus the money multiplier. But the credibility of the exchange rate target and of the CB requires the guaranteed implementation of transparency. Special contracts with the members of the board (and with the

[6] This limitation excludes the necessary revaluation of reserves according to variations in the market exchange- rates on the central banks balance sheet and adjustment of the monetary base accordingly. Otherwise the CB has the additional possibility of discretion. Therefore the government should have no direct access to revenues from coinage.

members of the banking supervision authority („Bankenaufsicht") are not necessary but may more or less make sense.

Ad 3.:
Output persistence effects, which are to be understood as a slow adjustment process, would generate a totally different income equation:

(4) $y = b\, y_{t-1} + ß\,(p-p^*) + v\,; \qquad 0 < b < 1.$

Output persistence and -hysteresis are neglected. This restrictive assumption seems to be acceptable for a country with homogenous expectations; a broad social consensus regarding structural adjustments and high flexibilities are necessary. Phenomena such as business cycle and (steady state-) growth are not depicted.

2.3 The CB as a Second-Best Solution

The three following cases will be briefly examined. A central bank with discretionary power (A), with a given optimum rule (B) and with a given inflation rate target (C) as the CB.

Ad A.:
Without public announcement p is optimized in order to minimize L. The rational expectations are conditionalized by the known parameters and the inflation rate of the last period. It holds:

(5) $p = p^* + a\,ß\,y^* - aß\,v\,/\,(\,1 + a\,ß^2)$

with the mean, moreover the expected value:

(6) $E(p) = p^* + a\,ß\,y^*$

It shows the inherent (average) inflationary distortion following from income and employment targets exceeding the natural output. Without the target distortion the bias approaches zero. Output corresponds to the natural output.

Ad B.:
With a given credibility p is optimized according to the exogenous shock and price expectations. There is no time inconsistency. It holds:

(7) $p = p^* - a\,ß\,v\,/\,(\,1 + a\,ß^2\,)$

with the mean, moreover the expected value:

(8) $E(p) = p^*$

There is no inflationary distortion and in the long-run p (as well as y) is equal to the social optimum (natural output).

Ad C.:

The CB has to accept the (given) inflation rate of the anchor currency country p^B. And a = 0 holds without an income target. But if additionally a y-target and thus a > 0 is assumed, there may come into existence some problems of inconsistency and of incredibility.[7] But each price target has an implicitly defined employment target and both values serve as an orientation in building (conditional) expectations. Countries in transition lack efficient money and capital markets for a long time. Here the fixed exchange rate as well as the implicitly fixed inflation rate serve i.a. to avoid structural uncertainty in the determination of v's distribution function and of ${}_tp^*$ for a temporary equilibrium. For the inflation rate and its mean thus follows:

(9) $$p = p^B + a^B \beta y^B - a^B \beta v / (1 + a^B \beta^2)$$

and

(10) $$E(p) = p^B + a^B \beta y^B$$

The mean is greater than in the optimum if p^B and y^B do not correspond to p* and y*. Then, however, the second-best solution is reached. If the inflation rate according to the temporary equilibrium is higher than the one of the anchor currency, then the restrictive money supply would accelerate the re-inflationary process. The costs of adjustment are crucial in the question of optimality. The advantages of a so-called shocktherapy (versus gradualism) lie within a broad concept of a CB within a system of (free)markets. And if the results of an optimal monetary policy are attainable with a CB, then further advantages of the CB are seen, not only in situations of a regime shift, in the easiness of institutionalizing a CB compared to the implementation of contracts or to the determination of a national inflationary target. Credibility is dependent on:

- the chosen anchor currency; it has to be the most important (directly and indirectly) invoicing currency for the countries trade as well as for capital transactions,
- the credibility of the structurally economical orientation striven for by the choice of the anchor currency,
- the ability to defend the fixed exchange rate (moreover the countries foreign currency reserves).

---

[7] The employment target and its weighting may be too "ambitious". Then the inflation-rate of the non-tradeables will increase (absolutely and relatively) and the CBS credibility, which has already been limited by a (governmentally-given) y-target, will be reduced.

Estonia has become a shining example. The recommendations of the IMF in favor of the introduction of a CB rely on it, as well as the EU-discussions on the Baltics and on enlargement. Estonia's economical success (compared not only to Latvia or Lithuania) is based on the choice of the anchor currency (DM instead of US-$, Fmk, ECU or SDR), the common consensus to accept international competition immediately, a quick privatization and a consistently pursued (i.e. economical and juridical) integration with European countries.

2.4 On the Money Supply

The national money supply has to be equal to the money demand, given by the wellknown Cambridge equation. This equation has to be modified, if foreigners hold domestic legal tender or if in the country itself foreign legal tender is used as a medium of exchange (a kind of currency substitution) and if these shares alter with integration. An analysis of the money supply has to explain the money multiplier as well as the base money restriction, since the stock and the changes in the monetary base have to be equal to the CBS foreign currency reserves. An increase of the reserves and of the monetary base by the CB require a positive excess supply of foreign currencies (moreover of the anchor currency). It requires a surplus in the aggregated current account and capital movements, which mirrors the tendency of appreciation of the CBS currency.[8]

A CB is not an optimal solution in all cases. The monetary rule of the CBS supply mechanism does not take into account all kinds of (great or lasting) asymmetrical shocks in the CB- and in the anchor country. In a case of great disturbances in the CB-country itself even stronger distortions (and output variances) can be caused by a CB, compared to a central bank with a discretionary policy. Discretionary policy can be superior to a CB.[9]

[8] Due to this foreign-exchange restriction politicians frequently only regard a CB to be a temporary strategy and many of them (especially autonomy orientated) very quickly put in a claim for the transition to a central bank with a money supply based on domestic-assets (as recently in Lithuania), thus reducing the CBS reputation, increasing the countries capital costs and risk premium on international markets, and lowering domestic income and employment.

[9] The loss can be lower with a discretionary policy if the variances of the disturbances are high relative to the inflationary bias underlying the objective function (Garman and Richards (1989)).

3 Transitory and Permanent Changes

3.1 A Stationary Equilibrium with Transitory Fluctuations

3.1.1 The System without Inside-Money

Two aspects are to be analyzed. These are the effects of transitory and of permanent disturbances as well as the implications of an inside-money creation in the CB-country.

The stability of the fixed parity, of the whole monetary system and hence of the CB, as well as the ability of the CB to control the inflation rate is, with a money multiplier equal to one, a priori given by the base money restriction. If money creation by other (commercial) banks is restricted because of reserve requirements (or a leakage rate) of 100 percent and if the only source for base money is the sale of anchor currency to the CB, then the coverage of the whole money supply is constant at 100 percent in units of the anchor currency. The money supply is (totally and permanently) endogenous.

The currency risk of creditors and investors is "perfectly" covered. Because the CB has no option for a revaluation, profits from speculative attacks cannot be expected.[10] The CBS currency is a perfect substitute for the anchor currency. This is a priori even valid without unlimited credit lines with or access to the central bank of the anchor currency.[11] The stability and credibility of the CBS seems to be perfect. Investors, fond managers and the public have a perfect transparency concerning the money supply (and mechanism), the exchange rate fixing and the competence of the CB, which is able to follow the rules perfectly at any time. The supply mechanism is sustainable because of the 100 percent coverage.

However, this "perfect" credibility is restricted. Firstly, it is limited by the parliaments ability to change the parity (especially if this is a governments right) and the discredibility increases ceteris paribus with the shadow exchange rate moreover with the loss of reserves. The discredibility will be higher, the more accurately the date of the total loss can be estimated moreover the necessary devaluation be discounted, and thus the higher the probability of profits from a speculative attack will be. Additional judicial or constitutional stipulations, self-commitments and the settlement of the CB as well as of the foreign currency

[10] Here it is assumed that the CB cannot change the parity or the money supply mechanism, in order to avoid a conceivable total loss of foreign currency reserves. Of course there may be a previously fixed escape-clause.

[11] The greater the supply of inside money is, the more necessary (unlimited) stand-by credits will be. To avoid problems Estonias central bank pushed commercial banks to cooperate with foreign banks and to build up own foreign working balances and credit lines. The overall foreign reserves increased. But the systems credibility is endangered, if the short-term foreign credit engagements blow out the (multiplier and the) money supply and real estate speculation. Then reserve requirements can stabilize the CBS.

reserves abroad will improve the credibility gradually. Secondly, it is limited by (i.e. defense-, social-, distributional-, and) fiscal policy, the countries foreign debt and the governments weighting on efficiency and allocational optimality. Finally the credibility of the CB depends on the flexibility of wage rates and product prices, because they have to decrease in the case of an outflow of reserves and a co-integrated monetary contraction. Decreasing prices (relative to those in the anchor country) have to stimulate capital imports and product exports. Decisive is the price inflexibility (moreover of the real sector) relative to capital mobility.

A currency union with the anchor currency country or the introduction of the anchor currency as domestic legal tender, in which case the anchor currency country then handles all domestic monetary matters and transfers the seigniorage gain back, evades the problem of monetary credibility. The problems with high rigidities in labor and commodity markets remain. A currency union creates neither a kind of real sector credibility nor a social consensus.

3.1.2 A CB as a Target Zone Approach

As a system with a fixed parity and a band equal to zero a CB can be analyzed within a target zone approach.[12] Then the CB is to be understood as an objective function which defines the admissible and a non-admissible value range for the exchange rate. And this (pre-)fixed parity then enters into all policy decisions and reaction functions and, thus, it restricts all (!) other economic variables - politicians have to recognize and to accept it.

The vector of all fundamentals, the money supply included, has to be in line with the fixed exchange rate. To rephrase it: this parity determines the target zones for all fundamental variables as well as the publics conditionally expected exchange rate variation which in the case of a CB is equal to zero (with a domestic interest rate equal to the foreign one).[13] Expectations do not only refer to the exchange rate, but also to the whole market system and the institutional framework.[14] The target zone approach, with the known S-shaped curve following from credibility

[12] For a literature survey and for the approach including many computerassisted statements from simulations see Scheunpflug (1997).

[13] Within a crawling peg system a revaluation according to the divergent developments of the fundamentals is to be expected. At the end of the transformation process and reaching the countries specific steady-state there will be a tendency of appreciation for the currency of this country.

[14] The assumed credibility evades systematic errors of the exchange rate expectations as well as problems with an economically perfect rationality and lasting deviations from the uncovered interest parity. But the learning model has to be extended to all fundamentals; the concept of rationality becomes even more restrictive. See Lewis (1989), Garretsen, Knot and Nijsse (1997).

and the stabilization effect of expectations, clearly shows for the case of a CB[15] to be stable:

- other news of policy (e.g. structural policies) may not disturb exchange rate expectations (and create speculations about a change of the parity),
- other (non-monetary) policies may take the task of stabilization, and if so then the effects on the exchange rate expectations must be taken into consideration,
- no long-run drifts between the home and the anchor country may occur, in order to avoid a collapse of the fixed rate system (and of the CB) - naturally or by speculative attacks.

The compulsion for the adjustment of the domestic fundamentals and the transfer of the stabilization tasks to non-monetary policies elucidates that an institutionalization of a CB has to be understood as a social strategy enforcing an integrative development of the domestic economy. The necessity of establishing a consistent CBS is made clear. Attempts to secure this strategy are:

- the CB or an other department of the central bank additionally holds free foreign exchange reserves or standby credits or credit lines for the purpose of intervention and to stabilize expectations,
- the CB or an other (banking-) department has legitimate instruments with regard to monetary policy and banking supervision at its disposal, and tries to neutralize fluctuations in the non-controllable fundamentals by the management of the money multiplier.

3.1.3 The System with Inside-Money

A money supply by commercial banks can be destabilizing and therefore it implies an effective banking supervision and discretionary monetary measures. Within narrow limits the money supply is independent from the balance of payments. Thus, the central bank has to consist of a modified CB or a pure CB and a banking board (BB).

This is important because as a result of the experiences with the CB the relative importance of the cashholdings will decrease, the efficiency of the banking system and the cash management of the firms and the government will increase, and even foreigners will increase their stocks of domestic money (and assets). The multiplier will increase, and without a CB or BB in the position of a lender-of-last-resort, the variance of the interest-rate in the money market will be higher in cases

[15] If the (non-monetary) fundamentals reach their upper limit then the money supply must decrease in order to compensate. This upper limit denotes the loss of reserves; the CB holds no free foreign exchange-reserves.

of strong (transitory) fluctuations and speculative capital movements, and this will cause liquidity shortages of some banks and jeopardize the stability of the CB.

In general a CB is endangered, if any (spot-) speculation on devaluation of the CB-currency seems to be profitable moreover if the interest rate differential leads to the expectation of a parity change. This expected exchange rate change has to be compensated by a change of the multiplier moreover of the domestic component of the money supply (inside-money). This component, combined with the endogenous change in the monetary base has to absorb all transitory (and permanent) relative changes of the domestic fundamentals.[16]

The credibility of a CB increases with restrictive monetary policy and banking surveillance. The solvency and international competitiveness of the commercial banks are significant factors. Just as important as the monetary rule and the tied base money supply process, is the banking supervisions orientation to strict international standards (at least to those of the anchor country). The burden rests on the modified CB or on the BB; it needs monetary instruments immediately, i.e. a reserve requirement policy and (for countries in transition to be developed) an open-market policy (OMP).

3.1.4 On Substitutability

The credibility of the CB depends on the publics perception of the intention and ability to defend the fixed parity, and thus on the stock of foreign reserves.[17] From the view of capital owners, the CB-currency (I) is stable, if it is a nearly perfect substitute for the anchor currency (A). Their indifference curves have an absolute slope of 45 degrees. This is the case, within a system of coordinates with the domestic money supply (I) and the stock of foreign reserves (A) on the axes, in each point on the parity line (PP) which goes through the origin with a slope equal to the fixed exchange-rate. The PP-curve denotes for each stock of A the amount of (I) which is covered with 100 percent.

Since the coverage of the money supply (I) will be smaller than 100 percent for a multiplier of greater than one, a steeper equilibrium line for the money market (MM) can be plotted for each value of the multiplier. The lower the coverage-quota and the greater the multiplier is, the steeper this equilibrium line (MM) will be. In an array stretched between the PP-line and a critical MM-line the indifference curves (still) have a slope of 45 degrees. This array is the target zone

---

[16] The literature focuses attention on the external equilibrium; monetary policy and rational expectations are normally analyzed concerning their effects on the external equilibrium, the internal equilibrium is (neo-classically) assumed to exist. But this is far from being adequate. If politicians follow this theoretical recommendation, it must ultimately lead to a collapse of the CB.

[17] For collapse scenarios of regimes with a fixed exchange rate regime see Krugman (1979).

for the money supply. This critical MM-line follows from the upper limit of the fundamentals according to the (pre-)fixed exchange rate. Within this array the system is stable; no one expects a change of the parity or of the anchor currency; the CB is regarded to be credible, the honey-moon-effect is at work.[18]

3.2 The Drift and Permanent Changes

While a common type of an exchange rate fixing as well as a crawling-peg system tries to determine the equilibrium exchange rate for a given market system, the strategy with a CB is to develop the market structure and improve price flexibilities endogenously and optimize with respect to an advanced (anchor-) economy.[19] The fundamentals do not determine the exchange rate, but the fixed parity determines the (adjustment of all) fundamentals without disturbing the potential growth and excludes a drift.

The intlation rate of the anchor currency country marks an upper limit for price changes. An arising drift must be compensated; it requires a change in the money supply moreover a stimulus to expectations. This may be done by a reduction in the reserve requirement (or of the coverage-quota). The critical MM-curve turns and the array broadens. But, exchange rate options may not exist to the CB, since with such options expectations will arise, the more likely a parity change (i.a. dependent on the stock of foreign reserves) will be. Then a successful speculative attack may be possible; the "divorce-effect“ counteracts the "honey-moon-effect“. The variability of the interest rate and money supply will increase, the substitutability from the CB-currency to the anchor currency will decrease.

The central bank (moreover the modified CB or the BB) has no discretion with regard to the exchange rate and it has limited discretion with regard to the price stability. Changes of the money supply and of the foreign exchange reserves are no longer cointegrated. Problems exist in strengthening the independence of the central bank (Rogoff) or in arranging special contracts (Walsh) or in introducing credible types of self-binding commitments.

---

[18] For further problems (besides the missing empirical confirmation of target zone approaches relying on the S-shaped curve) see Fuhrmann (1997).

[19] The choice of the anchor currency (the German Mark as the directly and via the Finnish as well as the Swedish currencies indirectly the most important foreign currency to Estonia) and of the relevant international markets guaranteed the time-consistency of the CB-strategy and its credibility in the sense of Kydland and Prescott (1977). The Lithuanian CB with a tie to the US-Dollar but divergent developments in Europe and in the U.S.A. seems to be time-inconsistent and to be not optimal. These considerations become increasingly valid for Asian countries with their US-Dollar ties and rising integration with Japan and China.

4 Summary

A currency board is not an institution that could be compared with an anchor holding a ship on an uneven sea. It is a part of a future orientated strategy to avoid an everlasting running aground; that means an anchor in the sense of a tie to a well defined area of integration with a free market system being wished for and supported for by all socially decisive groups in the society. It is effective and stable only within a comprehensive institutional frame.

The difficulties of a CB, which is to be institutionalized as a strategical investment, prima facie are based on the credibility of the choice of the anchor currency as well as on the parity. Then a CB can be understood as a specific objective function within an extreme target zone regime. The ultimate target lies in the endogenous adjustment of the domestic fundamentals to those of the anchor currency country moreover of the anchor currency community. The pre-determination of an exchange rate, of the base-money supply mechanism and of an implicit price target puts a strong adjustment pressure on the whole domestic system. In accordance therewith all kinds of politics are dominated by and geared towards this monetary institution. The credibility of a CB lies with all other policies. Non-compatible policies will lead ultimately to a devaluation (in most cases a depreciation is to be expected), a change of the anchor currency or (temporarily) even to capital controls. Half-hearted reforms and a disregard of the underlying market mechanism and of the credibility, as practiced by diverse countries, with the exclusive introduction of a CB causes either, a growing economic consensus or only short-run stabilization, like a drift anchor.

The advantage of the CB is based on the immediate implication of a higher credibility due to the transparency and to the endogenity of the money supply as well as of the rules for exchange rate changes. It rests with the stabilizing repercussions of the conditional expectations of the market. An option of the CB for the change of the anchor or the parity eliminates this advantage and leads to known cases of instability of a fixed exchange rate. But the CB is only one department of the central bank, the banking board is another. A CB creates credibility, but it depends for its part on the stability of the whole domestic banking system as well as on the standards and effectiveness of banking surveillance.

References

Frenkel, M. (1997), Chartists, Fundamentalists and Rational Speculators in the Foreign Exchange Market, *Journal of International Business* 2, 1-24.

Froot, K.A. and M. Obstfeld (1991), Exchange-Rate Dynamics Under Stochastic Regime Shifts - A Unified Approach, *Journal of International Economics* 31, 203-29.

Fuhrmann, W. (1994), Ein Currency-Board System; Econ. Dep. of the University Paderborn (ed.), International Economics Working Paper No. 9403 and http:// 141.89.32.20/u/ls_ makrooek/index.htm .

Fuhrmann, W. and R. Richert (1995), Ein Währungssystem mit einem Currency Board, *Wirtschaftswissenschaftliches Studium* 12, 1035-39.

Fuhrmann, W. and R. Schweickert (1997), Zur Theorie des Currency Boards, Econ. Dep. of the University Potsdam (ed.), International Working Paper No. 9704 and http://141.89.32.20/u/ls_makrooek/index.htm .

Garman, D.M. and D.J. Richards (1989), Policy Rules, Inflationary Bias, and Cyclical Stability, *Journal of Money, Credit, and Banking* 1, 409-21.

Garretsen, H. K. Knot and E. Nijsse (1997), Learning about Fundamentals in a Target Zone: The Widening of the French ERM Bands in 1993, De Nederlandsche Bank NV (ed.), DNB- Staff Reports No. 11/1997.

Gesell, S. (1920), Internationale Valuta-Assoziation (Iva), Sontra in Hessen.

Hanke, St. H., L. Jonung and K. Schuler (1993), Russian Currency and Finance: A Currency Board Approach to Reform, London, New York.

Illing, G. (1997), Theorie der Geldpolitik, Eine spieltheoretische Einführung, Berlin.

Krugman, P. (1979), A Model of Balance of Payment Crisis, *Journal of Money, Credit, and Banking* 11, 311-25.

Kydland, F. E. and E. C. Prescott (1977), Rules rather than Discretion: The Inconsistency of Optimal Plans, *Journal of Political Economy* 85, 473-91.

Lewis, K. K. (1989), Can Learning Affect Exchange Rate Behavior? *Journal of Monetary Economics* 23, 79- 100.

Lewis, K. K. (1989), Changing Beliefs and Systematic Rational Forecast Errors with Evidence from Foreign Exchange, *American Economic Review* 79, 621-36.

Lockwood, B. and A. Philippopoulos (1994), Insider Power, Unemployment Dynamics, and Multiple Inflation Equilibria, *Economica* 61, 59-77.

Lohmann, S. (1992), The Optimal Degree of Commitment: Credibility versus Flexibility, *American Economic Review* 82, 273-286.

Meltzer, A. H. (1993), The Benefits and Costs of Currency Boards, *Cato-Journal* 12, 707-10.

Neely, C. J. (1994), Realignments of Target Zone Exchange Rate Systems: What We Do Know?, The Federal Reserve Board of St. Louis (ed.), St. Louis 76, 23-34.

Persson, T. and G. Tabellini (1990), Macroeconomic Policy, Credibility and Politics, *Fundamentals of Pure and Applied Economics* 38, Chur, London.

Persson, T. and G. Tabellini (1994), Designing Institutions for Monetary Stability, *Carnegie-Rochester Conference Series on Public Policy* 39, 53-84.

Rogoff, K. (1985), The Optimal Degree of Commitment to an Intermediate Monetary Target, *Quarterly Journal of Economics* 100, 1169-90.

Scheunpflug, I. (1997), Wechselkurszonen und Währungsbandbreiten, Frankfurt.

Sell, F. (1995), Stabilizing the Rouble: Is There a Case for a New Fisher Rule?, *Intereconomics* 30, 31-35.

Svennson, L. E. O. (1992), An Interpretation of Recent Research on Exchange Rate Target Zones, *Journal of Economic Perspectives* 6, 119-44.

Svensson, L. E. O. (1995), Optimal Inflation Targets, "Conservative" Central Banks, and Linear Inflation Contracts, Institute for International Economic Studies, Stockholm University (ed.), Seminar Paper No. 595.

Walsh, C. E. (1995), Optimal Contracts for Independent Central Bankers, *American Economic Review* 85, 150-67.

Werner, A. M. (1995), Exchange-Rate Target Zones, Realignments and the Interest Differential: Theory and Evidence, *Journal of International Economics* 39, 353-67.

Werner, A. M. (1996), Target Zones and Realignments Expectations: The Israeli and Mexican Experience, *IMF Staff Papers* 43, 571-86.

Williamson, J. (1992), On Designing an International Monetary System, *Journal of Post Keynesian Economics* 15, 181-92.

Comment

Rainer Schweickert
Institute of World Economics, Düsterbrooker Weg 120, D-24105 Kiel

1 Introduction

Since its implementation in Argentina and Estonia, the currency board idea celebrates a revival which comes quite as a surprise. With the exceptions of Hongkong and Singapore, all currency boards in former colonies were substituted by central banks when colonial times ended (see Schwartz (1993)). Hence, the abolition of currency boards in the past marked the beginning of an institutional reform. It is highly interesting that the recent introduction of currency boards were exactly motivated by full-scale institutional reforms starting either from scratch (transformation countries: Estonia) or chaos (developing countries: Argentina). Have the former colonies made a mistake when abolishing currency boards? What is the role of a currency board in institutional reforms? Fuhrmann touched this issues in his introduction but rather as a motivation for his interesting approach to formalize the currency board idea in terms of exchange rate policy.

This paper tries to complement Fuhrmann's paper by focusing on the relationship between currency boards and institutional reforms. The basic issue is that the revival of the currency board follows a switch in the emphasis in the literature on exchange rate policy in emerging market economies from efficiency to credibility. While 'traditional' currency boards were thought to implement an optimum currency area, 'modern' currency boards are thought to import the credibility of the country providing the anchor currency, thereby improving the chances of institutional reforms. Focusing on this possible trade-off between efficiency and credibility, the following analysis comes to somewhat different assessments compared to those to be found in the paper by Fuhrmann:

- It is more optimistic about real adjustment under a currency board regime, i.e. real exchange rate adjustment given a long-run drift in economic fundamentals between the home country and the country which provides the anchor currency.
- It is more pessimistic that a currency board creates an advantage in terms of credibility compared to a central bank free to conduct discretionary monetary policy.
- It gives room to an explicit discussion of exchange rate based stabilization programs and especially of the critical role of the real exchange rate in this type of stabilization program.

The discussion of these issues will be organized around the presentation of the Argentine stabilization policy implemented in April 1991 and its performance in comparative perspective. Two hypotheses can be supported by such an analysis.

- *Credibility* can not be imported by means of a currency board; a currency board rather needs radical complementary reforms in order to establish its credibility (Schweickert 1993a).
- *Stabilization* with a currency board is a high-risk strategy which is only optimal if the potential return is high as well, i.e. if monetary stabilization has top priority and a high potential for reforms is given (Schweickert (1993b)).

2 Currency Boards and Credibility

Synopsis 1 gives the stylized facts of the Argentine stabilization policy. It demonstrates that the currency board is just a technical rule for the automatic determination of money supply. This rule has been supported by a range of measures which can be classified into two categories. Orthodox reforms have been implemented to guarantee the feasibility of the stabilization policies by making monetary policy independent from fiscal policy and by making prices flexible; political economy policies have supported the sustainability of stabilization by making the market expect that the rule will not be changed. This overview shows that a 'theory of the currency board' has to be either trivial or complex. On the one hand, the technical implications of the currency board for money supply are explained by textbook versions of the monetary exchange rate theory. On the other hand, a complete understanding of the role of the currency board in a stabilization package needs to consider the theories of currency competition, optimal regulation of financial markets, sequencing of reforms, and the political economy of reforms.

As a consequence, the description of the broader theoretical background for explaining credibility must remain eclectic. Three aspects which are important in the Argentine case figure prominently in the recent discussion. First, Argentina implemented a type of currency board which allowed for some flexibility. Up to 20 per cent of the monetary base could be covered by Argentine public debt denominated in US Dollar, i.e. the minimum coverage with 'hard' reserves is 80 per cent. This gives some room for the central bank to act as a lender-of-last-resort. Because all other measures support a free play of market forces this loophole appears to be rather unsystematic. However, the theoretical literature is also rather indecisive whether or not lender-of-last-resort functions of a quasi currency board reduce or increase its credibility (see Fuhrmann on this point and Caprio et al. (1996)).

Second, the political economy of reforms gains importance in both the theoretical and empirical literature. While it seems relatively easy to win the support of voters which suffer from high inflation or even subsequent hyperinflations as was the case in Argentina, stabilization can only be sustained by avoiding resistance from employers, labor unions, and the military (see Starr (1997) for the case of Argentina):

- *Employers* control two sources essential to successful implementation, capital and reputation; in Argentina, employers, traditionally opposing Peronist governments, joined the government coalition because the Peronist government adopted market-oriented policies and distributed key posts in the administration to representatives of the internationally oriented segment of the private sector.
- *Labor unions* are expected to oppose against a large-scale dismissal of public employees, against significant wage cuts in the public sector, and against a flexibilization of labor market regulations; in Argentina, protest from labor unions, the traditional allies of the Peronist party, has been rather weak because moderate labor unions supported their party and because the government destroyed the stronghold of radical labor unions by privatizing state-owned enterprises.
- *The military* is likely to oppose sharp reductions in the military budget; in Argentina, the government pleased the military, in general pro-Peronist, by stopping human rights trials and, initially, supporting radical groups in order to force the military establishment to negotiate budget reductions - after a compromise has been settled, the radicals became isolated.

Hence, the government has to choose allies within the three relevant political forces outside government. The Argentine case demonstrates that this choice depends on the reform strategy and its implication for key macroeconomic variables - above all for the fiscal budget.

Third, the target system for monetary and exchange rate policy in developing countries is discussed more formally in the recent literature (see, e.g., Edwards (1996)). Generally, there seems to be a consensus that high and unstable inflation rates *as well as* an overvalued currency are to be avoided (see Schweickert (1993c): Ch. B). Unfortunately, the conflict between these targets is most pronounced in exchange rate based stabilization programs leading to the 'stabilization blues' (Guidotti and Végh (1992)): the fixing of the exchange rate curbes traded goods prices while non-traded goods prices still increase; the emerging trade deficit resulting from this real appreciation is financed by capital inflows; because of stock-adjustment and speculative effects, capital inflows are likely to dry up, the boom ends, the currency becomes overvalued, and foreign exchange flows out leading to a monetary contraction which should put pressure on non-traded goods prices; if non-traded goods prices increase slower than traded goods prices, the real exchange rate devalues and overvaluation diminishes. Typically, however, the end of the boom phase also marks the end of exchange rate based stabilization programs.

Synopsis 1 — Currency Board and Reform-Program in Argentina (April 1991–)

Currency Board
– Monetary base covered by foreign exchange
– Exchange of domestic currency against foreign reserves on demand given the official fixed exchange rate
Credibility I: Feasibility ('orthodox reforms')
– Consolidation of fiscal budget
– Deregulation of goods and factor markets
– Privatization of public-owned enterprises
Credibility II: Sustainability ('political economy' measures)
– Full convertibility
– US Dollar as parallel currency
– Limited lender of last resort function of the currency board
– Exchange rate fixed by law
– Strategic policies to secure support from voters and interest groups
Target
– Stabilization without overvaluation.

Source: Schweickert (1994; 1996).

These stylized facts lead to the conclusion that the loss function discussed by Fuhrmann is adequate for industrialized countries rather than for developing and transformation countries. The loss function for industrialized countries implicitly assumes either a closed economy or the absence of an external disequilibrium in the sense that a current account deficit could not be financed. While these assumptions make some sense for the more advanced industrial countries (certainly less so for the Spains and Portugals) they are not plausible for developing and transformation countries. Hence, a loss function for the latter group of countries has to contain both the deviation of the actual from the desired inflation rate (p-p^*) and the real exchange rate disequilibrium (r-r^*).

Additionally, the loss function discussed by Fuhrmann creates difficulties in the case of a fixed exchange rate. Assuming external equilibrium, the output gap (y-y^*) shows the disequilibrium of the real exchange rate, i.e. the need for real exchange rate adjustment, and (p-p^*) shows the actual real exchange rate adjustment.[1] This implies (p-p^*) and (y-y^*) to be perfectly (positively) correlated in the case of a smooth functioning of the nominal anchor. Hence, the minimization of the loss function makes not much sense, except for (y-y^*) = 0. In this case, however, the only remaining target is the inflation rate.

3 Currency Boards and Stabilization

The discussion of the target system for developing and transformation countries supports the second hypothesis given above, i.e. that stabilization cum currency board is a high risk strategy which only pays if stabilization has a high priority (a high weight for (p-p^*) rather than for (r-r^*) in the loss function) and the reform potential is equally high. This can be further demonstrated by looking at the Argentine experience in comparison with Mexico and Chile.

Synopsis 2 lines out reform priorities and reform potentials of the three Latin American countries. It shows two countries with a high priority for stabilization – Argentina and Mexico – and one country with high priority for real exchange rate adjustment – Chile. These choices have been rational given the initial conditions, in terms of monetary stability and monetary reputation, i.e. rule based stabilization had high pay-offs in Argentina and Mexico but not in Chile. Synopsis 2 also shows that Argentina and Mexico adopted distinct reform approaches. Argentina showed a high potential for radical, market oriented reforms adequate to complement the currency board exchange rate regime; Mexico with a lower reform effort and a preference for social consensus quickly eased the nominal anchor and adopted an active crawling-peg, i.e. preannounced devaluations smaller than the difference in inflation rates in the home and the anchor currency. Again, Chile provides the counterfactual: flexible exchange rates, orthodox reforms already completed in the 1970s and 1980s, and no need for political economy reforms.

Hence, all three countries implemented policies which would have been classified consistent in an a-priori evaluation. Moreover, the performance of the different regimes can be observed against a comparable background: increasing capital inflows and low US Dollar interest rates. Figures 1 to 4 present the development of the key macroeconomic variables inflation rate and real exchange rate (quarterly data) and real GDP and trade balance (annual data). The time series start one quarter and one year respectively before the implementation of the exchange rate based stabilization programs in the cases of Mexico and Argentina

[1] p^* depends on inflation in the anchor currency with (p^*-p^B) reflecting the desired (equilibrium) real exchange rate adjustment.

(for the data, see IMFa). Figures 1 and 2 reveal the significant advantages of the radical Argentine currency board system compared with the Mexican active crawl.

Synopsis 2:

	Exchange Rate Policies in Argentina, Mexico and Chile since 1987 – Initial Conditions and Reform Strategies		
	Argentina (1991-)	Mexico	Chile
Exchange Rate Policy	Currency Board	fixed exchange rate, active crawling-peg	passive crawling-peg, managed floating
Monetary Stability	no	no	yes
Monetary Reputation	no	no	yes
Reform Priority	stabilization	stabilization	real exchange rate adjustment
Orthodox Reforms	short-term, radical	short-term, mixed	long-term, radical
Political Economy Reforms	free play of market forces	social consensus	none
Reform Potential	high	medium	high

Source: Diehl and Schweickert (1997): Ch. C.I.

- *Effectiveness*: The impact on stabilization was immediate in Argentina and delayed in Mexico;
- *Sustainability*: The capital outflows after the outbreak of the Tequila crisis (4/1994) led to a complete stabilization of the price level in Argentina while

Mexico - because of the devaluation crisis - returned to inflation levels experienced seven years ago at the beginning of the stabilization process;
- *Costs*: Economic growth before the crisis has been higher in Argentina, the recession due to the crisis has been less pronounced in Argentina, and economic growth after the crisis is comparable in both countries.

Hence, compared with a less radical implementation of exchange rate based stabilization, the currency board solution, if complemented by comprehensive orthodox and political economy reforms, shows clear advantages in terms of efficiency.

Figures 1 and 2 also show the clear advantage of the Chilean strategy to weigh anchor when the tide is turning, i.e. when capital flows change their direction. During the period 1988 to 1990 when capital started to return to Latin American countries, the passive crawl with a band allowed inflation to increase. As shown in Figure 1, Chile did not only allow inflation to increase but also reduced it rather gradually. As shown in Figure 2, the return to two digit (annual) inflation rates did not distort the real economy significantly. To the contrary, Chile remained on the stable growth path which dates back to 1984. High growth has also been maintained during the Tequila crisis because, contrary to Argentina and Mexico, capital inflows have not been affected.

Figure 1: Inflation Rates in Chile, Mexico, and Argentina (per cent; log scale)

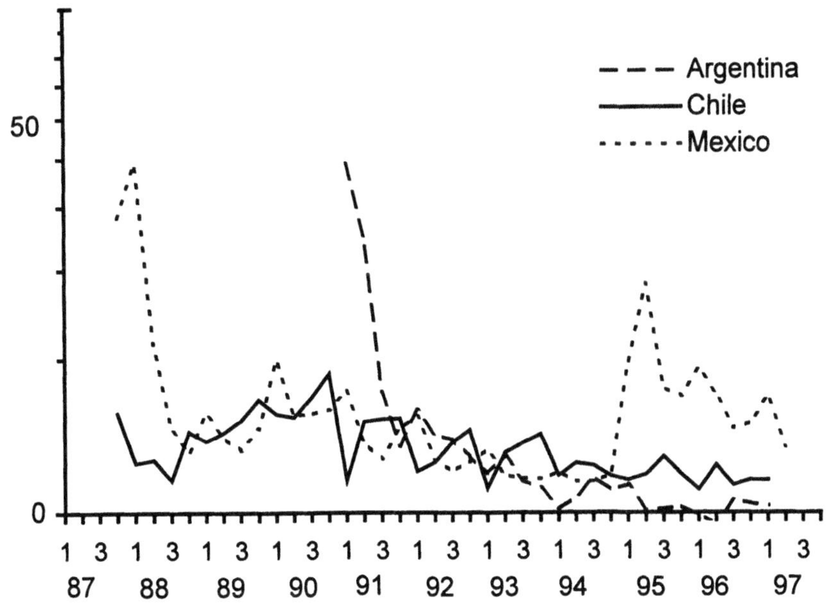

Figure 2: Real GDP in Chile, Mexico, and Argentina (Index)

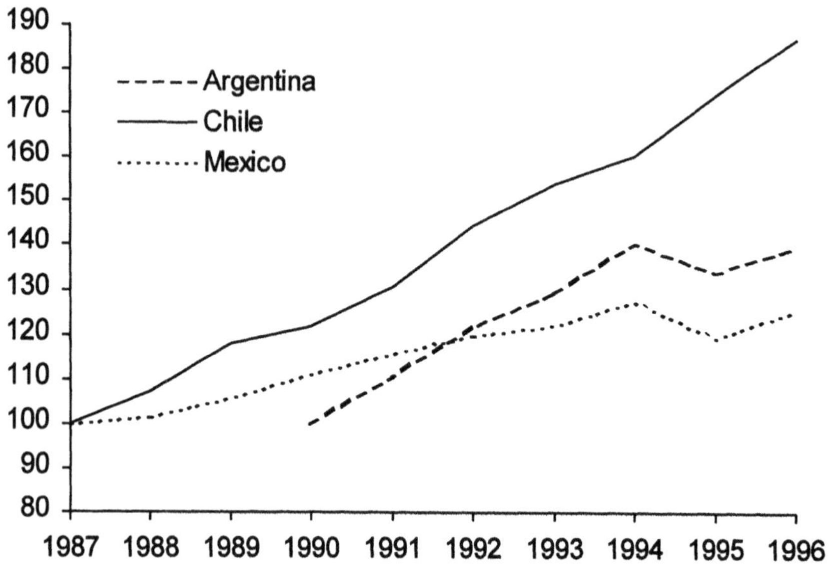

The reason for Chile being rated differently by foreign investors can be identified in Figure 3. It shows that the real exchange rate, defined against the major currencies using SDR weights, shows the same stable growth path as real GDP. Considering the high growth rates in Chile, real appreciation has been consistent with real exchange rate equilibrium. The stable growth path also shows that Chile targeted the real exchange rate rather than the inflation rate.

The motivation for this policy has been the experience with overvaluation produced by capital inflows and followed by a deep crisis in the early 1980s. In order to avoid such a situation, Chile systematically increased exchange rate uncertainty (see Ffrench-Davis et al. (1995)): The band around the passive crawl was increased from +/-2 to +/-10 per cent, the parity formerly defined against the US Dollar became defined against a basket of currencies, the parity was changed in a discretionary and unsystematic way, interventions from the central bank became intramarginal, and reserve inflows were sterilized. Additionally, short-term capital inflows became regulated and implicitly taxed by a reserve requirement for external credits of 20 per cent to be kept on a non-interest bearing account for at least 90 days. These measures show the room for manoeuvre of an independent central bank which built up reputation in the past. The Chilean central bank used this discretionary power to stabilize the real exchange rate and – in the medium run – the inflation rate as well.

To the contrary, the development of the real exchange rate was determined by the market in the cases of Argentina and Mexico finally leading to an overvaluation when capital flows changed direction. Again, the Argentine currency board reveals a significant advantage: although the nominal exchange rate was absolutely fixed, real exchange rate adjustment and the development of the trade balance was more stable than in Mexico. Hence, a smooth transition to a new real exchange rate equilibrium is possible in a fixed exchange rate regime but, contrary to a flexible exchange rate regime of the Chilean type, not without costs.

Unfortunately, it is difficult to disentangle how much of the (relative) Argentine success is due to the currency board and how much is due to the other reform measures. Synopsis 1 already showed that the currency board is but one item in a comprehensive reform package. One other item has been the parallel currency approach. The stabilizing properties of this measure are shown in Figure 5. According to unpublished World Bank data, the decrease in Peso deposits at the start of the crisis in early 1995 was partly compensated by an increase in US Dollar deposits. When capital returned, US Dollar deposits quickly surpassed their initial level. It is, therefore, reasonable to assume that the availability of US Dollar deposits stabilized the banking system and helped to avoid a full-fledged financial crisis.

Additionally, the Argentine central bank used its limited function as lender-of-last-resort to smooth the effects of declining foreign reserves on the banking system. A liquidity policy was possible because the monetary base was fully covered by 'hard' reserves at the beginning of the crisis. This reserves were smelted down to 80 per cent of the monetary base thereby switching the reserves held by commercial banks from Pesos into US Dollars. Hence, the Argentine central bank voluntarily helped the Peso monetary base to adjust to lower demand and increased the Dollar liquidity of commercial banks.

An advantage of such a limited flexibility is supported by the counterexample of Mexico. Contrary to Argentina, the Mexican central bank used its discretionary power to stop the decline of base money due to reserve outflows (Zarazaga (1995). The consequence was that the difference between money demand and money supply even increased and that the central bank supplied the liquidity for speculative attacks. This points to a main advantage of a quasi currency board of the Argentine type. After the monetary base has been covered by a maximum of 20 per cent by domestic public debt, the currency board can only gain discretionary power by building up excess reserves. This implies that both the potential and the direction of interventions are known by the market. However, in order to reach such a solution it would be sufficient to restrict the domestic component of the monetary base.

Figure 3: Real Exchange Rate Adjustment in Chile, Mexico, and Argentina (Index, SDR weight)

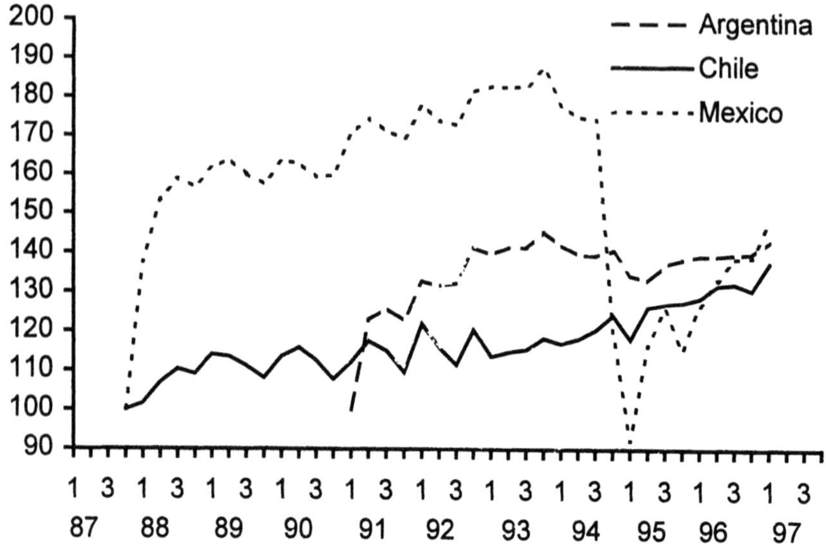

Figure 4: Trade Balance in Chile, Mexico, and Argentina (per cent of GDP)

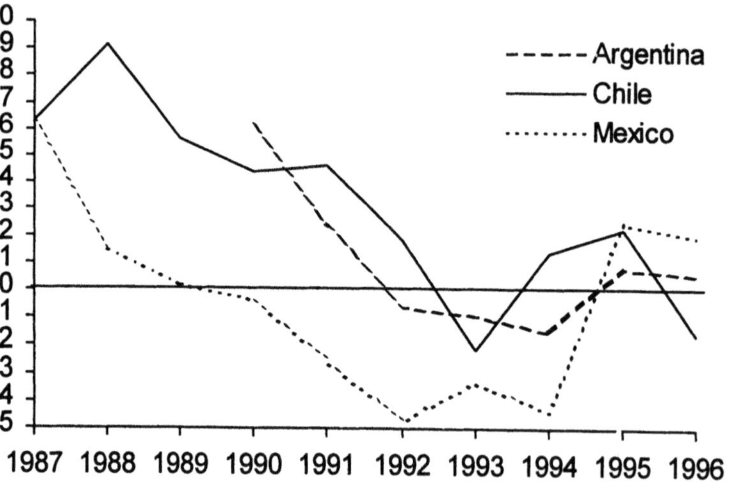

Figure 5: Bank Deposits in Argentina (Mill. Pesos)

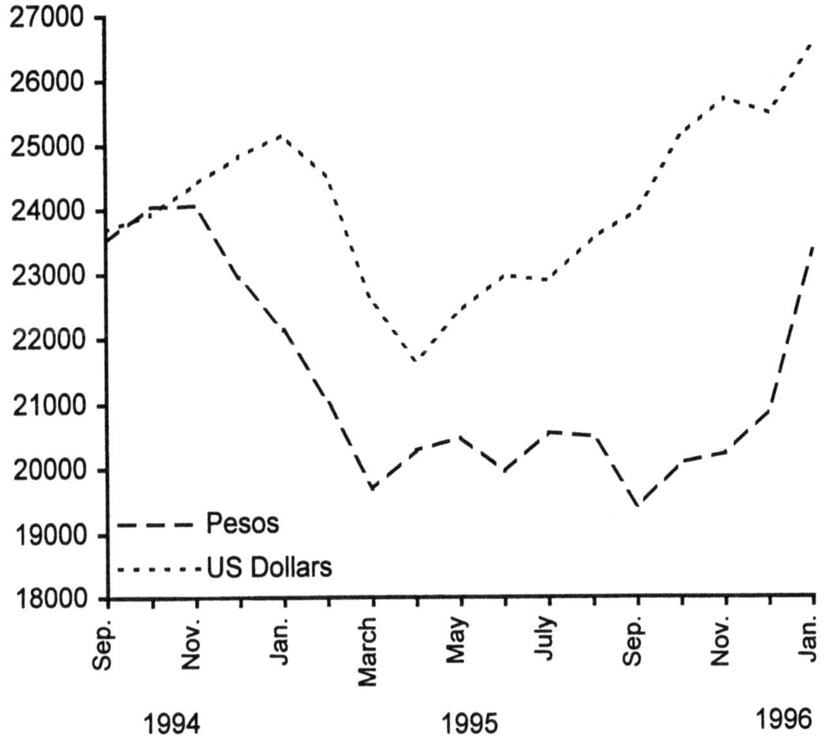

4 Conclusions

All in all, the currency board appears to be but one element of a stabilization package which aims at reducing inflation drastically in the short-run and which includes a complete and radical reform of all policy areas in order to improve the functioning of market forces. Only such a full-fledged program constitutes credibility; the currency board, as a rule to restrict money supply on the basis of domestic assets, needs rather than produces credibility.

Such a radical stabilization policy is only optimal if pay-offs are worth to take the risk, i.e. to accept the dependence on capital inflows. The Argentine example shows that there are high pay-offs in the case of high monetary instability, low reputation of the monetary authorities, and a high potential for market oriented reforms. The comparison with Mexico which implemented an active crawl, a compromise between fixing and floating, reveals that the radical currency board based solution has clear advantages over other forms of exchange rate based stabilization programs. However, in terms of real adjustment, the Chilean example shows that a flexible exchange rate is more adequate to smooth real exchange rate adjustment and to maintain real growth of GDP.

Hence, the general problem is to maintain credibility when switching from the currency board system which may be optimal in the short-run to a more flexible regime which is likely to be optimal in the long-run. At the same time, it becomes increasingly difficult to maintain support for the currency board after successful stabilization. Therefore, the most interesting unsolved and policy relevant questions concern the political economy of currency boards and the political economy of reforms in general.

References

Diehl, M. and R. Schweickert (1997), Wechselkurspolitik im Aufholprozeß. Erfahrungen lateinamerikanischer, europäischer und asiatischer Länder, Tübingen.

Caprio jr., G., M.P. Dooley, D.M. Leipziger and C.E. Walsh (1996), The Lender of Last Resort Function under a Currency Board: The Case of Argentina, *Open Economies Review* 7 (Suppl. 1), 625–50.

Edwards, S. (1996), Exchange-Rate Anchors, Credibility, and Inertia: A Tale of Two Crises, Chile and Mexico, *American Economic Review* 86, 176–80.

Ffrench-Davis, R., M. Agosin and A. Uthoff (1995), Capital Movements, Export Strategy, and Macroeconomic Stability in Chile, in: R. Ffrench-Davis, S. Griffith-Jones (eds.), Coping with Capital Surges. The Return of Finance in Latin America, Ottawa.

Guidotti, P.E. and C.A. Végh (1992), Losing Credibility: The Stabilization Blues, IMF Working Paper 92/73, Washington D.C.

IMF (a), International Financial Statistics, Washington D.C., var. issues.

Schwartz, A.J. (1993), Currency Boards: Their Past, Present, and Possible Future Role, *Carnegie-Rochester Conference Series on Public Policy* 39, 147–87.

Schweickert, R. (1993a), Implikationen alternativer geld- und wechselkurspolitischer Regeln im Transformationsprozeß, *Kredit & Kapital* 26 (2), 205–29.

Schweickert, R. (1993b), Alternative Strategies for Real Devaluation and the Sequencing of Economic Reforms in Developing Countries, *Kyklos* 46 (1), 65–85.

Schweickert, R. (1993c), Geld- und Wechselkurspolitik in Entwicklungsländern - eine Analyse alternativer Stabilisierungs- und Anpassungsstrategien, Tübingen.

Schweickert, R. (1994), Exchange Rate Based Stabilization — Lessons from a Radical Implementation in Argentina, *The World Economy* 17 (2), 171–89.

Schweickert, R. (1996), Neoliberale Wirtschaftsordnung und wirtschaftliche Entwicklung in Lateinamerika, *Zeitschrift für Wirtschaftspolitik* 45 (2), 249–61.

Starr, P.K. (1997), Government Coalitions and the Viability of Currency Boards: Argentina under the Cavallo Plan, *Journal of Interamerican Studies and World Affairs* 39 (2), 83–133.

Zarazaga, C.E. (1995), Argentina, Mexico, and Currency Boards: Another Case of Rules versus Discretion, *Economic Review* 4, Federal Reserve Bank of Dallas, 14–24.

Conclusion and Supplements

Helmut Wagner
University of Hagen, Feithstr. 140, D - 58084 Hagen

In this concluding chapter I will be showing in Section 1 overviews of the comments or supplementary papers and of the general discussions on the symposium. In Section 2 I will underline again some key issues which were encountered in a whole series of articles and supplementary comments as well as in the subsequent discussions.

1 The Supplementary Papers and the General Discussions[1]

In his supplementary paper on Illing's article, **Hans Peter Grüner** examines the time inconsistency problem in more detail. In this context he stresses the following aspects:

- *The credibility problem of central bank contracts*, although he attaches less importance to these than Illing. Grüner's reasons for this are that if the principal waives the punishment this would necessitate a change of the central bank law which would only be possible at great political costs. As a result, it may be assumed that a written contract will also be enforced (i.e. there is no renegotiation). A monetary policy based on the existence of a central bank contract is therefore more credible than one based simply on announcements.
- *Problems of non-availability of data* that is required to realize the Walsh contract on an optimum basis. The data problem refers above all to the influence of the central bank on real variables, on society's preferences, the central bank's own preferences, the socially desirable rate of inflation and on other macroeconomic variables. Uncertainty about central bank preferences in particular means that an exact contract cannot be formulated.
- *Problems of output stabilization.* Grüner questions whether central banks are able to stabilize output. According to Grüner, the empirical findings on the correlation of central bank independence and output volatility can also be interpreted to show that government-dependent central banks were unsuccessful in stabilizing output. In addition, it will have to be examined

[1] I would like to thank my assistants for drawing up submissions for this section. These were Wolfram Berger, Claudia Goldschmidt, Friedrich Kißmer, Ralf Sonnenfroh and Florian Späte.

whether more suitable mechanisms exist, for example, stabilizing output via the labor market.

- *Problems on determining the optimal rate of inflation.* Grüner points to the circumstance that the level of the optimal rate of inflation is very controversial, both theoretically and empirically. In this context he addresses the latest findings in a study by Lucas (1997).

The following discussion on the conference papers[2] from Illing and Grüner was centered on a critical examination of the approaches from Rogoff and Walsh and their differences. As a positive effect of contracts it was determined that contracts can provide incentives so that central banks do not support party-political interests before elections. In so far, contracts contribute to limiting the risks of political business cycles. In addition, different forms of shocks were analyzed and confronted with appropriate rules. A further central point in the discussion was the debate on credibility. The emphasis here was on the required consideration of the different central bank philosophies, which are sometimes expressed in the degree of accountability. In conclusion, the influence of the size of a country and international movements of capital were also discussed.

In his supplementary paper on Karmann's contribution, **Norbert Funke** emphasizes above all the following points:

- that a generally superior monetary policy strategy cannot be determined, because the best solution in each case must be orientated towards the reality prevailing in each country;
- that in the practice-orientated realization of the conception of central bank contracts one has to be extremely skeptical whether the suitable level of payment can in fact be stipulated in a simple, linear contract;
- that it is questionable whether an inflation bias can be canceled through changes to the preferences of central bankers, because, when a bias is to be substantiated, the roles of the formation of expectations and the role of wage/price formation processes has to be examined. The actual shape of short-term Phillips curves has not been granted sufficient empirical research;
- that in practice an escape clause can take several forms that e.g. can differ in the ex ante definition of a condition for escape, in the establishment of a committee that decides ad hoc on the legitimacy of an escape from the contract, and in the ex post examination of an actual escape;
- that a preferable alternative to state-contingent escape clauses might be to target (and make public) a modified price index that is appropriately adjusted for the impact of supply shocks. Against this background the importance of communication strategies is increasingly coming into focus. On theoretical grounds, a move towards greater transparency along with changes in the

[2] The articles and comments printed in this book, with the exception of James Tobin's contribution, are all more or less amended or revised versions of the papers presented at the conference.

communication strategy may have effects which are similar to a shift from a discretionary policy towards a more rule-based strategy;

- that different monetary policy strategies are more similar in practice than is to be suspected from the differences in the theoretical approaches.

In the general discussion it was pointed out that an inflation bias may indeed be rationally expected because external pressure that is only gradually perceived can bring the central bank to deviate from its ex ante targets. In so far, the deviation of the output target pursued by the central bank from the "natural" level of production is an endogenous variable that is determined by the respective general social framework. In fact, a positive deviation has been confirmed empirically in several studies for the USA, for example. In addition, the interpretation of stochastic shocks as exogenous shocks for the central bank was also discussed. Finally the question was raised as to whether an escape clause might really improve the results of the games situation examined.

In his supplementary paper, **Lukas Menkhoff** sets up a comparison of the two articles by Cecchetti and Fagan. In Cecchetti's article, which assumed the credibility of rules, it was argued that the political authorities should not restrict themselves to pursuing an inflation target, but that they should also take account of output variances, because according to Cecchetti's calculations output reactions are greater than price reactions on interest rate innovations. However, according to Menkhoff, this argument must not neglect the fact that Cecchetti's empirical finding in relation to the USA cannot simply be transferred to the European Monetary Union, with which Fagan is in fact concerned. Firstly, the respective institutional anchoring of central bank responsibility must be taken into account, and, secondly, the transition to an European Monetary Union is a completely new regime, so that stable relations, e.g. the stability of the velocity of money circulation, cannot be assumed.

Menkhoff states that he agrees with Fagan that in practice the difference between a money supply rule and an inflation target rule is slight. The fact that the Bundesbank has frequently deviated from its announced money supply corridor indicated that it can be supposed that it had an implicit inflation target.

In the general discussion there was criticism that Cecchetti paid little attention to the Lucas critique in his numerically substantiated arguments and that in his representation of the correlation between price and output variances considerable differences in the time lags of the respective reactions could be seen. Menkhoff's warning against exaggerated demands being made on the European Central Bank (ECB) was countered with the argument that an ambitious inflation target was practical for reasons connected with developing a reputation and stabilizing exchange rates. A pure exchange rate target was assessed on the other hand as being unsuitable. On the question of the credibility of ECB policies it was noted that initially it was not appropriate to see the credibility that had to be created as being dependent on whether a policy can be verified or not. In certain circumstances, a certain degree of inexactitude should be aimed for. This is also indicated by the fact that communication between the ECB and the European parliament has not yet been fully clarified. Finally, the meaning of the term "inflation targeting" was discussed. It is obvious that there is no agreement as to how this term can be restricted, and this can also be seen in the conference papers. This means that there is, of course, a danger that it will lose a good deal of its meaning if it is used as an all-purpose term. If it is to be used in a manner adequate to the problems, one must in particular examine what one wants to use as an intermediate goal.[3]

In his supplementary note on Frenkel's article, **Manfred Willms** refers to some points in Frenkel's arguments. The first point concerns the increased volatility (at least outside the EMS) of real exchange rates since Bretton Woods was abandoned. In Willms' opinion this was caused by bandwagon effects. He points to a recent study carried out at his own institute which showed that the high volume of exchange market trading was caused in the end by intrabank transactions. The fact that banks speculate on the exchange markets, although this is a zero sum game, is, according to Willms, the result of asymmetric information between bank management and foreign-exchange traders. The latter have an information advantage over the bank managers and this prevents complete control of the foreign-exchange traders' actions by management.

Another point addressed by Willms concerns the function of fixed exchange rates as a nominal anchor. It can be seen empirically that fixed exchange rates often lead to real overvaluation, because wage and price pressure based on past experience continues to exist. Currency boards are more suitable, because they are more credible, but they were unfortunately not discussed in Frenkel's paper.

Finally, Willms examines target zone approaches. He claims that the most frequent criticism of target zone approaches based on the monetary model of the exchange rate, namely that the monetary model is empirically not confirmed, is untenable, and he points here to a recent study by Hansen (1996). As an alternative to the unsatisfactory concept of the Fundamental Equilibrium Exchange Rate put forward by Williamson, Willms offers Stein's approach (1992), which Frenkel did not introduce (Natural Real Exchange Rate Approach). The fact that in practice no target zone approaches were implemented is, according to Willms, based on the difficulty of determining the right timing for the implementation, on shortcomings in the theoretical foundation, and on the difficulty of the adequate determination of the equilibrium exchange rate.

In the general discussion on the conference papers the main topics were the methods on which empirical studies were based, the negative effects of exchange rate volatility on investments when hysteresis is taken into account, the disciplinary effects of fixed exchange rates, the possibility of using fixed exchange rates as a nominal anchor, and the question why long-term capital flows into developing and transition countries if fixed exchange rates are unsuitable as a nominal anchor.

---

[3] Cf. Section 2 as well.

In his supplementary note on De Grauwe's contribution, **Ansgar Belke** analyzes first of all the effect of the institutional restrictions on the choice of euro conversion rates imposed by the Maastricht Treaty and the EU's Madrid Summit resolutions. He comes to the conclusion that the procedure decided on at the EU Summit in Luxembourg on 14 September 1997 of a premature announcement of bilateral parities cannot be credible. From a game-theoretic point of view, announcements of this nature should rather be seen as non-credible threats, because the European Central Bank is obliged by the provisions of the Maastricht Treaty to fix the rates that obtain at the end of stage 2 of Economic and Monetary Union.

With regard to the euro conversion rates Belke differentiates between uncertainty and indeterminacy. He argues that the Summit resolution on a 1:1 conversion of ecu to euro leads to random euro conversion factors with the consequence that attachment to national currencies is prolonged and investment delayed.

Belke then discusses the relevance of exchange rate indeterminacy analyzed by De Grauwe. His most important theoretical objection to the indeterminacy problem is again based on game-theoretic considerations. In his opinion, with the help of the standard monetary exchange rate model it can be shown that the expectations of market actors with regard to bilateral conversion rates can only be determined by the fundamentals as they are found on 31.12.1998. Announcements by participating states or European authorities do not have any effect on the formation of expectations.

Belke continues to address the three solution processes examined by De Grauwe which are claimed to enable a fixing of the euro conversion rates in advance by providing an anchor in the foreign exchange markets. Belke assesses the second and third proposal in a similar manner to De Grauwe himself. With regard to the first proposal, which provides for premature fixing of the euro conversion rates combined with adjustments of the currency composition of the ecu currency basket as reactions to exchange-rate movements of currencies that are not included, Belke doubts whether the countries affected are prepared to cooperate to the required extent.

Finally Belke raises the question whether De Grauwe develops solutions for an indeterminacy problem whose practical relevance he grossly overestimates. This question was taken up in the following general discussion and subjected to some controversial arguments. While some participants expressed their agreement, and stated that De Grauwe's analysis was theoretically very elegant but that the significance of the basic problem was in practice very slight, others were of the opinion that considerable consequences could result from the indeterminacy concerning euro conversion rates during the transition to EMU and this justified a complex theoretical analysis.

In his supplementary paper on Fuhrmann's article, **Rainer Schweickert** amplifies the former's contribution by placing the focal point of his arguments on the relationship between currency boards and institutional reforms. He explains the theoretical foundations of a stabilization program by using the example of the implementation of a currency board in Argentina in 1991 and compares this with the strategies pursued by Chile and Mexico. He emphasizes that an important aspect for the implementation of a currency board is importing credibility. Starting from this he arrives at some evaluations which deviate from Fuhrmann:

- Schweickert stresses that there may indeed be a long-term drift in economic fundamentals between the home country and the country which provides the anchor currency.
- He also contradicts Fuhrmann's assessment that a currency board per se has a credibility advantage over a central bank conducting a discretionary policy.
- Finally he emphasizes the problem field of stabilization programs which are based on fixing the exchange rate, in particular with regard to the role of the real exchange rate.

On the basis of the experience of Latin America Schweickert comes to the conclusion that it is essential for the credibility of a currency board that it is accompanied by radical reforms which guarantee the feasibility and the sustainability of the stabilization program. In addition, a currency board is only optimal if monetary stabilization and not the adjustment of the real exchange rate has top priority, and if there is the necessity and the potential for radical reforms. If these preconditions are given, using a comparison of Mexico and Argentina Schweikert shows that a currency board is superior to other strategies based on exchange rates. However, after successful stabilization it is difficult to switch to a regime offering more flexibility without losing credibility.

In the general discussion above all the difference between a monetary union and a currency board was dealt with and the question was debated of how to explain empirically determinable diverging inflation rates in a currency board system. In addition, the problem of variable money supply multiplicators was discussed, and the question was raised how real exchange rate adjustments take place in a currency board system.

2 Supplementary Aspects

When we take a final look at those issues which were the subject of the greatest amount of debate at the symposium, we find the three following:

- central bank independence,
- policy coordination, and
- inflation targeting.

I would now like to present these issues once again and point to the common context.

The argument for **central bank independence** in modern theory of monetary policy, usually runs as follows: Owing to lack of credibility, governments favor inflationary policies. This inflation bias can be mitigated by delegating monetary policy to an independent central bank.[4] Establishing an autonomous central bank is the most important way to make money supply exogenous, thereby raising the central bank's credibility and thus reducing the private sector's inflationary expectations that determine wage and price contracts and thereby the exchange rate as well. It may be concluded from this that each country should develop its central bank into an institution that formulates and conducts monetary policy independently. If this is done, it is claimed that the monetary authority will be protected from the influence of the fiscal authority and other political interest groups, and thus can prevent high inflation more easily.[5]

The latter conclusion, however, may be doubted, in particular with respect to developing and transition countries. Central bank independence may be regarded only (if at all) as a necessary condition for low inflation. For attaining low inflation with minimum costs, one could argue that central bank independence has to be associated with **policy coordination**. From a theoretical point of view, the problem lies in the fact that simply giving central banks independence may be counterproductive insofar as it is then easy for the government or fiscal authority (as well as for particular interest groups responsible for negotiating wages and setting prices) to shift the responsibility for not attaining certain stabilization targets to the central bank, which may de facto be powerless. Under asymmetric information and contract-bound decisions this may turn into a socially ineffective redistribution game where the "independent" central bank is blamed for failing to reach social targets. In other words, by itself the central bank may be too weak to attain the disinflation target (or to stabilize the economy) but have to bear the responsibility for missing the target because of its formally independent status. This means formal independence may be a necessary element for successful

---

[4] For more details, see, e.g., Eijffinger and De Haan (1996). See the article by Illing in this volume as well.

[5] Cf. Wagner (1993, 1996).

central banking, however, without the simultaneous implementation of other necessary elements, in particular coordination with fiscal and wage/price policies, it may prove ineffective or even counterproductive.[6]

One way to strengthen the position of the central bank and to enhance the credibility of its announcements in a situation like this is to choose an appropriate nominal anchor in order to conduct monetary policy successfully, i.e. to induce a (locally) maximum disinflationary effect. The question of nominal anchors is important because the credibility of the monetary policy strategy eventually determines the success of the central bank, in this case the attainable inflation rate. Credibility, however, is dependent not only upon time inconsistency aspects (namely the incentives of the central bank to deviate from its goal or announcement ex post), but also upon the expected implementability of the strategy that is a function of the reform stage.[7]

In the recent past a number of countries, such as (in chronological order) New Zealand, Canada, the United Kingdom, Sweden, Finland, Australia and Spain, have turned to pursuing a new monetary policy strategy referred to as **inflation targeting** (see, e.g., Leidermann and Svensson (1995)). These are mainly countries which have experienced difficulties in conducting monetary policy using an exchange rate peg or some monetary aggregate as the main intermediate target. In this context a theory of inflation targeting was developed which is discussed today in great detail in the theory of monetary policy and in central bank circles. This approach gains additional significance from the fact that it has been proposed to the future European Central Bank by the European Monetary Institute as the sole alternative monetary policy strategy to the monetary targeting strategy of the German Bundesbank. This modern monetary policy conception was analyzed, or at least referred to, in a whole series of papers in this book, above all in those by Illing, Cecchetti and Fagan. However, this was done in a somewhat heterogeneous form, given the different conceptions of what inflation targeting actually is. The monetary policy strategy of inflation targeting ("IT"), as a theoretical construction, may possibly be best characterized by means of the following conceptional elements:[8]

(1) the central bank is given an explicit quantitative inflation target;
(2) an operating procedure is applied, at least implicitly, which can be referred to as "inflation forecast targeting". This means that a conditional, internal,

[6] Cf. Wagner (1997a) and Mas (1995) in the context of transition and developing countries.

[7] Cf. ibid.

[8] For more details see, e.g., Wagner (1997b). The EMI (1997) proposal to the future European Central Bank with regard to the monetary policy strategy to be pursued by the Bank can be subsumed under the above arrangement. See Fagan's paper in this book.

central bank inflation forecast is used as an intermediate target and as an indicator variable.[9]

(3) Great importance is attached to a high degree of transparency and accountability of the monetary policy.

Element (1) is the indispensable characteristic of all IT. On the other hand, elements (2) and (3) are specifications or characteristic features intended to increase the efficiency of IT. However, it only appears practical to consider IT as a monetary policy strategy if the following institutional preconditions are given which themselves imply central bank independence and policy coordination:

- The central bank must be able to carry out an independent monetary policy. On the other hand, it is enough for this if the central bank enjoys a sufficiently high degree of instrument independence, i.e. is able to decide freely on the use of monetary policy instruments to achieve a defined inflation target. This inflation target itself may be imposed exogenously, i.e. it is not absolutely necessary for the central bank to be able to set targets independently. However, we can only refer to genuine instrument independence where a country does not display any symptoms of "fiscal dominance", i.e. the implementation of domestic monetary policy is not dictated by fiscal tendencies (such as a country's indebtedness). This could be prevented by coordinating monetary and fiscal (and incomes) policies, for example.
- The central bank must be confronted with an unequivocal inflation target, and must not be simultaneously obliged to maintain a defined exchange rate (band), because the government and the central bank would very quickly come into conflict regarding priorities once the limits of an exchange rate band were reached. This can most easily be avoided if the central bank is independent. Possible conflicts with other decision-makers can be prevented or reduced by a prior coordination of policies.
- In addition, the monetary authorities in a country must be in possession of the technical and institutional capacity required to model and forecast the domestic inflation process. Moreover, they need reliable knowledge or estimates of the time lags in the effects of the changes in many forecast variables on the inflation rate. The monetary authorities also require knowledge of the transmission mechanism and the transmission effects of the monetary policy.

---

[9] IT is sometimes understood as a strategy which does not require any intermediate goals. However, a strategy of this kind would be dangerous. The problem is that inflation reacts to changes of monetary policy only with long and variable time lags. This makes simple inflation targeting (i.e. without an intermediate target) difficult. Not only inflation control, but also controllability of monetary policy and accountability of the central bank would then be very imperfect. This, however, would restrict the credibility of the central bank.

- Finally, monetary policy actions and considerations must be kept transparent and imparted comprehensibly. Only then can the credibility of monetary policy announcements be generated.

Generally speaking, these preconditions for realization are only found conditionally even in industrial countries. In any case, the above preconditions appear not (yet) to be given at all in the case of most of today's developing and transition countries.[10]

It is to be expected that these three areas, central bank independence, policy coordination, and inflation targeting, will be counted among the main issues in monetary economics for some time to come. Other issues, for example the transmission mechanism in "globalized markets" and (in the context of EMU) in monetary unions, may gain (additional) relevance, as James Tobin also stresses in his introductory contribution to this volume. We will be able to be more precise in a subsequent conference in a few years.

[10] This is worth mentioning because last year there was a great deal of lively discussion, including in the International Monetary Fund, on the possibilities for applying IT strategy in developing countries. See Masson, Savastano and Sharma (1997) as well. See Wagner (1997a, part III) for applicability in transition countries.

References

Eijffinger, S. C. W. and J. de Haan (1996), The Political Economy of Central-Bank Independence, *Special Papers in International Economics*, No. 19, Princeton University.

European Monetary Institute (1997), The Single Monetary Policy in Stage Three: Elements of the Monetary Policy Strategy of the ESCB, Frankfurt am Main.

Hansen, G. (1996), The Mark-Dollar Exchange Rate and Purchasing Power Parity. Some Empirical Evidence. Arbeiten aus dem Institut für Statistik und Ökonometrie der Universität Kiel, No. 89, Kiel.

Leiderman, L. and L. E. O. Svensson (1995) (eds.), Inflation Targets, London: CEPR.

Lucas, R. E. (1997), The Welfare Costs of Inflation, Presidential Address, Econometric Society North American Meeting, Pasadena, CA.

Mas, I. (1995), Central Bank Independence: a critical view from a developing country, *World Development* 10, 1639-52.

Masson, P. R., M. A. Savastano and S. Sharma (1997), The Scope for Inflation Targeting in Developing Countries, IMF Working Paper 97/130.

Stein, J. I. (1992), Fundamental Determinants of Exchange Rate, *Journal of International and Comparative Economics* 1, 125-62.

Tobin, J. (1998), Monetary Policy: Recent Theory and Practice, in this volume.

Wagner, H. (1993), Reconstruction of the Financial System in East Germany: Description and Comparison with Eastern Europe, *Journal of Banking and Finance* 17, 1001-19.

Wagner, H. (1996), Transformation Process and the J-Curve-Problem, *International Journal of Social Economics* 23, 73-87.

Wagner, H. (1997a), Central Banking in Transition Countries, IMF Working Paper, forthcoming, Washington, D.C.

Wagner, H. (1997b), Inflation Targeting, Diskussionsbeitrag der FernUniversität Hagen Nr. 245, Hagen.

Notes on Contributors

Ansgar Belke is assistant at the Department of Economics at the University of Bochum. He studied economics in Münster, Kiel and Paris and received his Ph.D. in 1995 at the University of Bochum. He was visitor at the Center for Economic Research (CentER) in Tilburg, Netherlands and the Center for European Policy Studies (CEPS) in Brussels and was research fellow at the Institute of World Economics in Kiel and at the University of Cambridge, England.

Stephen G. Cecchetti is executive vice president and director of research at the Federal Reserve Bank of New York. He received his Ph.D. from the University of California at Berkley in 1982. He was professor of economics at Ohio State University 1992-97 and a visiting professor at the University of Melbourne in 1996, Boston College in 1994 and 1995, Princeton University in 1992 - 1993. From 1982 to 1983 he was on the faculty of New York University's Graduate School of Business and at Ohio State University. He served as a consultant to several Reserve Banks including the Reserve Bank of Australia in 1996 and the Bank of Israel in 1994.

Gabriel P. Fagan is head of the Monetary Strategy Section at the European Monetary Institute in Frankfurt. He studied economics at Trinity College Dublin, Ireland. Since 1985, he has been employed as an economist in the Economic Affairs Department of the Central Bank of Ireland. Between 1992 and 1994, he was employed as an economist at the Committee of Governors of the EU Central Banks, based at the BIS in Basle.

Wolfgang Filc is professor of economics at the University of Trier. He studied economics at the University of Berlin and received his Ph.D. in 1974 at the Technical University of Hannover. In 1987 he was visiting professor at the Clark University in Worcester, MA. He is member at the Institute for Empirical Economic Research in Berlin, of the Advisory Council for the Institute for Industrial Law and Working (Industrial) Relations at the EC and the Commission of Experts in Economics *'Progress 2000'*.

Michael Frenkel is dean and professor of economics at the WHU Koblenz, Otto Beisheim Graduate School of Management, Vallendar, Germany. He received his Ph.D. in 1985 from the University of Mainz. From August 1995 to August 1996 he was *Visiting Konrad Adenauer Professor* at Georgetown University in Washington, D.C. He worked for the International Monetary Fund in Washington, D.C. from 1985 to May 1988.

Wilfried Fuhrmann is professor of economics at the University of Potsdam. He studied economics at the Christian-Albrechts University in Kiel and received his Ph.D. in 1976. He was assistant-professor at the University of Kiel until 1987, professor at the University of Linz, Austria from 1987 to 1990 and professor at the University of Paderborn from 1990 to 1995.

Norbert Funke is an economist in the Financial Affairs Division of the Organization for Economic Cooperation and Development (OECD). He holds a Ph.D. from the University of Cologne. He has been with the OECD since 1994 and worked previously as research associate at the Kiel Institute of World Economics in Germany.

Paul De Grauwe has been professor of economics at the University of Leuven since 1982. He holds a Ph.D. from Johns Hopkins University in Baltimore. From 1973 to 1974 he worked as an economist at the IMF. He has been visiting professor at the University of Paris (1978), the University of Michigan (1981), the University of Pennsylvania (1983), the College of Europe (1985-1987), the University of Brussels (1988), the Institute of World Economics in Kiel (1989, 1991) and the University of Saarbrücken (1991-1992). From 1988 to 1991 he was research fellow of CEPS and CEPR. In 1991 he became a member of the Belgian Parliament.

Hans-Peter Grüner is assistant at the Department of Economics at the University of Bonn. He studied mathematical economics at the University of Heidelberg and received his Ph.D. in the European Doctoral Program in Quantitative Economics at DELTA, Paris in 1994.

Gerhard Illing is professor of economics at the University of Frankfurt. He studied Economics at the University of Munich and Cambridge, England and received his Ph.D. from the University of Munich in 1984. He was assistant professor at the University of Western Ontario, London, Canada in 1986/87 and visiting professor at the CERGE in Prag in 1992. From 1993-95 he was professor at the University of Bamberg.

Alexander Karmann is professor of economics at the University of Dresden. He studied mathematics and received a Ph.D. degree in economics from the University of Karlsruhe. From 1986-1993 he was professor of economics at the University of Hamburg.

Dietmar Kath is professor of economics at the University of Duisburg. He studied economics at the Universities of Saarbrücken and Hamburg. He received his Ph.D. from the University in Hamburg in 1966. Since 1977 he has been member of the Committee for Monetary Theory and Monetary Policy of the German Society for Economic and Social Sciences (Verein für Socialpolitik).

Lukas Menkhoff is professor of economics at the University of Aachen. He received his Ph.D. from the University of Freiburg in 1985. From 1986 to 1989 he worked as an economist at the Dresdner Bank AG and McKinsey &Co. He was professor at the University of Freiburg from 1989 to 1991. From 1992 to 1995 he was a visiting professor in Thailand.

Rainer Schweickert is deputy head of the research department for *Development Economics and World Economic Integration* at the Institute of World Economics in Kiel. He studied economics at the University of Mannheim and received his Ph.D. from the University of Kiel in 1993. He was head of the research project 'Stability and Economic Development' at the Institute of World Economics in Kiel.

Friedrich Sell is professor of economics at the University of Dresden. He studied economics at the University of Freiburg i. Br. and received his Ph.D. there in 1981. He was guest lecturer at the University of Santo Tomas, Manila, Visiting Fellow at the ISEAS Institute Singapur and did research for the World Bank and IMF in Washington as well as for the Institute of World Economics in Kiel.

James Tobin is professor emeritus at Yale University, where he has been Sterling Professor of Economics since 1950. He received his Ph.D. from Harvard University in 1947. From 1961 to 1962 he was a member of the US President's Council of Economic Advisors. In 1981 he received the Nobel Prize for Economics.

Helmut Wagner is professor of economics at the University of Hagen (FernUniversität). He received his Ph.D. from the University of Regensburg in 1976. He was professor of economics at the University of Hamburg (HWP) from 1982 to 1995 and visiting professor/scholar at the University of California from 1982 to 1983, at MIT in 1987, at Princeton University from 1991 - 1992, at the Bank of Japan's Institute for Monetary and Economic Studies in 1988, at the IMF Research Department and at the American Institute for Contemporary German Studies, Johns Hopkins University in Washington, D.C. in 1997.

Manfred Willms has been professor of economics at the University of Kiel since 1971. He studied economics at the University of Hamburg and received his Ph.D. in 1964. He was visiting professor at the University of Illinois from 1968 - 70, professor of economics at the University of Bonn from 1967 - 70 and research fellow at the Federal Reserve Bank of St. Louis from 1969 - 71.

GPSR Compliance

The European Union's (EU) General Product Safety Regulation (GPSR) is a set of rules that requires consumer products to be safe and our obligations to ensure this.

If you have any concerns about our products, you can contact us on ProductSafety@springernature.com

In case Publisher is established outside the EU, the EU authorized representative is:

Springer Nature Customer Service Center GmbH
Europaplatz 3
69115 Heidelberg, Germany

Batch number: 10725973

Printed by Printforce, the Netherlands